CW00395240

# Business Strategy

# Business Strategy

## Managing Uncertainty, Opportunity, and Enterprise

J.-C. Spender

OXFORD
UNIVERSITY PRESS

# OXFORD

UNIVERSITY PRESS

Great Clarendon Street, Oxford, OX2 6DP,
United Kingdom

Oxford University Press is a department of the University of Oxford.
It furthers the University's objective of excellence in research, scholarship,
and education by publishing worldwide. Oxford is a registered trade mark of
Oxford University Press in the UK and in certain other countries

First Edition published in 2014

Impression: 4

Published in the United States of America by Oxford University Press
198 Madison Avenue, New York, NY 10016, United States of America

British Library Cataloguing in Publication Data
Data available

Library of Congress Control Number: 2013943044

ISBN 978–0–19–968654–4

Printed and bound by CPI Group (UK) Ltd, Croydon, CR0 4YY

Since economics offers little in the way of practical insight, managers and entrepreneurs depend on their own business acumen, personal judgment, and rules of thumb in making decisions.

Coase, R. H. & Wang, N. 2012. Saving Economics from the Economists. *Harvard Business Review*, 90(12): 36–36.

In this article, published when Ronald Coase, the English economist, was 101, Coase continues to shake his fist at his colleagues for failing to address the questions about business firms and their strategies that he posed in his Nobel-winning 1937 paper.

# Preface

A preface helps position a book with comments that do not really belong in the text yet help the reader get a sense where the author is "coming from." For instance: how the book came to be written—from disappointment with the current literature, to fulfill a grant, for income, or as part of a larger project involving several volumes. It can indicate where key ideas came from. Plus it is personal and can name those who helped support the writer during the book's creation in whatever ways mattered. It is also an opportunity for the author to thank people who are not, of course, held responsible for the outcome. But as Jonathan Swift—of *Gulliver's Travels*—warned, if the preface is too good it lessens the incentive to read further—something to bear in mind.

My book's origins lie in my shortcomings as a manager and as a teacher. As one of my students chided me, "academics sometimes try to do with their heads what they cannot do with their hearts (or guts)." Right, Maggie, you nailed us. I became interested in management when I joined Rolls-Royce & Associates after time in Royal Navy submarines and at Oxford University. I quickly realized that, while I could survive, I was never going to be a great manager. Managing was not a "natural" medium for me—amply confirmed when I worked for one of those rare people born to manage. I would be a "journeyman" manager, like most. I also began to teach apprentices in the evenings at the Derby Technical College (now the University of Derby). I learned little about management in my engineering courses at Oxford, but soon discovered good things to read about being a manager. Urwick's *Elements of Administration*[1] was the first book into my management library—very British and military. At the same time I realized that teaching was not all that natural for me either. My strategy was more preparation. But the deeper I got into the material, the more puzzling it became; questions went unanswered, displaced by even deeper ones.

In 1971, after several business adventures, I entered the Ph.D. program at the Manchester Business School. There I had the good fortune to be taught by world-class scholars such as David Weir and Richard Whitley who introduced

[1] L. F. Urwick (1947) *The Elements of Administration* (2nd edn). London: Sir Isaac Pitman & Sons.

me to our discipline's great books and, to my surprise, changed my life. I was given latitude many of today's students are denied—I wanted to understand business strategizing *tout court*. The first hurdle was my Ph.D. thesis "Strategy-Making in Business," generously awarded the 1980 Academy of Management's A. T. Kearney Prize and later published as *Industry Recipes*.[2] This was OK as far as it went, but I knew I missed my mark, plus few grasped what I was about or found it interesting. The present book is a second shot at the same target. It is the generalization that brings that project to completion. At its core is a model of the individual as having powers of imagination and judgment along with powers of logic. This shift of underpinning distances my work from the huge literature that presumes every individual's principal attribute is rationality. Thus I see managing is an imaginative practice, an art form.

In the thirty years between my Ph.D. and this book I managed in several milieus—as an entrepreneur, strategist, director, investor, and business school dean. I also taught and wrote about business strategy and later about knowledge management (KM), especially about the interplay of knowledge presences and absences, the practice-framed discovery that we do not know that we are incompetent. At first KM seemed a diversion from strategy but it now seems central, for strategic work can be defined as dealing with the "knowledge absences" that impede competent progress towards our goals. As I explored the KM–strategy relationship I realized two things. First, there is no understanding strategic work without a complementary understanding of the entity being managed—the private sector firm—and the knowledge absences that characterize it. While the "nature of the firm" may seem blindingly obvious to managers, management theorists know we are not too sure of what firms are, or why they exist. Strategy theory reaches towards a theory of the firm, of course, and it follows—take my word for it—this means it is not useful to think of management as generic, that being able to manage well in one situation implies you will be able to manage somewhere else. Managing and strategic work is highly specific and contextualized, not at all general. Nor is it useful to think of the firm as a dumb object, an inanimate entity that does not require continuous managing, constant pumping to keep it afloat. At law the firm is easily described in terms of the rights and obligations written into its charter or articles of association. In contrast, the firm's managers must deal with its buzz of dynamic activities, imprecise, riven with knowledge absences, and not readily defined—forever "under construction," in part because of its many possible futures, and in part because of its ambiguous present and past. From management's point of view a firm is defined more by its practical capabilities and potentials than by its charter or the tangible resources

---

[2] J.-C. Spender (1989) *Industry Recipes: The Nature and Sources of Managerial Judgement*. Oxford: Blackwell.

shown on its balance sheet. These capabilities change all the time because people learn by doing—so strategic work is continuous and dynamic, and an ongoing challenge in a changing world. The firm the managers are creating continuously is like a long-lived rosebush; managing it is husbandry. All of which calls for a dynamic "theory of the managed firm" (TMF) before we can analyze or evaluate managers' practice.

I realized that to get into the heart of strategy and value creation it is crucial to turn the conventional analysis upside down, to probe for the knowledge absences that allow and call for the application of the entrepreneurial imagination—rather than presuppose economic value creation has external causes. Turning my back on Rational Man, I also turned away from rigorous economic theorizing. Microeconomics has yet to provide us with theories of the firm that explain strategizing or the firm's capability to generate profit or growth, or even its existence. Ronald Coase's questions about the "nature of the firm," posed in 1937, have not yet been answered, leaving non-econo-mists and others free to have a go.[3] What we do know is that the firm, and its profit and growth, are created by the enterprise of the firm's managers, so it is they who should properly claim to "own" these terms, not economists. My book is for these managers, as I admire their enterprise and creativity in the face of many management theorists who ignore it. By not presuming we already know what firms are, we shift the analysis onto the practice of con-structing them. I call this "strategic work," and this strategic art form powers our economy. Contrary to the popular view, I do not presume a firm's strategy is determined by its markets, competition, technology, or any similar external features of its situation, even though these "facts" clearly constrain the strat-egist. Strategic work is the process of bringing an entrepreneurial idea into a particular socio-economic context (where it appears as a "business model"). The entrepreneur identifies and chooses the markets, competitors, and situ-ation s/he wishes to engage, not the other way around. The resulting business model must answer the questions that arise as the firm's entrepreneur/s look out at their context from within their business model—with their chosen goals in mind: "What does it mean to us? What do we do now?" I offer an insider's value-creating view that stands against the conventional outsider's view that tries to map the world beyond the firm "objectively," to propose "strategy" as determined by circumstance and so hand the strategic initiative to someone or something external. An important guide here is Carl von Clausewitz, the nineteenth-century military strategist whose concept of stra-tegic work was constructive and dynamic *bricolage*. From a philosophical and

---

[3] R. H. Coase (1991) 'The Nature of the Firm' (1937), in O. E. Williamson and S. G. Winter (eds), *The Nature of the Firm: Origins, Evolution and Development.* New York: Oxford University Press, pp. 18–33.

methodological point of view I turn away from the positivism that underpins our notions of natural science and follow the twentieth-century turn towards language found in the work of, for instance, Wittgenstein, Habermas, and most importantly Heidegger. My book is about the construction and deployment of the firm's own language (jargon), what gives it its identity. Another way to put this as my argument's arc: that the discovery of knowledge absences in the course of purposive practice triggers the application of entrepreneurial judgment, thus *practice—Knightian uncertainty—entrepreneurial judgment—language—rhetorical activity—new collaborative practice—new economic value*. This arc opposes the Rational Man convention found in the strategy literature: *goal—environment—theorize action—apply—redirect*. Knightian uncertainty collapses the second.

Over the decade since my retirement from the Deanship at the School of Business and Technology at FIT/SUNY (New York), encouraging colleagues who found something interesting in my work, plus my wife Barbara and my friend and editor David Musson, exerted gentle but persistent pressure on me to write up my dissident view of strategy. Eventually David suggested the ever-expanding theoretical schema might be cut short and presented as a book for thoughtful managers, consultants, business teachers, and students without the full academic paraphernalia of sources, citations, theorizing, empirical data, and so on. This book is not written with the standard textbook in mind, a thirteen-week course-pack with cases and chapters-for-the-week that begin with a description of what would be learned and end with a summary of what should have been learned. Rather it is an overstuffed trunk of ideas I have found relevant to my own experiences of private sector strategic work, a portable supermarket of materials to be sampled according to interest, style, and context, for the entrepreneur/strategist to pick and choose, as is implicit in the practice and aesthetic of strategizing.

Strategists select and synthesize what is available to them, a *bricolage* of an extraordinarily important sort. The work can never be detached from the entrepreneur's context; no one invents strategy unconstrained or *de novo*. It begins with the entrepreneur who finds a "knowledge absence," something of interest in her/his world, anomalous perhaps, that pursued may lead on to economic value and profit—and surprise. It is described and brought into the realm of our reasoning by constructing a "local reality," of which history is a key dimension. Managers struggle with "Who are we and where? What are we going to be?" Eventually the focus is on the thoughtful and creative exploitation of what is NOT known about the situation and its possibilities, surfacing and resolving the "knowledge absences" that bring others to a halt. Consequently strategic work often benefits from but is never driven by data. At its core are the acts of imaginative practice that project the entrepreneurs' ideas (and will) into the world. This calls for moral and ethical awareness and for "practical wisdom" (what the Ancient Greeks called *phronesis*). My book is intended for those who appreciate this and know that managing carries irremovable social and human responsibility for actions that involve and affect others. Consequently it is personal and I use the first-person voice, sometimes unwelcome in scholarly work. Metaphorically, I hope to hold the reader's hand and guide her/him towards my conclusions, to be ignored or adopted as they feel inclined, part of their own strategic work.

Those seeking a teachable text on corporate strategizing that engages today's globally connected and ethically alerted situation can use the first three chapters as a textbook and/or consultant's tool-kit. Chapter 1 examines the nature of strategic work and familiarizes the reader with my "voice" and viewpoint: in particular my methodological shift from an "objective" stance to my "subjective" or "constructivist" stance. The argument begins by contrasting imagining against logical reasoning, proposing that strategic work is always about the first, never about the second. Logical reasoning complements and facilitates our imagining, but it does not have priority. So the rest of my book deals with how imagining can be managed. Most strategy books focus on managing others' reasoning, not their imagining. Though the switch from rational decision-making to imagining is challenging academically it seems no more than commonsense, especially to anyone who has held responsibility in business situations. We are creatures of imagination as well as of reason. The firm is an astonishing social and legal innovation precisely because it is an apparatus that can help us transform acts of imagining into socio-economic value. The firm's data collection, analysis, and reasoning support but do not delimit its ability to create value. Managing is imagination-intensive and clearly done without much attention to theory-shaped reasoning. But theory often has something important to say and this makes talking about theory both difficult and desirable. Strategic work is not easy; if it were it would not be valuable or important. Doing it well calls for a particular state of mind and way of looking, and von Clausewitz is especially good on this. It is hard to get one's head (and heart/guts) into that place, especially in the artificial environment of a classroom. At the same time much of our literature and commentary in the business press is too sloppy to show the heavy lifting of strategic work. It cannot be distilled down to five Ss, the seven steps of successful entrepreneurs, or the eight ingredients of *In Search of Excellence*. Consultants or teachers who argue that strategy is simple in principle, no more than a matter of being clear and logical, do their clients or students a grave disservice. Strategy only makes sense because things are unclear and difficult. What clients and students need is a workable practice for coping with knowledge absences—a handy methodology to carry with them into other uncertain times and situations. I describe and illustrate a practice, not a theory.

The scene is set in Chapter 1—the question strategizing must address. In Chapter 2 I review the inventory of strategy tools used by consultants and business practitioners as they frame and address this question. In practice strategic work answers no general question such as optimizing the chances of reaching your objective. Of course it deals with goals, but also with the situation's specifics, and the resulting singular challenges. These do not fit together tidily. Strategic tools can help identify these elements and there is interesting empirical data on which tools are popular and why. Chapter 3 reviews the complementary inventory offered by academic theorists and economists—in a non-academic way. The reader needs no prior academic knowledge. I have tried to make the text accessible to non-academics; though there are occasional footnotes and an Appendix D of further reading for those who want to dig deeper. The book is "theory-lite" though it sometimes calls for some rethinking of what the reader might have learned previously. Chapter 3 transitions from a static analysis towards a dynamic one, eventually focusing on learning processes. The discussion moves up a notch in Chapter 4 as I complete the pivot from the outsider (etic) view that underpins the first three chapters and dive into the insider (emic) view that is the true nature of value-adding practice. The key lies in seeing how strategic work must create the specific business model through which the firm's situation is to be viewed and imagined. The idea of "mental map" may seem helpful but it misses what business people know is so central about their peoples' skills and creativity, that they are often tacit and unmappable. Instead I focus on the formulation and construction of a firm-specific and practical language (jargon) in which the entrepreneurs' vision can be articulated and communicated to those with the skills required. The resulting business model is "double-acting"; on the one hand, the apparatus that shapes the imaginative judgments actors deploy in their work, on the other, how they use their imagination to learn from their doings.

It is curious how the majority of strategy texts—and journals like the *Harvard Business Review* or *Business Week*—often offer sweeping generalizations about how firms should go about their business—when anyone who works in a firm knows how particular is its situation. In contrast to the generalities, I say that a firm without a "local" language to describe itself and its context, and thereby capture its uniqueness, has no strategy. Along with Socrates, the strategist must borrow the ancient maxim "know thyself" on behalf of her/his firm and address the question "Who are we?" Again, the discussion in Chapter 4 has nothing esoteric or "theory-heavy" about it, though the material examines the structure and use of language and may feel unfamiliar on that account. But we all know a lot about language and use it all the time. Focusing on the work of language construction, Chapter 4 frees the analysis from the axioms and terminologies underpinning the strategic tools and models reviewed in Chapters 2 and 3, and sketches a generalized approach to constructing the entrepreneur's new business model, defining her/his firm as a practical language for engaging chosen aspects of its context.

In terms of method my book's first switch is from the objective "outsider" view to a "subjective" insider view, from fact-based to language- or discussion-based. Its second switch is from an analysis that is limited to logic and reason alone to one that also embraces imagination, judgment, and creativity. This calls for a switch from rigorous analysis to constructing language, and redefines the business model as double-acting linguistic artifact that shapes both judgment and learning. Entrepreneurial innovation is the core capitalist art form, pushing the boundaries of economic activity. Thus strategic work is not a science, though science frequently supports the art. We should reason as logically as possible but bear in mind that reason, on its own, is never sufficient to determine human action in uncertain situations. The firm cannot stop when reason fails—indeed this is where the heavy-duty strategic work really begins. To illustrate, a camera collects data objectively, scientifically "reasons" an image, and so does not (cannot) lie—but it is not able to select images as the talented photographer can, separating those that we find iconic and engaging from those we find lifeless and forgettable. We experience the world as an uncertain place onto which we project ourselves imaginatively, where we realize ourselves through our actions. We are never able to see anything "as it is," completely and unambiguously. We construct our memory, mediating all sense data with subjectivity. In the same way strategic data collection and reasoning must always be complemented by judgment (and memory). Why these data rather than those? What do the data mean for us? Strategizing creates the business model as a "local" locus of "relative certainty" about the firm's nature and way of engaging its uncertain world. It tells everyone involved "This is the way it will be." It lays out what should be taken as real and important by those involved.

Strategists, even sole entrepreneurs, never work alone. They are limited, so need the active help of those who know the relevant details and practices better than they do. Rockefeller did not understand the chemistry of oil refining. Steve Jobs did not understand how to make glass scratchproof. They depended on others who knew the theories and practices necessary to produce results essential to the business models they envisaged. Private sector businesses are always in the middle between inputs and outputs, between suppliers and consumers, people who charge, and those who pay. Creating value demands imaginative collaboration. Chapter 5 outlines how the strategist establishes collaboration or cooperation with creative others. The firm is a socio-economic institution of staggering power precisely because it is an apparatus for harnessing the imagination and creativity of many employees and others to its chosen goals. Such collaboration cannot be generated or controlled through force, instruction, or incentives alone, for these modes of governance risk suppressing the imagination of those controlled. Persuasion is key, and interpersonal persuasion is the entrepreneur or leader's core capability. Persuasion has been studied for millennia as rhetoric, the "art of persuasion."[4] I harness this ancient art to the strategic task—for the firm is not an impersonal machine. It is a buzz of difficult-to-define interpersonal activities of uncertain nature and duration. From the strategist's point of view the firm has no secure and identifiable "ontology"—the academics' term for "existence as an object beyond and independent of our thoughts." To the contrary, strategy cannot be comprehended if the nature of the firm is assumed, for it is the process in which managers create the firm. The result is ever changing and a constant challenge to management's continuing influence and control. Thus strategic work calls for an attitude of ongoing anxiety that these interactions will not continue but will collapse into chaos and disorder, arresting profit and growth. The challenge is always to bring human reasoning and imagining together, reducing anxiety and raising confidence without ever achieving certainty and predictability, with activities directed towards sustaining progress towards the firm's goals. The concluding Chapter 6 explores the personal, historical, legal, cultural, and technological contexts in which private sector firms are embedded, in which profit-producing value-adding practice must be created.

My hope is that managers, consultants, and students will find the text accessible and engaging enough to provoke their thinking—for I admire Donald Schön's "reflective practitioner."[5] On the other hand, some teachers may feel Chapters 4 and 5 are "too complex" or "advanced" for their students, a bridge or concept too far. This would shortchange many, especially those with business experience, for that will have familiarized them with the practical exercise of imagination and judgment. It may even be condescending, for there is nothing difficult about the material, beyond commonsense. Most readers know this stuff already, even if academics have trouble theorizing it. I do not expect to tell readers things they do not already know. Rather, I hope to persuade them to appreciate what they already know in new ways—itself a good metaphor for strategic work. Plus I would like my readers to share my sense that in Chapters 4, 5, and 6 I finally hit the target I envisaged as an inexperienced engineering manager and teacher fifty years ago.

---

[4] The foundations were laid in Aristotle—(1991) *The Art of Rhetoric*. London: Penguin Books—and a huge derivative literature. T. M. Conley (1990) *Rhetoric in the European Tradition*. Chicago: University of Chicago Press, is especially good.

[5] D. A. Schön (1983) *The Reflective Practitioner: How Professionals Think in Action*. New York: Basic Books.

The journey had its hiccups and restarts over the years but turned out to be fascinating as I learned many things that surprised me, especially about the economics and politics of capitalist democracy. Thirty years after my project's start Eduard Bonet's quiet mention that I might find the "art of rhetoric" interesting was transforming. This became the final piece of the puzzle and helped lift me upward and onwards. I am also grateful to many institutions, academic colleagues, and students, especially at ESADE, Lund University's School of Economics and Management, and ISM in Paris, who gave me the opportunity to work on so rich a puzzle, one that transformed my initial probing into a forty-plus-years academic career. I learned how tricky it is to frame the research question, the persistent temptation to engage the wrong question because it is easier to deal with. It took me a while to understand that I sought a "theory of the managed firm" (TMF) to contrast against the current bevy of models or theories of the firm that offer no strategic place for the creativity of the entrepreneur, leader, or manager—their fundamental nature. Firms only have a nature because of the people involved. Thus one answer to Coase's killer question is historical—the entrepreneur who wanted to bring it into existence, the firm as an artifact or enactment of its founder's vision and volition. This is not an economist's answer of course and does not help other entrepreneurs. My answers bear on (a) the practice of entrepreneurial management, and (b) the place of the firm in the capitalist democratic economy's value-generating processes.

I am far from alone in appreciating the need for a managerial theory of private sector profit, growth, and value addition, or a theory of the application of the human imagination in business. But for a long time I failed to appreciate the deeper methodological dialectic at work, the glass half full or half empty issue. I found it hard to overcome the comforting but naïve view that business school theorizing is "too abstract," "too quantitative," "bereft of moral and ethical content," or "too dismissive of real world managing."[6] Eventually I realized I was trying to complement and thus enrich the current theorizing on business matters, not simply bash it. Just as a talented driver complements the capacities built into a fine auto or a talented scientist can make use of good ideas, instruments, and metrics, so the manager's personal judgment is complemented by good rational resource allocation processes. But the reader who seeks theory-driven prescriptions will not find them here, for I write towards those whose strategic judgment complements the mechanics of careful data collection and rigorous decision-making, who know that being "in charge" means carrying a burden of responsibility for action and its consequences for others as well as for themselves. Managing is a morally and

[6] R. R. Locke and J.-C. Spender (2011) *Confronting Managerialism: How the Business Elite and Their Schools Threw Our Lives Out of Balance*. London: Zed Books.

ethically penetrated activity entailing responsibility for our choices; just as Keynes insisted economics was a moral science, not a natural science.

Strategizing is the process of dealing with anxiety. One of my anxieties is that readers will think I miss the strategic significance of recent advances in "big data," "cloud computing," "analytics," AI, automation, and robotics, and how they are changing business practice. To the contrary, I trained as a nuclear engineer, worked in the computer industry with expert systems, depend on the research materials I access, create, and store on-line, and am ever amazed by what computers can do for us. But in spite of my "geekiness," I have shifted focus towards people and their work, in particular towards how people differ from machines and must work in different ways. Human work is not machine work, so I am with Hubert Dreyfus and his *What Computers Still Can't Do*.[7] Likewise recent "brain science" is fascinating and important, but I see nothing to suggest computers will soon, or ever, imagine and strategize in the ways we humans do. Computers do not see the world as we see it; they cannot for they do not live it. The imagination and judgment we develop through living springs from abilities that complement our reasoning and enable us to inhabit our uncertain world in a purposeful manner. Here I am at one with John Locke.[8] Even if, one day, in a space/time context far away, computers command, for the moment we humans rule—for better or worse—and the business firm and the way it channels our creativity is at the center of our socio-economy.

The private sector firm and entrepreneurship have a pivotal place in capitalist democracy and its politics. One of the impulses behind this book is my sense that most strategy writers ignore or "disrespect" the politics of private enterprise along with its ethics and aesthetics. In part this is because it is difficult to meet the professional demands of an academic career in the management sciences without also presuming there can be an apolitical positivist science of managing—no matter how little fruit has come from this particular tree. We all know that it rejects Keynes's notion of morality and reflects the prevailing hegemony of positivist methods that are taken to be the litmus test of all knowledge. But we also know that our hearts (and guts) continue to function even when our heads fail to find logical or rational answers. Our bounded rationality means we differ profoundly from computers (and Spock), yet act purposefully despite that. Which is why managerial ethics matter so much. Management and entrepreneurship lie at the core of capitalist politics; perhaps its poetry or music making. It is the most influential art form in our

---

[7] H. L. Dreyfus (1992) *What Computers Still Can't Do: A Critique of Artificial Reason*. Cambridge, MA: MIT Press.

[8] John Dunn (2003) *Locke: A Very Short Introduction*. Oxford: Oxford University Press. John Locke (1997) *An Essay Concerning Human Understanding*, ed. Roger Woolhouse. London: Penguin Books.

democracy, what shapes and sustains our life-world. By the same token, natural science, important as it obviously is, has little relevance to the human condition whenever we lack the poetic imagination to bring it to bear on our society or the politics to fit it in. I explore how we might help correct the excessive quantification in today's discussions of managing. I show how our imaginings complement and make valuable the increasingly powerful analytic techniques we use to pursue our projects.

Additional questions arise because the boundary between the private and public sectors is managed via a political process that depends on how the two sides understand each other's language. Yet, as Coase reminds us, we lack a tenable theory of the firm and so can scarcely fault public officials' misunderstandings of the entrepreneurs' strategic process. Many presume the principal differences between the private and public sectors lie in ownership and that the mechanics are otherwise much the same, beliefs that underpin most proposals to regulate or deregulate the private sector. I offer an alternative view, that the two sectors employ profoundly different ways and means to harness the participating individuals' imagination. A public agency is not a private firm with taxpayers as shareholders. Thus it is quite one thing to debate the legitimacy and utility of an apparatus that harnesses citizens' imaginative capacity to the public good, quite another when it is being harnessed to private profit. The private sector's legitimacy cannot hinge on the value created "spilling-over" into the public good.[9] Its construction may entail a mode of citizen subordination that is undemocratic at its essence. These matters cannot be theorized using or presuming "theories of the firm" that cut people's imagination from the analysis, for the citizens' rights to their own imaginings are among democracy's most fundamental axioms—one of the reasons Locke sought the separation of Church and State.

*JC Spender*
*New York*

---

[9] Since the US Supreme Court judgment on Citizens United vs Federal Electoral Commission (2010) there has been renewed political debate about the nature of the firm (e.g. J. D. Clements (2012) *Corporations are Not People: Why They Have More Rights than You Do and What You Can Do about it*. San Francisco: Brett-Koehler Publishers). It resurfaces earlier debates about the firm as an "unnatural person" summarized in the judgments of Supreme Court Justice Stephen Field and Maitland (F. W. Maitland (1900) 'The Corporation Sole', *Law Quarterly Review*, 16, 335–54).

# Contents

# Contents

# Figures

# Acronyms

| | |
|---|---|
| AACSB | Association to Advance Collegiate Schools of Business |
| AFC | Arsenal Football Club |
| BCG | Boston Consulting Group |
| BM | Business Model |
| BS | Balanced Scorecard |
| CCTL | Christensen Center for Teaching and Learning |
| CEO | Chief Executive Officer |
| CISC | Complex Instruction Set Computer |
| DC | Dynamic Capability |
| EADS | European Aeronautics Defence and Space Company |
| EIF | External–Internal Fit |
| ESOP | Employee Stock Ownership Plan |
| FCPA | Foreign Corrupt Practices Act (1977) |
| FIT | Fashion Institute of Technology |
| GE | General Electric |
| GSK | GlaxoSmithKline |
| HBS | Harvard Business School |
| ICI | Imperial Chemical Industries |
| KM | Knowledge Management |
| LCAG | Learned, Christensen, Andrews, and Guth |
| LSE | London School of Economics |
| MIT | Massachusetts Institute of Technology |
| NIE | New Institutional Economics |
| PADR | Prospector–Analyzer–Defender–Reactor |
| PAT | Principal-Agent Theory |
| PEST | Political, Economic, Social, Technological |
| R&D | Research and Development |
| RBV | Resource-Based View |
| RISC | Reduced Instruction Set Computer |
| ROI | Return on Investment |
| s-a-p | Strategy-as-Practice |
| SME | Small and Medium-sized Enterprises |

| | |
|---|---|
| SRI | Stanford Research Institute |
| SWOT | Strengths, Weaknesses, Opportunities, Threats |
| TAM | Team, Action, Management |
| TCE | Transactions Cost Economics |
| TMF | Theory of the Managed Firm |
| ToF | Theory of the Firm |
| VOC | Vereenigde Oost-Indische Compagnie |
| VRIO | Valuable, Rare, Inimitable, Organizational |
| WW2 | Second World War |

# 1

# Introduction to Strategic Work, Language, and Value

## 1.0 Introduction

This chapter has two objectives. First, to familiarize the reader with my view of strategic work and how it goes well beyond rational decision-making and goal-oriented planning. Second, to present my general argument. I have tried to keep my language in the realm of everyday talk and commonsense and avoid packing the text with academic terminology and citations. There are footnotes, but I have tried to make the text understandable without requiring the reader to have studied other material, to be followable on the basis of their everyday experience of the business world. I have also tried to make the text gender-neutral—especially difficult in English—and avoid too narrow an emphasis on US management thinking. The explosive growth of business schools and management education worldwide has reinforced English as the lingua franca of business, so Anglo-American thinking too often dominates. We all hope to see important business literature in Spanish, French, Japanese, Chinese, and Russian soon—but that is for later. The reader will also see some circularity and repetition. This is not simply about style. It reflects my coming at strategy with assumptions that differ from those most strategy writers adopt, more "subjective" and less "objective," and my sense that I need to say some basic things more than once.

My focus is strategic work in business, on generating profit and growth, the artful practice of channeling the intuitions, thinking, choosing, collaborating, and practice of those involved towards the firm's chosen goals. The private sector firm is an amazing invention—a deliberately constructed instrument or process for value creation. My writing is for people engaged in real value-creating firms, or those studying them, and is intended to help them appreciate the work of firm construction and profit-making. This first chapter deals with talking about strategic work—and how we need a language. Few strategy texts pay attention to language or to the problems of selecting language appropriate to the topic. Yet strategy presents authors with considerable challenges in this respect. How should we talk about firms, strategies, and profits? Languages always revolve around distinctions; "left" is meaningful because we know "right"; likewise "up" and "down." A word indicates what it is not as well as what it is, and this is the basis of meaning. A pedal-cycle is not a motorcycle. To talk about strategy we need to know what strategy is not as well as what it is. We need to know what a firm is. Binary distinctions are often elaborated. Instead of "up" versus "down" we might have "which floor?" in a seventy-floor skyscraper, or elevations in thousands of feet or fractions of a millimeter, depending on what we want to do with the data. This chapter identifies some of the distinctions we use to say something meaningful about strategic work. Most strategy books plunge in without paying attention to their language, often drawing on fuzzy notions like "market share," "leadership," "competitive advantage," or "innovation." It is worth being careful with words because the structure of the language chosen determines the penetrative power of the resulting analysis, just as a clock that has lost its minute hand has shortcomings as a timepiece or a screen's resolution determines what can be seen—and what cannot. Academics have an advantage over the "man in the street" here; they may be no cleverer but they are trained to use language more rigorously and so waste less effort on arguments that pass by each other without informing.

The distinctions we use to build a language and discuss strategy are as commonsense as left/right and up/down, but they rise from the specifics of the business context rather than everyday life. We shall also see that strategy is an empirical concept, not a theoretical one. The language's effectiveness depends on the strategic work's context. So there is no single definition of strategy, just as there is no single definition of "the good life." The distinctions useful to talk about strategy include goal-directed/directionless, knowing/non-knowing, sustainable/unsustainable, static/dynamic, and so on. Note, too, that my notion of "work" goes beyond "decision-making," which is how many describe managerial practice. I lean heavily on the work/decision-making distinction; work being purposeful practice in the world, dealing creatively with something specific in difficult context.[1] The resourceful actor inhabits the lived context of her/his action. In contrast, rational decision-making inhabits only part of the head, a mental activity we might also do in a classroom, abstracted from everyday organizational life. In a sense my whole argument spins around this distinction because it tells us so much about strategic work—how it differs from rational decision-making precisely because it is in the "lived" world. So strategic work is less computable, more difficult, and more humanely dimensioned than rational decision-making—one of the reasons strategy professors, researchers, and students are so tempted to retreat into abstractions, away from the factual and moral complexities of day-to-day business. They keep the lived world at arm's length, presuming it is computable and rationally structured according to their theories. The real world that managers inhabit is not a classroom—and therein lies what is so complex and difficult about strategic work. Theory is logical, it powers rational decision-making and while theory is often relevant to evaluating action it is never sufficient to managers' practical needs. Strategic work, being in the lived world, reaches beyond computation and engages the messy and unavoidably compromising business of living. One caution: I eventually abandon the distinction between managers and managed because once strategic work is properly understood it becomes clear that it is widely distributed in real firms. Everybody is doing it. The firm's strategic work goes way beyond the senior "C-level" managers and engages everyone whose expertise is essential to the firm's existence and successful pursuit of profit. Or, turning this point around, much that is strategically important to a firm happens even when the C-level folk know little about it. All purposive activity in our uncertain world calls for strategic work—but the work of a business differs from the work we do in our private lives.

## 1.1 What Does "Strategic" Mean?

Academic writers are encouraged to define what they are talking about—but not all answers help when it comes to strategy. So much about it is like operating a new washing machine or videodisc player, all lights and buttons. You have to know how to operate it before you can understand the instruction booklet (it was written by someone who already knew). Likewise we may have to know more or less what we mean by strategic work before we can really understand the explanations offered. This is because the different definitions

---

[1] The papal encyclical of 1981 is particularly interesting on the notion of work and the distinction between work and "labor." Work leads to Man's "flourishing" whereas labor hinders it. Pope John Paul II (1981) *Laborem Exercens* (On Human Work). Boston: Pauline Books.

imply very different concepts; they are not differing definitions of a single concept. Strategy's meanings are always "situated" reflections of the knowledge absences the strategist chooses to grapple with in the pursuit of profit. "What are we going to do now?" is the key question, and time matters. In our capitalist system these choices are incredibly varied, and strategic work is a corollary of this freedom of choice. For instance, one firm offers sea cruises, another makes handguns, a third puts on rock concerts, and the meaning of "strategic" is different in each line of business, pointing to the myriad different ways in which firms make profits. The thing common to these different contexts is strategic work's "methodology," how managers gain awareness of the particular aspects that call for their judging and choosing, supported by whatever theory and analysis has to offer. Their judgments are contextualized and differ—and become the essence of what "strategic work" means in that particular situation. So this chapter moves towards a notion of strategic work as the practice of managerial judgment, choice, and persuasion rather than observation, computation, and instruction—and, like the bulk of my book, is about how this works in practice.

Strategy always begins with a chosen purpose, the idea of human activity directed towards a known end. "Intention" is absolutely central to the analysis, axiomatic. Human beings "intend"—other entities that seem to make choices such as rivers choosing to run here rather than there, or forest fires, are not conscious and do not intend. Human beings first imagine their intentions, though sometimes there are deeper intentions they are not immediately aware of. This happens because we lack complete knowledge of ourselves, our situation, and our future; we think there are choices. Strategy presupposes a goal freely chosen, and strategic analysis often aims to achieve or improve performance measured against that goal—which may not be known precisely but must be known well enough to provide a sense of direction, to discriminate between the options we see. Intention provides a sense of direction. Note the choice of goal lies outside the analysis and is logically prior to the strategic work, part of our freedom. First "intend" a goal then the strategic work begins. Often strategic work begins with a sense of "failed progress," goals missed, what used to be called a "strategic gap." Second, there is no strategic work to do if there is no difficulty involved in reaching the goal or resetting direction; strategy presumes difficulty. It addresses a difficult and non-trivial problem. My "definition" of strategy turns on the nature of this difficulty, on what is difficult about discovering and implementing the practice that reaches a goal freely chosen. The difficulty is not that of choosing the firm's goals, it is practical: "How to reach that goal?" Pondering what to do with your life is dealing with goals—it may well be "a problem" but it is not a strategic one. But if you choose to become a brain surgeon you have a strategic problem—how to reach that objective. In short, strategy presupposes more than just having a goal. The problems it addresses are grounded in a "collision" between the goal and the real-world context or situation in which it is found difficult. Business strategy reflects the vast variety of goals that lie open to businesses in a capitalist democracy and the difficulties achieving them. It arises precisely because (*a*) the business's goal has been chosen, not imposed, and (*b*) it can only be reached by engaging a difficult or "resistant" situation.

So far so good—strategic work deals with the difficulties of achieving a chosen goal in a particular and difficult situation. But can we distinguish strategic work from other forms of managerial work? Surely everything managers do is directed towards the firm's goal? Strategic work has characteristics that help us separate it from some of the other things that managers do. Before getting to these, our initial definition of strategy can be sharpened against some familiar academic definitions—we can test the words used. Academic definitions are sometimes less than clear, hiding what they mean under other assumptions. For instance, some distinguish "strategic" from "tactical," defining strategic as the "big" or "long-term" decisions, tactical being the "small" practical decisions. Perhaps the club's goal is to top the football league; the strategy chosen is to buy some top players, the tactic is to raise the money necessary. What gets hidden here is the "model in the middle" of the strategy's implementation; for instance the assumption that acquiring great players translates into success. This may not happen, as every fan knows, but herein is the nub of the club's strategy. It is difficult to transform great players into a winning team, which is why the coaches or team managers who can do this are expensive too. Providing the club can make the "model in the middle" work, the rest of the funding and trading strategy works too. So perhaps the real league-winning strategy is not only to buy a handful of players but also to get a top coach and the resources s/he needs to get the job done. How do we find this person? What is our strategy for hiring a top coach, given we are well down in the league? Now the "model in the middle" changes and may mean finding a top manager who wants to retire to our area (Barcelona is very inviting to those used to living in Northern Europe). What is our strategy for making this happen? And so on, an endless regression showing that relating causes to effects is not a fruitful way of talking about strategy.

Likewise the distinction between long-term and short-term does not work either. As the maxim "from acorns to oaks" reminds us, big things often start out small. Precedent works to show how small choices often escalate into major changes, that a winning business strategy often begins far from the big decisions that later seem to have been made. Wrigley got into the chewing-gum business by using gum in a marketing promotion for their baking soda—their real business at the time. Amazon has developed as a global player in cloud computing after deciding to sell the excess capacity on its book-sale-managing computers. Jobs and Wozniak's refusal to open the Apple II computer's operating system to app developers made Apple a very different company from Microsoft, though it did not seem strategic at the time. Later, as we now know, it revealed unanticipated "externalities" in the context in which Apple and Microsoft interacted with app developers and PC users. The point here is that strategy is not just about having an intention. Any definition that ignores the particularities and difficulties of the context in which the goal is pursued is useless "one-handed clapping." Because particulars are crucial to the nature of strategic work, no general definition can work. Second, not every distinction helps. Sometimes market segmentation will matter, sometimes not. Likewise technological evolution will sometimes matter and sometimes not. Strategic work begins with finding the specific distinctions that are appropriate to help us wrap our arms around the particular collision of intention, context, and difficulty that is the firm.

Another popular definition suggests strategy as "pattern in the ongoing flow of events or activities," distinguishing between patterned and unpatterned or random. The problems with this definition are different from those above—big/small, long-term/short-term—but the result is the same. No go. Theories propose patterns. But pattern is in the eye of the beholder, of course; watch one sparrow fly and it does not seem to know where it is headed. Watch a flock and the pattern impresses, though if you watch carefully you see each sparrow seems to move randomly within the flock. We see no "leader" sparrows that match the highly leader'd patterns of human activity. So there are deeper questions around the source of the patterns we see. Water flowing over a dam is patterned to the observer on the shore, though not to the cork bobbing downstream. Who controls or makes the pattern, and who sees it? Watching the pattern in a military parade or a ballet on stage, we know we are seeing the choreographer's intentions. But do non-coaches have the skill to see the choreography of an American football game—as compared with a soccer game? Patterns are sometimes intended by strategists, at other times they "emerge," the result of forces and relationships we do not control. In which case they may reflect the self-organizing characteristics and properties of the entities behaving—water or sparrows. Physicists and engineers know a lot about the properties of water and can explain why it "self-organizes" and takes up patterns—because it is in the equilibrium or "least energy" condition—nothing to do with our intentions or purposive activity. There may be no self-organizing tendencies on which strategists can lean. We humans do not cause the patterns in biology and botany. The study of fractals and chaos theory sometimes leads people to define strategy as "pattern at the edge of chaos"; presuming pattern is evidence of human intention. But the pattern might equally well be emergent. The patterns of Vietnamese mountain rice terraces are intended, part of the farmers' collective strategy of overcoming their specific difficulties, as compared with the different difficulties facing the rice growers in the plains' paddy fields. There are often patterns in economic activity—sometimes intended, as on a production line or an underpriced IPO, sometimes emergent as buyers move to lower priced suppliers, or in the "power-law distribution" of firm size that seems to deny management's impact altogether. Individual trades in a market place may seem chaotic. The larger view seems patterned, the "invisible hand" of a non-human choreographer as the market "clears." We think this the logical consequence of the economic agents' imperative to self-maximize. But in general the notion of pattern is incidental to strategy and reveals little about the presence or absence of strategic practice.

## 1.2 Intention and Context

Above, I suggest the regular textbook definitions of strategy are not very useful to strategic practitioners, and this is not mere academic nitpicking. Different people mean different things when they use the term "strategy." When I use the term I have something specific in mind that needs to be surfaced if the reader is to follow my explanation of how it leads to value, profit, or competitive advantage. Again I repeat myself a bit here, but only to ensure all are following my drift (most managers insist they have to repeat themselves several times if what they intend is to happen). Strategy writers often emphasize the need to analyze the firm's context, which is helpful, but then leave the strategist's intention undefined, presuming it is to maximize something—profit, performance, advantage, etc. There is the complementary tendency to equate having an intention with having a strategy, to think "be bold" is a strategy because it contrasts with "be cautious," or to have a goal is to have a strategy, such as "be #1" rather than not #1.[2] This is not helpful. An intention to be the industry leader may be a start, but we only get to strategy by understanding the difficulties of achieving this goal in a particular context. We can cut through the tangle by focusing on the interaction of (a) the strategist's intention, and (b) the difficulties s/he faces in that particular context. Most strategy writers' definitions of strategy confuse or miss (b), hiding the practical dimensions of the question to be answered, missing the "model in the middle" and the practices necessary to cross the space between intention and result. Intention or purpose is always specific to time and situation and precedes strategic practice. Plus, there has to be a real and specific context before any strategic question can arise. There are no generalities here. Merely being in a context does not mean you need a strategy; you

---

[2] R. P. Rumelt (2011) *Good Strategy, Bad Strategy: The Difference and Why it Matters*. New York: Crown Business. This is engaging on this approach.

may have no intention of changing your situation. Intention is not simply about reaching for a goal, it is also about purposively or intendedly moving away from your current position and towards another particular situation. Thus intention and strategy are bound up with the specific changes we want to make in specific situations. The essence of the managers' strategic work lies in the difficulties that stand in the way of satisfying their desire to make these changes. Paradoxically we have to know who we are—strategically speaking—before we can delineate the context of our goal seeking. Socrates was absolutely right on this—know thyself! Strategy is as much about choosing who we are as about choosing a goal or the context in which to pursue it.

Again, strategy lies at the intersection of the actor's chosen identity, her/his intention, and the difficulties s/he faces in a specific context. There can be no general definition of strategy, for it only arises among the actor's and the situation's colliding specifics. It is useful to turn this around and ask, "What question is strategic work supposed to answer?" Yes, it is to bring identity, intention, and situation together in reasoned action. And, yes, it indicates how best to achieve the intended goal—but that does not convey much until "best" has also been measured against the difficulties and options that are available to that specific actor in that particular context. A strategist needs a sense of expediency, of ensuring the best does not become the enemy of the "good enough"—the compromise that some call "satisficing." Beyond describing the context we need some way of classifying or calibrating the difficulties and available options, given our capabilities and idea of adequate performance.

## 1.3 Data Difficulties

As the analysis of the business context proceeds, never simple in the real world, we discover several different kinds of difficulty beyond finding the appropriate metrics like the easy/hard or costly/cheap that enable us to collect data. Anyone who has been orienteering, or hiking across unmarked country where there are no roads, trails, rivers, and so on, knows the challenge is keeping "oriented"; which is why it is called orienteering. We get lost. The story is that when there are no marks visible, as in the desert, we walk in circles, perhaps counterclockwise if we are right-handed. In dense forests there are too many marks for the non-expert trapper to handle, so people walk randomly until exhausted, getting nowhere. These tales indicate a completely different kind of contextual difficulty. It is easy to imagine the firm's context presents itself know-ably and unambiguously. The reality is generally different. We find the world is a "blooming buzzing confusion," as the pragmatist William James said. What can the strategist make of it? Today's term is "sense-making"—how we make sense of what we see, feel, hear, smell, taste, or think.[3] When our senses get baffled we get confused. Our "reading" of the context must be in terms of our capabilities and goals. First a strategy and then a reading, perhaps, inverting the sequence many assume?

The scientist's task may be to measure the context "objectively" with a calibrated means like a thermometer or GPS equipment. In contrast, the strategist's challenge is to see the context in terms of her/himself or, more specifically, in terms of her/his capabilities to negotiate the context competently in pursuit of her/his chosen goal. This is OK as far as it goes but it hides deeper sense-making complexities. Now we are rapidly closing in on the essential nature of strategic work, which arises precisely because real contexts are not like maps others have drawn for us. We must choose identity, intention, and content, and then draw our own map based on our capabilities. Real contexts have endless complexity and it is never obvious what matters and what does not. The mapmaker decides most of that for the map user. An additional difficulty in mapping a context is realizing that knowing "who we are" has a "when" in it as well, a "now" as opposed a "back then," when we were different, or a "perhaps who we might be" and aspire to be different in the future. Strategic work is typically time-sensitive because identities, intentions, and contexts are all dynamic. As marketers remind us, "timing is everything," so strategic work is often about getting the timing right, distinguishing "now!" from "too soon" or "too late." The real world is comprised of "windows of strategic opportunity," the granularity of lived time that matches the granularity of our circumstances—we do not engage either time or space as "seamless."

At this point we see that strategic work arises at the interface between a specific identity, an intention, and a context in a specific lived time frame—a specific moment. But what if the metrics for mapping these are not on the same footing and cannot be brought together? We may have multiple maps of the "same thing"—reflecting our multiple sense-making and measuring techniques. Firms are interested in profit, customer satisfaction, and product quality. Each of these metrics may be practical enough but they cannot be melded into a single scale for assessing action. It is tricky to synthesize data that have been created using different metrics. Thus everyday life is not readily "objectified." Witnesses to a crime often tell remarkably different stories. Much of the difficulty in sense-making work arises from the variety of metrics behind the rising volume of "big data" available in business today—what

---

[3] K. E. Weick (1995) *Sensemaking in Organizations*. Thousand Oaks, CA: Sage Publications. Weick's work has been dominant in bringing Gestalt psychology's notions into the analysis of management and organizations. However, the approach pays little attention to tacit knowledge or "best practice."

Donald Rumsfeld, who had a remarkable talent for language, called "connecting the dots." For example, business data might be about our customers' payment records, which pay on time, which pay late. We might also have data on customers' cash positions; or on their R&D expenditures, their advertising budgets, their CEO's pay, or their political donations. Perhaps we also have data on their market share, their rate of product recalls, labor turnover, etc. What are we to make of this multiply-dimensioned data? Payment behavior seems reasonably related to cash position but there quickly comes a point when we have more data than we can make sense of. In the past business people may have had to work with less information than they wanted. Today we often have too much and it may not be possible to connect the dots and make sense of it. Our different maps may not coalesce into a single coherent map. We are left with a number of alternative maps—and must use our goals to judge which of these maps are going to work best for us. Thus business intelligence has two facets: (*a*) getting the necessary data and (*b*) making sense of it. All of us are tempted to leave out what is not easily connected. Connecting the dots is hard work.

## 1.4 People-Based Difficulties

The challenges of mapping a multidimensioned and changing business context in which the firm's strategists have changing (dynamic) intentions are considerable. The strategic analysts' work is exhausting, though modern data collection and analytic techniques may be helpful. The business context hides a deeper dimension of difficulties. The mapping metaphor is useful but has little to say about people. People are peculiar—and tricky to "map." Sometimes they are predictable, "map-able," and can be made part of the definable context. In business situations people are often variable, such as when lining up at the checkout—but might still be handled as members of larger and thereby more predictable populations. "On average..." we say, and try to work with that, even though business is done in the particular—one customer at a time. Sophisticated traffic analysis can help a restaurant minimize its food wastage and queuing theory can help balance shoppers' impatience against checkout costs. But sometimes people are unpredictable—and creative.

The paragraphs above point to several kinds of problem that translate directly into the difficulties of describing the firm's context and reaching goals. These fall into distinct categories of "knowledge absence." First, there is a lack of the data necessary to seeing how to reach our goal, "ignorance" of what can be known, at least in principle because it is about something that exists objectively. Second, there is the multidimensionality or fragmented state of the data available that creates a very different kind of knowledge absence—connecting the dots—technically known as "incommensurability," the absence of a common measure of what we know. This chapter section explores yet another kind of "knowledge absence." Technically known as "indeterminacy," it arises because much of the firm's context is made up of other firms, institutions, and people who are responding to our actions in ways that may surprise us. Thus, in addition to "ignorance" and "incommensurability," people generate "indeterminacy" as they respond actively to each other and change in ways contingent on that action. The firm's context becomes interactive, dynamic in a different way.

Game theory studies these interactions and provides a very specific definition of strategy—what we can label "strategy/gt"—the/gt standing for game theory. (This is clumsy and will not be with us for long.) A player with a strategy/gt knows the appropriate choice to make at every decision-point during the interaction in order to reach his/her goal (to win probably but not necessarily, she might be playing checkers with her grandfather and wants to boost his ego by letting him win). In general the game theoretic definition of "a strategy" is the full set of unambiguous instructions for completing the game in the manner chosen. I distinguish this with the /gt tag because such strategy inheres in the game, not in the player or the collision between her/his intention and context. It positions "a strategy" as outside our lived world and in the specific world the game defines, like chess. Because of this different objective nature, game theory has grave limitations as a theory of strategy in the lived world. It offers solutions (strategies/gt) only under conditions of zero ignorance or incommensurability—for instance, in a zero-sum game like checkers or chess, when one person wins and the other loses and no collaborative gains are allowed (draws are OK). There are also game theories of shared non-zero-sum, incomplete information, and other situations, and they can provide valuable insights into auction bidding, alliance management, contract insurance, risk management, and many other aspects of real-world business. But even then, because strategy/gt applies to a realm of constructed certainty, it can only be applied after the strategic work identified above—the choice of goal, identity, context, and timing—has been completed. My focus is on the lived world and coping with its uncertainties and knowledge absences and not with playing games in an artificial world. Of course, if the reactions of the different people involved (customers, competitors, suppliers, labor unions, employees, etc.) to the firm's moves can be forecast with absolute certainty, they can be incorporated into a strategy/gt rigorously. But how should the strategist proceed when other people's moves can be neither forecast nor dismissed on the grounds that they do not affect the outcome? This is the point at which game theory analysis runs out of steam and real strategic work begins.

The strategic or entrepreneurial answer here—which the rest of my book unpacks—is to get around the stoppage, breakdown, or impediment by acting on and changing the situation, and understanding that people can be persuaded into a different universe of action possibilities. Then, instead of describing or forecasting the context, the emphasis of the strategic work turns towards changing the interplay of identity, intention, and context so that it can be brought into the analysis as a manageable variable: for example, the monopolist who decides for (and so "manages") the customer—"any color so long as it is black." In the real world the strategist is never the only actor vying for control, there are always forces beyond her/his control. Much strategic practice revolves around changing others so that they become aligned with the firm's intentions and do not introduce "indeterminacy" into the situation.

## 1.5 Four Paradigms of Strategic Work and Talk

Strategic work leads to changes in identity, intention, and context. Sometimes it makes good sense to adapt one's goals in the light of experience and more data. Sometimes the emphasis will be towards changing the people on whom the value-creating processes depend. At other times the way forward is to shift the firm's resources into a more amenable context. A firm faces an especially tough task when it has to change "external" people to achieve its goal. For many years the UK retailer Marks & Spencer was famous for successfully "educating" its suppliers to produce better quality, no mean task given suppliers' incentives to do the opposite. The same challenge exists on the customer side of the firm, changing customers to accept what you produce. The most important change in business practice since WW2 is today's emphasis on "market making," on creating demand for goods and services that were not even recognized as needed in earlier times. Macroeconomists sometimes distinguish "basic" goods from "luxury" goods, the first being essential and needed irrespective of price, the second only acquired when buyers have funds to spare. Luxury goods dominate the economy. The business of creating new luxury goods and changing consumers' behavior has made advertising into a huge and powerful industry with enormous budgets—seldom discussed in the strategy literature. Today the major part of the economy is in non-basic luxury goods (and services), so market making seems as important as making goods and services, if not more so. Effective use of verbal and visual languages is advertising's core.

Later in the book I emphasize talk as managers' principal method of generating strategically significant change in the people involved with the business. This is not to take away from the many other ways in which firms can change their contexts in the pursuit of better performance. Private sector lobbying is powerful and strategic in the US, but I see no strategy books on how to gin up and manage your lobbyists. FCPA (Foreign Corrupt Practices Act 1977) has also had a significant impact, penalizing those who give kickbacks, yet few strategy texts mention the problems of doing business when bribes are everyday practice. Likewise the Supreme Court's *Citizen's United vs Federal Election Commission* (2010) decision has made a huge impact, with more to come as corporations are given increased political voice. Less considered traditional ways to manipulate consumption and production are to help the local sports team to success (a sure boost to labor productivity), engage with trade associations to promote legislation and industry-related research, create appropriate educational facilities to ensure a good supply of trained labor (as so evident in Germany), take part in the procedures that shape local legislation in land development and ecology—and many similar. All these form part of the strategic work of real firms because a great deal of their legislative and socio-economic context is likely to be susceptible to engagement and manipulation by others. A full description of the firm's context includes all the ways in which it can be influenced by the firm to assist its progress towards its goals. But contexts are more malleable than most strategy writers admit.

Up to this point strategic work can be defined as arising through the dynamic interaction of identity, intention, and context—and there can be no theoretical definition of strategy because this is not a theoretical concept. Rather, it is an empirical concept about overcoming real-world difficulties that take their meaning from the situation's particulars—this chosen objective in this context, at this moment. So before we can talk about the strategic work of managing such difficulties we need a language based on appropriate empirically grounded distinctions. The generalizations we find in textbooks miss the particularities and thus the nature of the strategic work to be done. For example, there may be nothing difficult—in principle or theoretically—about expanding market share. We drop price or raise quality. It only becomes strategic because in the real world that action impacts elsewhere. Likewise in a particular market we might think of changing position because our present position is "too difficult." But this means nothing until we also identify the difficulties of getting into any alternative position we might think to occupy. We may be jumping from the pan into the fire, making a strategic error and exacerbating our difficulties. Perhaps the opposite also, we might be able to occupy the new market and defend it without difficulty. It all depends—and strategy turns on such empirical details. There are few, if any, generalities. Conversely, when "it all depends" does not apply there is no strategic work to be done.

We can categorize the strategic work the entrepreneur or management has to do as we move from static definitions of identity, intention, and context towards more dynamic definitions. The interaction of changeable intention, context, and identity suggests four common paradigms or basic orientations towards strategic work—labeled A, B, C, and D in Figure 1.1—depending on what we hold constant, what changes, and how. It is worth spelling these out so that they can be fitted into a more general framework within which further notions of strategy can be contrasted. Many of us have been trained into Paradigm A. Its basis is the "scientific method" and the hunt for objective theories about the firm's nature and context. The concept is sometimes illustrated as the final step in a sequence of (*a*) description, (*b*) correlation, and (*c*) identification of causal relations. It presumes the world comprises identifiable interacting entities whose existence we have no doubts about—such as automakers, grocers, or homebuyers. Logical cause and effect relationships or action networks connect the entities that comprise this world. Theories summarize these relationships as general statements about predictable interactions and effects in a particular milieu. We "explain" events by referring to this kind of theory. When the analysis suggests that X happens because of Y, we consider X explained. The explanation is judged acceptable because the theory relating X and Y is logical. This kind of theorizing is often at the center of our discussion about the business world and its doings. Sometimes the theories we use are solidly supported by scientific observation. Often our theories are less secure, even tentative. For instance, while global warming has a degree of scientific support, it is not regarded as a compelling explanation of Mid-Western drought or the West Nile virus epidemic.

As we dig into the strategy literature we can contrast its authors' choice of ontology (what is thought about) against their choice of epistemology (how it is thought about). Most of the literature (top row of Figure 1.1) presumes firms exist as non-problematic entities to be directed by strategic decision-making. The contrasting narrative (bottom row) is that strategic work is another term for the processes of constructing the firm. These would be trivial if following

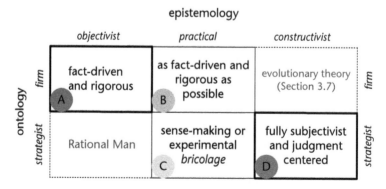

**Figure 1.1** Four Paradigms of Strategic Thinking

rigorous models or "blueprints" were all that was necessary. I presume the opposite, of course, that there are no rigorous models because uncertainty prevails. Indeed absent such uncertainty there is no reason for firms to come into being—the subject of my entire book. But whatever the nature of the resulting firm, the process of its construction must turn on the entrepreneur's judgment inputs rather than on the objectified facts of the situation, which are then supporting and secondary rather than determining. The discussion moves from the firm as the entity being thought about (top line) and onto the lower row in Figure 1.1 where we locate the entrepreneur or strategist who is the source of judgment.

The scientific method encourages us to formulate a theory or hypothesis (a particular statement of a theory) about the phenomena of interest (the entities and relationships we are looking into) and expose it to empirical test. Obviously a lot of academic research into strategizing and its economic impact is framed this way; for instance, we may have a tentative theory of market–firm interaction that says firms that respond to market needs will be more successful than those that do not. We explain Kodak's troubles on the basis of this theory, arguing the company failed to respond to the market's growing desire for digital cameras, resulting in the disappearance of their camera film business. The Paradigm A implication is that the strategist must construct a logical theory of how to achieve the goal chosen—and articulate it into a plan. It assumes reasonable people will follow along willy-nilly because of what has been scientifically proven. Many strategy writers operate within Paradigm A, and for many years it was the dominant notion of strategic work, adopted on the grounds of such thinking's popularity and effectiveness during WW2. Ultimately a well-constructed plan is a theory about how selected resources and their relationships must lead to the goal sought. The emphasis is on completeness and logicality and there is no distinction between theory/ plan and strategy.

Paradigm B is more realistic because it seems to bring "real people" back in. It suggests plans are never completely determining, gaps remain, people do not know or follow the right answers, and things are seldom as they were reported. Thus Paradigm B also presumes flexible and imaginative people are needed to provide creative inputs—for understanding is invariably incomplete and may not be rigorously logical. But it does not identify them or make them central to the analysis. OK, we discover our data is incorrect and our predictions do not turn out as expected. Likewise we are often ignorant of some of the necessary facts about the entities and their relationships until after we have acted. We get surprised. Then we muddle through. The alliance of AOL and Time-Warner did not go according to plan and called for considerable recrafting during the process of merging the firms into one. It was a bad surprise for many, though not, perhaps, for Steve Case, who made out well enough. Paradigm B does not hang on rigorous plans; just plans that are as-good-as-practicably-possible. It allows gaps, to be addressed later by competent and imaginative people. Many things will not be taken into consideration and the hope is that it will all work out well in the end. It is muddling through. Successful business people are those who make "good calls" in such situations, successfully judging which facts to take into account and which to ignore, and who guess well when there are no facts to be found. There is nothing much that strategy writers can say about this paradigm beyond "make sure your strategist has good judgment in this particular situation"—a tautology. There is no solid theory here. Which leads people to pay attention to the strategist's "track record"; a model that presumes experience is the source of (or a theory of) good judgment. The new CEO is hired on the basis of her track record, though that was in a situation quite unlike that this firm presently faces. This may lead to more surprises, as in the cases of Carly Fiorina or Ron Johnson. We might say that Paradigm B aspires to become Paradigm A by introducing and linking in a new concept—strategic judgment—that can establish, beyond the plan's dictates, what matters and how detailed it should be.[4] While we presume a relationship between experience and judgment, it is not very secure for we know experience is not always a source of good judgment. There is no causal connection between experience and judgment; we have no theory of good judgment or its source.

Most strategy writers position themselves within Paradigm A, though sometimes concede the need to move towards Paradigm B and admit the importance of business judgment, however acquired or applied. In Paradigm A the strategy writer guides the reader towards methods of collecting and analyzing data about the situation that will lead to a plan that is as complete and logical as possible. The plan is then implemented. The shift from Paradigm A towards Paradigm B is driven by the lack of complete objective knowledge, the inevitable knowledge absences. The gaps remaining must be "made up" by strategic judgment. Thus Paradigm B distinguishes theory/plan (not a matter of judgment) from strategy (which is). Under Paradigm B the strategic work of context discovery and strategic judging produces a compromise adapted to the situation, and knowledge absences are recognized. When ignorance renders a Paradigm A inoperable because not enough is known to construct a completely logical plan, Paradigm B admits the strategist's judgment into the analysis in order to create or construct a plan that is judged as-good-as-possible. Judgment is tough to define or predict, of course, but it provides a way to describe the strategist's fundamental contribution to the business—the

---

[4] There is a strange ambivalence here, for much of this literature seeks middle ground by sticking to the basic notions of rigorous causal relations, but rendering them practice-friendly by allowing them to be sloppy and "good enough." This cannot work, of course.

strategist as the person or group that provides the judgments necessary to complete the plan that theory alone would otherwise be insufficient for.

Paradigm A is hostage to missing facts. It defines the strategist as a planner, the person collecting facts and theories and computing a plan that is both logical and optimal. When the necessary facts and theories are available this task can be performed by a computer, indeed there are many expert systems designed to do just this in complex situations, such as working out the logistics of invading a foreign country. It takes a huge effort to develop the plans necessary to bring a fighting force's multiple components together and move them into theater. Extraordinarily powerful expert systems have been developed for this task. But note how it is made easier by the special nature of the goods and people covered—so many medium tanks, so many Master Sergeants, so many attack helicopter pilots. The resources are categorized as countable and replaceable—an army's basic operating assumption. As soon as we deal with individuals and their differences this kind of planning cannot work. Even in the army situation individuals with good experience and judgment can make all the difference between success and failure, especially when time or battle presses. Paradigm B defines the strategist as the source of whatever judgment is necessary while Paradigm A is silent because none is called for. Perhaps Paradigm A defines the strategist as a computer, a computational function aided by an expert system of stored heuristics. Strategy writers operating in the shadow of Paradigm A generally consider Paradigm B as unworkable because they cannot grasp, "define," or measure judgment as an abstract concept and bring it into their logical model. Thus Paradigm B writers are caught between their desire to use the nuanced language that business people use to talk about what they are doing and the scientific problem of defining terms closely enough to assemble them into testable theoretical statements. We know managers and others in a business do a lot of calculating. But note that when the desired result is hidden in the data it does not matter whose analysis digs it out. Computation reveals the answer—objectively. Thus when we think of a business as a logical machine we write judgment, whether that of the managers or others, out of the discussion. Yet people matter, indeed are the very core of the private sector enterprise, precisely because no firm fits into the specification of a machine. The most fundamental aspects of a business—its ability to add value and be an "engine of the economy"—lie in what cannot be calculated, what is not mechanical and predictable. Thus Paradigm B admits people and their judgment but subordinates their value to that of the plan—their judgment is needed to complete the plan. This turns out to be a very awkward option that ultimately collapses.

Paradigm C is very different and is sometimes evident in the strategy literature. People and their desires are central. Paradigms A and B are upended, goals are subordinated, judgment is prioritized. Thus Paradigm C moves away from the scientific methods as normally defined. It does not assume our socio-economic world is comprised of objective facts about things and logical causal relations between them. Rather the strategist's universe consists of ideas that lead people to do things, especially to produce and consume. For example, there is the urge to buy a better car than your neighbor's, or produce a wristwatch with more features. Paradigm C's relationship to Paradigm B is also a bit like that of luxury goods to basic goods. In Paradigm C the strategy's core is a production/consumption idea, the entrepreneur's idea. Strategic work surfaces that and brings it into the socio-economic world where its successful application leads to adding value and achieving goals such as profit or competitive advantage. The economic terrain here is made up of expectations rather than data or theories about economic actors' behavior—such as buying more when prices drop. But perhaps price is seen as the indicator of quality, so the regular theory does not apply in this case.

In Paradigm C tangible things, especially "resources," matter strategically because they "carry" or "fasten" our expectations and desires. Penrose, like Knight, whose work is central to my argument, pointed out that resources matter less for their objective (scientific, measurable) way of existing than for how they are perceived by producers and consumers.[5] Diamonds are interesting to engineers and chemists for their physical and chemical characteristics, reasonably "objective" and scientifically established facts that drive the "industrial diamond" business. The lady with a "rock" on her finger couldn't care less, and her very different needs and perceptions (and great expectations?) drive the jewelry diamond business. The power of the Paradigm C approach to strategy is evident in the fashion industry. What theory can explain Rolex's success, or that of Prada, or of those firms that sell diamond-studded mobile phones? Note that Paradigms C and B both spin on strategic judgment. But in Paradigm C the judgment needed is not about what is missing from what is known or knowable about a real situation (the market for 5-carat VS1 M pear-cut diamonds). Judgment is no longer subordinated to the logical plan. Rather the reverse. The strategy hinges on what people might be persuaded to think, how their expectations might be changed, and so induced to behave in a new way imagined by the entrepreneur.

Which leads towards Paradigm D. This is like Paradigm C in that it presumes the strategist's world is made up of malleable people with changeable expectations rather than an unchangeable reality. But it goes beyond Paradigm C towards the logical limit that embraces the changeability of the entrepreneur her/himself in addition to the changeability of her/his world. Paradigms A, B, and C presume a stable entrepreneur with a chosen goal. In Paradigm

---

[5] E. T. Penrose (1995) *The Theory of the Growth of the Firm* (3rd edn). New York: Oxford University Press.

A this goal drives the plan; in Paradigm B the plan + some judgments. In Paradigm C it is translated into an apparatus to persuade some other people to behave in a way that subordinates them to the entrepreneur's goal. Of course we are encouraged to presume the point of all business activity is profit. But profit is a far trickier notion with a more tangled and complex history than many admit. Perhaps the emphasis should be simpler and more direct, on creating activity, on process, the uniquely human/social notion of purposive living, of interpersonal interactions of which profit is simply an ex-post measure. The most fundamental outcome of strategy is reasoned and shaped practice. This may translate into profit, or it may not, it all depends. Section 1.13 shows that profit is a simple concept for accountants but is as complex as strategy for those managers whose most fundamental goal is activity, making things happen. In brief: no activity, no engagement with uncertainty, no value adding, no possibility of profit. There may be surprises and disconnections between the activity that the entrepreneurs generate and the accountants' bookkeeping. A firm might show a loss at the same time that its managers know all kinds of other good things happened that open up new strategic opportunities for the future. The recent initiatives to identify and report the firm's intangible assets, such as its learning or "tacit knowledge," attempt to shift the emphasis from what accountants are allowed to count towards the value the firm's managers know has been added through its learning processes. From the strategist's point of view it may be unwise to make managers' strategic work hostage to accountants' assessments. The assessment should turn on the managers' own views of how the firm's strategic situation has changed.

As the strategic work is detached from external measures and leans more on the subjective assessments of the managers themselves, their entrepreneurial identity also becomes more flexible. They control the whole game and are under no obligation to maximize shareholder wealth or resource utilization. The goals they choose might change opportunistically—something just came up—or because minds change and get changed. Real people are flexible, persuadable, not at all like monomaniacal Rational Man. The thrust of Paradigm D is that it admits the possibility of the entrepreneurs changing just as much as Paradigm C is focused on their changing others to align them to the goals chosen. The analysis then hinges on the entrepreneur's "desire" to bring her/his imagination and vision into the world, whatever it is or becomes, knowing it can shift and adapt for a multitude of reasons. Paradigm D is a fuller reflection of the private sector situation that allows business people a great degree of freedom, one aspect of which is that they are free to change their minds about what they are trying to do.[6] In practical terms one of the

---

[6] The classic case is made in J. Child (1972) 'Organisation Structure, Environment and Performance', *Sociology*, 6: 1–21.

reasons why start-ups succeed—or "fail to fail"—is that they learn "strategic-ally" to abandon their initial ideas, which they discover were not as workable or fruitful as they thought when they set up the firm. Amazon reinvented itself around a new vision—to sell books and outcompete the brick-and-mortar bookstore—as it abandoned its initial business plan to acquire and sell customer data. Likewise Microsoft reinvented itself, at considerable strategic and financial risk, when Bill Gates determined that all the company's products had henceforth to be web-oriented. The strategic capability to reach towards a desirable objective is matched and balanced by the ability to turn away from a less desirable objective. Goals are changeable. What remains fixed is the entrepreneurial urge to action that adds value, a fundamental "primitive" desire underpinning strategic practice as a manifestation of our purposiveness, like the fundamental human desire that underpins the production of art. Thus the entrepreneurial process creates and shapes all three aspects—identity, intention, and context. The firm arises at their intersection—from a specific desire and at a specific moment.

With these four paradigms in mind we can approach strategic work more closely. As noted already, explanations normally rely on identifying a "cover-ing theory." To explain is to propose a theory that covers an event. A theory enables us to predict the outcome of the event. Adding value, as Paradigms C and D allow, but Paradigms A and B do not, ultimately means going beyond what was predicted—the value-add is a "surprise," a departure from what was or could be forecast.[7] In this sense there cannot be a theory of "value adding" or, turning this comment around, value adding always takes us beyond what can be theorized because it surprises us. Strategic work precipitates activity that goes beyond the possibilities theorized. Seeking surprise is part of the way we are, our restlessness and desire to inquire into and change (improve) the human condition. We are strategic animals and strive to learn more. Research helps us reach beyond what is known already into anomalies and regions of surprise.[8] So my book can be read as a managerial handbook for dealing with business situations and discovering surprising possibilities—for instance the vast market for interpersonal communication opened up by mobile phones, or the market for education and the life improvements it can lead to, or

---

[7] George Shackle was an English economist (1903–92) whose work was way out of the mainstream. But he was also a follower of Keynes and critical of rational choice theorizing. Shackle believed in the importance of admitting "surprise" into the analysis of economic activity. He attempted—and failed—to interest his fellow economists in the importance of imagination. See G. L. S. Shackle (1979) *Imagination and the Nature of Choice*. Edinburgh: Edinburgh University Press. Around the same time Schumpeter (1883–1950) was more successful in generating interest in "innovation" without saying much about the human capacity to generate it or how or why it arose.

[8] T. S. Kuhn (1970) *The Structure of Scientific Revolutions* (2nd edn). Chicago: University of Chicago Press.

people's susceptibility to fashion. The challenge is to get beyond mere description of surprise in two ways. First, use the methods of science to capture it with new theory, so bringing the phenomena into the realm of the measurable and predictable, de-mystifying the event, as Einstein suggested gravitational forces could bend light. In the same manner, behavioral theories can uncover what we do without knowing we are doing it. But second, by adopting a method to direct the human desire to seek surprise deliberately in ways that are likely to be fruitful rather than simply flailing about hoping to be surprised by what turns up. This is the field of strategy—finding a knowledge absence to plunge into.

My method stands on theory but is directed toward the situated value-creating practices that go beyond the scientific method. It pays attention to the academic literature but is not dominated by it. Consequently this is not an academic book that employs academic style and detail to present its argument. My thrust is towards the constructive strategic work that turns on the crucial distinction between analyzing and doing. It is naïve to think real-world doing can be reduced to implementing an analysis. Certainly a plan may be the result of analysis and decision, and such a plan may well guide practice. But our world is characterized by surprise, failure, ignorance, interruption, and things never being quite as we expected them to be. It is a version of Murphy's Law, that if anything can go wrong, it will; so we are often surprised. Paradigm B says "OK, we know this, but we shall muddle along presuming the gaps are deficiencies that can be ignored in the interests of getting stuff done." I suggest this throws the baby (value-creation) out with the bath-water—we should focus on the baby not the decision to toss the bath-water. Thus I define strategizing as the judgment or imaginative response to what is NOT known, to the surprising, unexpected, incomplete, or illogical nature of what arises through our practice. Surprises come as reality "kicks back" at us, interfering with our "best-laid" plans to reach our goals. It makes their achievement difficult. If we knew everything there was to know about how to reach an objective it would be because we understand the world really is the determined clockwork-like mechanism some tell us it is. Frankly, the world of business is anything but this; it is under-determined. Indeed economic activity hinges on actors' disagreements about, for instance, the value of an asset. Without sellers and buyers disagreeing there would be no trade. Ironically, the situations in which things are most agreed and predictable are those farthest from everyday life—such as sending a rover to Mars. We can predict when the rover will arrive with great precision, precisely because in space there is nothing (or nobody, as far as we know) to interfere with its passage. In Earth-bound business the opposite applies, others are constantly interfering with everything we try to do. They contribute ignorance, incommensurability, and indeterminacy to ensure no human situation can be fully grasped by logical planning. This is what makes strategizing so interesting, so difficult, and so fundamental to the human condition. It lies at the very core of business and the managerial task.

## 1.6 Corporate Strategy's Beginnings

Strategic work has a long history. As many strategy authors point out with their first sentences, the literature takes in the Ancient Greeks, the Romans, Machiavelli, the Napoleonic Wars, Alfred Mahan, and so on. Of course, there is a similar long tradition in Asia (Sun Tzu, Sun Pin, the Book of 5 Rings, or Nguyen Gap)—and in India, and everywhere else that people struggle against each other. But political and military strategizing may not provide much insight into strategizing in business contexts. The post-WW2 history of academic work on corporate strategy (a term used more or less interchangeably with business strategy) shows a big shift in the 1980s. Prior to that time the dominant idea was to match the firm's processes and resources to the market's demands. Without a good fit between the firm and its market engagements (customers' needs, suppliers' offerings, labor availability, etc.) the resulting inefficiencies would reduce profit and threaten the firm's survival. Strategizing meant fitting the firm to the environment, thereby eliminating inefficiencies and maximizing potential. It followed that under-utilized resources had to be applied or disposed of, just as new market engagements had to be appropriately resourced and planned. These ideas fit well with the quantitative planning techniques developed during WW2 and with the industrial restructuring of the post military-dominated production era. But in the 1980s a different set of ideas became popular, largely propelled by Michael Porter's work on competitive strategy[9] but also by shifts in the political climate as Thatcher and Reagan pushed regulators back and freed up commercial markets. Mass consumption, branding, and services began to dominate the economy.

These principles were not new, they reintroduced ideas about industry and competition that were dominant at the end of the nineteenth century, the era of the "trusts" and "robber barons," such as Vanderbilt and Rockefeller. Instead of efficiency these men's focus was on monopolistic advantage and the active suppression of competition—collusion, legislative fixes, violence at times, and agreements made in cigar-smoke-filled rooms. Efficiency mattered less than being able to control the firm's market engagements and exposures so that its profits were secured against the competitive activities of others (and

[9] Michael E. Porter (1980) *Competitive Strategy: Techniques for Analyzing Industries and Competitors*. New York: Free Press.

government regulators). The technical term here is "economic rent," meaning above-normal profit, a return greater than that earned with a "risk-free" investment in, for instance, "gilts" or Treasury Bonds. Competitive activity exposes firms and so generally reduces whatever rents they have—these get competed away. We presume competition "improves the breed," delivering more value to customers by forcing businesses to look for new ways of gaining competitive advantage. The presence of rents indicates "imperfect" markets in which there are likely to be advantageous positions not easily competed away, sustained by government legislation perhaps, or by owning patents or brand-rights. Free markets are often regarded as basic sources of economic efficiency—and strategically beneficial on that account alone. But it may be a misunderstanding of how firms really work. The 1980s strategy theorists' shift towards "rent-seeking" or the pursuit of monopoly-based strategic advantage displaced the earlier focus on efficiency. It showed there was little future in pursuing efficiency if there were rents to be had. Rather the real strategic objective was to secure the rents to be derived from sustained monopolistic positions—such as Apple's dominance in the tablet business. A large research project that seemed to reveal the profitability (rent) impact of market share—PIMS—created a great stir.[10] Many firms and strategy consultants were persuaded to push for market share in the short term in the expectation that doing so would raise profits. Rent-seeking by expanding and protecting market share became the me-too "strategy" of the day, just as the larger and more complicated corporations post-WW2 led to "divisionalization" of the me-too efficiency strategy in the 1960s. Likewise today's strategic anxieties about "innovation" presume the overwhelming need (and possibility) to gain and secure sustainable economic rents though technological development or acquisition, especially where the "windows of competitive advantage" seem to be opening and closing with increasing speed. As we see in the law courts, a well-managed patent portfolio can be a major source of strategic advantage—in database software, for instance, or mobiles, or pharmaceuticals.

Thus the 1980s shift in strategy theorizing changed the way strategists thought and talked. Before the 1980s, when planning (as in Paradigms A and B) was still dominant, there was much talk about efficiency and "strategy implementation": something that happened after the strategic work was done. Nowadays the pursuit and protection of the firm's rent-streams is discussed more and seen as the ongoing challenge. As the distinction between planning and implementing has dissolved, strategizing is seen as a perpetual process. Other distinctions then become evident, especially between evolving products and services versus evolving markets. Indeed, a new academic

---

[10] Robert D. Buzzell and Bradley T. Gale (1987) *The PIMS Principles: Linking Strategy to Performance*. New York: Free Press.

discussion, labeled "strategy-as-practice," has joined the previous efficiency and rent-seeking discussions, and will be considered in Chapter 3. An inventory of "practitioner's strategy tools" has been developed. While the academic shifts and trends, especially from efficiency to rents, appear evolutionary, there seems to be little rhyme or reason to the way the practitioners' tools have developed. We have a list of a dozen or so, in no obvious order except popularity; and no way of comparing them or knowing when to adopt one rather than another. Chapters 2 and 3 get to the bottom of this puzzle. They show how the consultants' tools address questions that differ from those the academic literature addresses. In fact they refer to quite different notions of strategy, so the term strategy appears in different languages. This can be confusing. Not surprisingly, practitioners and academics see strategy as a topic characterized by a lack of common ground, fragmentation, and the presence of what academics label a "rigor-relevance" or "theory-practice" gap.

## 1.7 Convergence of Practitioner and Academic Inputs

Though practitioner and academic languages differ, they are not mutually exclusive. Often they can be melded. Practitioners and academics of strategy can support each other. But it is useful to explore the differences as a means to close in on the strategizing process. First, academic researchers pursue general theory while the practitioners focus on the specific action. The distinction leads to separate literatures. This is obvious when we compare influential books like *In Search of Excellence* or *Blue Ocean Strategy* against articles in the *Strategic Management Journal* or the *Academy of Management Journal*. The books are intended for "practitioner-readers," with illuminating instances and stories rather than statistics. In contrast, the journals publish data, generalizations, theories, tests, and principles—very dry. Practitioners wonder if the academic work is worth reading, given its esoteric language and subtle statistics, plus generally they find it difficult to see its relevance to their practice. Academics question the practitioner literature's homely assumptions and naïve simplicity, its lack of scientific theory and empirical testing. Dismissing one or other literature is an easy knee-jerk response that devalues both and misses the opportunity to have them inform each other. I stay focused on practitioners' objectives but draw on the academic literature in novel ways, specifically on literature that is more or less ignored in the academic strategy arena even though it is familiar to many practitioners.

To give the reader some of my personal context, aside from being an academic who has studied business strategy for a while, I have also been a nuclear engineer, sales manager, plant manager, director, investor, and Silicon Valley entrepreneur, and feel able to keep the manager's practical purposes in mind. As mentioned already, one of my main intellectual sources is Carl von Clausewitz. He was a remarkable and courageous man with real battlefield experience and a profoundly practical thinker. Even so there are fundamental differences between military and business strategizing—plus von Clausewitz's work is anything but easy reading. At West Point, the US's principal military college, the quip is "If you think war is hell, try reading von Clausewitz." But he grasped something profound about the nature of strategizing that seems almost lost today but is well worth recapturing. He argued it is only necessary because the strategist lacks the full information necessary to arrive at a logical (computable) solution, especially under the press of battle and in the "fog of war." Strategizing, then, has more to do with disciplined guessing than with rigorous analyzing. The numbers can never be conclusive for real human action; no strategist can say "the numbers did it."

Like John Locke, von Clausewitz presumed two different but complementary modes of human thought—one rigorous, driven by facts; the other less so, an "estimating" shaped by judgment and experience. Objectivity rises with generalities, which is why researchers are interested in large populations of events. What is common is surfaced as objective fact. But practice is always specific, calling for judgment to reconcile the multiple ways in which we know lived situations. Thus, as the earlier discussion of knowledge absences indicates, judgment will be present whenever we act. The tension here is the ancient one between generalizations and instances or, to paraphrase Nietzsche, between the high-flying eagle who coolly surveys the terrain far below and the serpent that meets the terrain's particulars face to face.[11] Strategic work relates to specific instances, not to distant abstractions; it is most definitely not a "helicopter view" that is detached from the details and sees only generalities. Strategy must have its "boots on the ground." We cannot have a general theory of business strategizing because it is a contradiction—strategy must deal with what is both significant and particular to the action situation. Also, when we judge, especially as we act under conditions of knowledge absence, we reveal our individuality, how we differ as individuals. Our strategic work reveals our nature and identity as we engage a situation's particularities. Jack Welch's choices were not like those of Steve Jobs. Neither were they like those of Lloyd Blankfein or Howard Stringer or Mark Zuckerberg. Generally there is not enough consistency in an individual's judgments to make them forecastable. Judgment is what cannot be foretold or foreseen. It emerges through our practice, our choices about what we do.

Individual judgment is also the pivot in our dynamic democratic capitalist system. Private sector business is incredibly varied and full of strategic

---

[11] F. W. Nietzsche (1966) *Thus Spoke Zarathustra: A Book for All and None,* tr. W. Kaufman. New York: Viking Press.

opportunities for different people to apply their judgment as they pursue different objectives (or dreams). Strategizing explores every business firm's capacity to be unique, different from every other one, a possibility that arises only because our world can never be completely known. There are always "knowledge absences" that are crucial to the discussion. If everything was known then we would always be in, or be heading into, a state of equilibrium, the end of life and time—and there would be no point in doing business, let alone in strategizing. In practice we have different views, live different lives, sense different presents, and pursue different objectives—all of which makes the world (and democracy) open-ended and the way it is. Thus strategizing is the very antithesis of generality, of following the herd, or imposed answers. But in the opposite direction, as we abandon generality and the undeniable power of rigorous theorizing from large samples and move towards uniqueness and intuition, we run into methodological difficulties. Here von Clausewitz's thinking is important, albeit neglected today, precisely because he showed us practical ways to handle the methodological tension between generality and particularity—in his case, of course, how to integrate military theory with the seasoned trooper's (and colonel's) practice and experience in bounded strategic situations. There are good reasons for business people to insist their situation is unique, for in that perception lies the possibility of gaining economic rents. So too when they sense thinking otherwise would lead them to disregard many of the particularities that their experience tells them will be essential to successful choice. Battlefield situations are likewise. Survival and victory depend on grasping the specifics as well as the generalities. As the nursery rhyme about Richard III tells it, "For want of a nail a kingdom was lost." Generalities float above the flow of the lived life, which is a succession of instances of practice in our real and not completely known world—where we are forever hostage to surprise, where Murphy's Law rules, and things often fail to turn out as we expect.

## 1.8 Methodological Questions

At this point I have more or less sketched the arc of my book; but several issues deserve attention before we can delve into the details of strategic practice. First, the reader may well have sensed a profound methodological puzzle—"If our objective knowledge of the real that lies beyond our minds is not anchoring our analysis and strategizing, what stops us drifting onto the rocks of subjectivity and anarchy?" The risk excites many academics' horror. If objective facts fail to anchor us, as in Paradigm A, how do we stop Paradigms B, C, and D descending into pure relativism and wishful thinking—being of no dependable value whatsoever? The first part of my answer points to optimism and belief in the capacity of human imagination and judgment to invent useful progress in the face of insufficient facts. But that takes us back to the earlier question "What question is strategy (or strategizing) answering?" Many, perhaps most, strategy books offer a prescription—do this and you will beat your competitors, maximize market share, or optimize whatever. Von Clausewitz reacted to the similar prescriptions being taught at the École Militaire in Paris, the authors of the military doctrine of his day—do this and you will be victorious. Napoleon, von Clausewitz's nemesis, was one of the École's most capable students. But von Clausewitz knew the weakness of this way of thinking (and training) when it came to battlefield conditions, for principles never fit situations well enough to allow commanders to ignore the particularities. Von Clausewitz was driven by the urgent realization that the French would beat the Prussians if the Prussians were not able to think "outside the French box" and strategize in a different way. Trying to implement the French army's principles better than they could was clearly high risk.

Von Clausewitz's schema was radical—and successful—because it set aside slavish application of the dominant me-too French theory and opened up a space for the imagination and judgment of the well-stocked military mind. The balance between revered theory and innovative practice was restored. He did not simply pursue superior objective knowledge of the real. He put his faith in the military imagination, suitably trained, encouraged, invigorated, constrained, and applied. Second, in the battlefield situation he appreciated strategizing had to be a collaborative enterprise, not the purview of a senior officer acting on his own (as Hitler and Stalin sometimes did). Von Clausewitz's approach dissolved the artificial and unhelpful distinction between the strategist and the other participants. Just as the strategic process must get onto the battlefield, be brought into action, and adapt, so practice must come off the battlefield to shape the generals' strategizing without losing contact with its reality. These notions led to Prussian officers training with their men and colleagues in the field, not segregated in classrooms far away. The communications activities relevant to their circumstances and objectives likewise become integral to the strategizing process. Along with the division of labor articulated into the military order of things comes a specialization of battle experience—and the learning that shapes individuals' judgment. Artillery troops learn little of the infantry's experience, and vice versa. Thus von Clausewitz's notion of training was not simply about theorizing military doing—cavalry charges, storming ramparts, shelling—but also embraced establishing human communication in the field, especially opening the senior officers' thinking to the experience and imagination of those with a better grasp of specific details that might have grave strategic consequences. The fundamental question military strategizing must address is to grasp the battle's details and possibilities and so see through the fog of war to develop and sustain the confidence appropriate to the commitment of blood and treasure. As von Clausewitz noted famously, all military strategizing was embedded in military service to the State, and war was an instrument of politics, another of its means. In a similar way business action, while very different from military action, is an instrument of the entrepreneur's freedom and desire.

## 1.9 Consultants' Inputs

My first proposition is that strategic work addresses the knowledge absences at the interfaces between identity, intention, and context. All are fluid—uncertain. No uncertainties, no strategic work, no innovative activity, no learning experience. The strategic work of fastening these down comes first, before any decision-making. The second proposition is that we are able to respond to knowledge absences with relevant judgments because we humans are gifted with imagination that can be channeled by others as well as by ourselves. Often the strategic work must be persuasive, directing our imagination towards knowledge absences discovered by others, the entrepreneur perhaps. Third, we would be wise to make all this into a "structured practice," a methodical way of dealing with uncertainties that begins with the discovery and analysis of the constraints to what can be usefully imagined. Fourth, strategizing is almost always a collaborative multi-person activity to which a fully adapted form of communication is central. This chapter explores these ideas and their interplay, setting the stage for the main body of the book—Chapters 2 and 3. Then Chapter 4 springs us free and proposes the structured practice mentioned above, but leaves the burden firmly on the strategist—it is not a prescription that relives her/him of that burden.

To prepare the reader for this task it is useful to see how others have addressed these issues. In Chapter 2 I review some of the strategic tools that consultants have developed since WW2. Pre-WW2 writings about management had very different flavor. They presumed managers were completely in charge of the enterprise and knew it holistically from top to bottom—but needed to take their social duties more seriously, see how they were beholden to their fellow human beings, to society, and even more narrowly, to their customers. Most senior managers had worked their way through the firm, from the bottom up, as did Andrew Carnegie. This holistic style of thinking has re-emerged in "stakeholder theory," which seeks to restore a balance between shareholders' interests and those of the rest of the people and social institutions that interact through the firm's activities.[12]

---

[12] R. Edward Freeman, Jeffrey S. Harrison, Andrew C. Wicks, Bidhan L. Parmar, and Simone de Colle (2010) *Stakeholder Theory: The State of the Art.* Cambridge: Cambridge University Press.

Post-WW2 strategy consultants developed tools towards rather different goals. The focus was less on social duty—especially as that vague concept was disaggregated into the divergent and often contradictory interests of the various stakeholders—and more on the firm itself as an independent economic actor, distanced from all of the people involved—investors, managers, employees, customers, etc. Eventually Milton Friedman pronounced that managers' function was to maximize shareholder wealth. This simplification made it possible to be precise and rigorous, and the habit has stuck to the point that almost all strategy books presuppose the firm as an entity whose nature is not problematic, ignoring our doubts about what firms really are.[13] The strategic questions are then around choosing the goals to which the firm should be directed. In contrast I see the firm as extremely puzzling and that strategizing is the non-trivial process of constructing and sustaining it. With their own interests in mind, consultants borrowed copiously from the formalized statistics and modeling techniques developed during the war that led to the new discipline of "operations research" (OR). In this way their work took on the vestments of a science, seeming independent of the strategist's judgment. In Chapter 2 we review these strategic tools. But there is a curious twist. At first sight the tools seem to be scientifically powered prescriptions, proto-theories. But closer inspection shows they only ever go part way towards such definitive conclusions. They leave a crucial place for management's judgment input. The tools are diverse and not readily compared precisely because they leave different kinds of "opportunity space" open for the strategist's final inputs—another way of saying the tools answer different questions. They do not provide prescriptions; they merely help those executives who must do so. The variety of tools then implies there is no single overarching strategic question or theory that might address it. Chapter 2's pluralistic view is extended in Chapter 3.

## 1.10 Academics' Inputs

In this section my focus is on academic theorists' contributions to the management puzzle. Today's strategy theorists tend to ignore Coase's questions and presume the firm's nature and existence, in the typical post-WW2 manner. The strategy questions focus on what is left undetermined after the firm's nature is assumed, most often the firm's "direction." Generally, whatever the nature of the firm's resources, even if some are specific to particular markets, others will be more liquid and the firm's market engagements can be changed.

---

[13] R. H. Coase (1937) 'The Nature of the Firm', *Economica,* ns 4(16), 386–405.

As noted, academic theorizing was transformed by Chandler's proposal that the firm's internal organization could be changed too, with strategic consequences.[14] Chandler linked these two options and proposed the environmental-internal fit (EIF) approach that dominated the academic approach to strategy until rent-seeking took over in the 1980s.

Despite this shift, much of the academic strategy theorizing since continues to explore variations on Chandler's theme, considering the impact of vertical and horizontal integration, alternative modes of governance, alternative incentive schemes, and so on. At the same time management theorists have done little to extend the rent-seeking approach beyond Porter's formulation. In sharp contrast, microeconomists have seized the academic initiative by effectively turning the rent-seeking approach upside down, implying rents arise only because of market imperfections. Alongside rising interest in the strategic thinking about rents, a new generation of economists has begun to explore the implications of Coase's conjecture that the nature of the firm was intimately tied up with market imperfections. There would be no rents if markets were perfect, nor would there be firms. These microeconomists have shifted the strategic question from directing firms that already existed (via pricing and resource allocation decisions) towards probing the strategic implications of the imperfection/s that brought the firm into existence in the first place. Each of their answers is a distinct "theory of the firm," proposing a specific language for framing the judgment needed and the strategic work to be done. In Chapter 3 we review a variety of the theories produced so far. Again, at first sight they seem to be prescriptive, but closer inspection shows they frame a complementary set of "opportunity spaces" for the managers' entrepreneurial judgment. Again, there is no single overarching model—a final totalizing theory of the firm. Indeed, we can wonder if this is a mistaken academic goal, for if we were to find a universal theory of the firm the knowledge presence/knowledge absence distinctions would collapse, annihilating the very questions strategic work addresses.

Chapter 4 pulls the preceding three chapters together into a comprehensive approach to developing situation-specific languages for framing the strategic work involved in constructing a private sector business firm. It is the "main event" after the appetizers of the first three chapters. Chapter 1 introduces strategic work, Chapter 2 reviews how consultants do it, Chapter 3 how academics see it, Chapter 4 clarifies how the strategist shapes the entire analysis according to her/his choice of identity, intention, and context. The public and private sectors are very different, for firms focus on profit, public agencies on quite different goals. Yet the private sector's historical, political, legal, social,

---

[14] Alfred D. Chandler (1962) *Strategy and Structure: Chapters in the History of the American Industrial Enterprise*. Cambridge, MA: MIT Press.

cultural, and technological constraints must be brought into play in addition to the obvious ones of market position, industry structure, strategic intent, human relations, sustainability, business ethics, and so on. Entrepreneurship, strategizing, and leadership converge as strategists choose from among the knowledge absences private sector businesses are permitted to engage. Some think strategizing should be called "entrepreneurship" when dealing with a sole proprietor or SME situation and "strategizing" in the larger firm, but I think any distinction between entrepreneurship and strategizing is inherently artificial. It merely obscures the essential judgment-based nature of the task, which does not differ between the small firm, single proprietor, family firm, or major corporation. No question these contexts differ, so I defend this opinion in due course. My argument hinges on the assumption that strategic work is profoundly individual because the individual is where human judgment is seated. Technically speaking, my approach is "micro-foundational." Firms do not make decisions or have judgment—though there might be some attention to collective and team creativity. Firms large or small depend on individuals and have no capacity for judgment beyond those of these individuals. Also, when it comes to leadership and the distinctions between "leader" and "led" it is useful to distinguish between being a "leader of men," as they used to say, a notion that applies equally to business, church, military, and politics, versus focusing narrowly on private sector managers' thought and talk as they persuade others to act towards the firm's goals. Put differently, business leadership is contextualized strategizing.

## 1.11 Talk and Communication

Chapter 5 focuses on the firm's talk. Earlier I mentioned von Clausewitz's interest in training military officers to engage in collaborative strategic work, to learn how to carry the strategic debate forward by communicating within the strategizing team.[15] We know human communication is extraordinarily complex. The idea that it is analogous to computer communication hides almost all its interesting complexities. Von Clausewitz recognized the importance of communications carefully adapted to the specifics of the ongoing situation, dispersing the "fog of war." Given our age's tendency to define everything in terms of systems, and computer systems in particular, it is easy to forget that human and computer communication differ fundamentally—a point illustrated, for instance, by the 1941 US high command not paying attention to the reports of an impending attack on Pearl Harbor, or the more

---

[15] J. T. Sumida (2008) *Decoding Clausewitz: A New Approach to 'On War'*. Lawrence, KS: University Press of Kansas.

egregious example of the ignored reports about the 9/11 terrorist pilots' training in Arizona, Florida, and elsewhere. Computers do not have the "blind spots" we do, suggesting "total surveillance" is possible (also mistaken). The problem is that data differ from meaning; more data is not the same as better communication. Meaning shapes human action, data do not. Computers know nothing of the meaning of the data and couldn't care less. In contrast, people know there is a vast range of meaning to be attached to any data— some may be highly significant, much is irrelevant. So even if we perfect the mechanics of communication there is the deeper question of changing the meanings people attach to the data they are getting. Much of the strategy literature presumes that it is easier to come up with a strategy than to promulgate it through the firm and get people to accept it, getting them to change the meanings they attach to the data swirling about them. This literature, which often takes off from the assumption that people are "resistant," results from a grave misunderstanding of the nature of human communication.

The strategic communication issues here do not merely parallel the interesting problems in computer networks; they go much deeper, beyond the transfer of data and beyond the idea that a firm can be enveloped by a single coherent set of meanings (note that a computer program's data structures must be consistent). Adam Smith taught us the importance of the division of labor, but made little of the consequence that employees (and managers) think differently as a result of their different experiences and practice-based learning. In many respects strategizing is as much about coordinating internal differentiation and divergence as it is about dealing with external divergences and uncertainties, such as competitors and grouchy customers. How can the many different practices and meanings within the firm be brought under control, given the communications problems resulting from divergent work's learning? In the background to our learning, meaning, and resistance lies the concept of persuasion, the idea that strategic change boils down to persuading other people to think and behave differently—in particular, to behave in ways that converge on or are aligned with the firm's goals. Barnard made a great deal of this and of the central place of persuasion when discussing the functions of the executive.[16] The challenge is not new, of course, and goes back to the earliest days of democracy—how to develop a community when people know they are discrete individuals with citizens' rights to act independently? The social sciences take this as their foundational question and have a great deal to say about how social organization comes about. Four basic mechanisms are proposed: coercion (the use of force), calculation (the use of incentives), acculturation (indoctrinating individuals into an existing

---

[16] Chester I. Barnard (1968) *The Functions of the Executive* (30th anniversary edn). Cambridge, MA: Harvard University Press.

community), and communication (persuading people to act together).[17] I prioritize the last as a description of the communication task in the context of the firm—to find (*a*) a way of looking at the situation or "meaning" that opens up potential for value-adding, and (*b*) communicating that meaning to others in ways that persuade them to collaborate. This process is ancient, and so is its study. Like strategy, the literature on persuasive communication goes back to the Greeks and is the study of "rhetoric." Chapter 5 explores how the study of rhetoric can inform strategizing today.

This leads to my concluding Chapter 6 that considers the contemporary business situation, the strategic challenges managers now face, and business schools' part in it all. The chapter is not intended to be complete, more of a commentary practicing strategists might choose to consider. The choice is always theirs. Likewise I assert there is no single "silver-bullet" theory or model of the firm that can usefully underpin strategic practice. To the contrary, every firm is different and the strategist's task is to grasp its possible uniqueness in ways that give their firm its demarcating competitive advantage. In an earlier book I explored ways in which the individual firm's uniqueness might be based on sharing or imitation of others, especially those in the same industry.[18] I argued many firms are "cookie cutter" imitations or "instantiations" of a shared way of doing business (of strategizing) that has been worked out by someone else, as in franchising. That book argued that much strategic practice was based on imitation as new strategic moves spread through an industry. But firms are always different strategically, so the present book deals with the construction of uniqueness, even though much of what gets drawn into the strategic practice might be either (*a*) already theorized or (*b*) directly imitated. Von Clausewitz taught us how to borrow from others' work without losing one's sense of identity. A degree of uniqueness is inevitable because no two firms can occupy identical spaces in the universe of strategic opportunities—every franchisee is different. There must be some separation of location, history, product, ambience, or pricing. Thus one route to strategic understanding is to examine the differences that make survival possible. Maybe it is a matter of geography or different consumers'

---

[17] R. Collins (1994) *Four Sociological Traditions: Revised and Expanded Edition of Three Sociological Traditions.* New York: Oxford University Press.

[18] J.-C. Spender (1989) *Industry Recipes: The Nature and Sources of Managerial Judgement.* Oxford: Blackwell. As mentioned in the Preface, *Industry Recipes* was an attempt to theorize private sector business strategy. My failure lay in my going along with the herd in presuming the firm as an unproblematic entity. I had not paid sufficient attention to Coase's questions. In the present book I claim strategizing is about creating the firm, not simply its direction. The industry recipe dodges this bullet by presuming firms—or rather the concepts and knowledge that enable entrepreneurs to create firms—are created collectively, by the industry. The idea was intended as a direct critique of the "sole entrepreneur," much mythologized in the American Horatio Alger tradition, implying the great entrepreneurs of the past learned nothing important by looking at, or working in, other firms they had not created.

different tastes. It might also be a matter of historical timing, just as bicycles today are technologically different from those of thirty years ago and now serve as cheap means of transportation and expensive means of recreation.

## 1.12 Historical Methods

The strategizing process is ongoing so a sense of history is essential to grasping its nature. Von Clausewitz urged ambitious young officers to study military history deeply. Sadly, business history is not given much of a place in business schools today, even though many managers are history buffs and find reading economic and business history engaging and educational. Understanding something of the historical sweep of business strategizing can clarify the task of creating uniqueness. History often suggests a typology; for instance it seems clear that business strategizing in the era of monopolies, before the Anti-Trust movement and its legislative achievements, was far different from strategizing today when global competition makes monopoly-based strategies far rarer—though Microsoft, Prada, and Aston Martin show such strategies are far from extinct. Indeed, the pursuit of monopolistic "rents" drives much of today's interest in branding for non-commodities, including business schools. History shows the shift towards a consumer-dominated economy in which the bulk of purchases are not basics like flour and walking shoes but high-margin luxury products such as McDonalds hamburgers, Nike sneakers, or iPods. Business strategies are now very different.

There is a history of business strategizing implicit in Khurana's history of the US business school. He suggested three phases.[19] Pre-WW2 business schools saw management permeated by a sense of duty to customers and their community. In the second 'tween-war period, precipitated by Frederick Taylor's Scientific Management, management was charged to maximize the efficiency of the firm's purchasing, production, and distribution activities. Efficiency was the thing. This was the era of "managerial capitalism." More recently, encouraged by Friedman's comments, "shareholder capitalism" has taken over. Shareholders now hold senior management accountable for the firm's short-term financial performance to the point that little else matters and managers can expect to be fired if financial performance falters. The three phases suggest quite different contexts and objectives—and languages—for the strategist.

---

[19] Rakesh Khurana (2007) *From Higher Aims to Hired Hands: The Social Transformation of American Business Schools and the Unfulfilled Promise of Management as a Profession*. Princeton: Princeton University Press.

I elaborate Khurana's typology, seeing a distinction arising in the 1960s between (*a*) conglomerates seeking to expand the firm and (*b*) the shareholder wealth maximization that brings the investment portfolio to the center of the strategy rather than the firm—maximizing the investment return gets to be more important than any particular firm's survival. Crucially the investor can "exit" through the market for the stock.[20] I also suggest (*c*) a post-1980s phase of financial market activity, borrowing Keynes's label of "casino capitalism," marked by almost complete detachment from typical firms' value-adding activity. Firm's debts and revenues become tradable objects in a specialized (and possibly rigged) market game. This latest phase is evident in the packaging and trading of sub-prime house mortgages, an activity that calls for quite different notions of strategizing. Driven by the historical shift in strategic problematics, there is a growing feeling that business schools are out of synch and failing both their students and those who recruit them, one aspect of an expanding education "bubble," especially of student debt and university expenditure, with serious economic dimensions. I certainly believe business schools fail to prepare or equip students well to deal with the real strategic work presented in my book. While today's students are increasingly well-trained to collect and analyze information (knowledge presences), we have abandoned them when it comes to helping them face knowledge absences—which is when they must call on the judgment that lies at the core of strategizing, entrepreneurship, and leadership practice. The remedy? No question business schools should continue to teach analysis, but that should also be balanced, humanized, and enriched by the kinds of training and self-preparation von Clausewitz explored. Outside the structured military environment, wherein selfless duty and uncompromising obedience are mandatory, the rhetorical practices of contemporary business management come into play and deserve particular study—so it is Chapter 5's topic. Casework is a laboratory to bring strategic analysis and judgment together, but this requires a talk-intensive situation in which we can discover and teach the rhetorical practices that lie at the heart of effective managerial practice.

## 1.13 Profit and Growth

The private sector firm is normally presumed to be strategizing to generate value and seize some of it as profit. Accumulated profits then drive growth. The firm that makes profits can also attract further funding and grow by accumulating debt. While start-ups often grow by investing and accumulating

---

[20] A. O. Hirschman (1970) *Exit, Voice and Loyalty: Responses to Decline in Firms, Organizations and States*. Cambridge, MA: Harvard University Press.

debt without making a profit, this happens in expectation of later profits. Profit, then, is central to the idea of the private sector firm and to what managers do and shareholders expect. But while profit seems pretty straightforward to business people, it is not so simple when we get to the details the strategist must engage. Profit is not only the game's score when the players have left the field. It has a complex history. Part of the problem revolves around who has the right to keep the profit: the workers whose labor creates the added value, the manager who organizes the work, the entrepreneur who set it up, the investors who finance it? The differences matter to the strategist. Second, is profit-seeking socially legitimate? This affects the relationship between profit-making and the rest of society, and maybe regulators too. Does profit come from the value created, the value added, or is it a mere transfer? For instance, I see a painting in your closet and buy it for $100. It turns out to be a Picasso that I sell for $8 million. No value has been created, I simply realized your property's value as my profit. The profit comes from your ignorance. Another example might be that I spend $100,000 while inventing a way of making synthetic rubber that significantly reduces the cost of manufacturing all kinds of product and, protected by an effective patent (another $100,000 for the lawyers), I net $12 million per annum profit. The added value comes from Mother Nature, available to other inventors until the patent is filed. Alternatively, you need cash to pay your driver in Polish zlotys, and I sell you zł 1000 for dollars at a hefty discount. The profit comes from others' opinions of the currency's value versus the imperfect nature of the deal between us. From a business point of view all these gains can be regarded as profit. But they have very different implications for the profit-seeking strategist.

Profit—a central idea in microeconomics—has economists and many others puzzled. Textbooks argue a distinction between "normal" profit and "economic" profit. The first considers both income and opportunity costs, relating to what I can earn by spending my time in some other way. I demand a normal profit if I am to stay in the business, so my revenue must be greater than my expenses, but I also want to do better than I might by investing my time doing something else. While economists take note of income, costs, and opportunity costs, accountants focus on net income. So, leading to one set of puzzles, business people tend to follow the accountants and see profit as total revenue minus total costs, the residual. The complications are two-fold. Which costs are considered and which not? Plus there might be social costs that the business does not have to carry yet incurs nonetheless. Secondly, there is the problem of deciding when to "strike" the account and write out cash flows that might accrue further into the future. Presuming these questions can be handled, economic profit is the difference between the revenue and all the costs, which include the normal profit sufficient to keep the business together and the implicit costs of not investing in an alternative opportunity. The business/accounting notion of profit contrasts with the economists' notion. The economists are interested in profit theory because it helps explain why firms come into being, presuming it is in order to make a profit that cannot be earned by doing something else.

As economists probe deeper into profit they conclude that, in the long run, given perfect markets, all economic profits get competed away, so profits only arise in the short/medium term and/or in imperfect markets. In which case the profit reflects a return grounded in some market inefficiency or monopoly that might arise through government action, information asymmetries, or innovation. Schumpeter argued for a distinction between (a) the economic profit (quasi-rent) to be earned by an innovation that would eventually be superseded by another, and (b) the return (or rents) to be earned when the economic profit became legally protected and perpetuated by, for instance, a patent. The first may be due to the entrepreneur while the second is due to the social arrangements that protect the rent-stream. This leads on to the notion that economic profits should be treated as the return to the entrepreneur, the residual after all costs have been accounted. These include the return to the suppliers of capital (interest), as well as all other costs. Some economists separate entrepreneurial effort (good) from state-perpetuated profits (bad) and argue the latter are not in the general interest and should expire. Another part of the puzzle is whether there should be a return for risk-bearing. Investors risk their money. Labor, in contrast, is paid wages and is not considered to bear risk or deserve additional return. Economists may argue that the entrepreneur who does not invest money is not taking a risk that deserves a specific return that should be accounted a cost, even though s/he "risks" her/his judgment and, perhaps, standing in the eyes of others. Rather the entrepreneur's "profit" should be the residual after all accountable costs. This return is sometimes called "pure profit" and raises questions that parallel those Coase asked about the firm's nature, "How can pure profit arise?"

Knight's intuition—the core of my book—was that pure profit could only arise from engaging uncertainty with imaginative practice, leading to what some call the "uncertainty theory of profit." Perfect markets that have equilibrated allow no uncertainty—or profit. Innovations engage and resolve previous uncertainties—in which event innovations generate pure profit. Whether these accrue to the inventor, the entrepreneur, the investor, and so on, is a separate question, important of course. When all costs have been allocated—wages, interest, and other contractual obligations—the profit is a residual. Rights to the residuals may be assigned to the inventor, the entrepreneur, or the investors, or others such as the authorities that grant the firm the right to exist. But they might also be assigned to the firm itself as a legal entity, and then be reassigned to those who own the firm. Everyday talk is of a firm making a profit, not of the people who produce the added value or those who may eventually own it. Hence it makes no sense to speak of profit without identifying and managing the uncertainty from which it flows—which helps show why profit is a curious and puzzling topic. The "uncertainty theory of profit" is pretty vacuous if the relevant uncertainty cannot be defined. Strategizing in pursuit of profit therefore begins with analyzing the relevant uncertainties and goes on to analyzing engaging them, thereby going beyond merely asserting, as Knight does, uncertainty's central place in profit-making. Profit arises from the creative ways strategists engage selected uncertainties and manage the resulting practice. Weston unpacked the uncertainty theory of profit in a series of papers about how firms might be uncertain and the implications for these strategists.[21]

My approach will be different, largely because I deny the firm the kind of identity that allows it to be uncertain—or knowledgeable. Firms cannot be usefully said to be uncertain so long as they have no corresponding power of judgment. The micro-foundational position follows since I presume that capacity inheres in human individuals alone, so in section 1.4 I argue that uncertainties arise only from the different ways in which we humans know. Neither firms nor situations are uncertain, the term is a reflection of how people feel about what they know. As noted already, I distinguish between ignorance, indeterminacy, and incommensurability—three types of knowledge absence—and between data, meaning, and practice—three corresponding or complementary types of knowledge presence. It follows there are three types of profit that the strategist might seek, and there may be some value in going over these distinctions again. Innovation is often technology-driven, a new way of doing something as technological advances overcome ignorance. Here Man is expanding his limited knowledge of Mother Nature—dealing with his ignorance. The resulting profit gets competed away as others copy or realize what can be done and imitate, overcoming their ignorance and making similar advances—unless prevented by institutional arrangements (patents) or secrecy (the Coca-Cola recipe locked in a safe that needs two keys, as in a missile-silo). Ignorance also appears in knowledge asymmetries—the Picasso mentioned above; there are profits to be made from the ignorance of others. The core of arbitrage is asymmetric knowledge of both the present and the future. People can also be persuaded into ignorance—"a pig in a poke" when the meat content was not pork. There are profits to be made from people's persuadability and gullibility.

Indeterminacy and incommensurability suggest their own manners of profit-seeking. Indeterminacy puts ignorance into motion but focuses on

[21] J. F. Weston (1954) 'The Profit Concept and Theory: A Restatement', *Journal of Political Economy*, 62(2), 152–70.

pursuing dynamic knowledge asymmetries against particular others. Poker can be profitable to those who play it well. But knowing how to play poker will not translate to profit unless you get on the riverboat and find others to play against. This is not the same as playing poker (or dice) against Nature, planting corn in anticipation of a bumper crop, which others can see you doing, only to experience drought. Incommensurability, coming from the fractured condition of human knowing, is overcome by intelligence and imagination, bringing things together in new ways and combinations, and is an inherently competitive activity, as academics can attest. Schumpeter's innovations were typically of the new combination type rather than pushes against Man's ignorance.[22] It follows there are profits to be made by making new sense of what is already widely known. Schumpeter initially saw the economy as a cycle that would tend towards stability as profits were competed away. Later he argued innovations disturbed the cycle, provoking other entrepreneurs into a new round of innovations—what he dubbed "creative destruction." He concluded the economy would never stabilize and so could never be understood so long as neoclassical economics dismissed Knightian uncertainty; rather it must be understood as evolving through time, a very different kind of economics with a very different notion of profit.

The conclusion drawn from this section is that the pursuit of profit becomes strategizing only as the interplay of identity, intention, and context is analyzed to uncover and identify knowledge absences in Nature (ignorance), in each other (indeterminacy), and in ourselves (incommensurability). This cannot be done in general, only in the specific as particular uncertainties are engaged with specific practice. There can be no engaging uncertainties without leveraging (standing on) what is known, selected knowledge presences. Then profits arise from leveraging the known into knowledge absences that can be related. In short, there can be no "theory of profit" for it is not a general idea that can be defined in the contexts in which profits arise.

## 1.14 Summary

This chapter introduces the reader to my view of strategic work as the essence of profit-seeking and value-adding business practice. The work is specific rather than general and the outcome is practical language—*phronesis*—rather than an appeal to covering theory and rational choice. The present literature, practitioner and academic, offers a variety of languages for deploying knowledge presences in ways that frame the knowledge absences that strategic work

---

[22] J. A. Schumpeter (2008) *Capitalism, Socialism, and Democracy* (3rd edn). New York: Harper Perennial.

addresses. Every language stands on some chosen terms (axioms). This chapter opens with a number of distinctions: generalities/specifics, academics/practitioners, judgment/fact, and moves on to discuss language, talk, experience, and history. I treat strategizing as a constructive or creative art form in the medium of language and tacit knowledge rather than either the application of a theory or a mode of analysis. The private sector firm's strategic work is collaborative and lays stress on the communication that must take place between those participating and contributing their judgment. The rest of my book unpacks strategizing as a skillful managerial practice centered on the creation and use of a firm-specific language that successfully grasps the firm's intents and context.

It is easy to throw in the idea that strategizing is an art,[23] but art is tricky stuff too. We know there can be no deterministic "theory of art production"; it would be a contradiction in terms since the outcome is unique—which is what makes it art. A great deal of art is impelled by critique of what others take to be the taken-for-granted aspects of their lives. The best art impels us to look at the world and ourselves in new ways, so is inherently "critical." Entrepreneurship is similarly critical in that it proposes better products and services, it teaches us that our refrigerators, air travel, bakers, or accountants can be bettered, an endless frontier. Entrepreneurs are often more driven by this challenge—producing a better mousetrap—than by the prospect of profit. They see their achievements as in the realm of human possibility not wealth. Overall I follow Knight and frame private sector business as an artistic medium of great economic, social, and political—and personal—significance, and expand on this in Chapter 6. Strategizing is practical work that goes well beyond adopting a theory. It calls for a sympathetic feeling for the materials at hand (especially for selecting good people, Knight's definition of executive judgment),[24] for arranging appropriate financing, for controlling the value-chain, for encouraging customers, etc. Artists learn to "read" other artists' work to get a sense of the question being addressed. Likewise business people who keep up with the business press, stay informed about what their regulators, customers, employees, and competitors are doing, are less likely to be nastily surprised by what happens. Most of all, strategizing is the process of maneuvering competently in a real-world context that is stunningly heterogeneous, dynamic, and pitted with unexpected value—and traps for the unwary. Instead of approaching this in the abstract, presuming perfectly formed people and information, strategy is about responding to the imperfect nature of the real terrain, the specific individuals, challenges, resources, and circumstances at hand.

---

[23] F. H. Knight (1923) 'Business Management: Science or Art?', *Journal of Business*, 2(4), 5–24.

[24] F. H. Knight (1921) *Risk, Uncertainty and Profit*. Boston: Houghton Mifflin Co., p. 229.

It is clear that business is one of democracy's most politically important activities. Private firms are legally, economically, structurally, and ethically at the root of our socio-economy. Most of us aspire to work in them and spend much of our lives there. Parenthetically many also assert the political importance of free markets. They may have a point, for markets facilitate the distribution of resources to higher uses. But markets are socially and economically irrelevant without the private firms that interact across them. No firms, no markets—and our capitalist democracy stops dead. Given the recent economic upheavals it is increasingly obvious that we need a better understanding of how private sector firms actually generate jobs and value—especially as we see the private sector can also destroy value, ecologies, and lives. Without a better understanding of strategy we cannot begin to design the social or legal institutions that might protect society at large from such destructive activity— even as Schumpeter made us aware of destruction's inevitable part in economic advance. Nor can we discuss the balance of public and private sectors or the government's proper role; matters that concern all private sector business managers, whether they like it or not, as they look towards their firms' future.

# 2

# Strategic Analysis—Consulting Tools

## 2.0 On Method

This chapter reviews some of the tools that consultants and strategy teachers use to analyze a firm's strategic challenges. The inventory reflects the post-WW2 impulse to formalize management thought with new theory, or as much structure as seems useful. Many believe the pace of change and strategic problem generation has accelerated and that strategy tools have become more important. Perhaps this is correct. What seems clearer is that the exact nature of strategic tools is often misunderstood. Whatever some theorists hope, they do not provide managers with strategic prescriptions. To the contrary, their principal use is to simplify situations that would otherwise be too puzzling for judgment to be applied and strategy to be developed. This chapter's premise is that managers face a variety of the strategic challenges, more than can be captured in any single analysis. Dealing with them calls for selection and judgment as well as logical analysis. These are slippery concepts but a better understanding of strategic tools helps clarify them to the point of making them practical. Practice, not theory, turns out to be key. Strategic tools are not low-quality theories. On the contrary, they support managers' judgment and value-production precisely because they are not rigorous theories. They facilitate the transformation of managerial judgment into economic value and profit. This chapter shows the strategist's judgment works at two levels: first in the selection of the tool, second in its application.

Here we get down to the practicalities of strategic work. Chapter 1 presents strategic judgment as the necessary complement to rational decision-making, a yin-yang relation. Judgment drives the strategist's imaginative responses to the three types of knowledge absence that arise in business: ignorance, incommensurability, and indeterminacy. It selects the knowledge presences (data, meaning, and skilled practice) used to frame the opportunity space. Most strategy texts do not venture beyond rational decision-making and presume the data to be computed are readily available. At worst they allow for some degree of ignorance and presume it can be dealt with by some research, such as market research or systematic product or process development. They deny the place of judgment in the strategic work process. This chapter shows many of the tools that consultants have developed since WW2 are subtler and make a specific place for the strategist's judgment. This achieves three things. First, those using the tools are reassured that strategic work calls for the application of judgment, which they intuit—correctly—is strategy's defining characteristic. Second, the nature and scope of the judgment required is radically narrowed and made attachable to the firm's context. Third, the strategic tool provides a language the participants in the strategy process can use to describe and debate the judgment to be applied. Leaving judgment out of the picture, as most strategy texts do, puts discussion of these three issues beyond the strategic process, and so provides the people engaged with no means to deal with the uncertainties that can only be resolved by the exercise of their judgment.

Chapter 2's list of tools is far from complete and some readers will see I have missed tools they have used and find valuable (please let me know so I can improve my list). Nonetheless the list's variety is interesting in itself. The tools differ. This shines light onto their nature, for knowing what something is not is often as useful as knowing what it is. Surfacing these models' differences helps clarify the judgment in choosing what seems to be the appropriate tool to capture the situation. The list lets me re-emphasize my book's underlying assumption—that strategic work is the exercise of managerial imagination and judgment in under-determined business situations. Preparation means extending one's thinking and inventory of ideas by learning what to pay attention to—through close and critical observation, talking with others, reading, researching, and reflecting on one's experience. Strategic work calls for a critical and doubting approach to the world. It begins by sensing the knowledge absence to be engaged, its possibilities, and then choosing a tool from a tool-kit.

Framing the work this way helps show there can be no universal, rigorous, totalizing theories or models to which every strategist must subordinate her/his judgment and intuition—and the academic project to discover such universals is a methodological error, a misspecification or hangover from our commitment to positivist methods that are ill-suited to strategizing as the practical problem in hand. Fortunately this has only minor consequences for practicing strategists, though it might distract them from their proper function—to focus on their firm's specific challenges. But it has regrettable consequences for many of management education's providers and consumers. Given that many of their students get into doing real strategic work they might need reassuring that the firm is very different from the classroom, as are the strategic responsibilities they carry as managers. Reality is marked by uncertainties and responsibilities not normally admitted into the classroom.

Listing a tool begins with a description. This seems simple enough but it hides a couple of things. Again, the strategist's task (and value) grows out of the absence of certainty. This hits immediately. Who knows when the description chosen is "correct," given there is no "truth" to test it against? The true impulse to strategic work is doubt, especially that things are not the way they are presented and will not turn out as expected. That things are often misrepresented opens up the possibility of seeing them in a new and strategically more valuable way. Is the glass half full or half empty? Is this market just pausing or changing direction? Are the customers buying our product our market's "long tail" or its future mainstream? Second, a description is not an explanation. Every strategic tool proposes a language as a way of seeing, but also implies a business model, how the firm works as a value-adding mechanism. Plus it is not helpful to declare the product of strategic work "a strategy." Who knows what that means? A document on a shelf (or in the trashcan)? An idea? A practice? A policy or a set of rules promulgated throughout the firm? A language the organization will then speak and use to describe its world? My book is about action, and the aim of strategic work is action that is considered and directed, that embraces what has been learned from action in the past. I see strategic work as artistic with an accompanying aesthetic, a way of looking and acting, and calling the result a language is simply to indicate how the strategist must (*a*) select what matters, (*b*) pay attention to practice and (*c*) the situation's dynamics, aspects than often lie beyond the grasp of language, and (*d*) communicate to those others whose judgments are needed to bring the value-adding processes to life.

In this chapter I begin to use the term "business model" (BM) more consistently. I do not mean anything like a blueprint, mechanical design, or computable model. These reflect an analyst's ways of thinking that presumes the world is fully knowable, controllable, or determinable. There is no definition or necessary format for the business model—for it is a notion that belongs in a world marked by knowledge absences and judgments and is the apparatus of the imagination able to exploit these to advantage. There is a huge literature on business models that tends to treat them as mechanical designs—a view I dismiss.[1] My BM is a language specific enough to grasp the situation's possibilities in an actionable way, making them discussable. It identifies and characterizes a situation and thereby the specific "collision" of identity, intention, and context discussed in Chapter 1. It implies elements or axioms with connections and relations, and its structure goes some way to "explain" what happens, how the situation will be changed, corrected, or transformed by the strategy-directed business activity that follows the actors' commitment of resources, energy, and emotion. But my BM is not a theory that fully determines the outcome or eliminates the possibility of being surprised by the value added arising. It is unlike a theory in being open and flexible enough to describe and embrace the surprising aspects of the outcome as the value added.

A simple example might be craftwork, the potter working at the wheel. Her BM embraces the potter, her training, her aesthetic, the clay, wheel, kiln, her customers, and so on. But there is nothing in this that either determines the outcome or excludes the possibility of something surprisingly beautiful (or ugly) coming out of the process. We might say the beautiful vase produced is a projection of the potter's imagination into her real-world context through the specific activities and choices of its production—constrained by the properties of the materials to hand and the time- and production-sequences appropriated. The BM is the time-space-resource-transformation-framed context in which the entrepreneur's imagination is projected into the socio-economy to appear as a product or service that surpasses its inputs and adds value—which may lead to profit. Thus by BM I mean a workable synthesis of the differing ways in which the firm's managers identify and secure the various resources their firm needs, the customers and other external actors they serve, the processes (like the value-chain) by which value is created, added, and delivered—plus, of course, the ways in which the managers identify those others in the context who either support or threaten their activity and the "boundary maintenance" processes they deploy to articulate and protect their strategic choices.

A BM is not a rigorous or coherent theory of the firm for it must frame and engage uncertainties if it is to lead to the possibility of adding value. But it must be workable and coherent enough to provide an interior logic and language, and an external one too, that reflects the business's being embedded in and constantly interacting with the wider socio-economy. The business has to have an "actionable sense" of itself and of the wider world it engages, and this calls for a BM that is complex, multidimensioned, and multi-level. The BM can never be a direct (isomorphic) reflection of the wider situation precisely because no coherent and rigorous model of the whole socio-economy exists. If one existed it would (a) tell us everything about the future and the

---

[1] J. Magretta (2002) 'Why Business Models Matter', *Harvard Business Review*, 80(5), 86–92.

past, everything history and the social sciences seek, and (*b*), closer to the firm, show there was no possibility of it adding value or making a profit. Imaginative practice under uncertainty, engaging knowledge absences, and value-adding outcomes are all tied together. Thus a BM is never determined by outside circumstance, only by the strategic work of its construction. Nor is it detachable from its context; to the contrary it is an ever-evolving pattern of shaped interaction between the human beings who share and comprise the context. It is typically incomprehensible to those who have not inhabited its context, time, and history. Nor is it fully expressible. It is organic, tacit, and vitalized, a dynamic form of knowing that is forever a "work in progress" as it responds to the strategist's unfolding experience of applying the BM in its shifting context. But, equally, it is not organic in the strict biological sense of having a form of vitality that is independent of the human elements that, interacting through the BM, bring it to life. Its only vitality is that of the human beings involved, their practice of projecting their imagination into the context as intentional value-adding practice. Perhaps DNA is Nature's business model for the production of the entity arising. We know that no amount of analyzing the DNA enables us to forecast what comes out of it, yet we also know it totally delimits the range of possible outcomes—in ways we do not yet understand.

The uncertainties in the socio-economy open up an economic space for the firm's value-adding processes. Another way to put this is that firms exist only when their markets (shorthand for "the broader socio-economy") "fail" to be fully determined because, perhaps, full information is not fully available to all economic actors. Real markets are not fully prescriptive, and they cannot determine the nature of the firm. There are other "causes" or determinants. Typically the firm has features and aspects imprinted on it by the imagination of its creators. Business historians often discover the entrepreneurial activity of developing and implementing the firm's initial business model gets shared between two individuals—"inside man" and "outside man"—McGraw-Hill, Rolls-Royce, Ernst & Young, or Ben & Jerry's. Being organic, the BM also has a time dimension. Unfortunately much of the literature on BMs is produced by economists whose training and search for equilibrium prevents them from bringing time into their thinking—neoclassical markets clear instantly, making time irrelevant—and their BMs tend to be time-independent restatements of their originating notion of the firm as an economic production function linking determining markets. Perhaps the BM's "strategic time" is the characteristic that most distinguishes it from theory (which is time-free)—hence the practitioners' maxim "timing is everything." Each BM implies the firm's "strategic time." For example, most farming runs on an annual cycle—Mother Nature's strategic-time. But salmon farming is determined by that fish's gestation and fattening time and can be detached from the annual breeding cycle of wild salmon. Likewise some cattle-feed plants can be "cropped" twice each year. Hydroponic farming can be decoupled from the sun's cycle. Much of high-tech runs to different clocks, such as the "windows of opportunity" in the smartphone market, or the cycle of discovery and marketing controlled by the FDA in the pharmaceutical industry. The strategist must deal with and maybe select the BM's timing or "heart-beat."

The strategic tool chosen sketches the BM as its implementation in the same way that a hypothesis is a specific instance of a "covering theory." The comparison of strategic tools is not just a matter of seeing which best captures the situation, it helps reveal the ways in which value gets added through the firm's activity, illuminating the enormous variety of business models and opportunities available in a democratic capitalist economy. It is easy to speak of "the situation" as if there was some objective socio-economic reality to be observed and discovered. This is a positivist or "modernist" tic and makes it difficult for those who have become completely absorbed into the modernist way of thinking to get an intuitive sense of the business strategist's art and talent. There is no "real situation," there is only what the strategist admits, constructs, or intuits through her/his thinking, reasoning, and imagining. Hence honest and hard-thinking people get to disagree about, say, whether there is a human-generated ecological crisis in the Antarctic—yet the ice is melting. Who can say if this explanation is "correct"? From the strategist's point of view her/his necessary doubting attitude makes the question irrelevant. The relevant question is always what, if anything, are we going to do or what can we do? Such questions cannot be addressed by rigorously analyzing external circumstances, for the answers turn on us—and our choices. While there may be many constraints on our choices, there is no complete picture that would determine that choice and eliminate our "subjective" input. This includes how we "feel," our hunches, so given the uncertainties on which strategy feeds, there is always a relationship between the strategist's thinking and feeling. Optimists view the world in ways that pessimists do not. Sometimes optimism opens up the strategizing process in ways that pessimism cannot. Likewise pessimism sometimes flourishes by denying aspects of the situation that optimistic others take as facts. The BM proposes a unique world to be inhabited as a result of the strategic work that impacts those whose actions make the world and makes them feel different. Good strategy empowers and inspires others' imagination; bad strategy alienates and depresses it.

It is not easy to wrest a strategic tool's value-adding mechanism from its description. Getting at it requires the special doubting aesthetic of strategic thinking—the radicalism, impatience, or anarchy that underpins Schumpeter's notion of "creative destruction," distinguishing it from mere destruction.[2] How

---

[2] J. A. Schumpeter (1975) *Capitalism, Socialism and Democracy* (3rd edn). New York: Harper & Row.

can a fresh vision of the situation be made to work in practice, and with whom? In the background is doubt about whether it is possible to understand a business model without actually living or inhabiting it. Can a description of a business model explain IBM's or United Airlines's profitability? Or Lehman Brothers' demise? Many City and Wall St analysts work hard to follow and predict firms' results and would have no work to do if this was simple or could be readily computerized—even if that was with an expert system able to absorb the information these analysts gain from talking with the firm's executives, board members, and shareholders. Warren Buffett reports he never invested in a company he did not understand. No question he is a financial whiz and may well have understood Goldman Sachs or the Bank of America, but did he really understand the subtleties of running a railroad (BNSF), or the medical insurance business (MedPro)?

The BM is a powerful concept because it helps move the discussion beyond the limits of positivist "theory" to grasp something of the value-adding power of the firm, the aspect a positivist analysis is forced to ignore. But a BM can only be sustained and provide a long-term competitive edge when it is hidden, far from transparent. Coca-Cola has made much marketing capital by telling us that its syrup's recipe is secret, known to only two executives at any one time. This is clearly a myth, especially because these executives are not actually making the syrup, lots of other workers around the world do that and even if the ingredients are not transparently labeled they can surely get the gist of it. The real point is that it is impossible to sustain an edge in the face of competition if "reverse engineering," workers who leave and join competitors, industrial espionage, and so on, render the BM transparent and so public. In 1982 the strategy theorists Lippman and Rumelt coined the term "uncertain imitability" to capture this necessary obscurity, precisely what the economist Veblen identified in 1904 as the secrecy crucial to the firm's survival.[3] Business people seek secrecy for good reason. When it is threatened, as in a patent dispute, the firm's strategic options change rapidly. The firm discovers others are able to manipulate its world and it may be forced to switch from exploiting the patent in its own time (and uninvaded opportunity space) to selling whatever intellectual property rights remain at the end of the legal dispute.

The expectation that a BM's value-creating process can be completely understood or "explained" is another part of the modernist fallacy. If it could be completely explained as, say, a causal model is an explanation, then the value-creation process would not be creative, it would be rendered mechanical. So along with the notion that strategic work is creative comes the

---

[3] Steve A. Lippman and Richard P. Rumelt (1982) 'Uncertain Imitability: An Analysis of Interfirm Differences in Efficiency under Competition', *Bell Journal of Economics*, 12, 413–38. T. Veblen ([1904] 1965) *The Theory of the Business Enterprise*. New York: Augustus M. Kelley.

implication that it can never be fully explained. Does any successful horse-breeder know precisely and fully what they do? Are they never surprised? Does any painter really know precisely why some of his/her paintings "work" and others do not? This is not to say that they do not know anything about what they do; one has to know a great deal to set up the creative process, not only what French chefs call *mise en place*, getting everything ready, but also getting into the right frame of mind to engage the creative process. This probes the subtlety of the interplay of reason, analysis, and imagination, of identity, intention, and context. In the same way that we cannot know the world completely, for if this was possible the world would then be unchangeable, we likewise cannot and do not know ourselves completely. If we ever achieved complete self-knowledge, as Socrates urged, we would then be immune to surprise and no longer organic, adapting, and learning—living a normal human life. Rational Man, of course, cannot learn anything—he merely computes. So outlining the BM is not a search for a logical or coherent deterministic model, a notion that quashes its human and creative dimensions. Rather it is an attempt to grasp enough about the resources, aspects, and constraints of the situation to illuminate some relevant particularities and singularities, to give one a sense of how one BM (such as Coca-Cola's) differs from that another (such as Google's).

To summarize, I shall explore the different consulting tools as "proto-business models," ways of looking that can be easily adopted as tentative foundations to the firm's BM. Several questions must be answered in the process of creating a BM. First, a description of what the business is and, by implication, what it is not. Second, a consideration of the language and categories proposed so that the entrepreneurs and strategists can operationalize it. Third, an explanation and assessment of its value-adding practices, how the categories link together so that time becomes integral to the BM, for there can be no value-add without a specification of the strategic process's time. Fourth, where in the process, and how, the strategist's imagination, judgment, or creativity is drawn into the BM. The examples in the sections that follow illustrate this. I do not hope to provide complete clarity—impossible given the uncertainties on which profit and added value hinge—rather to inculcate an attitude, a habit of mind, that sense of doubt that is the strategist's basic aesthetic about whether things are as they seem or have been reported. Doubt is the practicing strategist's most defining characteristic—the awareness of uncertainty.

## 2.1 Strengths, Weaknesses, Opportunities, and Threats (SWOT)

The inventory of consultants' models begins with SWOT, goes on to the BCG matrix, Porter's 5-forces, the Balanced Scorecard, and so on. Many of these models are illustrated with well-known diagrams, so the reader is urged to go on the internet and bring up the appropriate images (that would otherwise have occupied many pages in this book—fancy but superfluous).

SWOT remains managements' most popular strategic tool in spite of the large number of "more sophisticated" tools that have become available since its appearance in the 1950s. At first sight SWOT is just an appraisal of the situation, what Fayol (a major nineteenth-century French management theorist) called "the all-round look." Something happens and you have to do something about it. You look around. What resources are available? What are the opportunities or options? What else might happen? It is just commonsense. But as Voltaire noted, commonsense is not so common. There are three points here. Commonsense is deeply situated; perhaps only those inhabiting a situation can grasp fully the difference between commonsense and other views. Commonsense is shaped by experience, reflection, and practice rather than by analysis or education. The Ancient Greeks recognized the difference between *phronesis*, translated today as "practical wisdom," and *episteme*, the ability to think rigorously and logically from universal truths, or *techne*, the ability to do things with materials.[4] Both *episteme* and *techne* are often misplaced in social situations: knowing how is not the same as knowing when or where. The gap between *techne* and *phronesis* captures this. Commonsense relates to acting wisely or proficiently in a specific situation, plus it presumes we are complex sentient social practitioners rather than coldly calculating analysts. Michael Polanyi captured the nature of *phronesis* in the notion of tacit knowledge, a mode of human understanding inseparable from timely proficient practice, what stands behind language and makes it seem relevant to our projects.[5] Hence his quip "we know more than we can say" and his illustration of our inability to help bicycle non-riders become riders through explanation alone; we must learn through practice. Strategizing engages our tacit knowledge and is likewise embedded in practice. Strategic practices both follow from tacit knowing, opening us to learning, and precede it, shaping our practice.

The desire that drives strategic practice is to make an improving change in the situation. The change we have in mind is a reflection of (a) our view of the situation as changeable through our practice, and (b) our choice of how and when to make the change—which acts reveal us and our intentions. Put differently, we can only change a situation that is open to being changed,

---

[4] The Greek philosophers appreciated the philosophical absurdity of trying to define "knowledge." Their strategy for dealing with it was to realize (a) knowledge is not about the thing known, rather it is about how we humans think and know, and (b) the nature of our knowing could be best explored by contrasting the different ways in which we think we know as a matter of our own experience.

[5] M. Polanyi (1967) *The Tacit Dimension*. Garden City, NY: Doubleday Anchor Books.

and the change we make is inevitably a reflection of us and our feelings about the world. We thereby make ourselves responsible for our actions, especially as they affect other people. There is no human action that is fully determined by non-human factors, about which we can argue we have no choice. This follows from the limited or "bounded" sense we have of ourselves and the world. Our view of a resource is always through the lens of our understanding and intentions, the activity we have in mind. As we look at our situation there is no certain and universal metric available. The classic business question "What does it mean for us?" is central here—strengths, weakness, threats, and opportunities must be framed by our intentions. There is no point in attending to someone else's evaluation—especially the anonymous people who comprise the market. If they knew what we know about extracting value from the resources they sell us, they would not sell.

SWOT works when strategists trust their "subjective" judgments about categorizing and estimating its components. There are no strategically useful informing "objective" metrics. We create the analysis through the lens of our judgments, so our conclusions are always hostage to our bad judgments. For example, most business people know IBM turned down an opportunity to acquire the patents and processes offered them by Chester Carlson—that were the foundation of the Xerox Corporation. This was not a matter of not knowing their potential; IBM was already working on developing their own photocopying machines using a different technology. They judged the market too small—perhaps a couple of machines at the Pentagon, one at the Library of Congress, and so on. As a counter-example, Intel were the dominant suppliers of DRAMs when they choose to get out of the way of the low-cost invasion from the Japanese companies and moved into micro-processors at a time when neither the market potential or the manufacturing challenges were well understood. Yet they judged they could build an impregnable position. History showed how right they were—at least for a while. Strategic changes to the BM are probably best thought of as "paradigm shifts" into a different world in which everything—especially strengths, weaknesses, threats, and opportunities—differs. In spite of its simplicity, SWOT is a tool of considerable sophistication because its focus is the judgments the strategists make about their external and internal situation, and their resources. As these judgments bring SWOT together it provides a picture of the firm as a pattern of strategic judgment.

Perhaps a good metaphor is that SWOT is like a mirror held up to reflect the firm's self-image, prompting the strategists to discuss and debate the answer to the most fundamental of strategic questions "Who are we?" and, bringing in the time element, "Who do we want to be and when?" A SWOT analysis can be an exploration of a possible world rather than the present one to be left behind. This is what makes it a strategic tool rather than an analytic one. It is not a search for the external determinants of how our BM should or must change—we have lots of acreage so we should grow something or we know lots about office calculators so we should make photocopiers. Thinking of SWOT as a causal analysis of the external determinants of the firm's future hands the strategic initiative over to the "business environment." Such a passive "objective" reading abandons both the creative dimension of strategic work and the managerial responsibility for the judgment the firm needs if it is to create added value in an under-determined situation.

A SWOT analysis has two quite distinct stages. First, it begins as an all-round look to articulate what has happened, where, and what is the nature of the impulse that leads us to re-examine our strategy. Is the current strategy aiding our achievement of our purposes? Second, SWOT moves into an exploration of what happens if we make changes to ameliorate the current strategy's unsatis-factoriness or open up some beneficial impacts. We can think of this as explor-ing what happens to our resources as we move them into the new world imagined. Perhaps we are strong in mainframe computers—as IBM was—what happens to the firm's strengths, weaknesses, opportunities, and threats as we imagine moving these capabilities into the mobile computer market? We know the answer to this, of course. The technologies are quite different, as are the customers and their performance criteria. Mainframe strengths turn out to be weaknesses when they get in the way of seeing the PC market's new possibil-ities. Another example: if we are strong in the manufacture of small high-performance gas engines, should we get into the chainsaw and snowmobile businesses? Again we know this can work out well, our current strengths are sustained and extended by moving into such allied businesses. It turns out that a chainsaw is mostly a small high-performance gas engine, and the comple-mentary technologies of chain and saw are peripheral and not likely to be a source of competitive advantage. The opposite is true of the mobile computer; it is not a shrunken and portable mainframe. It is a very different entity with very different strategic marketing and support implications.

The third point is that, while SWOT is a handy vehicle for surfacing and discussing strategic judgments rather than objectively measured matters of fact, it offers a degree of systematization. It is a tool rather than "an approach" or "a statement of a principle." There are lots of business principles, such as "buy low, sell high" or "give the customer what she wants" or "look after the pennies and the pounds will look after themselves," but they are not system-atic and not a good language with which to discuss the firm's strategic options. After WW2 there was a widespread move to try and systematize many of the principles of good management that business people already knew and used, and which were evident in the existing rich literature of management.[6] As best

---

[6] T. M. Porter (1995) *Trust in Numbers: The Pursuit of Objectivity in Science and Public Life.* Princeton: Princeton University Press.

we know, SWOT emerged in the 1960s from the Stanford Research Institute in California where a consulting team led by Al Humphreys was researching the human and social dimensions of effective teamwork. Their ideas were taken up by the British management consultants Urwick & Orr (originators of the POSDCORB analysis) and first applied at the UK booksellers W. H. Smith.

From the beginning SWOT was a critique of the post-WW2 rational-planning trend driven by the success of wartime planning methods. These centralized the decision-making on the data-driven and numbers-oriented planning staff attached to corporate HQ, army-style. That led to the development of "operations research" (OR) and today's dominance of quantitative methods. The insight behind SWOT was different, that human judgments are needed to make actionable sense of the firm's strategic situation and possibilities, precisely because of the uncertainties penetrating real business situations. The judgments sought were those of the operatives engaged in the relevant practices. Even though they lacked the quantitative analytic skills of the HQ staffers, their intuitions should be brought into the planning process rather than kept separate. The SRI team saw that most firms' "group dynamics" were counterproductive and inhibited open communication, especially preventing "lower level" non-professional employees from suggesting the senior people had got it wrong while their staffers, looking only at the numbers and blind to the practice, were telling them they had it right.

The deeper point is that strategic tools—and management education too—are only valuable because the senior executives do not know enough about the strategic implications of what is going on in their firms. Strategic tools are devices and procedures to collect and present data that can help the strategists find their way through the "fog" of the real business situation. Another way to put this is that in the "old days," especially prior to WW2, those senior managers who did not start their own business and shepherd it through its history only got to head up the business after working their way up from its junior levels, during which time they gained a thorough understanding of what was going on; from shipping clerk to CEO perhaps, like Andrew Carnegie, who started on the factory floor. Plus business models were not changing as rapidly as they seem to nowadays so what they learned on the way up remained relevant when they arrived. Especially since WW2 it has become increasingly common for people to "parachute" into senior positions from other businesses or even from other professions entirely, such as law. MBA programs are thought to equip the best and brightest to parachute accordingly. Plus the stable business structures through which people clambered in the old days are now under constant reconstruction through merger and acquisition. All of which makes business models more changeable. In which event senior managers never have the old-timers' opportunity to understand the subtle details of the business—and we see CEOs at Senate hearings insisting on their ignorance of their own firm's activities. Strategic tools are relevant and valuable precisely because they may save knowledge-challenged managers from the consequences of their ignorance.

SWOT was elaborated into the (a) PEST (political, economic, social, and technological) and (b) TAM (team, action, management) models. There is lots of information about these tools on the internet. The PEST model looks at some different dimensions with which to describe the business environment. It is more outward-looking than SWOT. A substantial degree of managerial judgment, and the study and observation that helps one develop such judgment, is necessary to make any of these tools "work." This desire to formalize strategic work into a structured process leads on to "sensitivity analysis," an even more systematic and sometimes mathematical or statistical modeling development of similar multidimensional ideas. The TAM model is a process in three stages: (1) senior-management-led objective setting and team building, (2) discussion and conclusion drawing, and (3) implementation. The PEST components are separated into categories—products and services, value-add processes, customers, distribution channels and methods, financing, administration. The TAM model anticipated the Balanced Scorecard (see section 2.14), though that has a somewhat different orientation and is more closely tied to the tradition of management accounting.

Many consultants "sell" the SWOT, PEST, and TAM models, proposing them as practical languages to shape strategic discussion with their clients. Looking at their literature it is clear these models are sometimes presented as if they were rigorous with a strong internal logic—even as consultants know this is not the case. There is no rigorous model of the socio-economy—made up of the firm, its environment, and their interaction—nor of the firm as the collision or synthesis of identity, intention, and context. The consultants use SWOT to generate discussion and then listen to the client to pick up those judgments the client's management has put in place, and to surface, critique, and improve on them. Using these models to shape the discussion reflects the practical rhetoric of consulting; the sense conveyed that systematic methods are more powerful than non-systematic ones. On the other hand, too dogmatically adopted rigor means the most important aspect of the strategizing process, the collaborative development of an actionable judgment about "what to do" based on experience-driven assessments, gets silenced. Successful strategy consultants learn to transition from data-driven discussion and to bring judgment into play—but only after a solid consultant–client relationship has been built up. Strategic consulting is too often a process of executives handing over their power and responsibility to others on the grounds, perhaps, that they have wider experience or more powerful concepts. Whether such responsibility ever can or should be handed over is another matter, as Fayol noted.

In summary, SWOT-type models offer a language for describing or mirroring the firm as a pattern of strategic judgments. These are management's own assessments of its current resources—assets and liabilities—and current relationships—opportunities and threats, and how they might be changed and re-synthesized into a different image of the firm. The models show how strategic imagination and judgment is necessary to arrive at a coherent picture, a sense that the firm "exists" and has unique identity, intention, and space-time context; including (*a*) whether any particular resource or relationship is an asset or a liability and (*b*) how these conclusions might be changed by moving to a new arrangement or BM. SWOT-based models offer little sense of the firm's value-adding processes or their clock-time. At best they suggest it might be useful to develop "snapshots" of, say, increasing threats to the present business model. Thus Intel "looked ahead" and concluded they would not be able to compete with the Japanese companies expanding into the DRAM business. Or one might look to a particular increasing strength as an R&D project progresses and delivers a new technological edge.

## 2.2 Learning and the Experience Curve

If SWOT is like a mirror that presents an image of the firm's identity, so as to facilitate strategic discussion of what the firm might become, experience curve analysis brings time to the center of the strategic analysis. Long before Adam Smith, business people grasped that learning a better practice was a powerful business strategy, perhaps its most basic one. The private sector's freedom to pursue learning, and thereby add value and gain profit, is what distinguishes it from the public sector. The public sector's strategies, like von Clausewitz's military strategies, turn on public service criteria that get defined by the political process. The private sector is different, permitted to stand free of the public interest and act in the interests of private investors. Profit is an incentive to secure private gains from the firm's practical learning. Beyond Smith's analysis, Marshall, the British marginalist economist, noted business learning was often collective as groups of entrepreneurs shared or collaborated informally in their learning processes—Sheffield cutlers, Dalton GA carpet makers, Swiss watchmakers. He spoke of their know-how being "in the air" of the industry rather than within firms, and today we speak similarly of "strategic groups."

At the end of the nineteenth century psychologists began to research human learning more scientifically and coined the term "learning curve," which was drawn on in an influential 1936 economics paper that summarized the steady increase of labor productivity during the production run of military aircraft. After WW2 Bruce Henderson, the founder of the Boston Consulting

Group (BCG), made the idea basic to his new consulting business model.[7] The WW2 data on long production runs of complex equipment such as Liberty ships, Grumman F4F Wildcat fighters, or M4 Sherman tanks was compelling. Productivity improvements were persistent and kept on appearing. Henderson argued that, so long as these productivity gains were passed through to customers as lower prices, the experience curve suggested a winning and self-reinforcing "first-mover advantage" strategy. The later explanations of the downward sloping curve of cost against cumulative production drew on Adam Smith's division of labor propositions and considered rising labor efficiency and improved tools and methods. These could be added to gains from technological advances, product redesign, and network effects or positive externalities, the best-known being the QWERTY keyboard and the beneficial consequences of "everybody's doing it." Moore's law about the steady advance of computing cost-effectiveness is another well-known application of the experience curve—especially dependent on network effects, both electronic and social.

The first point to be made about experience curves is that the strategically appropriate metrics are not necessarily those evident in the textbooks. Time is fundamental and inescapable, but what "time" is strategic? And where is change to be measured? Declining cost may not be the most important consequence of more production. Experience can also translate into other customer-attractive attributes: product reliability and user awareness, even design adaptation. Network and geographical effects may overtake all of these so that customers end up buying, for example, a Windows PC when other (better) operating systems are available—because they are not supported at their location. The experience gained in producing Windows in huge volume is obviously incredibly valuable to Microsoft, which achieves huge gross margins as a result, but the experience of using Windows also leads to an after-sale situation of user learning that favors the most-used, a winner-take-all result. As with the SWOT model, strategic attention to the learning curve means learning to look at the world through the lens of a particular BM and its impact. The learning curve applies both to the firm, and to those involved in the world beyond, as consumers and suppliers (and support personnel) get more experience of the firm's products and activities. Clearly if the experience curve was the only strategic option there would never be a move to the next generation of product or service. In fact learning is disaggregated by use; learning to produce is not the same as learning to consume, use, or repair, or teach others. Experience also operates against the status quo as more gets learned about shortcomings of present practice and the possibilities for

---

[7] B. D. Henderson (1979) *Henderson on Corporate Strategy*. Cambridge, MA: Abt Books.

change. Likewise, just as early adopters may desire the new product, so there are late adopters who do not wish to be beta-testers and would rather wait for others to learn and help flush out the bugs.

The value of the learning curve is the way it highlights the impact of production-based or market-based learning on the BM. The knowledge produced in one period can be carried forward to the next period where it becomes a means of adding new value. The model presumes that the firm's world is not changing so rapidly that the learning at time $T_1$ is obsolete by time $T_2$ as the next production period arrives, so the product's or firm's "cycle time" matters greatly. But the learning curve's weakness is that the performance dimension impacted by the learning process is not given and needs to be judged in the context of the firm's BM. For instance, the EADS and Boeing bids for the $35 billion contract to build US air-refueling tankers depended heavily on estimates of the impact of their production-based learning, which is not the same as economies of scale. These exist without additional learning. For instance, given the auto industry's competitive intensity, the commoditized nature of its product, and resulting slim margins, auto manufacturers must defray the model and production development costs across a long production run. The first units produced are very costly. The manufacturers forecast sales and price accordingly, hoping to reach break-even or better within the model's viable market window. They must produce "at scale"—millions of units—with huge investment if they are to open up the possibility of a profit. Learning curve effects and economies of scale differ when the economies of scale are due to being able to defray start-up and capital costs via larger scale production. The air-tanker bids looked to economies of scale and network effects through sharing parts and maintenance procedures with other aircraft being produced, as well to learning curve effects. Likewise some airlines, especially new ones, try to stick to a single base model aircraft for similar reasons.

The learning curve helps illuminate the BM's strategic timing and its importance to strategists. Calendar time may mean little. One quarterly reports plops on top of another. The financials are no more than scoreboards, their timing-clock run by regulators and investors who demand financial reports (e.g. annually). Yet the auto companies, for example, take around two years to get a new model into production and so have to carry huge investment and R&D expenses across accounting periods. In the same way that financial accounting differs from managerial accounting—the production of accounts to help managers—financial reports may shed little light on the strategist's game—the value-adding process. Financials need not reveal the declining market share or the growing inventory of patents or the approaching retirement of key workers. The business's strategic time is a complex notion that always has many threads but needs to reveal the principal urgencies of the firm's situation.

There is also the notion of "human capital"—what individuals have learned by doing and now know how to do, capital in the sense of something that can be carried forward into a new time period. The employees' skills and tacit knowledge are a major component of what they can contribute to the firm. It may—or may not—be useful to distinguish human capital from the firm's financial, organizational, social, or structural capitals. But clearly the learning curve draws attention to managing the firm's human capital as this is being developed or renewed in the value-adding processes of purchasing, producing, distributing, and supporting the firm's products and services. The change in human capital is not visible in the financials. Nor is it readily captured by rigorous scientific or accounting methods. Ironically those who urge more rigorous SWOT-based methods and metrics are actually pressing managers to identify and count those assets that can be measured, implicitly suppressing and devaluing the human and social capabilities that cannot be so measured. Given the accessibility and clarity of Adam Smith's analysis of the economic impact of human learning it is surprising how little the strategy literature engages those assets (and liabilities) that are "off the books" and beyond the metrics. Indeed, many now argue these "intangible assets" drive the firm's strategy, that "employee knowledge" is the most strategic of the firm's assets, so that identifying and husbanding them becomes the core of strategizing. SWOT analysis is dominated by resources and relationships susceptible to management's judgments, so management is always in the best position to know what the employees do or do not know, what they can or might be able to do. Such intuitions lead on towards the notions of the "knowledge-based view" of the firm (2.10) and "dynamic capabilities" (Chapter 3).

When the learning curve is judged strategically significant, that brings managing the firm's learning into the core of the BM. The strategists' challenge is to pick useful categories and metrics—what exactly is being improved and by how much? Good strategic work depends on management having a workable sense of the business model for their particular firm. There is a chicken and egg question. The strategic process creates the firm's BM. But the relevant metrics depend on the BM chosen, for it is the "lens" through which the world must be viewed to distinguish the relevant from the irrelevant, between what should be attended to and what ignored. So which comes first, lens or metric? This helps show why doubt lies at the center of the strategizing process. There must be a way of looking at the world to get the process started, but along with the developing sense of certainty and confidence must come the habit of mind that questions whether one is being led "up the garden path" or "into an enemy trap"—is this the right way to look at things? Is it just a crutch? Thus declining production cost may be an indicator of knowledge being generated and applied—or that something essential is being missed out. There may be better indicators. Should the design be changed, taking the firm back to the start of the learning curve but leveraging off the experience gained in a different way, opening up a new universe of possibilities that will eventually prove richer or more defensible than the product-markets already engaged? Thus strategic work is as much about propitious questions as it is about answers, for while it is necessary to generate answers to communicate to others, these answers should be doubted, reproblematized, and turned back into questions—"Is this right?"

There is a substantial literature on the learning curve and it suggests the possibility of a mathematical relationship between the cumulative averages of the metric (Y) chosen to measure the learning (production cost, production time, product quality, etc.) and the cumulative production (X). The result is of the form Y = aX(b). But the empirical research shows wide variation in learning rate across different kinds of business—aircraft production, Kibbutz farming, petroleum refining, pizza making, etc. This reinforces the earlier point that fitting a learning curve to the firm involves strategic judgment, in particular the choices the metric (Y) indicates, through the learning, and the firm's time-dimension—for instance it might be better to focus on maintaining the pizza production costs while ensuring the quality improves.

Summarizing this section, the learning curve is strong in its implications but maddeningly vague in its application. Yes, learning by doing leads to knowledge that can be important strategically, but what is being learned, by whom, and how might we measure it, and can we do more than simply point towards it? It also shows how the value of learning is contingent on its being both carried forward and remaining relevant in subsequent time periods. The learning curve literature has suggestions about the learning mechanisms and how they might translate into value adding, but they are likewise vague and controversial. The approach's great strength is how it points towards the BM's strategic-time.

## 2.3 Life Cycle

Another approach that brings time central to the analysis is the "organizational life cycle." Social Darwinism became a popular and powerful philosophy at the end of the nineteenth century and it shaped a great deal of thinking about sociology and economics.[8] Firms were often thought to be "organic" entities and it became common to speak of their birth, life, and death. The organic assumption leads on to evolutionary models and evolutionary economics will be considered briefly in Chapter 3. But the degree to which firms

---

[8] R. Hofstadter (1955) *Social Darwinism in American Thought* (rev. edn). Boston: Beacon Press.

can be thought of as biological entities is limited. The idea that they have some kind of life independent of the human beings that manage them and whose interactions bring the firm to life is curious, since it seems to question or even deny management's strategic role. If the firm is an independent entity like a truck, the product of some non-managerial entity or activity, then management's role would be to drive it this way or that. Likewise, as an organic entity like a species member, it has its own inbuilt direction and selection mechanisms. Horse-breeders try to get into the middle of the evolutionary process, replacing chance mating with selected ones, though their control over the outcome is marginal at best. Some theorists, such as population ecologists, have moved to the extreme here and argue managers have no significant strategic impact on the firm or its life cycle.

There is also the curious and as yet unexplained empirical support for this line of thinking from researchers into firm's sizes and how they seem to conform to a mathematical "power law"—implying firm size is independent of the differences that strategizing presumes.[9] Nonetheless it is not usual to think of firms coming into existence spontaneously in the way we think new species members come into existence as new ecological niches open up. Business strategists, by definition, presume firms are "caused" by the strategic choices of entrepreneurs rather than by the appearance of economic opportunities. It may be useful to think of firms springing up to meet these, just as many entrepreneurs jumped into business to provide iPhone apps or wireless services, but human beings (the entrepreneurs) and their strategic choices always mediate the process. Much government economic policy aims to foster entrepreneurship by creating "ecological" conditions that increase the chances of new firms being formed and surviving. This is a nice metaphor, but the firms always need an entrepreneur to "read" these conditions and respond imaginatively to the opportunities presented.

But thinking of firms as biological entities gives them a life cycle. This is their BM's strategic-clock, the period between birth and death. Biological metaphors are all very well and it might seem useful to try and capture something of the firm's tendency to change through time, but are they clarifying? Must the firm mature and die? Can strategizing change this? Ironically many scholars of corporate law define the firm as a social institution (unnatural person) with eternal life, the very opposite of having a life cycle. But if the firm's strategic timing can be established, like the human reproductive cycle, we might be able to draw some strategic conclusions. For instance, demographic analysis can illuminate how the passage of time expands or contracts a BM's reach. Given a recession and rising gas prices we might forecast that

---

[9] Y. Ijiri and H. A. Simon (1964) 'Business Firm Growth and Size', *American Economic Review*, 54(2), 77–89.

recent of-age drivers will choose better-mileage autos. The demographic analysis is based on human biology, and this puts the gas and auto industry (in this particular respect) onto a definable timescale. Likewise demographic analysis, coupled with an understanding of the impact of improving health care, makes it possible to forecast the emerging "senior market" and its special needs.

These life cycles are of people, individually or collectively, nothing to do with firms as evolving or "living" as independent entities. Likewise it might make sense to think that a particular form of firm, such as a restaurant, will find itself to be a member of a population whose vital characteristics can be usefully aggregated—leading one to conclude that the average lifetime of a restaurant is X years or that the restaurant life's distribution curve has a certain character. But, as this example suggests, there is nothing to tell a specific restaurant's owners where on this distribution they fall. One common BM in the restaurant business is to open and then use various publicity techniques—including discounted meals and free meals for celebrities—to create a good "buzz." Then, as the business expands and develops a reputation, and heads into profitability, the owners sell to that ever-present population of novice entrepreneurs who want to get into the restaurant business. Their lack of knowledge leads to the establishment's swift decline. Meanwhile the "start-up specialists" have moved on with their very different BM. There is an endless variety of ways of making money, even in the restaurant business—part of the mysterious magic of our capitalist system.

Presuming a firm has a life cycle means imbuing it with a measure of independence, implicitly denying complete dependence on its strategists and maybe on external circumstances too. When it comes to restaurants we see determination rather than luck stands behind keeping them open, in spite of the fact that they eventually get ragged and need refurbishing, providing indifferent food with indifferent service. Many restaurants are new, but some are venerable; Maxim's in Paris opened in 1893, Set Portes in Barcelona opened in 1836 and is Europe's oldest. The life-cycle approach may capture little more than the commonsense idea that even the best ideas eventually go "off the boil," and that much of strategizing is about preventing this from collapsing the BM. But there is no real model here.

Consultants have also made something out of the idea of curing or exploiting interruptions to the life cycle—such as Geoffrey Moore's notion of the "chasm" between early adopters and the main part of the market. If the firm is a prisoner of a life cycle over which managers have little control, then repairing interruptions seems like a useful thing for them to do. But the distinction between market segments hides subtler assumptions. If we treat the early-adopters and late-adopters as different market segments, we are presuming they have different BMs. It might be better for the strategist to spend less time thinking about repairing the life cycle or "bridging the chasm," and more about targeting the two segments with different BMs. Putting them together expresses the intuition that the late-adopters will only buy something they have seen the early-adopters buy and report well on. On the one hand all who report buying for that reason can be then categorized as late-adopters. But hidden here would be the belief that these folks can only be convinced to buy as a result of some behavior that is out of the control of the management. How come their marketing armamentarium is so empty?

Summarizing then, the life cycle is clearly not a very useful tool for it does not provide what it claims, seizing the timing of the cycle from birth though maturity to decline. It is more of reflection of the attitude that presumes the BM is a socio-economic concept that is management-independent—denying, for instance, the firm is a money-making machine whose superb design can be sufficient to ensure its long-term viability. But as we know, moth and rust corrupt all worldly things and the firm is a human artifact. At best the life cycle is a metaphor for an attitude of constant vigilance about the unmanageable and surprising changes that happen all the time, the doubt that drives all strategizing.

## 2.4 What is Going On Here?

With three different "strategic tools" in hand we begin to see the practical nature of strategic work and judgment. SWOT, the learning curve, and life cycle analyses clearly differ. They make completely different assumptions about the BM and its strategic possibilities and problems. They imply very different strategic languages. Which is right? Which is best for this situation? This provides a practical definition of what strategic work is about, to wit, using judgment to assess which of these tools, or any others, best illuminates the firm's situation. But notice that the contrasts between the tools are often more illuminating than their definitions, which are none too precise and irritate academics because they are not "objective" and have not been exposed to empirical test. In practice each of these strategic tools probably has something pertinent to say about almost any business situation, but it is unlikely that any one will fit precisely enough to enable the strategist to exclaim, "Got it!" The contrasts are easier to handle. Is strategic time important here? Is learning important here? The strategic question is always "Which tool seems to surface best the possibilities for added value and profit?"

The purpose of leading the reader through this list is to provide her/him with a set of tools or diagnostics, to be tried out just as a mechanic might try out various wrenches or screw-drivers from his tool-box to see which fits the nut best, prior to applying force, to committing resources. This is a test of the mechanic's judgment. Anyone who has done this knows there comes a moment of commitment when getting it wrong and stripping the screw-head or nut makes things much worse. Actions have consequences, especially strategic actions. Having to search among a set of strategic alternatives is a consequence of the situation's uncertainty, there being no external referent, no objective way of establishing "for sure" the nature of the challenge the firm is facing. "It all depends" is the ruling maxim. The immediate result of choosing is confidence enough to commit—showing that the unsettling effect of engaging uncertainty has been coped with and that practice should proceed. In the end all of us are driven by the desire for the confidence that attends the sense of our competence. We abhor risk and uncertainty because it reminds us of our incompetence. The entrepreneur has the judgment and technique to create confident practice, just as the skilled pianist successfully engages a complex piece with the same resources—eyes, hands, nerves, muscles—as the novice, but with very different results. These three tools are a start to analyzing the judging technique, but many more tools are available to the aspiring strategist. The practice of strategic judgment can be framed as looking though one's strategic tool-box—after adding a few other tools as a result of study, instruction, and experience—and choosing which to use in a particular situation. My book's intent is to put some tools into the reader's tool-box, and thereby illustrate the real nature of strategic work—but not select for the reader. In due course I shall connect choosing a tool to "doing cases." But first a few more of today's appreciated tools.[10]

## 2.5 Break-Even

Most investment projects graph their finances as the familiar "hockey-stick"— a period of negative cash flow followed by a period of positive cash flow. An estimation of the point in time at which the initial investment will be recovered is useful, especially when the firm sees several alternative investment opportunities and wants to compare them quickly without considering much beyond their financial basics—such as the investments' different returns and product-market risks. It is easy to introduce a base or cut-off rate of return such as the firm's strategically chosen internal rate of return (IRR).

---

[10] Á. B. Cyrino and R. A. de Miranda (2008) *Strategic Management Tools: Usage Patterns of Companies in Brazil*. Nova Lima MG: Fundação Dom Cabral. R. Gunn and W. Williams (2007) 'Strategic Tools: An Empirical Investigation into Strategy in Practice in the UK', *Strategic Change*, 16, 201–16. D. Jarratt and D. Stiles (2010) 'How are Methodologies and Tools Framing Managers' Strategizing Practice in Competitive Strategy Development?', *British Journal of Management*, 21, 28–43. P. Jarzabkowski, M. Giuletti, and B. Oliveira (2009) *Building a Strategy Toolkit: Lessons from Business*. London: Advanced Institute of Management Research. S. Stenfors (2007) 'Strategy Tools and Strategy Toys: Management Tools in Strategy Work', *Helsinki School of Economics*, A-297.

Break-even analysis is also a handy way to gauge the impact of a sudden decline in sales. The US Big Three auto companies were thrown into turmoil as the economy collapsed in 2007/2008 and their sales fell well below their break-even levels of production and sales. Ford's response was to resist government funding and cut back savagely on its fixed costs to bring its break-even point to somewhere close to or even below its post-crash sales levels. This was one alternative to the impractical strategy of maintaining its sales by, say, massive marketing expenditures that would have substantially increased its share of the declining national and global auto market.

Break-even analysis is still a popular management tool and it can be enriched by doing the analysis on a project-by-project basis, or by using a more strategically relevant time-base, given that different projects may vary in the time they take to come to fruition and into profitability. The analysis can also be enriched by bringing the impact of the learning into account, which again might vary from project to project and so materially change the return to the firm, adding intangible capital. The intangible capital developed can be added into the revenue. While break-even analysis can help the strategic discussion along, it clearly calls for considerable strategic judgment in its application—which judgment is very different from that needed in implementing the previous tools. On the one hand it can be used to compare investment opportunities, on the other to indicate how the balance of costs and revenues must be readjusted when new rates of production and consumption apply.

## 2.6 Porter's 5-Force Analysis and Economic Rents versus Chandler's "Fit" Approach

I shall cover additional simple tools, but the merit of moving on to Porter's more complex analysis at this stage is that many of the tools I mention later, such as Ansoff's strategy matrix and the BCG matrix, are specifically designed for multiple investment opportunities or business operations. The tools covered already are mostly focused on single operations or lines of business. The later ones are tools for managing a portfolio of different lines of business rather than discrete units, and so more appropriate for the modern large firm. Note, though, that the vast bulk of our economy's firms are small—family firms, SMEs, start-ups, and so on. We often assume the economy is dominated by the large firms whose names are in the financial pages every day, but there is an ongoing debate among economists about whether they or small firms are more characteristic of democratic capitalism, and whether small firms are the major source of new jobs and of innovative products and services. Porter's analysis applies to a single business unit, it is not a portfolio management tool. But we cannot consider the 5-force model in any depth without first doing some homework that gets us into more complexity; so this section will cover other matters as well, reconsidering "economic rent" and Chandler's strategy-structure model.

In spite of its global popularity and impact, Porter's 5-force model is widely misunderstood.[11] First, it is not an "industry analysis" as many insist. On the contrary it is pretty much like a PEST or SWOT analysis in that that its five forces are merely the dimensions or categories Porter chose as he used his own strategic judgment to describe the firm's environment rather than simply borrowing SWOT's four. Yet his choice of dimensions seems no more rigorous than those chosen for the SWOT or PEST models. Perhaps it seems easier to identify customers and suppliers than identify strengths and weaknesses, but these become equally tricky when potentials and possibilities are taken into account in future time periods. Many of the 5-force model's users see it incorrectly as determining (telling the strategist what to do), just as many see the SWOT models' dimensions as determining (equally incorrectly). But there is more to Porter's model than an idiosyncratic choice of SWOT-like descriptors. The principal difference lies in Porter's implicit model of the firm or BM. He did not make this explicit—at least not until his later work on the "value-chain." But many strategy writers noted his 5-force model precipitated a major shift from efficiency-based strategic analyses to those that focused on "economic rents" and market imperfections.

Rent is the economists' term for "above-average return on investment" or, more correctly, persistent above-average return or, even more precisely, the circumstances that make a persistent rent-stream possible. A landlord charges a shopkeeper a rent for the use of his building. He might charge whatever gives him a "normal" rate of return, perhaps the Fed rate + 2%. The economists' idea is that an "economic rent" arises when the landlord is able to get away with charging something like Fed + 7%. This means the landlord is able to borrow from the bank at the "normal" rate of Fed + 2%, buy the building, rent it, and pocket the 5% difference as the economic rent. This might happen because the landlord bought the building from his father who charged him less than its "real" market price as a way of helping him get into business or for some other reason, or because a new development has been built nearby and its residents are eager to shop at the store which, doing well, can afford the raised rent. Economic rents draw attention to the various kinds of market distortion that give rise to above-average returns. They are empirical facts about the real-world economic situation—market distortions exist as matters of fact so there is no need to explain how or why they arise, just as some people swim better than others. The possibility of rents is a way of describing the difference between the observed economic situation and imagined notions of "perfect markets." Alternatively we can see rent as part of a language for describing the firm's real context in ways that highlight its profit potential (the glass half full) rather than its failure to meet the "perfect market" standard (half empty). A context that offers rents is unlike one that does not.

In business, rents often arise through R&D—there are many things yet to be discovered. Science proceeds and our ignorance about Nature and how she works is overcome. Institutions such as patents might protect ownership of the resulting knowledge or technique. Thus Glaxo-Smith-Kline developed what the world knows as Tagamet, an ulcer treatment that by 1981 was the world's best-selling drug, and hugely profitable. But Tagamet was actually developed by James Black, a researcher who had previously developed a successful heart treatment drug, Propranolol, for ICI. While Tagamet and Propranolol generated huge rent-streams, there were questions about where the rent-streams flowed. How come James Black, eventually knighted for his services to medicine and awarded a Nobel in 1988, was not able to scoop the lion's share of these rents for himself rather than their going to the ICI and GSK executives and shareholders—given they were generated by his work? Yet he did not. Ray Dolby, in contrast, was able to garner a much greater share of the rent-stream that his audio and stereo-reproduction inventions (Dolby Digital) produced. The appearance of rents is empirical evidence of the real economic world's patchy, lumpy, and obscured nature. It is not at all like the fully known and brightly lit homogeneous market in the economics classroom.

Rent-streams are obviously of great interest to the business strategist. Perhaps strategy is no more than a search for securable rents. SWOT-based and learning-based models do not discriminate between efficiency-based and rent-based BMs. When the ability to charge or escape a rent appears in the analysis—as a strength or a weakness—the efficiency- and rent-based models can both be applied. The distinction is clear in microeconomic discussions of the "theory of the firm"—the microeconomists' term for "business model." Macroeconomists are not concerned with the theory of the firm, their focus is on the whole economy and its management. I shall deal with microeconomists' approaches to strategizing in Chapter 3, but the distinction between efficiency and rent strategies points to an axiomatic fault-line separating the economists' thinking into two different universes or "languages" that lead towards very different ideas of strategizing—efficiency-based and/or equilibrating versus rent-based and dis-equilibrating.

Today's general awareness of the efficiency/rent distinction shows the impact of microeconomic thinking on the strategy field over the last thirty or so years, given it was earlier characterized by less rigorous thinking that made no such distinction. First, to clarify the distinction, the bulk of neoclassical economic thinking presumes all economic actors have complete information, and the resulting economic behavior spins around the concept of the "efficient market." Under this circumstance the markets "dominate" the actors' choices or, more precisely, the collective behaviors that result from widespread information and maximizing behaviors dominate (and punish) actors who choose differently. The strategic theorizing then focuses on discovering the market's dominating behaviors. Firms are little more than production functions obliged to adopt these rules as they link efficient supply and demand markets. In these markets, market prices rule—oil at so much a barrel, plastic jugs made from oil at so much a gross—all prices known. Vigorous competition ensures any economic rents get competed away. If an oil supplier or plastic jug seller tries to charge above the market price he will not sell much. If he underprices he will be deluged with buyers, unable to meet their demands. In this way the market works to eliminate all but those producers setting market-clearing or "equilibrium" prices.

Strategists accept these as the inviolable facts of a competitive market. Firms might then try to compete on the basis of their internal production efficiency—the non-market aspects of their firm that include all sub-activities such as financing, purchasing, designing, production, warehousing, distribution, and managing. Note these non-market aspects are only strategically significant because they are not influenced by—are in some way insulated from—market behaviors. Perhaps two firms have different technologies, one being more efficient than the other. But then there are questions about how much each paid for the technology, when will it need replacing, how long are their production runs, and so on. In the long run a firm may be unable to prevent its internal aspects from being exposed to market pressures, for the more productive equipment suppliers will raise their prices, as does labor. In general, so long as all firms have the same access to the various technologies, and the market for technology is efficient, externally provided technology cannot provide the firm with a source of strategic advantage. An internally generated technology could achieve this so long as it is not "reverse engineered" or copied by others—so long as it remains "inimitable."

Learning models are attractive to those who think strategizing is about rent-seeking because they get around the impression that rents can only be acquired in getting lucky in less-than-efficient markets—and there is no useful theory of these, given that a market's specific imperfections are of an empirical nature and not theorizable. Learning is a concept that allows each firm's production experience to be unique and internal, with its benefits not tradable, in which event it seems possible for one firm to become more efficient than another through superior knowledge management—the discovery, and application of its own learning. No doubt learning can become a source of sustainable rent, as with successful R&D. But this may not be as simple as it seems, for only people learn. If the firms are also in efficient labor markets, competing firms will simply attract away those whose learning gave the firm an advantage—like recruiting Sir James, who actually quit ICI when they showed no interest in the research that led to Tagamet and decamped to GSK. Firms can trade in the people who create rents, like soccer stars, rather than the rents themselves. Perhaps every aspect of the process and benefit of learning can be traded. If everything capable of producing advantage can be traded, the rents will get competed away. If learning is to be the basis for a rent-stream there must be some mechanism to prevent erosion or leakage.

One argument is that the learning is collective. This is tricky. If James Black needs a whole team of researchers, so be it, and the competitor buys his whole team—something seen regularly in the City and on Wall St. In high tech, go one step further and buy the whole R&D apparatus, just as Google, Amazon, and Microsoft regularly buy small firms that seem to have achieved or be capable of interesting innovation. If this people trafficking goes on, suggesting there may be a perfect market in rent-generating resources, firms may be left with, stuck with, even defined by, those characteristics or features that cannot be traded. One implication is that IF firms are competing with others in well-managed and efficient markets THEN they actually end up competing only by better managing their naturally arising inefficiencies—for instance the inefficiencies that arise from human failings (such as inattention to the market's information, miscommunication, miscalculation, etc.) that they have not learned how to eliminate. Perhaps the founding entrepreneur is averse to discussing her strategic plans with the other executives, so compounding her strategic errors. In fact most start-up firms go through strategic crises as the founding executives get to see the firm's future differently and fall out. Start-ups are high-pressure and high-emotion situations. No doubt human-sourced inefficiencies can be reduced and possibly eliminated by superior management, but this simply points back to the possibility of these superior managers leaving to work for a competitor and so "monetizing" their personal talents elsewhere—just as the founders of Intel left Fairchild Semiconductor because they had a different vision of micro-electronics' future.

When we look at strategizing based on economic rent we go around and around in circles until we find a rent-producing mechanism that cannot be traded—perhaps because it cannot be separated from the firm, such as its reputation, or because the firm gets stuck with a "negative rent," something costly that no one wants and that cannot be traded for that reason: perhaps an internal inefficiency that we cannot eliminate, such as a burdensome labor or delivery contract—like that which drove Rolls-Royce into bankruptcy in 1971. Another way to express this is that we cannot escape the inexorable rent-eliminating logic of the assumption that markets are perfect—until we abandon it. Thus the axiomatic divide between the two microeconomic languages sets out from their differing concepts of "the market"—the neoclassical concept being abstract, theoretical, and perfect by assumption, versus the rent-based approach that sees real markets as lumpy and imperfect, an essentially empirical concept. Instead of looking at the economics textbook for the latter we might look, for instance, at the available facts about financing, managing, and distributing British tea-imports in the eighteenth century, or the market for tulips in 1630—sometimes stable, sometimes crazed. History becomes important to understanding the economic situation's heterogeneity. The neoclassical presumption of market efficiency automatically prioritizes markets over the firms that thereby end up containing all the inefficiencies, leading to major questions about why firms exist if they are nothing but trashcans for economic inefficiencies. But given the uncertainties of the real world's lumpy and unstable markets, the analysis should be the other way around.

Many would argue that firms are only necessary when perfect markets do not exist, which amounts to the same thing as saying firms are made up of things that cannot be traded and are not available in the markets that do exist. But there is no explanation of these markets' imperfections or why there are "gaps" in the markets that do exist. The presumption that markets are efficient simply shifts all the economic system's inefficiencies into the firms that exist. That cannot stand as an explanation of why firms exist. When firms do exist, markets may well "police" them, forcing them to compete by, for instance, learning how to squeeze out inefficiencies or killing them off. Such "economic cleansing" could be a reason why markets and firms both exist, like an explanation of why garbage trucks exist—overlooking any explanation of why society evolved to deal with its economic garbage rather than simply ignoring it, leaving the landscape littered with odious and inefficient firms. Markets reveal the politics behind presuming the beneficial effects of competition, viewing market pressure as the principal or even sole driver—competition improves the breed. But perhaps competition does not do this, playing instead to the market's lowest common denominator, and so on. There is no really solid reasoning available here.

Of course some would consider this entire discussion curious, even ridiculous, seeing no reason to wonder why firms exist, and would point to IBM or Microsoft and say "see! They exist!"—even as they declare an interest in strategic work and the task of inventing new business models. But we cannot make a good analysis of strategic work if we have no good ideas about why firms exist; or, turning this around, only by presuming something about their nature can we set about analyzing strategic work. Many take firms' existence as unproblematic. For me, in contrast, strategic work is irrevocably tied up with why we think firms exist. If we assume they exist there is little to be said about strategizing. This goes beyond saying firms are purposive and have objectives, the collision between identity, intention, and context discussed in Chapter 1, and that strategic work is about reaching for these. This simply presumes firms can exist. Clearly markets do not really exist in the same way that firms do; to say the market does this or that is simply a way to summarize a vast number of discrete transactions, all made by human beings and potentially riddled with the inefficiencies we find within firms. The trade that sets the "market price" at a particular moment may have been made in error, a broker misunderstanding his client, or on the broker's wrong advice about how "the market" was moving. Economists conclude wrong guesses are flushed out, presuming whatever the market "eventually" does is something like "the truth."

Whatever the strength of these points, the idea that management was mostly about the elimination of internal inefficiencies was attractive at the end of the nineteenth century. At the time the firms needing managers were mostly in manufacturing, using tangible materials, and waste and scrap were major concerns. Frederick Taylor and his colleagues developed Scientific Management to help their managers minimize waste, first of the firm's tangible resources and then of its labor potential.[12] Managers were valued because they were experts in efficiency, in helping firms "do for a shilling what any fool could do for a pound." In the period between WW1 and WW2 there was widespread enthusiasm for product and process standardization in the interests of increasing efficiency. This thinking led to what is now called "managerial capitalism" wherein strategizing was about the pursuit of firm efficiency in order to meet the dictates of increasingly efficient and competitive markets. A key presumption about an efficient market is that it is beyond being affected by anything any single firm does. It also throws into question whether a collection of firms, such as an industry, can collaborate to impact the market and make it monopolistic. Both efficient market and monopolistic market strategizing are compatible with the SWOT-based and learning models already covered.

The increasingly efficient national and global markets post-WW2 gave rise to what many consider the principal source of modern academic thinking about business strategy, the work of Al Chandler. He argued that, while a firm may not be able to affect its efficient market, it could influence its internal efficiency in ways that went beyond the value-chain efficiencies that were the focus of Scientific Management. Chandler focused on administrative efficiency as opposed to Taylor's production efficiency. Some see administration as the firm's "vertical" structure in contrast to the "horizontal" production-function structure of the firm. Both presume a division of labor and managers

---

[12] J.-C. Spender and H. Kijne (eds) (1996) *Scientific Management: Frederick Winslow Taylor's Gift to the World?* Norwell, MA: Kluwer.

able to harness it effectively to reach the firm's goals. Chandler argued that, given the firm could not influence any part of the market, its strategy lay in in its judgments to engage or not engage specific market-segments, choosing the lines of business it wanted to be in. Structure was the complementary judgment made about how to organize and administer the firm's operations in the light of these market engagements. The idea was that, as firms became more complex, such as when they expanded beyond their originating regions and "went national," the rising complexities and inefficiencies could be managed by adept specialization in the firm's administrative structure—seeking a "best fit" and so maximizing efficiency. Senior management were "generalists" who would delegate the firm's legal, purchasing, marketing, and production management functions to specialists who would be separated and structured in a more efficient way. Structure had to adapt to strategy, otherwise the firm would be inefficient or less efficient than the competition and its viability threatened.

Chandler's work reflected senior managers' concerns at the time and attracted considerable attention. As the complexity of firms grew in the 1960s managers were increasingly concerned by the changing ratio of indirect and direct workers, the rising proportion of "white-collar" workers and declining proportion of "blue-collar" workers, especially accentuated as technological and other improvement led to significant gains in blue-collar productivity. This impelled business interest in IT systems as a technology for both controlling administrative costs and raising administrative efficiency. Indeed business interest in IT has a great deal to do with the way technology made it possible to "deskill" white-collar work as well as blue-collar work. Internet-connected laptop-equipped salespeople, for instance, could gain competitive advantage by offering contract terms and book orders in "real time" while meeting with customers. The types of work that could be outsourced extended from, say, subcontracting making windows for a new office-tower to supporting intangible data-products, such as reading X-rays or providing mobile phone support.

With his focus on structure, Chandler analyzed the widespread move towards multidivisional firms as they further separated the functions that would remain at HQ once the manufacturing and marketing decisions had been delegated to the divisional level. For many strategists and consultants his thinking remains the core of corporate strategy, which is odd given it was actually about administrative organization. In fact Chandler's analyses are little more than explorations of the evolving bureaucratization of the firms he researched. But we know bureaucratization often leads to inefficiency and moving to more complex administrative structures is often associated with declining efficiency. Chandler was not an organization theorist and did not explain why the new administrative structures, such as divisionalization, were more efficient. He was a historian and merely observed their more frequent appearance. McKinsey turned prescribing divisionalization into a vigorous line of business. Eventual doubts about its effectiveness, and how to generate or even measure administrative efficiency, threw Chandler's thinking into question. While Chandler did path-breaking work as a business historian, his strategy-structure discussion clearly does not meet the four-fold Coasian questions about why firms exist, why their boundaries are where they are, why their structure and process is the way it is, and why their performance is so varied. At best they shed some light onto the third and fourth question.

Porter's work moved in a different direction. Rather than emerging from neoclassical economics it drew on the even more venerable tradition of theorizing about monopolies. The 5-force model is not a mere application of an economic theory of monopoly—which might consider, for instance, the public welfare loss occasioned by a monopoly. Porter provided a managerial or strategizing model and its differences from an economic model are crucial. Instead of seeking efficiency, the implication that efficient markets maximize public welfare, Porter focused on how managers might set about protecting a firm's existing rent-stream against competition, efficient market operations, or other processes. The subtlety and usefulness of his model lay in the variety of means and ideas that could be brought to the analysis. It offered a very inclusive language of rent-affecting possibilities in contrast to the parsimony of the microeconomic model that took account only of prices and costs, whether average or marginal. The way Porter used the term "force"—as in 5-force model—was interesting precisely because its many meanings helped encompass a variety of the practical means available to firms that wished to protect their rent-stream or attack others'. Note the term "force" is seldom encountered in neoclassical economics—it is an older term. The notion of efficient markets is likewise relatively new. Prior to Adam Smith's time business was more likely to be about acquiring and protecting a monopoly than anything remotely concerned with efficiency and market competition.

The notion of business and strategizing in the context of efficient markets was largely irrelevant until the sorts of infrastructural changes that facilitated efficient markets had come about: good transportation, banking institutions and systems, powerful commercial law, rapid technological diffusion, and so on. Especially, of course, the good information on which we know efficient markets depend. There was no radio, no internet. Even though there was nothing else available, newspapers were not very good for telling rural pig-farmers in Ohio where prices stood, how much pork bellies were selling for in Chicago. Business history shows that at least until the end of the nineteenth century US business managers mostly busied themselves with obtaining, creating, and protecting monopolistic positions. Sometimes these were short term; as in the apocryphal story of bankers whose carrier pigeons informed them of Napoleon's defeat at Waterloo, who were then able to get a useful edge in the currency market.

Monopoly theory accepts that firms may be able to influence their markets; the "boundaries" separating firm and market that most take for granted dissolve. The notion becomes exceedingly muddled. In the extreme, when a firm has complete control of its market, the firm becomes the market. The firm is then less of an economic entity than a socio-political one, for the boundaries around the firm become determined by socio-political processes rather than by economics. By socio-politics I mean "the way things social and economic work in practice," rather than any specific political processes of election, legislative debate, and decision-making. Alternatively we can say the firm is redefined as situated in a less-than-efficient socio-economic process. Whatever firms are, and why they exist, they are certainly not the efficiency-seeking production function so often presumed. In which case the firm's strategic work becomes a socio-political process, a situated political practice with political judgments vital.

Along these lines, Porter drew on the industrial organization (IO) approach that developed out of economic theorizing about rent-streams and, conversely, the analysis of their social merits and demerits. There was considerable theoretical progress between 1850 and 1950, in part to support the US government's efforts to control the sometimes predatory behavior of the "robber baron" trusts through anti-trust legislation. The theory was deployed to help convince those arguing against or for anti-trust activity or similar restraints of trade. While governmental control of business monopoly goes back to the Roman era, serious US legislation began with the 1890 Sherman Act. Business lawyers easily worked around its provisions and it was not until the Clayton Antitrust Act of 1914 and the Robinson-Patman Act of 1936 that anti-trust legislation began to have teeth and impact on US business strategy. Executives were made personally liable.

The 5-force model is grounded in the theorizing of that time and is more than an application of the industrial organization (IO) work of Mason and Bain that Porter mentioned in various papers. It was also shaped by the Harvard Business School approach Porter experienced as an MBA student. He was taught that strategizing meant searching for a sweet spot between the contrasting socio-political ends that were open to private sector managers. The LCAG model was set out in Learned, Christensen, Andrews, and Guth's strategy text, a book that underpinned MBA courses everywhere for decades.[13] Their matrix reminds one of SWOT, but the criteria are less about resources and competition and more

---

[13] E. P. Learned, R. Christensen, K. Andrews, and W. Guth (1965) *Business Policy: Text and Cases*. Homewood, IL: Richard D. Irwin.

about coexisting with the socio-economy. Drawing on the work of the labor economist John Commons, they argued that a good strategy called for judgments about (*a*) what the firm might do, (*b*) what it could do, (*c*) what its managers wanted to do, and (*d*) what they felt it should do.[14] Teaching strategy meant helping students grasp the subtlety of these questions and develop the judgment required to synthesize viable answers. In contrast neoclassical economics collapsed these four questions into a single question, such as "maximize profit and/or shareholder wealth." The LCAG matrix implied a personal set of judgments from managers. As they answered them they revealed themselves and their view of the firm's situation. The synthesis was inevitably shaped by their moral and ethical concerns as well as by their political and scientific understanding of the firm's situation. The LCAG matrix also mirrored Chester Barnard's image of the executive function.[15]

Even though the LCAG matrix did not address Coase's questions or illuminate the collision of identity, intention, and context, it remained central to Harvard's teaching for decades. Porter's 5-force model advanced beyond it, replacing the LCAG matrix's social and ethical notions of might, can, want, and should with private sector commercial concerns. The 5-force model's popularity and power as a teaching tool arose from the subtlety with which these were brought together. Estimating the likelihood that someone inside or outside the firm's industry would be able to develop a substitute product—as quartz movements proved to be vastly cheaper substitutes for mechanical watch movements—was always going to be tricky. Perhaps it called for technological forecasting by a scientific expert judging what was happening in quartz crystal development. This person was clearly not the same person who knew how to negotiate with suppliers of mechanical watch springs and get the best possible price. The model did not make any assumptions about people and their skills. It assumed the firm had the necessary capabilities available, that the implicit division of labor was effectively administered and did not lead to internal inefficiencies. The different kinds of analysis were then brought together through the lens of the potential impacts on the firm's existing rent-stream—the lens of the current BM. They were not brought together in a rigorous model of the firm, quite the opposite. The way they are brought together defines the firm strategically, illuminating how it adds value and protects that process.

Porter's categorization of impacts or "forces" was derived inductively from an analysis by teams of student aides, duly noted in his books, who reviewed

[14] J. R. Commons (1957) *Legal Foundations of Capitalism*. Madison, WI: University of Wisconsin Press.
[15] C. I. Barnard (1968) *The Functions of the Executive* (30th anniversary edn). Cambridge, MA: Harvard University Press.

hundreds of the case studies HBS had available. It generalized evidence of the many ways in which firms found their rent-stream diminished by others. It is useful to note the different levels and strategic timings buried in the 5-force analysis. The pressures that customers and suppliers can bring to bear as they negotiate prices, delivery schedules, and other contractual matters with the firm are easily recognized. They are immediate and their timing set by order size, contract period, contract renewal, and so on. Likewise rivalry is immediate, related to competitors' price changes and product introductions. While these are not everyday events in, say, the laptop or mobile phone business, they happen regularly in many industries. Their frequency is influenced by the break-even times characterizing the business. For instance, competitive activity between supermarkets is higher paced. Predicting the arrival of new entrants is quite different. We see three levels of analysis in the 5-force model: the upper level of short-term competitive interaction and signaling between those already in the business (rivalry) and a middle level of rent-management against suppliers and customers trying to claim some of that for themselves. These matters are relatively close to a microeconomic analysis. The lower level and slower timing of scanning for the entry of new firms or new technologies is closer to macroeconomic and historical analyses of the whole economy. The three levels of strategic timing are very different.

The 5-force model meets the criteria noted in section 2.0 at the start of this chapter—especially where and how the strategist's judgment enters the BM. In addition to describing the BM and loosely suggesting how the synthesis adds value, how the strategizing demands imagination at every level is clear—such as the selection of the categories. The categories Porter chose may well seem arbitrary. For instance they do not include labor unions or government regulators, in particular those administering anti-trust legislation, matters central to the oil and telecommunications industries, and their firms' rent-seeking. Imagination is also required when relating the behavior observed to the rent-stream, such as aggressive contract negotiation. If you supply Wal-Mart you have to decide how far you can push them and protect your margin if you still want their business, when the present cycle of pricing will be renegotiated, who else they can go to, their business situation, and so on.

## 2.7 Ansoff's Strategy Matrix

The Ansoff matrix is a simpler affair, but useful nonetheless because it captures a very different strategic intuition. Igor Ansoff was a mathematician and VP in charge of thinking through diversification possibilities for Lockheed in the late 1950s. Lockheed, a major US aircraft builder, had already moved on from their WW2 activity producing P-38, B-17, and B-34 airplanes, and had begun to build civilian aircraft such as the Constellation and longer-run military cargo aircraft such as the C-130 Hercules (launched in 1954 and still in production!). But widespread interest in diversifying into other sectors of the economy led to the conglomerate movement, to firms such as LTV (Ling-Temco-Vought). By 1969 many of the conglomerates were unraveling, suggesting they had become too arbitrary in their portfolios and too complex to manage, an intuition made famous later by Peters and Waterman with their "stick to the knitting (the business you know)." Ansoff anticipated all this, advising Lockheed against moving into completely new lines of business and to focus on what they knew best about. His matrix is an excellent example of a tool that is probably more useful as a rhetorical device than as an analytic device; it helps support the senior management's strategic discussions and presents the strategist's guidance as a SWOT-like picture language.

The anchoring quadrant was the "today situation"—current lines of business and current customer base. This defined Ansoff's BM and, as with all of these strategic tools, was the lens through which the rest of the analysis was to be viewed. The adjacent quadrants were existing products/new customers and existing customers/new products. The thrust was towards leveraging existing knowledge, facilities, and relationships. The final "no-go" quadrant was new products/new customers—risky, yet precisely the sort of thing the conglomerates were getting into. They were looking at firms as nothing but investment opportunities and, if their financials suggested an attractive ROI, they would be purchased and brought into the network. The fashion led to a spike in mergers and acquisition activity between 1965 and 1969. The conglomerate companies presumed the business's financials alone could provide managers with most of the information they needed to control the firm and direct strategizing. The archetype US conglomerate was ITT, largely built under Harold Geneen who had a variety of memorable managerial maxims such as "you can't run a business on a theory"—implying it could be run on the basis of accounting reports—and "better a good decision made quickly than the best decision too late." He also argued that "leadership cannot be taught, only learned." ITT had its troubles but did relatively well until it was broken up in 1995, getting out of the telecommunications industry just before that was reinvented by the mobile phone and began to grow explosively. Berkshire-Hathaway remains a successful conglomerate (at this writing). While Ansoff's matrix was conservative in the investment sense, the enormous amount of work Geneen, Buffett, and their analysts actually put into understanding their acquisitions tells us how the publicly available accounting data are seldom adequate to inform the investor, whether individual or institutional.

The Ansoff matrix describes the firm as a portfolio of products and customers. It has little to say about whether an operation's BM is rent- or efficiency-based, nor about how the BM's categories are linked up to generate value, nor much about the BM's strategic time. Its conservatism is an articulation of the American Mid-Western maxim "if it ain't broke, don't fix it." But it success-fully captures the anxiety the strategist should feel about assessing when the current BM is going to become obsolete—its most basic strategic time. There are also timings issues about the development of market segment, how long it takes to persuade existing customers to buy new products, and so on.

## 2.8 BCG and Some Other Matrices

Bruce Henderson, the founder of the Boston Consulting Group (BCG), grasped the strategic significance of learning-by-doing, as we noted in 2.4. But he also grasped the strategic implications of relating learning to profitability. The possibility of converting learning into a rent-stream raised practical ques-tions about how long that rent-stream would persist, even when managed along the lines the 5-force model suggests. One answer, as we have seen, is that the firm's rent-stream was determined by an organic life cycle such as the learning curve whose characteristics lay beyond management's grasp. Then the right thing to do is to channel the profits of one line of business into a different line of business promising a brighter future. The BCG matrix was a tool for managing a portfolio of investment opportunities whose rent-streams could not be regenerated. Instead of merely loading up on the investment that offered the greatest ROI, ignoring time's impact, the BCG matrix links the portfolio together as a cycle, rolling the funds from those in their mature phases into the development phase of younger "question marks." Unlike the SWOT, PEST, or 5-force models that emphasize (a) cat-egorization and (b) synthesis into a single BM, the BCG matrix made no demands for relatedness in any respect save funds-flow. Unlike the Ansoff matrix that implicitly considered how the knowledge gained from one line of business would be reapplied in another line of business, the BCG matrix was concerned only with cash flow.

There are many other strategic matrices—two additional ones are worth mention. The PIMS project noted in Chapter 1 suggested a causal association between market share and profitability. Further research undermined this finding and led analysts to pay more attention to the relative attractiveness (potential) of different markets. McKinsey/GE matrix is sometimes considered a development of the BCG matrix, replacing market share by market attract-iveness. Again the GE matrix is a scheme to assist in the categorization of a large firm's portfolio of investments and opportunities. As large firms became more complex they were also more likely to engage in international business. I note attention to the analysis of relative political risk in section 2.11 but Bartlett and Ghoshal provided an interesting structural analysis with a strategic tool to address the rather different concerns of globalization.[16] They contrasted two archetypical growth routes—globalization and multinationalization. Globalization began with establishing overseas sales outlets, concentrating production in order to maximize economies of scale in production. Sales outlets would be supported by after-sales maintenance activities, for instance for CAT earthmoving equipment or John Deere agricultural equipment. The alternative "multinational" growth path paid more attention to local mores, tastes, and practices with product or service design adapted appropriately; examples would be beverages or accounting services—these being manufactured or provided locally. The matrix contrasted pursuit of economies of scale against the benefits of local responsiveness. Bartlett and Ghoshal coined the term "transnational" to label those global firms that balanced these two growth trajectories to best strategic and economic effect. Their matrix shows the judgment involved in assessing the fruitfulness of strategic alternatives. Finally, rather than focusing on marketing, several matrices focus narrowly on the firm's finances, such as the McKinsey Strategic Control Map that plots market capitalization against stock performance.

## 2.9 Organizational Change

Discussions of organizational change hide a variety of metaphors or models of organization and of change. The most familiar ideas are that organizations exist with their own ontology and that, being situated in a changing environment, have to adapt if they are to survive. This seems so obvious it barely deserves comment. But the discussion stands on the EIF metaphor, separating firm and environment, and sees management as standing apart from both, directing the organization to this destination or that, and redistributing and reconnecting internal resources and arrangement to do that efficiently. Chandler embraced this model of organization; organizational change was setting up new administrative structure. The commonplace observation is that people resist change because it takes them from their "comfort zone." Likewise bureaucracies, we are told, are ponderous, with the kind of inertia that challenges those trying to change them. Argyris has been especially influential in regarding organizational change as problematic on this account, and thinking about the processes of organizational change as typifying Lewin's well-known unfreezing–refreezing theory of psychological change. The literature is well supplied with nostrums and methodologies to help managers create

---

[16] Christopher A. Bartlett and Sumantra Ghoshal (1991) 'Global Strategic Management: Impact on the New Frontiers of Strategy Research', *Strategic Management Journal*, 12 (summer special issue), 5–16.

change along these lines. But they fail to connect with strategizing as the process of constructing the firm.

Like the EIF paradigm, these discussions of organizational change presume certainty and exclude any discussion of uncertainty and its impact. It is planning all over again and makes no sense unless new processes can be designed that lead logically to new goals or old goals in new ways. The major part of the literature on organizational change presumes it is spurred by failure to reach previously established clear goals. It follows that to create change, managers must have (*a*) the knowledge necessary to create new plans, and (*b*) the power and resources to put them into place in a situation they assume is "resistant." But once uncertainty is admitted it is impossible to start out with "the organization" as unproblematic entity or to adopt the EIF and planning metaphors, or be so sure about the nature of the situation. Any notion of organizational change must obviously reflect an underlying notion of organization as an identifiable entity—but under uncertain conditions, as argued throughout this chapter, the organization does not really exist, rather it is the locus of purposive interaction constantly regenerated by strategizing. Along these lines Weick has suggested that it is more useful to think of organizing (verb and activity) than "the organization" (entity with a discoverable ontology such as a structure or balance-sheet).[17] But with this different notion of organization, what can organizational change mean?

Given uncertainty, it might be more useful to start out with the idea that organizational constancy and predictability is a considerable strategic achievement. The firm manages to exist from week to week in spite of the buzzing, blooming confusion of the world and the transience of its constituting elements and relations. Change, perhaps, is the one constant; sometimes enhancing order and predictability, at other times not. The metaphor here is of organization as a complex of change, change being its normal mode.[18] Sometimes change is predictable, as in the value-chain that changes inputs into outputs; sometimes not, as R&D shows. As soon as we dispense with the assumption that the firm is time-independent, bureaucratic, and machine-like, it becomes a locus of constant change. We learn to take time and uncertainty seriously. The firm's existence and predictability is the result of ongoing strategic input because, as Heraclitus reminded us, we never step into the same river twice. It is the result of a flow of strategic judgment into the knowledge absence chosen. When the situation calls for constancy, strategic judgment is so directed. When the situation calls for adjustment and change, the judgment

---

[17] K. E. Weick and R. E. Quinn (1999) 'Organizational Change and Development', *Annual Review of Psychology*, 50, 361–86.

[18] H. Tsoukas and R. Chia (2002) 'On Organizational Becoming: Rethinking Organizational Change', *Organisation Science*, 13, 567–82.

must be directed in that direction. In this metaphor the problem of organizational change is nothing to do with adaptation to external change, but is actually defined by the problems of communicating the strategizing to those others whose judgment inputs are crucial to the firm's continued operations—the topic of Chapter 5. At the same time, if the firm is the consequence of a flow of strategic judgment into a chosen knowledge absence (itself ever changing) that flow is not necessarily continuous. It might be smooth, intermittent, or episodic, in which case it changes radically from one episode or period to the next. Time and history become crucial to a strategic understanding of the firm because its nature is fundamentally dynamic. The answers to Coase's question are neither (a) universal, as most microeconomists presume, nor (b) static, even in a specific known context.

## 2.10 Knowledge and K-Flow

Knowledge management (KM) consulting has become a huge industry. Its emphasis has been on IT, the gathering, analysis, storage, and distribution of increasing amounts of corporate and market data. The IT aspects of KM have strategic implications based on how IT is used to support traditional planning and administration. The judgments required have often been ignored, with the result that many—perhaps most—KM projects fail to deliver what was promised. This is unfortunate because the KM literature covers several initiatives highly relevant to strategic work. The modern firm is increasingly dependent on computer technology for fact gathering and analysis as well as the control of production. Quantification of production was already important in Josiah Wedgwood's pottery factory in the 1760s, long before Frederick Taylor's Scientific Management developed it further in the early twentieth century. Modern real-time data collection and analysis techniques derive directly from this earlier work and have revolutionized production lines, inventory management, logistics chain management, and so on, especially when aided by today's mathematically and statistically sophisticated "big data" techniques. But the strategic questions always revolve around the exercise of judgment rather than being driven by quantification and data. The BCG matrix, for example, focused on the strategic judgment involved in classifying the firm's investment opportunities and judging how to flow the firm's funds between them. The Ansoff matrix classifies the firm in terms of the familiarity of products and markets, a notion articulated later by Rumelt and others who classified different lines of business as "related" or "unrelated." Conglomerates got into difficulty when there was too little relatedness and the firm became an unmanageable ragbag of businesses. KM helped shift the analytic emphasis from funds flow to "knowledge flow" and especially onto what the senior management needed to know beyond the accountants' reports.

It is difficult to define or measure knowledge, though it is alarmingly easy to speak about. It is easy to sound wise when explaining that learning produces knowledge, that communication moves knowledge, and so on. But justifying this is more difficult and a great deal of "knowledge talk" is pointless puffery. KM researchers added a completely new dimension to the analysis by distinguishing different types of organizational knowledge. After the publication of Nonaka and Takeuchi's book *The Knowledge-Creating Company*[19] many managers became familiar with the distinction between explicit and tacit knowledge, the first associated with what the firm knows that can be "objectified" as numbers and logical models, the second being especially associated with skilled practices that remain "subjectified," embedded or "embodied" in the actors' practices, difficult or impossible to articulate. This knowledge typology leads to different types of learning and has immediate managerial implications. Acquiring explicit knowledge—especially data—is what IT systems can do well but acquiring tacit skill is a more complicated affair. As soon as this knowledge-distinction is admitted to the analysis most of the strategic tools considered so far get much more sophisticated and increase the demands on the judgment of those doing the strategic work. Planning a new operation then requires attention to the skill bases implied as well as to the more typical resources. In the BCG framework, new projects need more than funds—they need skills. At the same time there is no objective separation of explicit knowledge from tacit knowledge. Using the distinction calls for judgment based on its impact on the BM and the firm's processes. Many presumed that tacit knowledge was practice that was known but had not yet been made explicit. Much of Scientific Management was about surfacing, codifying, and so explicating the workplace's tacit knowledge. Reflecting Smith's pin-makers, in the *Principles of Scientific Management* Taylor comments that shop floor workers developed 90 percent of the practice improvements eventually implemented by the planning staff.[20] Then managerial decisions to allow one practice and disallow another could be made on the basis of quantitative analysis.

Others argued that tacit knowledge implied distinctly different modes of human knowing, contrasting, for instance, "knowing about" against "knowing how." KM researchers still struggle to clarify the problems of managing different knowledge types. Those aspects of KM that go beyond the data that IT systems can handle have not yet provided insights or techniques that are explicit or

---

[19] I. Nonaka and H. Takeuchi (1995) *The Knowledge-Creating Company: How Japanese Companies Create the Dynamics of Innovation*. New York: Oxford University Press.

[20] F. W. Taylor (1911) *The Principles of Scientific Management*. New York: Harper & Brothers.

operational enough to warrant inclusion in this chapter's review of strategic tools. But the exceptions indicated some of the potential of focusing on knowledge flows and embracing the tacit dimension of the firm as a body of skilled practice and resource deployment. Nonaka and Takeuchi proposed the SECI (socialization, externalization, combination, internalization) matrix. Its focus was the internal flow of knowledge between those work-groups whose task is to generate new knowledge, such as innovative products and production practices, and the senior management who make the major resource allocation decisions. The difficulties of relating them has also been addressed by those interested in promoting accelerated innovation in the firm's product and services.

Much of the fruit of investment in R&D gets lost without ever being drawn into the firm's strategic choices. Too often R&D is accused of "throwing new stuff over the wall" into production without trying to design in ways that facilitate production or paying much attention to customers and their needs. The SECI matrix went beyond many innovation management prescriptions because it paid specific attention to the internal flow of tacit knowledge. At the same time many theorists argued the greater part of the firm's "strategic assets" were likely to be "tacit," tough to identify and difficult to manage. Nonaka and Takeuchi paid careful attention to the management of the knowledge-generating work-groups and their interactions with others in the firm. The crux of their analysis was the "codification" or transformation of the tacit skills developed by the knowledge-generating groups into more explicit knowledge (and language) that could be communicated more widely. Eventually this knowledge could be integrated with the firm's other departmental policies through the senior management's strategic work, along with whatever quantitative data they had available. Had they adopted the view that tacit knowledge was of a different type that could not be "converted" into explicit knowledge, their knowledge-flow argument would have collapsed.

Nonaka and Takeuchi's work popularized the "tacit" term and gave senior managers new language with which to explain why the firm's people were so often its most important assets. Their analysis converged on a number of attempts to quantify the firm's "human capital" and so redescribe the firm in terms of its financial, structural, organizational, and human capital, which initiative was partially impelled by accounting research and concern with Tobin's "q"—a measure of the difference between the firm's market and book values, the latter being the accountant's formal valuation. Many firms, especially many of the stockmarket's highest fliers, are notable for high market valuations in spite of little or no profit and little book value. The implication is that the market's valuation is strategic, placing a high value on the firm's tacit or non-financial capital, and thus a better indicator of future performance than the accountants' valuation. Nonaka and Takeuchi's matrix is a theory of the firm as a knowledge-generation and transformation process. It is not a scheme for classifying firms, as is the Bartlett and Ghoshal matrix or the Miles and Snow matrix in section 2.12 below, nor for classifying the firm's assets, as is the SWOT matrix. It is more like the BCG matrix, a knowledge-type portfolio management model. It combines (a) attention to the internal workgroups coupled by the knowledge flow (from bottom to top) with (b) the transformation of the organizational knowledge from tacit to explicit, thereby enabling it to be integrated into the overall planning, and then back to tacit as it shapes a new round of organizational practices. It is difficult to see the SECI matrix as a strategic tool, but it has considerable significance as a knowledge-based way of thinking about the firm, the K-flows between its parts (as opposed to its authority relations and structure) and, most importantly, what aspects of the firm should be attended to. It addresses the Coase questions that deal with internal arrangements but not those about boundaries or existence.

Earlier, Edith Penrose advanced a "theory of the growth of the firm"[21] that made knowledge its central concept—and her vision lies at the core of my book. Penrose was also influenced by the distinction between explicit and tacit knowledge. Her analysis was a critique of the neoclassical economic notion of "resource." While economists are inclined to value a resource in terms of its cost or market value, she observed there was no necessary connection between either of these and the resource's strategic value to the firm, what she called the "services" the resource was able to supply to the firm's process. She argued the connection was mediated by the management team's knowledge of how to extract economic value from the resource. This redefined the firm's identity as a body of managerial knowledge about how to transform resources into added value—in contrast with regarding the firm as a bundle of identifiable resources (such as those on the books) or even a group of individuals (those listed as employees). The management team's knowledge is likely to be largely tacit, the product of their experience and reflection, so her analysis took the learning curve on board. The resulting "Penrose Effect" was that the firm could not expand at a rate faster than its management can learn how to use further resources.

Her work also identified the firm's "strategic timing." The firm's accumulated resources can be carried forward from one strategic time-period into the next—retained profits facilitate further investment. While tangible resources are costly to produce and reproduce, knowledge, as noted in Chapter 1, is not a tangible resource. It is "non-rivalrous" or "extensible." It is an intangible resource that is seldom consumed by being used, indeed is often increased.

---

[21] E. T. Penrose (1995) *The Theory of the Growth of the Firm* (3rd edn). New York: Oxford University Press.

Penrose focused on the value gained by carrying forward—into future production cycles—the knowledge generated by learning. Such knowledge is often less costly and more likely to be a powerful driver of growth than any tangible resource. Penrose's focus on learning made it the core of the firm's nature—the firm as a learning management apparatus—with major implications for managing. But while learning may well lead to growth it is extraordinarily difficult to bring into a rigorous analysis. Nor have the efforts to quantify the firm's intangible capital or learning led to the development of any viable strategic tools.

## 2.11 Scenario Planning

Long-range corporate planning became popular immediately after WW2—along with associated new professional societies and journals—and brought time to the center of strategic analysis. It addressed a fundamental uncertainty of business and of the human condition: "What is going to happen?" In this book I stress the importance of differentiating this widespread concern with the future from the subjective strategic business question—"What is going to happen—to us?" I have also noted the chicken-and-egg problem—we need an approximation of the BM before we know what aspects of the future to pay attention to—and yet our assessment of the future is one of the main shapers of the BM. The interplay is an aspect of the dialectic between identity, intention, and context—never completed, always a cause for doubt. Given that long-range planning was a popular strategic method in the 1960s, there was much talk about the "relevant environment," simply because the whole environment is beyond being analyzed and planned. The search for relevance was a corollary of long-range planning's assumption that the future would be independent of the firm in question, just as a perfect market is unchanged by the actions of any particular firm. Then the only kind of knowledge absence relevant to the firm's strategic work was ignorance of the future. We know this is inadequate on many counts for it presumes full knowledge. In the same way we can never know what we are ignorant of without contrasting what we know against certainty (such as the full knowledge circumstances that neo-classical economists presume). More to the point, for the strategists, the "firm's relevant environment" is never independent of the firm and its actions because there are incommensurability and indeterminacy issues to be considered as well as those of ignorance. The firm is not an isolated actor in a socio-economic vacuum.

In the 1960s US researchers such as Herman Kahn and French researchers under Gaston Berger began to develop "scenario planning." There were four major differences from long-range planning. First, the scenarios were more thoroughly structured with cause and effect relationships, less "forecasted facts" than carefully considered stories about how the firm's future might unfold. Key connections were considered. For instance, a rise in disposable income would lead to more autos and more driving, with a subsequent increase in the number of road accidents and hospital emergencies. Second, the scenarios moved the firm into the center of the analysis and a "relevant environment" was established by looking at the environment to see which variables were strategic to that specific firm. Third, the interactions between the firm and the scenario could be modeled or simulated over several time periods, setting up a more game-theoretic approach and mapping changes in the firm's context and in the firm's strategic thinking and responses. The simulation could be run at high speed, so that several years or decades of firm and context interaction could be compressed into a "war game" lasting only a few hours. In the auto situation above, increasing disposable income would also allow cars to be engineered with better safety features that customers would be prepared to pay for so long as they felt they were buying a measure of insurance against rising accident rates (think Volvo). The time taken to develop such features, and their cost and market share consequences, could be simulated. Fourth, several distinct scenarios or alternative futures could be worked up. A review of alternative futures was especially valuable for firms involved in extractive industries that were operating in politically unstable countries. One scenario would be that the dictator's regime fell, another that it nationalized all resources, a third that it effectively outsourced exploration and exploitation of its natural resources to the host firm. Alternatively a pharmaceutical company might model the broader implications of their "breakthrough drug" getting FDA approval or not, and their competitors' and customers' responses.

Scenario planning deserves a place in the list of strategic tools because it can be used to help senior management get a sense of the judgments they might have to make in the future in response to specific situations—both external and internal—often called "drivers." The technique allows alternative scenarios of considerable sophistication to be developed and simulated. Noting the judgments involved, quantitative data, theories, demographics, technological forecasting, government planning, and so forth could be integrated into coherent stories about getting to the future. Unlike long-range planning, which depends entirely on the "correctness" of the logical linkages in the plan considered, scenario planning throws more emphasis on the judgments associated with the contrasts between alternatives and moves closer to being an environmental sensitivity analysis. The parties affected—stakeholders, perhaps—can be established and contrasted similarly. The analysis's drivers can be analyzed into an importance/uncertainty pattern, emphasizing the "What does it mean to us?" question and drawing the firm further into the center of the analysis. Equally the sequence of the firm's responses to each scenario can be assessed using "real options" ideas. These look at non-financial as well as financial consequences. For instance, one scenario might be the appearance of tighter "fracking" legislation in the natural gas industry. If the host firm anticipated this and developed a different "fracking production technology" it might be able to license it profitably to other energy companies who would be surprised and otherwise be hard-pressed to remain in business when the new legislation came into force.

Scenario planning was especially associated with Royal Dutch Shell, which used and developed its techniques from the late 1960s onwards, finding them especially useful at the time of the "oil-shock" of 1973, when OPEC raised the price of crude.[22] One merit is that like many simulations—from pilot training and lunar landing to rehearsing candidates for Presidential debates—they offer the participants an opportunity to learn-by-doing in a less threatening situation than the real event. In this way they can be used to analyze the consequences of actions before they happen, a test of the strategist's ability to evaluate a strategy ahead of its implementation—a most important matter.

Some consultants specializing in scenario planning suggest a seven-step "structured process." First, discover a scenario's drivers and assumptions. Second, bring them together in a multi-causal framework—structurally similar to the 5-force model. Third, generate a number of force configurations or 'mini-scenarios'. Fourth, winnow these down to two or three principal alternative futures and their appropriate narratives. Fifth, prepare these for presentation to senior management. Sixth, set the management discussion going, and record and review the outcomes. Then, seventh, cycle back to the start again until good agreement has been reached across the management team about the "future-story" the firm chooses to take as "future fact." Each scenario is a story-specific pattern of strategic judgment, and promulgating it helps everyone involved locate and align their judgment contributions. But, like all of the strategic tools in this chapter, scenario planning has its critics. As always, academics complain about the subjectivities involved and the lack of empirical evidence of its impact on organizational performance. More important from the strategist's point of view, the technique inculcates a certain passivity, defining strategic work as the firm's response to externally induced change. In this book I turn this around and emphasize that the essence of strategizing is to explore the context's malleability and then, choosing to act proactively on it, to change it and lead the firm to un-forecast profit and growth.

[22] P. Cornelius, A. Van de Putte, and M. Romani (2005) 'Three Decades of Scenario Planning in Shell', *California Management Review*, 48(1), 92–109.

## 2.12 Culture and Stakeholders

Long-range planning stresses logical relationships and quantified data. From the 1970s onwards there was some pushback against the rising tide of rational approaches to management, especially to their strategic work. A number of strategy writers turned to "organization culture," arguing that the in-place culture was the organization's strategy "enacted." The planning scenario adopted is likewise a declaration of the firm's organizational culture and aesthetic. The senior management team might choose to displace a passive aesthetic with a more aggressive attitude. Miles and Snow suggested a matrix of Prospector–Analyzer–Defender–Reactor (PADR) aesthetics.[23] Prospectors are aggressive and seek out new markets. Analyzers act only on the numbers. Defenders try to maintain their place in the market. Reactors lack a definitive strategy; more opportunistic, they respond to short-term changes in the firm's context. The PADR typology was like SWOT in that it mirrored the management's own view of their firm. It remains well liked because firms do indeed display a certain strategic aesthetic. PADR's academic critics have pointed to the usual suspects: lack of objectivity and little empirical support for the relationship between aesthetic and performance. But from the point of view of this chapter there is value in combining the PADR matrix with some of the more instrumental strategic tools covered already—SWOT for one; almost any of the other tools would be illuminated by the strategists' paying more attention to the firm's cultural and non-instrumental aspects.

There has been a gathering interest in opening up the conventional notion that the firm's strategy must focus on maximizing shareholder value and management's fiduciary duties to stockholders. Stakeholder theories embrace a broader range of interests of those involved in the firm and its activities: resource providers, employees, the employees' families, customers, suppliers, alliance partners, local communities, voters, taxpayers, unions, and so on. At one level the implication is that the firm's strategic context comprises many dimensions of outsiders' interests, so considerable strategic judgment is called for in selecting those interests that must be attended to—beyond those given by corporate law and the firm's "articles of association." Relative power is one obvious dimension for the analysis, when different stakeholders can be ranged so that more attention is paid to the more powerful. Unfortunately power is as problematic a notion as strategy and there are many types of power. Porter's 5-force analysis was a specific form of stakeholder analysis, the power being defined as the outsider's ability to disturb the firm's rent-stream. Other theorists have suggested other kinds of power, especially political, that might be

---

[23] R. E. Miles and C. C. Snow (1978) *Organizational Strategy, Structure and Process*. New York: McGraw-Hill.

able to redefine or reshape the firm's identity, intentions, or context. Some business ethicists have argued for social or ethical legitimacy—that, as a constituent part of society, the firm should pay attention to wider social responsibilities and ethics—emphasizing "should" over "can" or "wants to," recalling the LCAG analysis (see section 2.6).

One aspect of this way of thinking is that the boundaries between the firm and its socio-economic context become increasingly problematic, to the point they eventually dissolve. In Chapter 1 the dialectic of identity, intention, and context presumed firms are "bounded." Likewise the public sector is separable from the private sector, the former made of up of organizations directed by the political process, the latter directed by the board of directors and left relatively free to pursue whatever goals they choose. My book is directed at private sector firms precisely because their strategic work is a consequence of or corollary to the freedoms they have been granted in the democratic political process. The firm is treated as an "unnatural" person with many of the rights that citizens have—especially to own resources and be held accountable for its actions. But strategy writers who treat the private firm as a socially and/or ethically responsible entity are missing something both legally and strategically profound as they reframe the firm as, more or less, a public sector agency with public responsibilities. Today's corporate legislation does not require the firm to be managed with public sector criteria in mind. More specifically, the only social and ethical responsibilities it has are those articulated into corporate law. This reflects the oft-cited Friedman quip that "the only responsibility of firms is to maximize shareholder wealth," which he was moved to say because it is implicit in neoclassical economics. This was not a "value judgment," simply his drawing attention to an axiom underpinning the analysis. But our democracy is not organized around economic ideology alone; there are additional constraints embedded in corporate law, for the firm is part and parcel of a legally institutionalized society. It follows that the most pertinent means to make firms more socially responsible is regulation, to act on corporate law, rather than by trying to make managers or boards more "ethics aware." Unfortunately neither strategy writers nor business ethicists have paid much attention to corporate law and its evolution. This is especially regrettable in the area of labor and employment law, for that shapes the relations between managers, firms, and their employees.

Culture is a collective characteristic, encompassing individual members. Thinking of the firm as a culture implies its shared ideas or modes of institutionalization might be achieved through persuasive means, as opposed to calculative (incentives) or coercive (force) means as these are embedded into the firm's administrative structures and processes. When those doing the firm's strategic work arrive at the entrepreneurial vision or "business idea" to be articulated as a strategy then the process of persuading others begins—discussed in detail in Chapter 5. But shared ideas and behaviors may also emerge unbidden from the individuals' interactions. Such networking and "small world" effects are interesting and have prompted a new line of strategy research.[24] Many theorists presume the firm's organizational culture is the principal source of resistance to strategic change. Small world effects, popularized by talk of our "six degrees of separation," may be very powerful, pushing back against management's attempts to change the firm's culture. Small world theory also shows the firm's culture can be changed by restructuring interpersonal relationships—making new communications connections and preventing others. For example, security forces take a special interest in tracking communications to find those exerting most influence in a terror cell or network.

## 2.13 Triple Bottom Line and the Theory of Sustainable Society

In spite of corporate law's evolution—especially the US Supreme Court's 2010 *Citizen's United* decision that extends the firm's "freedom of speech" and so its political power—major change seems to be coming in the public discourse around private firms and their strategic work. The private firm is being reconceptualized as an instrument, perhaps our democracy's principal instrument, for implementing politically determined social goals. As the trend to privatization of public agencies and functions continues, the narrow notion of the firm as serving only its shareholders' interests has dissolved somewhat. The future of the private firm may well be as a privately owned instrument of public policy, perhaps an NGO somewhat reminiscent of the Victorian cooperative movement, but at a different level. One effect is to add social, environmental, psychological, and ecological dimensions to the financial dimensions used to evaluate a firm's performance. Given "purpose" as the organization's anchoring concept, the elaboration of purpose beyond financial gain makes the firm a more complex idea and practice. The main impetus today is ecological rather than political, moral, or ethical. Planet Earth is a more practical political concept than the idea of management as a social duty or that private firms should exist only to provide the goods and services society needs—even though both ideas help dissolve the private/public distinction.

Private firms are clearly complicit in consuming the planet's non-replaceable resources and generating objectionable pollutants, such as heavy metal poisons and $CO_2$. The public's increasing desire to regulate these may provoke a new

---

[24] D. J. Watts (2003) *Six Degrees: The Science of a Connected Age*. New York: W. W. Norton & Co.

generation of regulations. Sustainability is becoming a major worldwide concern, with new legislation and education being promoted by an increasing number of organizations such as Greenpeace or the Stockholm Environment Institute (SEI). Many universities are seeing theorizing sustainability as an opportunity to attract new students anxious to inhabit a more responsibly managed socio-economy. But the deeper tensions between these new ideas and the economic, managerial and legislative institutions that currently define the private sector and its operations have not yet been surfaced or analyzed. The nature of the socio-economy implied by adopting sustainable objectives is far from understood.

## 2.14 The Balanced Scorecard

I consider the Balanced Scorecard (BS) late in this chapter because I believe it is quite close to my book's methodological and practical objectives, though there are some fundamental differences and it would not be correct to think of my approach as an extension of the BS. Yes, I see its four dimensions as (*a*) constraints to strategizing, and (*b*) incommensurate between each other. But at the same time I believe the BS is generally misunderstood. It has certainly been widely adopted, with surveys suggesting that over half of all major firms have adopted some form of performance measurement. Yet anyone looking at the academic literature must wonder whether its adoption indicates management's susceptibility to marketing hype, executive fad-ism, or some other not very complimentary view of managers. Its history and basic propositions are well known, and there is a substantial literature. Its principal expounders were Robert Kaplan and David Norton. The history is that it emerged in California in the 1980s. It added non-financial performance criteria to the financial ones already in place. The general formulation is four reporting dimensions: financial performance, customer response, internal business process improvement, and learning and growth initiatives. The academic criticisms are, as usual, its inherent subjectivity and lack of empirical validation. Indeed the persistent lack of empirical evidence associating BS adoption and performance boost remains curious and worthy of further research. Most of the later work on the BS deals with two kinds of development. The first is a move towards "better metrics" for all four performance measures. Many consultants propose around twenty metrics and a large variety of commercial software packages have been developed to facilitate their collection and tabulation—sometimes as a "strategic dashboard." Second, there is the development of alternative reporting dimensions or "headings." Some have argued the "first-generation" BS formulation was oriented towards SMEs and that reheading was necessary to make the BS relevant to large or global corporations.

But the seeming contradiction between the BS's high adoption rate and its lack of financial or competitive performance impact may point in a different direction—that the managerial incentives to adopt the BS may not be driven by financial or competitive performance as academics presume. Those who think management must be understood as the process of maximizing performance are seldom ready to entertain other possibilities, of course; they think it axiomatic. But several decades ago one of the more interesting management research projects revolved around the balance between task performance and group maintenance in small-group problem-solving. The proposition was that when problems were unclear and "dimly felt" the group's attention would be split between (a) addressing its evident problems and the tasks implied versus (b) maintaining the group's integrity against the disturbing uncertainties of the group's situation. The BS may be valued because of its impact on group maintenance. Recall the most obvious benefit of using a strategic tool is that it helps the strategist push back against the unease provoked by knowledge absences, increasing the management's confidence sufficiently to facilitate commitment to action. Many users of the BS find that it helps moderate the debate between the senior executives as they discuss the firm's strategic challenges. Many BS users also find this usefulness drops off sharply below the senior management level. The history of the BS helps here too. Many valued it as a "discussion control" mechanism that would help prevent the senior management meetings being overwhelmed by the financial data, especially the sheer weight of quantitative reports and accounting data. These data are necessarily retrospective, shifting attention away from strategic work's real focus—managing and shaping the firm's possible futures. Using the BS helps re-establish a better balance between learning from the past and shaping the future.

Throughout this book my emphasis is on strategizing as the process of language construction, for I see the firm as activity shaped by a language constructed specifically to engage selected contextual uncertainties. Each of the strategic tools in this chapter offers a unique language for characterizing some aspect of the dialectic interplay between identity, intention, and context. The BS is especially interesting because it helps the firm's strategic work at two levels. First, like the other tools, it offers the strategists a vocabulary with which to grasp the situation—in the "first generation" BS, covering financial, customer, internal process, and innovation performance. But it goes beyond being another classificatory matrix, such as the SWOT or Ansoff matrices, by focusing on the contrasting languages that dominate private sector talk—past/future, provider/customer, financial performance/reputation. So, second, it provides senior management, as a discussion group, with a way to structure their talk more "democratically" in the sense that prevents the dominance or preferment of any single theory or language. The BS's history is that it provided a way for managers to push back against the rhetorical power of financial language that threatened to define the firm as a purely backward-looking financial entity and so shut out the possibilities of surprise and profit. But strategic judgment, not some external source or rule, must always determine which languages to include. There may well be firms for whom the first generation BS languages—finance, customers, internal processes, and innovation—are not the most appropriate. Subsequent literature suggested second and third generation versions of the BS with changed topics. Kaplan and Norton later shifted their attention to "strategy maps" that explore alternative headings.

There is no reason to stick with any given version of the BS's categories. The four offered should be considered suggestions or exemplars. The strategists' own judgment determines the topics, a choice guided, perhaps, by the search for a comfortable balance between inclusiveness, exclusiveness, and operability, just as the 5-force model can be rearticulated with different headings to engage different strategic situations. But—uniquely—the BS addresses the firm's "internal politics" and focuses on the firm's (management's) language's rhetorical functionality and richness. A firm is clearly disadvantaged when its internal strategic conversation is poorly managed, enabling or encouraging some positions or ideas to dominance to the detriment of others that might well serve the firm better, insufficient "voices" to be heard. The BS helps characterize the firm's strategic work as a conversation between four classes of executive, each representing a specific interest group. This is the conversation from which the firm's strategy and strategic language emerges—always attended by strategic doubt about what is being "silenced." In Chapter 4 I detail the mechanics of the construction of the firm-specific language that shapes the strategic discourse. There is good reason to think that the popularity of the BS among business people lies in how it facilitates and structures this crucial managerial task. Academics pay little attention to this capability—or need.

## 2.15 Goldratt's Theory of Constraints

The BS is similar to my analysis in its focus on language and the firm's internal debates. Goldratt's theory of constraints has a different approach towards my analysis—for I see what the strategists choose to take as knowledge presences constrains their judged responses to their selected knowledge absence, rather than eliminating it as deterministic theory does. Too much uncertainty makes it impossible to generate closure, so things must be narrowed down if they are to be analyzable. Constraints are essential. But presuming they shut down all uncertainty cuts out any possibility of profit. The mathematics of dynamic programming deals with such bounding of the open action options. Goldratt was a physicist who became an industrial process consultant and brought dynamic programming into management in a novel *The Goal*, first published in 1984. His books, including the *Theory of Constraints*,[25] sold widely and generated much managerial discussion. The contrast between my analysis and Goldratt's is illuminating. Dynamic programming presumes the constraints are commensurate and so computable. I presume the contrary, that the constraints are incommensurate, reflections of the many different ways in which we humans know. But Goldratt's formatting his analysis as a novel was a brilliant way to present dynamic programming—an abstract methodology—as a subjective situated project, undertaken by managers inhabiting a particular space/time context. The constraints selected were not given but chosen by the actors. The novel, like the business comedy *The Office*, shows the struggle between competing interests, visions, and languages—between the identities, intentions, and contexts that collide when strategizing.

## 2.16 Summary

This chapter's first purpose is to add to the strategic worker's tool-kit, to add to the three familiar tools mentioned in section 2.4 above—SWOT, learning curve, and life cycle. Its deeper purpose is to illustrate the variety of strategic languages that have been developed to help strategists in the private sector grasp their firm and its context, illustrating the judgments that lie (*a*) in the implicit connections between the concepts embedded in each tool, and (*b*) in the fundamental choice of judging one model appropriate to the firm and its situation rather than another. But strategic doubt remains. At every moment those doing the firm's strategic work are left pondering whether they should best see their firm in, for example, terms of the McKinsey-GE matrix or the 5-force model, or a broader stakeholder model? Is the tool applied silencing something crucial, preventing them from seeing something important, locking them into an exhausted or competitively disadvantaged view? The academic intuition is to seek empirical support for each tool, presuming there is a relationship between the tool chosen and the resulting performance, but this may not be too helpful to the managers doing the strategic work of keeping the firm's practices moving. Doubt ultimately brings reasoned practice to a standstill. There is a constant tension between (*a*) doing nothing until plans have been analyzed and evaluated fully, and (*b*) doing something that keeps the firm's essential nature alive as a body of interlocking value-generating practices. An old adage is "ensure the perfect is not the enemy of the good."

---

[25] E. M. Goldratt (1990) *What is this Thing Called Theory of Constraints and How Should it be Implemented?* Great Barrington, MA: North River Press.

When continued practice is essential, as for organizations, doubts that arrest practice are a serious threat to existence, just as some say sharks must keep swimming. While this is not strictly true of real sharks, the metaphor works well enough. Perhaps the private sector firm is best understood as a shark that must keep swimming—in any direction—to survive until its next strategic profit opportunity turns up or is created.

There are many interesting strategic tools missing from my inventory here: performance prism, critical success factors, 3Cs, root-cause analysis, value mapping, and parenting styles...the list goes on. At this point the reader will see the essential features of every tool is to illuminate or frame the managerial judgment called for if the strategic work is to go forward to the point of resource commitment and practice. The tools differ in what they pay attention to, and whether some interplay is implied. A simpler categorization schema, such as SWOT or the GE matrix, leaves the description of the inter-category interplay open. At bottom the 5-force model is a scheme to categorize the focal firm's "rent-disturbers"—at three strategic time levels. Stakeholder theory is weaker, inviting the strategist to set up her/his own categorization schema on the basis of social power or norms, but having no strategic time or multi-level features. Scenario planning has time content but is weaker in that it captures neither identity nor intention, merely focusing on alternative contexts and using them to provoke senior management's reflection, helping them become more comfortable with the strategic doubt that is the mark of their role and service to the firm. In these tools the strategic imperative is left entirely to management's judgment. Some other tools, such as the BCG matrix, consider inter-category interplay and suggest a strategic imperative: do this to succeed. The cash cow's lot in life is to provide funds for question marks. The SECI matrix focuses on the flow of knowledge rather than funds— obviously interesting to any analysis of profit and/or growth—but is extraordinarily difficult to operationalize, given the complexities surrounding the notion of knowledge.

Above all, this chapter shows the emptiness of the concept of the private sector firm as an easily comprehended mechanism to make money—a contradiction, for mechanisms cannot add value, they only transform resources from one state to another. The chapter illustrates the strategic work necessary to bring human judgment into the world of real economic activity where value is added and profit may result. Strategic work cannot be captured as the instantiation or application of a theory or as following a plan, as if the firm was a machine for transforming inputs into outputs in an orderly and predictable manner. It is not that a firm cannot be modeled in this way—as by its value-chain, for instance. But choosing this model shuts down the discussion of uncertainty and strategy, for if it is so considered the analysis cannot show how the entrepreneur or strategist selects and engages the uncertainties that mark the real world and generate value. The value eventually added springs from the strategist's choices, not from the firm's existence. The firm is simply her/his instrument to engage the world—in Barnard's terminology, the firm's physical, social, and psychological sub-economies.[26] To enquire into strategic work the researcher must abandon the objectified "etic" approach exemplified by the dominant management research journals and switch to a subjective "emic" approach that turns on bringing the entrepreneur's imagination and judgment into play. The thinking must leave some kind of "space" open into which her/his strategic judgment is "projected." Ultimately strategic work focuses on the managerial task of constructing the firm's identity, intention, and context—addressing the questions "who are we, who do we want to be, what do we want to achieve, when, and where?" The fundamental Coasian questions about why firms exist, why their boundaries are as they are, why their internal arrangements are as they are, and why their performance varies so widely, are corollaries to the multidimensioned freedoms granted private sector entities. Strategic workers cannot presume the firm's ends are given, such as shareholder wealth maximization, leaving only the means to be decided as a matter of rational choice, excising judgment.

---

[26] C. L. Barnard (1968) *The Functions of the Executive* (30th anniversary edn). Cambridge, MA: Harvard University Press, p. 240.

# 3

# Strategic Analysis—Academic Models

## 3.0 On the Academics' Method and Questions

The previous chapter deals with the strategic judgments involved in (*a*) choosing from the small inventory of strategic tools available to consultants, and (*b*) applying the tool chosen to a real situation. Each tool stands on different ideas (axioms) about the firm and its components, but all presume the firm comprises valuable resources and the people able to exercise judgment about their selection and application. Each tool offers the strategist a language for describing the firm and its situation—normally developed from practice-derived heuristics rather than from axioms or theory. There is little consistency among these tools beyond being alternative ways to describe the firm's chosen knowledge presences and knowledge absences, the questions the entrepreneur must answer to bring the business to life. Note Chapter 2's assumption is that the firm being described already exists, and that the strategic work begins with the question "How can the firm be best described?" and not "How can the firm be created?" Different descriptions open up different action options but none promises the security of a deterministic model that can predict the consequences of acting. Without an overarching theory of the private sector firm and its economy it is difficult to evaluate the consequences and compare the options. This is a state of uncertainty wherein the option chosen is a matter of strategic judgment rather than logical deduction from objective facts.

Most of Chapter 2's strategic tools were developed by "strategy consultants" to facilitate their practice and marketing. Chapter 3 looks at some complementary "theories of the firm" developed by academics, principally but not solely by microeconomists. Contrary to much commentary I think economists have important things to say to practical managers. But note a crucial shift in the questions addressed. It is often difficult for non-economists to appreciate the way economists think, their special view of Man and his doings. Economic thinking has lately "colonized" a great deal of academic territory and that has led to a widening gap between managerial and academic thought. Economic theorizing reaches beyond the specifics and descriptions that help particular managers get a sense of what is going on in a particular situation. Managers are interested in performance, but academics are interested in generalities (and in publishing them). Theories can be useful to many people, managers are focused on their firm. The academics' questions are "How can we best characterize firms in general?" or even more abstract questions like Coase's "What is the firm?" Addressing these obliges the analyst to get into the "black box," the economists' term for the firm considered as an unproblematic "production function," an apparatus to transform inputs into outputs, for linking demand markets to supply markets, without any internals or other defining character. This metaphor ignores every real firm's particularities and internal heterogeneity and treats the entrepreneur's strategic work as irrelevant; just compute what the markets tell you. "Black boxing" means there is no need to deal with anything inside the box, just the inputs, outputs, costs, and market relations. Opening up the black box is rather like splitting the "economic value-creating atom" and discovering its components—the economic correlates of the electrons, the protons, and the various forces that hold physical atoms together. Most importantly, Chapter 3 examines the firm's components and "forces" to discover where strategic judgment is needed to hold the firm together while it generates value. For those who know their science I suggest an allusion to "binding energy." The discussion is shaped by the academics' hope of finding a theory so complete that no strategic judgment input is required—just as no judgment is necessary to predict the behavior of a dropped weight or the next high tide because the theory on this is complete; it has evolved to the point of closure and is predictive and trusted.

Some microeconomic theories are "evolutionary," based on the biology of self-sustaining or self-organizing organic entities. These theories do not depend on human judgment and presume the firm emerges and reaches closure without requiring external strategic inputs, much as plants propagate and reseed without human intervention (though they need nutrients, of course). A different type of theory leads to closure as the firm is presumed to be an efficient and self-stabilizing market in which managers, suppliers, and workers make the deals necessary to assemble people and resources into the firm's production function. Here market forces rule and, again, no judgment is required. Neither the market nor self-regulating circumstances admit the need for strategic work—but nor will there be the profit that results from engaging uncertainty with judgment and imaginative practice. Profit cannot arise when markets are perfect or when an organic entity remains independent of entrepreneurial inputs. The middle territory between market equilibrium and self-organizing evolution arises when there is no closure without strategic judgments—and these make profit possible. Real firms are structured towards their goals and populated by individuals who project or commit their judgment to the firm's activities. They are not self-organizing, nor are they perfectly designed machines, nor do "perfect market" forces determine their behavior. The middle ground is marked by managers' use of various techniques of (*a*) design and administration and (*b*) incentives to shape the behavior of the people involved. Each of this chapter's "theories of the firm" explores an aspect of these techniques and frames a knowledge absence that can be met by strategic judgment; what can also be thought of as a kind of "market failure." The theory of the firm in question goes some way to frame the imperfection the strategist must deal with if the firm is to arise and persist. Equally, each theory points towards one aspect of the firm's multifaceted nature. Again there is a handy inventory of models, but without an overarching integrated framework there is no comprehensive theory that melds them all into a coherent field of analysis. There is no single theory of the firm. Thus strategic judgment still determines the adoption of one theory rather than another and further judgment is required to fit it to the situation's specifics. More importantly, the chapter explores the interplay of judging and learning, and shows how learning must be brought into the analysis as the source of the strategic judgment necessary to negotiate the residual knowledge absences. Chapter 2 paid little attention to how strategic judgment develops. Chapter 3 probes this and suggests managing learning is a corollary to managing uncertainty. In particular it points to the imperfect connection between experience and learning. With these ideas in mind Chapter 4 examines the firm's "local language" as the vessel in which the strategic judgment developed can be captured, shared, managed, and applied.

The consulting models covered in Chapter 2 are gross simplifications of real firms and their workings. But chosen wisely the model can capture something important about the situation, labeling the strategic issues well enough to make them discussable while leaving much of what is going on unsaid and ignored. Judgment begins with deciding what to pay attention to, choosing what to label. Crucially, Chapter 2's models do not pay much attention to "people"—save in regard to the interplay of knowledge presence and absence—though we know business is always about working with, through, and for other people. But what are "people"? When people are reasonably or "intendedly" rational they become like each other and their particularities can be ignored. The analyst can ignore them. Perhaps they become more like computers, just another beige box running Windows. Rational Man is a generic rather than heroic figure. People's imagination and judgment is pushed into the background. Ultimately the theorists' goal is to excise peoples' subjective idiosyncrasies or particularities and thereby, of course, deny what we relish about others—their idiosyncrasies, how they differ and make judgments. Seeming in the grip of a rationality-favoring way of thinking, the collective sense of the Chapter 2 models is that strategizing does not require close attention to people, just attention to the external and internal facts as the tool frames them. Many see the tools as proto-theories. But strategic judgment, and the possibility of profit, arises precisely and only because the situation is uncertain and beyond being captured by theory. Under such conditions practice calls for the idiosyncratic personal inputs that generate varied answers.

Lived situations and firms are unique, what some economists call heterogeneous. The homogeneity of perfect competition, in which all differences have been competed away, eliminates the possibility of profit. Strategic work is the pursuit of the heterogeneity that can lead on to profit. Human subjectivity is its source; it is not the product of rationality. So the management theorists' attempts to airbrush people's heterogeneity out of the analysis is counterproductive and a sad commentary on the dehumanized nature of much of our thinking about business—even though we know it is about people. Few strategy texts discuss people or imagination, most presuming the analysis should be "computable" and that everyone involved should be as rational as they are able. Judgment is not part of this picture. Indeed, the authors of strategy texts normally presume the reader only wants to hear about how to look at situations rationally, not about how to see them as opportunities to apply their imagination and creativity. The strategist, analyst, and reader are all constrained to approach the situation on the same rational basis—denying the relevance of the profit-generating judgment each may bring to dealing with the situation's knowledge absences.

The academics trade off the useful insights they gain by simplifying and generalizing against the losses—such as the actors' heterogeneity—that get left out. But so long as we keep heterogeneity in mind as the essential impetus to strategic work, we may be able to make good use of theory without letting it suppress heterogeneity. This chapter shows that, while many of the academic models prefer rationality and avoid any discussion of judgment, they can still be interpreted as important ways to constrain or frame business uncertainties and, thereby, the strategic judgments needed. Where these theories fail to achieve closure they leave space open for strategic judgment—and value creation. So in this chapter we look at academics' theories to see what they fail to do rather than what they determine. In contrast to the consultants' models, they have also evolved over time through the discipline's constant iteration of presentation, critique, and re-presentation. Looking at a theory's history helps clarify the questions it addresses, and its strengths and weaknesses. There is little scholarly analysis of Chapter 2's models, no apparent development or sequence, no explanation of why some came into favor and others declined. Nor is there any sense of improvement with one model supplanting another in usefulness, precision, or diagnostic power. The absence of progression in strategic consultants' thinking, in spite of the great changes to the economy at large and to how business is done, suggests their inventory of tools should be treated with caution. To argue, perhaps, that SWOT reflects old-style managerial capitalist thinking while the BCG matrix reflects the post-1960s turn towards financial management neglects the fact that SWOT remains the leading "strategic tool" around the world, in advanced economies as well as advancing. Nor would it explain why the Balanced Scorecard became so popular. Is ease of use preferred over analytic power?

Academic models have a traceable history and development path. There is explicit attention to the question/s being addressed and the way one answer leads on to more interesting questions. So long as we do not get bogged down in the technical details, a look at the microeconomic theories of the firm shows interesting sequences and signs of progress. As Keynes quipped, theorists sometimes have unanticipated impacts long after their death. The history and literature here is considerable but Adam Smith, Alfred Marshall, Ronald Coase, Edith Penrose, and Oliver Williamson stand out among the economists—mostly English language, but a few French and German—who have theorized the private sector firm's components and forces. Again, there are many simplifications, but economics survives and prospers because it provides insights into the socio-economy, many valuable to business strategists as long as they do not expect too much of them.

Arguing that strategizing leads to the creation of the firm as well as to determining its direction puts a question mark behind the firm itself. In what sense can we say it exists or comes to life? Firms are not found objects or grown on trees; they are human artifacts. Early writers did not use the term "firm," referring instead to "projects" (Defoe) or "enterprises." The continuing puzzle is their nature, in particular whether they have some nature that is not put there by the individuals who create them. The potter can make a vase. Some aspects of the vase's nature are given by the clay and glaze, materials the potter did not create. As the potter learns to work the materials, s/he is constrained by what Nature provided. Yet the vase is also an artifact, a specific solution in an opportunity-space that reveals something of the potter's nature. If the firm is a pottery does it only reflect the potters and their managers and nothing of the materials? It is not immediately clear whether firms have any nature of their own, or whether they are determined by the resources employed, or by what their creators knew when their judgment came into account.

Originally "firm" meant only "*firma*"—the signature of the firm's partners. It has now become the label for many types of private sector business, not just a partnership. Adam Smith saw firms (enterprises) as the "engines of the economy" compounding capital, land, and labor into economic value. Unlike many theorists, especially today, he saw people and their abilities complementing and leveraging the firm's resources. Smith regarded the enterprise as important, a context in which the most mundane kinds of learning-by-doing by workers could lead to value creation at the level of the firm and, ultimately, the nation. The wealth of nations, he wrote, lay in the workers' capacity to apply their imaginations to improving the tools and methods they applied to the work the division of labor framed for them. Following Sir William Petty, he argued the nation's stock of imaginative people (its human capital) was its real wealth, not its bullion (gold or capital reserves), its territory (land and produce), or its international treaties. This is a profoundly political or political-economic view. It follows that entrepreneurs have a central role in the politics of democratic capitalism as well as being expected to do the strategic work necessary to set up the division of labor that might produce the crucial value-creating effect. Entrepreneurs have to coordinate practice towards the firm's overall objectives. The work tasks designed had to be modest enough to be done by ordinary people—be "doable"—yet significant enough to generate productivity gains that were material to firm and the nation, overcoming the normal frictions of real-world economic activity. Training could enhance workplace learning so that people could specialize and perform as skilled in their particular type of work. Smith's key concepts (with regard to the enterprise) were (1) division of labor, (2) specialization, (3) practical work, (4) learning, (5) coordination—leading to (6) economic growth. He paid less attention to (5) than modern theorists do. But his work helps entrepreneurs discern the different aspects of the value-adding process and judge how to bring them together into a viable enterprise.

The strategic work implied included creating (*a*) a "horizontal" value-adding apparatus, the "value-chain," and (*b*) a "vertical" administrative structure and process—and then populating the resulting structure of work roles with appropriately trained and resourced specialists. Technology, and its evolution, mattered to both horizontal and vertical arrangements because it shaped tasks and their administration. Smith's under-specified organizational ideas were formalized later by other theorists; in the early decades of the twentieth century in particular, as Max Weber developed the theory of bureaucracy and Frederick Taylor and other engineers around the world laid out Scientific

Management.[1] Their "classical organization theory" ideas have since dominated managers' notions of what "getting organized" means—setting out tasks, planning, resourcing, monitoring, etc. While there are many other ideas around, such as Senge's "learning organization" plus various "new wave" and evolutionary notions, classical organization theory still dominates business talk. The *Wealth of Nations* appeared in 1776 and was shaped by the work of earlier French economists and the managerial practices Smith saw around him during the heady days of the English Industrial Revolution. He believed what he was writing down was generally known, though he communicated the ideas exceptionally clearly. Indeed his reasoning and writing were superb and immediately appreciated. But he was not an entrepreneur himself and did not speak directly to the strategic work that is the entrepreneur's defining task. Richard Cantillon, an Irish-French banker writing in the early 1700s, coined the term "entrepreneur" that eventually replaced Defoe's earlier term "projectors".[2] Smith's was a time of great social, technological, economic, and political turmoil and this helps explain why he was writing more about the economic and political implications of the enterprise than about its creation, administration, or direction. As we know, he went onto to emphasize market forces as external constraints on the entrepreneur's imagination.

There are major differences between the models in Chapter 2, which assume the firm already exists and address its continuance and redirection by applying judgment and choosing to reallocate resources or rearrange categories, versus Smith's interest in understanding firms' nature. It took more than a century for microeconomists to get back to ask their "killer" question: "Why, when reasonably efficient markets exist, do firms exist?" Being focused on the national political economy, Smith did not reason much about the modern enterprise he observed emerging, certainly not their management. He was more interested in seeing how the entrepreneurs' choices would be affected by the "invisible hand" of market forces and in showing that, even as entrepreneurs selfishly pursued their own ends, the outcome would be socially beneficial. He paid little attention to a feature that concerns us greatly today, that the modern consumer demands goods and services that can seldom be produced by lone entrepreneurs, no matter how ingenious. Even "hollowed-out" corporations need subcontractors and agents, and even authors (like Smith) require printers and publishers. The modern economy requires more than a "village" and calls for extensive collaboration in production and

---

[1] R. Kanigel (1997) *The One Best Way: Frederick Winslow Taylor and the Enigma of Efficiency.* New York: Viking Press. J.-C. Spender and H. Kijne (eds) (1996) *Scientific Management: Frederick Winslow Taylor's Gift to the World?* Norwell, MA: Kluwer.

[2] R. Cantillon (2001) *Essay on the Nature of Commerce in General, with a New Introduction by Anthony Brewer,* tr. H. Higgs. New Brunswick, NJ: Transaction Publishers. D. Defoe (1887) *An Essay Upon Projects.* London: Cassell & Co.

distribution. The seemingly simple matter of being a baker or a candlestick maker turns out to be complicated. Should the baker's "means of production" (the oven) be purchased—as is typical of those making French bread, which requires steam in the oven—or be home-built, as is typical of those making pizza and unleavened bread? Should the baker raise and mill his own wheat? How should the baker treat and pay his assistants? Should he set up his own store or go to a public market to sell the bread baked? Is there an intermediate market for pre-mixed frozen dough? The point here is that the creation of the enterprise is shaped by the existence or absence of markets for the supplies needed and the people and firms who constitute the demand that reconverts finished goods and services back into revenue and the prospect of profit.

After WW2 Coase's pre-war paper got economists back to asking "Why firms?" once again. During the 150 years between Smith and Coase, European microeconomists were mainly focused on theorizing markets, thinking about their nature, if and why they were necessary, when they (their Invisible Hand/s) were able to efficiently distribute the nation's resources so as to maximize the general welfare, how they might be regulated, protected from interference, etc. Smith was an academic philosopher and rhetorician, adept with philosophical languages and concepts, and saw firms as components of the broader nation-level political economy that was changing rapidly in his day and so the target of his theorizing. In contrast, Alfred Marshall, initially a mathematician, and his peers wrote at a time of rising attention to the natural sciences. They moved economics towards a science by developing rigorous methodology. Marshall eliminated a lot of the existing firm's real-world particulars and details, inventing the "representative firm," a firm that was not in a distinctive state, for instance, of having just been founded or protected by a state monopoly or affected by some other "market disturbing" circumstance.

The representative firm, from my point of view, has no heterogeneity. Its strategizing has been reduced to responding rationally to the dictates of the knowable markets, as in Marshall's famous picture of crossed supply and demand curves. No entrepreneurial judgment is called for or admitted. Yet most of the questions and strategic opportunities entrepreneurs deal with arise from the idiosyncratic details Marshall cut out of the analysis, helping create the mistaken impression that economic science is not useful or relevant. Ironically, and contrary to those who regard neoclassical economics as an abstruse and a-social science, Marshall was very concerned with the social impact of economic thought and was very liberal by today's standards, supporting women's education, socialism, the co-operative movement, and policies to reduce poverty. Nor was he was a slave to quantitative methods. He used them to advance his analysis, not to methodologize economics so that solutions arrived at without mathematics would be trivialized. But, like Smith, he was not much interested in the practicalities of entrepreneurship and presumed the firm's existence and value. His impact on economists working on the "theory of the firm" was to direct them towards theorizing about markets: perfect, monopolistic, imperfect, and so on.

Between WW1 and WW2, when Coase began writing, the principal micro-economic questions were about the firm's size. Given the economies of scale evident in many industries' production functions such as learning curves why did the largest firms not expand to monopolize their entire market? Some management theorists proposed dis-economies of scale, as the firm's growth led to it becoming complex, unwieldy, and perhaps unmanageable. Implied was an equilibrium point as the firm grew its value-creating to the point when administrative diseconomies kicked in to nullify further gains. But management scholars were also aware of periodic improvements in administrative technique, such as the new modes of corporate governance analyzed in Chandler's work, and these meant internal efficiency was not as easily theorized as market efficiency. Perfect markets arose as economic agents traded without interference. Perfect governance, a single entrepreneur fully controlling every employee, seemed very different. Microeconomists saw market-based opportunities and possibilities. Coase's intuition was that there might be some relationship between real firms and their less-than-perfect markets, perhaps that there would be no firms if markets were completely efficient. Given the economists' preference for market-based explanations, eventually the question "Why are there firms?" was rephrased as "When might market transactions be so inefficient that firms become more effective modes of organization or governance?" In other words, if the firm was simply an apparatus for combining the work of individuals into increasingly sophisticated products and services that modern consumers consume—bread, trans-atlantic air travel, mobile phones, health care—why would that combining not be done more efficiently through markets, each worker acting as an independent entrepreneur or consultant selling her/his capacity under an hourly rate plus costs type of contract?

Clearly there are many reasons why real markets might not work well. One is that no market exists for the thing in question, such as a partially manufactured piece in the middle of a value-chain, a freshly made piecrust awaiting its apple filling. There is little market for an uncapped bottle of beer, save at a brewery or a party, so the steps between filling and capping the bottle must be organized. To some extent factory production can be organized as an internal market, with each worker and each department negotiating prices as part of a "putting-out" system. This way of administering manufacturing was widespread in Europe and North America in the eighteenth century but declined after Smith's time, being replaced by the "inside contracting" system, especially as production equipment became too large to be moved around or so capital-intensive that it lay beyond the financial means of most workers and required financiers and institutionalized methods of collecting funds. Increasing capital intensity meant the fixed costs of overall production rose, and accounting for specific tasks and properly allocating the overhead costs became so difficult that it was more effective to move from "putting out" and inside contracting to fixed wage payment in the factory. Then management could exert direct control over the equipment, the production processes, and the workers themselves. The employment contracts were increasingly "incomplete," meaning many detailed instructions would be left until later. Instead of contracting for so many finished pieces, such as shoes, the employment contract would be "come to work and you will be told what to do." Markets need prices and when these cannot be properly determined non-market forms of coordination become essential—as in the horizontal and vertical coordination structures so familiar today. The economists' conclusion is that firms only exist when the other more efficient, rational, and computable modes of coordination—markets—will not work properly. They do not, of course, see firms as a remarkable social apparatus that enables entrepreneurs and their employees to inject their imagination and judgment into the socio-economy and so add value. Neglecting value creation, the economists presume strategic work focuses on discovering (a) a typology of market failures and (b) alternative means of coordination and governance to deal with them. Chapter 3 looks into what microeconomists say on this. Ironically they do not do what consultants in Chapter 2 do: identify and frame the knowledge absences that, if addressed, might lead on to profit.

Markets fail for many reasons, not simply because there are no prices. Firms too need appropriate knowledge about their operations and how to coordinate them. Knowledge is a commonsense notion but hides many subtleties and complexities. For instance, it is not easily priced and traded. In particular one cannot put knowledge "on display" as in a shop window without actually revealing it. The technical issue here is that knowledge is "non-rivalrous." Neoclassical economics presumes goods and services (and resources) are "rivalrous," which means title is clear and can be passed from seller to buyer without ambiguity or loss. If I sell you an orange, I do not have it when you have it. This makes it easy to separate knowing about the orange—here it is, now you know about it, but I still have it—from possessing it, both knowing and having it. When you buy a house you have your attorney do a title search to be sure the seller actually owns it—maybe it belongs to his mother or a bank. You can be shown the real house, with the boundaries shown on the deeds. Either the seller owns it or the buyer does. The fact that title can be determined unambiguously, so separating knowing and possessing, means the thing being sold and bought is only in one place or economic state at one time, which leads to the notion of scarcity on which neoclassical economic theories and market processes depend. Knowledge is not like this. If you tell me how to make synthetic rubber, I get to know, but you have no less knowledge as a result of having told me. It is impossible to separate knowing and owning. But the separation is crucial to scarcity. Scarcity makes pricing rational, so pricing knowledge is trickier, and an economics of knowledge may be impossible.

Another mode of failure is triggered when production methods must be kept secret if there is to be any prospect of sustained profit. As production equipment became more complex and costly, the knowledge about how to use it became more valuable and strategic. When a newspaper press can be run by one operator, his threat to strike is a bigger threat than if one of the newsroom staff makes a similar threat. Nowadays we say the economy has become "knowledge-intensive" and that competitive advantage lies in the knowledge that one firm possesses and others do not. But knowledge does not fit easily into an analysis of market behavior. The more the firm's nature is grounded in its unshared knowledge, as opposed to its financial assets, the less market-based notions illuminate the firm's nature. Knowledge is often costly to generate, and the results are often valuable, so there should be some economic reasoning behind managing it. But what? There are further complications in that knowledge's application, rather than consuming it, like most resources, often improves it. The economics of knowledge is more like the economics of the real world and markets that turn more on expectations than on objective facts. The things economists are comfortable with, such as the expense of a beer-bottling plant or newspaper press, are only valuable because there are people with the knowledge of how to operate and maintain them. But the firm does not own their knowledge, as it owns the plant and the press. The values of all corporate assets are always mediated by and conditional on people's know-how, something not easy to identify, control, or price. We may pay a lot for something we do not know how to use and realize it is of little value to us. Strategists must be as conscious of managing, generating, and protecting the knowledge that underpins their profitability as they are of managing the firm's price-able resources and contracts. This focus on what those within the firm do know complements strategies of rent protection based on what outsiders do not know. Eventually the non-rivalrous knowledge-mediated view of strategic work will dominate my analysis.

Coase's four questions—(a) Why do firms exist? (b) Why are their boundaries located where they are? (c) Why is their internal structure as it is? (d) Why is their performance so varied?—provoked some microeconomists to develop generalized models that complement the models inventoried in Chapter 2. But their answers lack coherence. They are not yet able to show how the models interrelate or whether they are progressing towards a totalizing theory of the firm. While most are optimistic, feeling their field is progressing, others are more cautious.[3] There are several ways to analyze these models. The microeconomic literature seldom does more than recite the various theories and examine their axioms, caveats, conclusions, and so on.[4] Going through this may be important to economists in training but is not very useful to managers. However, when we turn these theories upside down and see where they fail to reach closure then they can be used to sketch the variety of strategic judgments needed to achieve closure—the same methodology as applied to the models in Chapter 2. So I shall make a list and work through their implications, knowledge presences, and knowledge absences to help working strategists get an added sense of what must be done. The first item is the value-chain, a reformulation of Smith's division of labor. Thereby Michael Porter makes a connection to Scientific Management.[5] As well as being a consultant he is also a credible microeconomic theorist. While Porter did his PhD under Richard Caves, he notably moved on from such Rational Man theorizing to the judgment-based synthesizing at the core of his 5-forces model (see section 2.6).

The value-chain presumes a division of labor. Once formulated, the work roles opened up must be filled, employees hired, instructed, and coordinated. The key to understanding the relationship between a microeconomic theory of the firm and the strategist's task is to see how the theory takes one or other single facet of the firm's nature and expresses it rigorously. Facet 1, then, is the division of labor. Facet 2 is the employment arrangement. Facet 3 is the relation between the firm and its market. Facet 4 is the assignment of property rights, and so on. This list of elementary concepts has not yet been completed; indeed it may not be possible to separate out the various facets that, taken together, would capture everything important about the firm. Or, to put this differently, the firm cannot ever be satisfactorily comprehended without addressing the many non-rigorous dimensions of the strategic work and judgments that are required to bring its identifiable facets together into a value-creating relationship. It may not be possible to complete this. But microeconomists progress by carving off and systematizing one or other of the firm's facets and so illuminate the strategic work to be done to bring the firm to life. They are microeconomic in that they presume people act rationally in their own interest and are able to calculate the results of their choices. In Chapter 2 the motives for action are not explored. Chapter 3 touches on alternatives to rational choice, as in behavioral and evolutionary theories.

---

[3] H. Demsetz (1988) 'The Theory of the Firm Revisited', *Journal of Law, Economics, and Organization,* 4, 141–61.

[4] An exception is N. J. Foss and P. G. Klein (2012) *Organizing Entrepreneurial Judgment: A New Approach to the Firm.* Cambridge: Cambridge University Press.

[5] M. E. Porter (1985) *Competitive Advantage: Creating and Sustaining Superior Performance.* New York: Free Press.

The archetypical arrangement for populating the firm as a value-chain is the incomplete employment agreement between firm and employee. This can be examined from different angles and traditions, as, for instance, a manager–employee or master–servant relationship. Relationships between superior and subordinate are as old as human history, and are inherently problematic if only because our inner thoughts and motives are private and inaccessible to others. Yet we often act on them. "Did you not do as I told you?" In recent years microeconomics has explored this through principal-agent theory (PAT). Note that principal-agent issues are often mislabeled "agency theory"—which is actually the analysis of how we humans act and make a difference in our world, presuming a degree of free will or "human agency." The insight in PAT is that when one person (the principal) hires another (the agent) to execute some task for him, the principal may well be anxious about whether the agent performs as well as he might, irrespective of how the contract is worded. There is knowledge asymmetry. Perhaps the agent is working at a distant location where the principal cannot see what he is doing, so he goofs off, or steals part of the value added, crops raised, or pies baked. Perhaps there is asymmetry of intention: the principal wants one thing, that agent another. Likewise managers are the shareholders' agents and instead of devoting themselves exclusively to maximizing shareholder wealth—or whatever corporate goals the board has dictated—they might be more interested in their own ease and welfare. Do they really need that corporate jet? Should they be paid a bonus when the firm is losing money and the stock plummeting? PAT is important because it captures something fundamental to every real firm as it considers people's relations, and, at the same time, recognizes that people normally have differing and sometimes conflicting interests. PAT (covering Facets 1 and 2) treats people as heterogeneous, an imperfection to the homogeneity-presuming analysis that must be dealt with. It explores how managers might spend to monitor employees or incentivize them to align their behavior with the firm's goals. Likewise it explores how shareholders might spend on management incentives and oversight (surveillance) to maximize their own benefit.

Theorizing the relationship between the firm and its market (Facet 3—supply and demand) moves us away from thinking the firm's boundaries could be determined by internal factors alone. Chandler proposed the EIF paradigm, matching the firm's structure to its strategy. Coase focused on economic transactions rather than on the firm as a whole. He suggested attention to the make-or-buy decisions that would adjust the firm's boundary and so the relationship between the firm and its markets. This disaggregated the firm into a set of allocation, acquisition, or sales transactions, just as the value-chain disaggregates the firm into a series of value-adding steps. In a manner reminiscent of Marshall's "representative firm" Oliver Williamson reformulated Coase's ideas, drawing on John Commons to propose a "representative transaction." The make-or-buy choice would involve computing the relative cost of conducting that transaction within the firm or across a market. If cheaper within the firm, the firm should expand its boundary to embrace the transaction. Otherwise it should be outsourced. Williamson went further to bring the make-or-buy analysis together with PAT problems in the outside vendor and internal employee contracts. These are normally incomplete and leave the task's precise details to be specified later. Since finite time is involved between contract and execution this opens the relationships to "opportunism" as employees and subcontractors are tempted to take advantage of the contractor, or vice versa. One variant would be when Firm X persuaded its subcontractor to invest in some capital equipment that had no use except under this specific contract and could only be sold at a loss. Firm X could then squeeze the subcontractor by threatening to cancel the contract. The transactions cost economics (TCE) analysis leads on to analyze alternative (a) modes of contract, and (b) allocations of property rights. The PAT and TCE "theories of the firm" showed a firm could not be understood as a "stand alone" entity but only in relation to those markets that might enable the same transaction to take place if the firm did not exist. Coase also argued a firm could not be understood without reference to the legal apparatus that shaped the relevant contracts and property rights that comprise it.

The point of going through these various theories is to review their widely differing notions of strategic work as the judgment necessary to create a firm. Economists' commitment to rational decision-making and lack of interest in strategic judgment leaves them with certain blind spots. Turning their theorizing upside down reveals these—"deconstructing" their theorizing to reveal what part of the analysis is being suppressed. Chapter 3's list of characterizations of strategic judgment complements that of Chapter 2 where the strategic problem being dealt with was to describe the firm, not its construction. The microeconomic theorists who looked beyond theorizing prices and markets took a significant step forward with these attempts to explain the Coasian approach to the firm. Ironically, each depends on identifying and axiomatizing a specific departure from full knowledge (market perfection). By doing this microeconomists have taken the theoretical initiative away from organization theorists who, since Weber and Taylor, have made little progress towards theorizing the nature of the value-generating firm or its creation. It follows there has been little progress towards theorizing what managers do or how management education should work. Some classical bureaucratic and machine-design notions remain, not yet taken over by economic thinking.

Against this, the resurgence of interest in entrepreneurship and leadership shows the hunger among managers, students, and academics for richer models with more scope than either neoclassical economics or classical organization theory (OT) can provide. In spite of opening up the black box, OT and microeconomic theories have not yet been pulled together into a coherent analysis of creating and managing the firm. But admitting strategic judgment makes some advance possible. Then, with the consultants' and the academics' lists in hand, comparing and contrasting them reveals something of the deeper nature of the firm and the managerial strategic work that brings it to life. It is also useful to consider which of Coase's questions have been answered, if any. Have we learned why firms exist? All becomes clearer when we understand that strategic work is not producing a plan to be implemented in some other process—nor a goal to be striven for even when unrealistic. Rather, strategizing is the creation of the firm itself as a persisting pattern of value-creating practice by those engaged. Ultimately we see the firm as a living strategic artifact that addresses the knowledge absences (questions) chosen— and when framed by the knowledge presences available define the firm's strategy. In similar fashion a sculpture may be an object of beauty or derision—but it is also an answer to the specific question the sculptor chooses. Henry Moore's sketches, interesting as they are, make a very different impression on the viewer than do his finished sculptures. They answer different questions, though they are related in the sculptor's intellectual and aesthetic practice—and biography. The point is that the artifact is not just an object to be considered on its own merits. On the contrary, it is an answer to a question contextualized in the artist's life. Likewise the firm is an answer to the knowledge absences the contextualized strategist choses to engage.

It is easy to get confused about the outcome of the strategic work process. The convention is that it is a plan that can be fully described, isolated, that persists across time. In fact, as Chapter 2's models show, the litmus test is its ability to capture the participants' judgment in the firm's "strategic time." As von Moltke, one of von Clausewitz's more prestigious students, quipped, real-world strategy is dynamic for "no strategy survives the first engagement with the enemy." He saw plans quickly become "dead letters." Rather than a plan, the need is for a human strategist who continues to respond, however badly or pleasantly surprised. Going back to sculpture, what the sculptor intends is her artifact's relationship with the viewer, something that exists in the moment, the viewer's "here-and-now," and penetrates (shocks) his consciousness. The sculpture's significance is not that it persists through "calendar time" as an object. Note the viewer's experience depends on how the object is lit at the moment of being seen. Many sculptures are majestic, as at the Lincoln memorial; other times sculptures can achieve visual ambiguity and, in some cases, an out-of-world mysteriousness, seeming to change in the light. At which point we appreciate the sculpture's essence is how we see it right now, not it being there centuries from now for others to see. Hayek considered this tilt towards the immediate and subjective to be the principal development in modern economics.[6] It is especially evident in performance arts, such as ballet. A concert or a "happening" is an artifact too, like a melting ice-sculpture, here but for a moment, like our "strut upon the stage." Strategies and business models can be likewise short-lived—perhaps to execute a single transaction. Business is within the strategist's here-and-now time as a complex of value-adding practice, employees laboring and learning, products being designed, sales being made, alliances working, and so on.

## 3.1 Value-Chain and Team Production

The next sections are not intended to be thoroughgoing explanations of the theories or ideas labeled. Rather I try to surface the character of the judgments the strategists must make to bring the firm to life. To begin with Adam Smith, the division of labor has long been recognized as one of a firm's most fundamental characteristics. His memorable description of the separate steps in pin making was actually derived from previous French descriptions, the literature rather than his own observations.[7] The division of labor goes a long way back in history. The production of sandals for the Roman legionnaires was organized systematically, as was the twelfth-century production of rope-blocks for the Venetian Navy. Descriptions of the division of labor make for some confusion between work roles, such as the separate stations on a production line or the separate offices in a bureaucracy, versus the production activities within one work role, for there might also be several of these. The wood-turner mounts the blank in his lathe, trims it, turns it, eventually applies the gauge and de-mounts the finished piece; a sequence of several work steps at one location. Bearing this in mind, later authors, such as Porter, focused more on the specific activities than work locations. All work seems to proceed in a sequence, so it seems perfectly reasonable to talk about upstream and downstream activities linked into a chain, with value being increased as the finished product is approached. The ideas have been formalized into "Value Chain Analysis" (VCA).[8] Debates swirl about where the analysis should start and stop. Should the wood-turner's value-chain start with the factors of production, timber blanks, or with the negotiations with suppliers, timber merchants, or foresters, and with customers, furniture stores, and wholesalers? Accountants may want to restrict the analysis narrowly to what is owned and can be put on the firm's books. Entrepreneurs might reach wider, to search

---

[6] F. A. Hayek (1948) *Individualism and Economic Order*. South Bend, IN: Gateway Editions.
[7] Smith, A. (1979) *The Wealth of Nations*, books i–iii. Harmondsworth: Penguin Books.
[8] J. K. Shank and V. Govindarajaran (1992) 'Strategic Cost Management: The Value Chain Perspective', *Journal of Management Accounting Research*, 4, 177–97.

upstream for opportunities and funding, or their downstream expectations that there will be "halo" effects in other business—as happens when another business carrying the Virgin brand opens. Other analysts might be critical of the idea of a serial flow from inputs to outputs since it implies focusing on the forward flow of materials and ignoring the backwards flow of information and funds. To focus only on one side of these interactions is to imply they do not need to be seen as a circular flow. Other analysts might go further and argue for even a complex interactive network.

The strategic point is that there may be little given about the value-chain. One firm might bring many activities into a single work role while another may not, choosing greater specialization. Most presume there are some limits to management's options here. When the flow is of physical materials the limits seem tied up with material properties that are not open to management's choices. The sequence of steps in refining uranium—through fluidizing to a gas, spinning in a centrifuge, separating the isotopes, and solidifying—is set by the chemistry and the chemical engineer has little choice. On the other hand, if the task is to translate a text from Spanish into Chinese the work structure does not necessarily mean only one translator can work on it. Spanish and Chinese sentence structures differ, so clearly it is not possible to parse a single sentence into its separate elements or to translate each separately, for the translator has to get a sense of what the sentence means and use that to reconstruct the meaning in the second language. The sentence is the minimal linguistic transaction. But perhaps the deeper flow of meaning in the text means the work cannot be disaggregated into less than chapter-sized blocks, or the entire work. Also the value-chain makes no sense without its administration and coordination. This stands on a perceived logic to its components and their relationship to the value-chain's purpose. There may be a "vertical" division of administrative labor, raising "second-order" problems of administration about who monitors and administers the administrators—and how all of this depends on how value is added. Thus the seeming simplicity of the value-chain hides complex strategic choices. Should the firm be administered on the basis of common product lines and customer groups or on the basis of shared production knowledge? What is the most effective logic of coordination, since none is given? Should the furniture business be organized into separate departments for chairs, tables, and cupboards, or by customer groups and marketing channels—government, hotels, residential?

The strategic choices turn on what are chosen as the value-chain's most significant attributes. In spite of the physical aspects of many value-adding processes, these attributes are often remarkably hard to discover—indeed, given the multidimensional nature of our knowledge, they may not be there to find. Like Democritus, Herbert Simon believed everything is composed of smaller elements into which they could be broken down or "decomposed." But there are limits and levels that become barriers to the transformation process so that real things are only "partially decomposable." There are complex energy barriers between metals, atoms, and sub-atomic particles that imply three quite distinct levels of analysis of how physical transformation processes might be described and managed. Though Porter's value-chain took the analysis to the level of the discrete activities below the firm's actions as a single entity, it is not clear which attributes actually provide the logic of value-chain separations and coordination. "Modularization" and "black boxing" see the firm as made up of modules of discrete activity that are "naturally" bounded and distinct. The conventional distinctions between, say, R&D, manufacturing, and selling—the "primary activities" in many value-chains—are complemented by support activities and perhaps administrative activities. "Business process re-engineering" (BPR) often turns on discovering these "natural" heterogeneities. But there is no theory to tell the strategist about which to take into account. At best they seem to be driven by (a) technology, and (b) learning. Technology is a complex and baffling topic, seeming so obvious in our lives yet deeply puzzling in its nature and impact, and I shall discuss it later. Maybe it is learning at the societal level—a manifestation of the growth of human knowledge—data, meaning, and skilled practice. There is little value in describing it as the application of science to the real world, though a great deal of what we call "technology"—in terms of the activities involved—is highly shaped by scientific knowledge. Much work activity is determined by the technologies the firm provides and as technology changes, so do work roles, modularization, and the problems of administration. In summary, the value-chain seems a great deal simpler in the classroom than it is in practice and there may be few generalities about its construction and administration.

## 3.2 Principal-Agent Theory

No question Adam Smith was a major theorist, applying his prodigious analytic capabilities to the economic and industrial activity around him. He was also a diligent student of commercial history. Earlier I noted two main analytic traditions in our subject area. One, the microeconomic tradition, sees firms as bundles of price-able assets. The other sees firms as networks of relationships between people with valuable producing and obeying skills that can be brought to bear on selected goals. This is the organization theory tradition that leads CEOs to say "our people are our most valuable assets." The meaning of "strategizing" differs between these two traditions. One is about asset allocation; the other is about setting up and controlling interpersonal and interinstitutional relationships. Real private sector strategic practice, of course, must bridge or synthesize these—and some other issues as well. The point of the list in Chapter 2 and in this chapter is to help clarify just what needs to be synthesized before the strategist has a strategy able to add value—as opposed to something developed in the classroom and never implemented. This chapter deals with microeconomists' moves to bridge between these traditions at a theoretical level, rather than as a matter of firm practice.

Being about people and their interaction, principal-agent theory seems to be in the organization theory tradition. Yes and no to that. What economists mean by people—and principal-agent theory—turns out to be rather different to what non-economists think. Economists see people as defined by (a) their rationality, and (b) their "objective function," the parameter they are attempting to maximize. Markets stabilize when everyone is maximizing. (I deal later with the recently popularized behavioral and psychological notions.) When people are fully rational and self-maximizing there is some possibility of bringing the asset management and people management traditions together. Principal-agent theory (PAT) takes economists towards a different notion of people, in this case defined by their relative power, knowledge, and capabilities in addition to their rational nature. These people work through and with each other—rationally and collaboratively—even as they pursue diverging interests. The divergence introduces a "market failure" because power, incentives, and knowledge differentials bring in the specific imperfections that principal-agent theory deals with. Most people have experience of dealing with an agent—a lawyer, real estate agent, or doctor. They will have discovered there may be times when their duly appointed agents do not seem to act as they have been instructed to, perhaps because the agent has some non-professional involvement with the other parties that prefers an interest other than yours, perhaps your doctor is protecting you from his diagnosis to spare you or your partner. In a sense, if professionalism is not being diverted from the facts as best as they are known, then PAT is about managing people's non-professionalism.

Economists locate their problems within economic frameworks where there are only facts; opinions do not apply; rationalism is their regular profession, so the principal-agent problem takes them into a new area. PAT is an attempt to resolve a "real" non-economic relationship problem using economic principles—a move some see as economists' "colonizing" areas normally considered the purview of the social sciences. At issue is exactly how much the agent deprives the principal because their interests diverge. PAT tries to determine how much the principal should pay out to prevent such loss. Hovering in the background is the idea of a break-even or equilibrium point, the economically correct answer to these questions at which the principal's return is maximized. The ordinary person's experience of using an agent can seldom be measured so precisely. You cannot know how much more you might have got for your house had you not accepted your agent's advice to take the offer you took. Likewise when you ask your friends for an opinion about someone you are thinking of hiring as an agent you do not expect a number. On the other hand economists got excited about the PAT discussion— especially in the late 1970s—because it suggested a rational analysis that would illuminate a key non-economic aspect of the firm, its authority relationships, providing something like an "internal" make-or-buy analysis. The make-or-buy decision is that, if internal costs are P and market price Q; if P > Q buy, otherwise make. Likewise if you spend M on monitoring your agent and N on performance incentives that end up saving you K that would otherwise be taken by your agent then setting M + N = K tells you what to do.

This is a clumsy way of saying that microeconomic theorists look for computable determining models. Then "the numbers speak for themselves" and the strategist does not need to make a judgment. Put differently, if the theory provides a rigorous solution no strategic judgment is called for, under which circumstances the managers do no more than collect data and run the numbers. But do any of the microeconomic models deliver the goods promised? When it comes to PAT is there any way of calculating *ex ante* the effect of M and N on the agent? This is like the game theory situation (see section 1.4). If the impact of monitoring and incentives can be calculated then it amounts to game player A knowing how game player B will respond to all his moves— and "the strategy" become a property of the game as defined by its rules rather than a game between the two partially uncertain human players. The economist wants to excise the players' idiosyncrasy and judgment in their responses to uncertainty. The indeterminacies of the relationship are translated into matters of ignorance which, when resolved, lead to rigorous solutions. When this happens it may be important (and strategically useful) to see how the theorist accomplishes this—for it shifts the discourse from judging or persuasion and into calculating. The excision maneuver illuminates the nature of the strategic judgment that would otherwise be called for—in PAT the players' idiosyncrasy is captured as quasi-calculative responses to monetary incentives.

A famous 1976 paper by Jensen and Meckling seemed to offer a deterministic solution to one of mankind's oldest questions—how principals control agents.[9] Closer inspection shows the solution/s offered—for the paper considers several variants of the PAT situation—depend on the availability of market prices. The paper presumed the PAT relationship is embedded in efficient markets. Thereby the analysts were able to ignore the uncertainties

---

[9] Michael C. Jensen and William H. Meckling (1976) 'Theory of the Firm: Managerial Behavior, Agency Costs, and Ownership Structure', *Journal of Financial Economics*, 3(4), 305–60.

(idiosyncrasies) around the impact of the principal's spending on the agent, a heroic assumption. But at a deeper level the requirement for efficient markets raises questions about whether the interests of principals and agents' interests can ever diverge in efficient markets—for all actors are then self-maximizing principals and there is no conceptual space for "an agent" as a non-principal. In efficient markets all actors are fully informed principals and no knowledge differentials or interest divergences arise. Thus Jensen and Meckling's assumptions seemed to deny the very phenomenon their theorizing addressed. In the real world of imperfect markets, when principals cannot ignore uncertainty, the principal (strategist) is left to make a non-computable judgment about how to deal with an agent. But even though Jensen and Meckling's portrayal of PAT "fails," it provides good insight. If the principal-agent relationship is axiomatically incompatible with and cannot be embedded within perfect markets, it is because PAT hinges on the particular imperfection of actors' diverging interest and intentions—whereas in perfect markets all actors pursue the same goal.

In Chapters 1 and 2 there was little discussion of strategizing in a context of divergent intentions; convergence was assumed except in game theory. A glance at the broader literature of principal-agent relations—given they are mentioned in all humankind's great books, including the Bible and the Muqaddimah—shows it is among the fundamental questions all sociology addresses, how order can arise in a context in which individuals act in their own interest (see section 1.11). The alternatives available are the exercise of power (coercion), incentives (calculation), acculturation (aligning interests), and communication—the four basic modes of human interaction. PAT implies the possibility of using just one of these (calculation) to solve the problem of creating order and predictability under uncertainty between divergent (real) individuals—and it should be questioned on that ground alone. A more commonsense approach is to do what we all do, learn from the experience of interacting with agents generally, and with this particular agent over time.

The crucial point here is time, the difference between single-period and multi-period solutions. Jensen and Meckling's paper suggested there was a computable mix of monitoring and incentives that would produce the optimum balance immediately, versus the more realistic multi-period solution in which these two particular actors learn about each other and use that knowledge to stabilize their relationship. One version of this learning interaction is Rapoport's "tit-for-tat" (TFT) approach in which each interacting actor presumes cooperation but if this is not forthcoming, the actor "retaliates" on the next move—but also "forgives" and readopts a cooperative strategy for the subsequent move.[10] In general when the analysis embraces rather than

---

[10] http://en.wikipedia.org/wiki/Anatol_Rapoport.

ignores actors' divergent interests there can be no theoretical solution, only a multi-period historical one, reflecting the accrued experience of the particular actors involved. The commonsense solution to the principal-agent "problem," as opposed to the monitoring and incentive one, is to pay attention to the history of the relationship, learn its nature and dimensions, and make a judgment. But, as with all real-world strategizing, irrespective of past behavior, doubts must remain about whether, this time, either agent or principal is going to welch on the deal. Perhaps the next interaction is the "last period" for one of the actors, in which case the history of acting in the expectation of future interaction may not apply. For instance, the barman puts the drink on "my tab" because I always paid up in the past; little does he know I am leaving town for good tonight and intend to stick him with the cost.

The point of listing the handful of available microeconomic theories is to show the different kinds of judgment that must be made as their theories "fail." In this respect they are similar to the models in Chapter 2—but they are more precise and deal with more fundamental aspects of the firm. They draw attention to the many incommensurate judgments required to bring the firm into being and so suggest how Coase's questions might eventually be answered. PAT considers the basic authority relation, clearly a fundamental aspect of every firm. The judgment required pays attention to the heterogeneous experience of particular people rather than backing away into generalities and presuming computation. The relationship between this particular principal and this particular agent is particular, not general. Without doubt any theory about, for instance, how people "generally" respond to monitoring or incentives might well be taken into consideration—but it cannot determine the judgment to be made. Note that, inasmuch as Coase suggested answers to his own killer question, he observed firms were distinguished by being "islands of power" wherein the price mechanism is "superseded." The result is that one factor of production (employees) agree to obey the directions of an entrepreneur "within certain limits" in return for a certain remuneration. One integrating "force" (the entrepreneur's power) has been substituted for another (the price mechanism and calculation). Coase went on to suggest that would work when the entrepreneur could supply the judgment necessary to deal with Knightian uncertainty. In general the idea that an employee can compute the costs and benefits (and risks) of entering into an employment agreement is absurd—the contract is underdetermined or "incomplete," leaving precise specification of the work to be done until later. Plus in real-world situations there are halo effects and externalities affecting other decisions. Good performance might lead to future engagements, promotions, bonuses, and so on. This is another version of the value of experience-based knowledge being "carried forward" into future time-periods (see 2.10).

## 3.3 Transaction Cost Economics

PAT is about interpersonal relationships—fundamental to every firm—and it pays little attention to the firm's economic resources or their ownership. We assume the firm comprises several kinds of resource—capital, land, and labor, perhaps. Transaction cost economics (TCE) is a melange of discourses about resources, their heterogeneity, and their ownership.[11] The firm's employees are not owned, of course, so people and resources get analyzed separately. Yet the firm has to bring people and resources together to create value. So in some ways PAT and TCE are complementary and suggest the possibility of a comprehensive theory of the firm. Many have commented on the complementarity of "capabilities" (asset allocation) and "contractual" (people relationship) approaches, though few appreciate their synthesis would be situation-specific rather than general, because it would turn on the strategic judgments necessary to make both theories "work" in that particular context. Just as PAT points to judgments about time, people's interests, with their interaction experience, and the resulting presence or absence of "trust," so TCE examines complementary strategic judgments about modes of governing and allocating resources to economic activities that change their value.

The ramifications of the TCE approach are complex and puzzling, though it is clear that important methodological issues are being raised; in particular, conflict between methods seeking general prescriptive theories versus inherently subjective approaches to clarifying human commitment to action in uncertain situations. In PAT, responding to the principal's and agent's divergent interests cannot be generalized, the interests are particular facts of the situation. The strategist's judgment ("What to do now?") will be contingent on these facts—the personalities, upside and downside risks, and "strategic timing" of the principal's and agent's interactions. Likewise cost and use-value differ, so the value of the firm's resources will be contingent on its business model—identity, intention, and context—and the strategist's expectations of the results of committing them at that particular time. Following Coase's comments about the cost of gathering the information necessary to conduct trade, some see TCE's defining characteristic as analyzing the effects of the costs of acquiring, exchanging, distributing, and protecting property rights, and analyzing the impact these costs have on economic behavior. Property rights are an economic agent's rights to consume and obtain income from specific resources, and to deny them to others. TCE pays attention to the difference between economic resources and the property rights attached to them, and so to the legal arrangements that relate them. Some of the costs,

---

[11] P. G. Klein and M. E. Sykuta (eds) (2010) *The Elgar Companion to Transaction Cost Economics*. Cheltenham: Edward Elgar.

and resulting behaviors, arise from the difficulty of measuring resources and property rights.

A little history helps clarify these ideas. Coase's 1937 questions provoked post-WW2 microeconomists into developing PAT and TCE—aspects of the new field of "new institutional economics" (NIE). In 1932 Coase was 21 years old and traveling around the US on a scholarship gained at LSE (London School of Economics).[12] He had just completed an undergraduate business degree and had become interested in questions about industrial integration— why industries organize and integrate as they do—a variant of the firm size question. He was also intrigued by corporate law and, seeing it as one mode of industrial organizing, wondered how it meshed with economic reasoning. He had powerful letters of introduction (including from the Bank of England) to senior US business people and meeting them, pressed them with his questions. He found they fully appreciated the risks of bilateral monopoly, what both parties to a contract would feel when one party made a significant investment purely to enable it to supply the other. Such commitment introduced "imperfection" into an otherwise computable business situation exemplified by the make-or-buy decision—do whatever is most economic. "Holdup" became possible. This upset the economic calculation and needed "organizing" through a legally enforceable contract that would allocate the risks and temptations and provide remedies for default. But the risks could not be priced, so were evidence of a different incommensurate or non-cost dimension to the contract.

Coase intuited a link between organizing and cost that was absent from the one-dimensional framework of neoclassical cost minimization. If the link could be formalized, the theory of the firm would be significantly advanced— and Coase's questions answered—and business people would be able to negotiate the bilateral monopoly situation without having to exercise strategic judgment. During his US trip Coase visited Chicago and attended a few of Knight's classes, without taking away much about Knightian uncertainty. Nonetheless Coase associated the costs of gathering information with uncertainty (both ignorance and incommensurability) and intuited that absent transactions costs there would be no need for firms—for any of the legally available relationships (including markets) would be equally effective. He concluded firms comprised activities that were not coordinated by the price coordination mechanism, wherein it was superseded, but by management "fiat"—because that would reduce the transaction costs. It followed that corporate law mattered—and private sector firms differed fundamentally from

---

[12] R. H. Coase (1991) 'The Nature of the Firm: Origin', in O. E. Williamson and S. G. Winter (eds), *The Nature of the Firm: Origins, Evolution, and Development*. New York: Oxford University Press, pp. 34–47.

public sector organizations or agencies. Coase's use of the notion of transaction cost "problematized" both people and resources without resorting to the notion of uncertainty (Knight's way of doing this), bounded rationality (Simon's way), or "learning" (Penrose's way). Problematizing both opened up the possibility of bringing them together in a coherent theory. Yet transaction costs arose from ignorance of resources' use-value and from ignorance of peoples' productive capabilities—which made people and resources heterogeneous and pricing difficult or impossible. Costs arose from the indeterminacy generated by people's interactions—requiring contractual non-market modes of organizing people. They also arose because of the incommensurability between the market and managing modes of integration—requiring strategic management.

We can illustrate the transactions cost issues as Coase himself did, by leveraging from a make-or-buy decision—and then seeing how the economic frictions or non-zero transactions costs would affect the actors' behavior. When the firm can price and compare the cost of manufacturing something (a particular transaction) against the price it would pay to buy it, it has all it needs at arrive at a rational decision about where to source. There is no knowledge absence and no judgment is required. Likewise when the information needed is findable but costly, the transaction cost can be brought into the calculation. But real make-or-buy decisions are not simple and they get to be of strategic interest when the costs cannot be computed because there are features that cannot be priced—such as halo effects (the promise of future business) or the risk of holdup. Difficulties may arise in many ways. Ignorance is a major impediment to rational resource allocation. Internal costs are seldom transparent, even to those inside the firm. The cost and works estimators of yesteryear (Coase took courses in this) are less evident today, perhaps because labor is less often the major constituent of the typical firm's costs. Even if costs can be determined there are judgments to be made about allocating overheads, for these now form an increasing portion of the costs. White-collar costs are rising far faster than blue-collar costs. Often firms gradually impose a greater overhead load as the production costs decline down the learning curve, so the allocation of overheads is itself a strategic choice.

In principle it might be possible to calculate the fully loaded internal costs of production. But the calculation would also hinge on the way the rest of the firm's operations were treated, not simply in overhead allocation. Instead of being the costs of a particular transaction they would be the allocated proportion of total costs. It is also tempting to think costs could be determined at a particular point in time, but as we know from the treatment of time in Chapter 2, this is a gross over-simplification. It would neglect the intellectual capital—individual and organizational—being built up that pushes the process down the learning curve. It would also neglect shadow or spillover effects. Learning by producing Product X may lead to changes and cost reductions in the firm's other products. Equally strategic are the results of the market's learning about the firm's ability to produce. Put another way, if the make-or-buy decision is computable, the costs considered are unlikely to include the impact of learning-by-doing. Note the proper comparison of the costs would also include allocations (perhaps through taxes) to cover the social costs of the transaction, the costs of setting up and operating the legal system that makes the contracts valid and enforceable.

The interpretation of a bid by another supplier across the market is no less troublesome. Does this supplier know his costs in ways we cannot? The answer may seem to be "Who cares just as long as the deliveries are up to spec? Do I care if he drives himself out of business?" Perhaps yes. The supplier may be taking a loss now in the hope of gaining more business later—or otherwise making a strategic judgment about how to price, a strategy that differs from ours and therefore opens up indeterminacy between his strategy and ours. At the same time the focal firm's interpretation of its own cost is no more than an aspect of its own strategy. Economists may be blind to the nature of strategic judgment and presume maximization—but of what? Perhaps management wants to get into a new line of business and creatively reduces the cost figures presented to the board. There are endless permutations as two firms' strategies interact, forming a field of contractual indeterminacies only negotiated with judgment. Behind this lies the suspicion that such costs are, in principle, never determinable because of the penetration of Knightian uncertainty into both the firm's and the market's affairs. In the real world it is never possible to do more than estimate them—make a judgment. The make-or-buy decision seems simple and computable but in practice always turns on judgments and estimations rather than computation alone.

The TCE discourse ranges far beyond holdup, contracting, and information costs. It (a) embraces the real-world imperfections that interfere with a purely economic analysis, and (b) appeals to non-price modes of coordination of both resources and people. Williamson, who received a Nobel Prize for his work on this topic, is often credited with opening up the discussion of governance and relating it to the previous cost-based economic resource allocation discussion. When the firm decides to buy it makes a contract with a supplier and is exposed to more than just an invoice. The perfect market "spot" timeless contract means the strategists need pay no attention to either past or future. In their place are "real" contracts, typically "time-full" and "incomplete," leaving many matters to be determined later including, perhaps, enforcement. These can become "imperfections" through which strategic questions enter, especially around time. For instance, the pricing that leads to a contract is shaped by the relatively large number of suppliers in the market of those able to bid on the contract being offered. But once the contract is drawn up and signed the situation changes—Williamson called it the "fundamental transformation"—because both sides now deal with specific partners (small numbers) and are open to non-pricing behaviors (and power plays) that might have a material impact on the conduct of the contract. This may happen because of irreversibilities associated with getting the contract. For instance, bidding to build a major bridge it is an expensive business for an architectural/engineering practice. There may be a competition, in which case it may seem a good strategy to spend lavishly on preparing the strongest possible bid—and, perhaps, "looking after" those who evaluate the bid.

The contractor's spending cuts two ways when the actor (contractee) for whom the bid is prepared is not covering the cost of the bid work. First, the out of pocket: a small practice might not have the funds required to prepare a bid, no matter how superb and competitive its content. Thus the competition mechanism is constrained and far from perfect. Second, the spending exposes the successful bidder to post-contract pressure from the contractee (recipient) to reduce bid price further, often by reducing their fee. This is a holdup. Any non-spot arrangement between firms, as well as within them, is open to either partner's "opportunism." For instance, some key workers in the contracting firm might see the contract's signing as an opportunity to strike for a bigger share of the proceeds. Commitment adds "imperfections" and irreversibilities that, somewhat like transactions costs, mean the subsequent relations are far from as "perfect" as those of the market in which the contract was first mooted. When the contract obliges the contractor to make significant investments in equipment or some other expense that cannot be easily recovered outside the contract in question, commitment leads to "asset-specificity." Sometimes the risks can be managed more equitably by reallocating the ownership of the property for which funds were expended. For instance, the contract may specify that the contractee must pay a portion of the contractor's capital outlays if the contract is terminated before the final period. In principle the property-rights approach can be extended to intellectual capital such as patents, R&D findings, and, perhaps, to any learning or work that has taken place. If the research consultancy does work for Client A then the consultancy retains a measure of ownership of the results if the contract is terminated early. The non-rivalrous nature of intangible assets makes this tricky. But the property-rights discussion can also provide a reason for the firm's existence. When the way the value-chain adds value is unclear and it is not possible to identify individual contributions, as is common in team or collaborative activity, it is not easy to reward the workers or contractors proportionately. The firm can then be the legal and administrative entity in which the residual value remaining after the workers have been paid is carried forward to the next time-periods.

Without getting into it any deeper we see TCE embraces at least two distinct discourses that call for strategic judgments of different types—(a) comparative cost assessment and (b) people management. Effective accounting can support the cost assessments but ultimately they will turn on what has been learned and what might be learned in the future, and how that intellectual capital might translate into revenue. People management means understanding how contracts work in practice and then judgments about choosing appropriate modes of governance, including the issues covered by PAT. TCE brings the people concerns of PAT together with microeconomics' traditional resource-based concerns in a rich way. But it is weak in that it is a bundle of concepts that do not finally come together into a rigorous deterministic theory. It is incoherent as it stands on several mutually exclusive axioms. In contrast to PAT, which is relatively clear, the TCE discussion is less so, and it is difficult to see the nature of the strategic judgments required to hold the TCE-model-firm together. If full rationality and perfect market conditions applied, then it would be possible to bring it all together into a rigorous solution—but then there would be no reason for the firm to exist. Economists are optimistic these concepts can be clarified sufficiently to build a rigorous relationship between them. But until that happens the choice situation exhibits substantial incommensurabilities that must be resolved by the participants' strategic judgment. While PAT emphasizes imperfections associated with indeterminacy (between people), TCE emphasizes the imperfections associated with the incommensurability—that rise markedly when the contract has been signed and opportunism and holdup become possible.

TCE focuses on "the representative transaction" while PAT focuses on what might be labeled the "representative relationship." Both suggest answers to Coasian questions about why firms exist or, conversely, indicate the kinds of strategic judgment required to bring a firm into existence. The PAT relationship it is typically "incomplete" and may be managed better within the firm because the employment contract, with its specific subordination of the employee to the boss, can provide the necessary longer term stability. Coase suggested employees might be those attracted by stability and wish to "insure" themselves against the market's uncertainty, clearly a matter of judgment on their part since the consequences cannot be foretold. The contract entails a specific sense of the time during which employees judge the entrepreneur's offer acceptable, when they give up a measure of their independence or free agency. Note this does little to explain why the entrepreneur makes them the offer. If it is in anticipation of making a profit—at some time in the future—the explanation for the firm's existence cannot be complete until it includes an explanation of how the employee's subordination translates into profit in that time. Equally the make-or-buy analysis compares transaction costs in two areas, and this cannot happen before the firm is in existence to incur the costs estimated. To argue the entrepreneur can anticipate favorable costing, and set up a firm on that expectation, is to move the analysis back one step to the justification for the expected costing—surely a previous firm. Ultimately the modes of governance available to managers to control others' opportunism in the TCE analysis are the same monitoring and incentive mechanisms discussed in PAT. These can be formalized into four principles of contract design—informativeness, incentive-intensity, monitoring intensity, and equal compensation—that complement the principles of administration.[13]

Overall the PAT and TCE discourses successfully open up the "black box" of the neoclassical production function. They deal with matters that are central to practical strategic work under uncertainty—knowledgeable individuals who may not be measurable or trustworthy, instruction, signaling, incentives, interests, contracts that are open-ended and incomplete, the passage of time, and property and its ownership. But they have failed to provide the coherent "theory of the firm" microeconomists seek as they surface many aspects of the strategic judgments necessary to bring the firm to life. Some judgments relate to relationships with other people—Knight argued these were the most crucial (strategic), as did Barnard. Other judgments relate to resource evaluation and allocation. PAT introduces divergence of actors' interest. The strategist's response is to consider monitoring and incentives. But since these can never be determining, the strategist must also allow time to pass so that mutual learning and trust can develop. TCE introduces purchase, production, and governance costing. It also pays attention to Coase's interest in corporate law, social costs, and the legal constraints to private sector business. The strategist can choose from a panoply of contracting techniques while evaluating the present value of learning, spillovers, and opportunism to arrive at a choice. Many of these analyses are axiomatically distinct, so call for strategic judgment to resolve the resulting incommensurabilities. While Knight and Coase disagreed on many matters, they shared an intuition that firms would not exist if markets were perfect and the actors' information complete; conversely that the nature of the firm is tied up with the ways in which markets are imperfect and actors are uncertain. Coase, not especially interested in uncertainty or strategic judgment, may have felt a better understanding of corporate law would advance the analysis, moving towards a final theory of the firm. Knight, in contrast, doubted the possibility of a deterministic conclusion and looked to strategic judgment as an art form whose practice could never be avoided even if it was ignored.[14]

---

[13] P. Milgrom and J. Roberts (1992) *Economics, Organization and Management.* Englewood Cliffs, NJ: Prentice-Hall.

[14] F. H. Knight (1923) 'Business Management: Science or Art?', *Journal of Business*, 2(4), 5–24.

## 3.4 Horizontal and Vertical Integration[15]

Horizontal and vertical integration seem to be extensions of the internal division of labor and its coordination—already covered in section 3.1. But it is worth dwelling briefly on the judgments required to implement them. Their premises revolve around the aggregation and disaggregation of the firm's value-adding practices—to their modularization into subsidiary companies or divisions or work units or whatever seems to be the most functional choice of elements to be connected, reshuffled, and perhaps bought and sold through merger or acquisition. Most firms, to use Simon's terminology (section 3.1), are "partially decomposed" into different levels of activity as well as value-chain modules.[16] Simon assumed the way operations are most usefully modularized manifests an internal logic rather than management's decisions; thus brick-making gets split up into shipping clay, preparing the molten mix, molding individual bricks, firing them, stacking them on pallets, shipping the pallets, and so on—different logics at each step. There is not much management can do about these stages because they are set by the materials, their properties, and the production process. In practice the boundaries around each module and between layers change constantly under the impetus of learning within the production unit, between production units, and among the players implied, for instance, in Porter's 5-force model (section 2.6). Much of the learning will be technological, part of the long-run trend that leads to increasing productivity. Much will be administrative as new modes of management and governance percolate. Many of these changes overlap, especially as better communications technologies improve administrative, marketing, and organizational efficiency, and force management to revisit their boundary-setting make-or-buy decisions. Outsourcing, sale-and-lease-back, customer financing, new financial instruments, and open innovation are among recently popularized maneuvers illustrating the dynamism of the strategizing about both relationships and resource allocation.

At all times the decision-making logic may seem to rest on cost minimization, especially transaction cost reduction. But this does not work well when Knightian uncertainty renders the situation non-computable. Strategic judgment is called for and many issues other than cost will enter in—the business risks of holdup, of the supplier going out of business or being acquired by a hostile competitor, of substitute products, and so on. What is computable may

---

[15] R. M. Grant is especially good on this topic: (2010) *Contemporary Strategic Analysis* (7th edn). Chichester: John Wiley & Sons.
[16] H. A. Simon (1973) 'The Organization of Complex Systems', in H. Pattee (ed.), *Hierarchy Theory: The Challenge of Complex Systems*. New York: George Braziller, pp. 3–27.

well be important, but eventually it must be synthesized with what is not computable. Along the lines of "follow the money," following the rent-streams generally leads to a good analysis. A classic example was Standard Oil's control of "downstream" oil transportation and refining. This enabled them to keep competing oil producers out of the market and transfer the monopolistic power gathered at one point in the circular flow of their business to other points more vulnerable to competition. Today Apple's app-policing and control of iTunes enables them to sustain the rents to be earned from elsewhere in their OSX/IOS "ecology." Zara's tight integration of design, manufacturing, and retailing enables them to maintain the rapid rate of product turnover that is at the core of their business model.

There have been many developments of private sector business relationship and resource allocation governance in recent years, often in response to changing legislation and regulation. Some have been credited with having a major impact on "clusters" of regional competitiveness, the Silicon Valley and Route 128 phenomena or the Italian Emilia-Romagna textile region. The drivers are not easily identified for they may be more to do with the complex social networks that exist in a region that lead to what Marshall called "the trade know-how that was in the air." As the strategists look out at their environment, their firm is at the center of a network of value-creating relations that span from the individual work roles within the firm, where the operative's judgment is projected into the knowledge absences of practice, through the vertical and horizontal relationships that are not likely to add value in themselves, to the peripheral others' judgments, culture, and tacit knowledge. The network is dynamic, so the firm can draw on, and perhaps help sustain, the wider regional and national economy—a tree with a vast complex root-system.[17]

## 3.5 Penrose on the Growth of the Firm

Penrose's theorizing is crucial to my argument and has been mentioned already. It draws attention to learning at the level of the firm, and to two other matters ignored in much of the strategy literature—tacit knowing and strategic time. She remarked that, as far as she knew, no economist had yet attempted a general theory of the growth of firms, and the absence seemed of some concern.[18] My argument, that profit and growth result from the exercise

---

[17] S. G. Checkland (1976) *The Upas Tree: Glasgow 1875–1975. A Study in Growth and Contraction.* Glasgow: University of Glasgow Press.

[18] E. T. Penrose (1995) *The Theory of the Growth of the Firm* (3rd edn). New York: Oxford University Press.

of entrepreneurial judgment in skillful practices that engage Knightian uncertainty, simply restates Penrose, though it elaborates on some aspects of her work while overlooking others. From the strategist's point of view it is crucial to appreciate how Penrose's analysis sets out by distinguishing two kinds of knowledge—which she labeled "objective knowledge" and "experience," corresponding more or less to explicit and tacit knowing. The second destabilized the conventional microeconomic notion of resource. She separated the notion of a resource available in the market from the services it might supply the firm—because a resource's value to the firm depends on someone knowing how to use it. A resource has no necessary value to the firm, so a resource-based analysis is fundamentally flawed. A resource's value is always mediated by some person's knowledge of how to deploy it. This might also be thought of as changing the meaning (and value) of the firm's resources, especially under Knightian uncertainty. It also implies the firm is a dynamic (evolving) universe of knowledge, discourse, and skilled activity (data, meaning, and practice). But not all of the firm's knowledge is ever "in play." The firm always "knows more than it is doing." Thus the incentives to expand are two-fold: first, to put retained profits to good use; second, and more important to Penrose's analysis, to put unapplied knowledge to work. The first reason assumes resources as universal (liquid, readily transferred); the second that their value is context-specific. The drive to apply the second springs from their having little alternative or comparable use, while the retained profits are liquid and might be used to invest in quite different activities. Penrose's division of knowledge types clarifies the strategist's task and room for maneuver.

Her notion of strategic time arises because doing is not the same as learning by doing. *Inter alia* there must be some time differences between the practices that generate the learning and those that apply it remodeled. Anticipating Nonaka and Takeuchi (section 2.10) she saw a knowledge cycle running within the management team between time $T_1$ when it initiates a new practice and time $T_2$ when it applies the new learning to subsequent practice. Nonaka and Takeuchi's knowledge cycle runs in a different way and on a different time-base, between the firm's shop floor and R&D operations and its senior management. Penrose's strategic time has different implications. The interplay of setting up a new process, whether to generate a product or a service, and putting it into motion with irreversibly expended resources, and then learning from what happens implies a different time-based granularity or modularity. The processes of doing, learning, and changing the doing cannot be continuous; processes, such as the process of innovation, tend to be serial, despite management's hopes to have them overlapping and accelerated.

## 3.6 Resource- and Capabilities-Based Views

The resource-based view (RBV) is included here because of its popularity among business school academics sympathetic to a microeconomic approach to strategizing. But it is not clear it provides working strategists much insight into their task. The RBV focuses on resources and not on people, so missing the synthesis discussed in this chapter's earlier sections, and it misses Penrose's critique of resources. Notwithstanding, it has wide appeal in that it suggests competitive advantage flows from the possession of valuable, rare, inimitable, and organizational (VRIO) resources that can be integrated into the BM, such as a patent or drilling rights, or a unique craft skill like Red Adair's putting out well-head fires. It does not deal with how VRIO resources are acquired at a cost that lets their possession and deployment lead to profit, nor whether the production process simply extracts the value inhering in the resources acquired or adds to it. The RBV's fundamental intuition is about the heterogeneity of the firm's resources and an implicit relationship between competitive advantage and the resources possessed.[19] Note the firm is presumed to exist and possess these resources; the discussion is not about creating it—or them. It is unfortunate many of those writing about the RBV claim Penrose as a forerunner since her views differ markedly from theirs. Most egregiously, while Penrose's theorizing stands on problematizing the notion of resource, most RBV writers' views of resource are neoclassical—possession is everything, deployment is based on objective analysis, and use is presumed unproblematic. Yet Penrose's attack on the neoclassical notion of resource is what makes firm growth (and her theory) possible. Her analysis was of the continuous creation and regeneration of the management team's knowledge, thus about the firm as a growing corpus of practical knowing rather than of tangible resources possessed and listed, perhaps, on the balance sheet. Hence it is difficult for those following the RBV to break out of its implicit tautology around valuing resources—they know a resource is valuable because it generates a rent, but we have no other way of valuing it.

The neoclassical view of economic value often adds confusion by differentiating cost, use-value, and market value. The bridge between cost and use-value is the theory of the firm that shows how inputs are transformed into outputs. Absent such a theory business people are as vexed about the value of their resources as about whether they possess them or not. Penrose pointed towards this by suggesting the firm as a coordinated "bundle of resources." It is difficult to determine the portion of profit realized that might be attributed to any one resource. What is the value of an expensive machine that is only

[19] J. Kraaijenbrink, J.-C. Spender, and A. Groen (2010) 'The Resource-Based View: A Review and Assessment of its Critiques', *Journal of Management*, 36(1), 349–72.

being used part of the time (one shift) when it could be used for three shifts? Other complications are created by indivisibilities, you may not be able to half-buy a machine or half-hire a person. If we take Adam Smith's notion of the enterprise as compounding land, labor, and capital their cost might seem plain, but estimating their use-value or contribution to the outcome is more complicated. As I suggested earlier, the use-value of a resource can only be discovered when viewed through prism of the firm's business model, the strategist's view rather than the accountant's. If RBV writers were to provide a theory of the firm through which to view the resources central to their analysis, to help the strategist discover their use-value, the confusion might be lessened. In the classroom it is easy to declare Coca-Cola's syrup recipe, Standard Oil's drilling rights, or Dolby's patents "obviously" crucial to their rent-streams, but it is quite another thing to explain their acquisition or the BM that translates them into profit. Of course, this explanation would be a resource-based definition of the strategic work to be done—noting the heterogeneity of the relevant resources. But it would not work well if it was blind to the heterogeneity of the people skills involved. In short, while PAT, TCE, and value-chain are potential theories of the firm, it is difficult to see the RBV this way.

This is more than academic bickering, for my book's focus is on strategic work and how this is illuminated by current theories about firms and competitive advantage—and the RBV is the leading academic theory whatever its weaknesses. My book stands on the pervasiveness of Knightian uncertainty and argues the RBV pays it no attention—something others may well dispute. The point of listing all the tools and economic models (Chapters 2 and 3) that are now available is to show how and where Knightian uncertainty renders them open-ended and incomplete, calling for situationally framed strategic judgment. There can be no judgment "in general" for it is always intentional, towards some specific situation, and personal, expressing the individual. As each of the tools or theories considered is exposed to or "deconstructed" by Knightian uncertainty, it opens up a spaces for strategic judgment. The tightness of the RBV's tautology does not allow this. The theory's extension into "dynamic capabilities" (DCs) does not help much either. DCs are defined as "the firm's ability to integrate, build, and reconfigure internal and external competences to address rapidly changing environments," which seems to be resource by another name, a resource with the capacity to create other resources—perhaps even itself. It is not clear how this magic differs from "imagination" or "judgment," except that it is attributed to firms rather than to individuals. Again it is not clear how firms can acquire DCs under terms that allow them to generate rents. How a firm is able to transform them into profits—and their relevance to resources and knowledge—is also unclear. Instead of DCs being the firm's basic building block, they seem to be more like resources possessed, so standing apart from the firm. But the emphasis is clearly on organizational learning, which makes intuitive sense because firms are generally able to change and adapt. But this means the nature of DCs hinges on the relevant theory of the firm rather than the other way around. Is what has been learned a resource like any other resource or knowledge embodiment—a patent or a machine—or something different, and what are the managerial and strategic implications of the difference? And what of Penrose's notion of unapplied knowledge as the driver of growth?

Penrose's distinction between objective knowledge and the fruits of managerial experience opens up her analysis and advances it sufficiently to provide her theory of growth. A deeper question is why the costs of learning—of any type—do not wipe out its benefits just as the cost of additional production wipes out some or all of the revenue resulting. Knowledge is not free, especially in a Coasian world of non-zero transaction costs. Penrose's is a theory of the firm as a complex of modes of knowing and learning. It is not a theory of the firm as a bundle of consumable economic resources, though many cite her seeming statement to that effect—overlooking her earlier destabilization of the notion of resource into at least two different types, one extensible and non-rivalrous, the other neoclassical and not. Hers is a theory of the firm as a people-based apparatus for generating and applying knowledge, with the knowing mediating all neoclassical economic resources into the services they provide the firm, not as a resource-based model. Thus neither the RBV nor the DC literatures cross the methodological bridge from neoclassical notions of economic resources to Penrose's subjective notions of the services people help the resources provide.

Organizational learning is key to understanding strategizing as a dynamic time-full practice. Instead of thinking of a strategy as a one-time answer to "What do we do now?" it implies an entity that can continue to learn as it moves through time in an ever-changing context. But what learns—a firm, its people, the market? Much of the organizational learning literature is based on "adaptation," the idea that the firm finds it is unable to meet its goals and adapts itself through internal change to perform better. This is the dynamic version of the EIF paradigm and was informed by the work of Ashby[20] and others on early forms of machine intelligence. It was based on control-systems theory and led to the distinction between single-loop and double-loop learning—the latter like resetting the thermostat that in its first-loop mode controls the room temperature already set. The analysis is engineering-based and presumes there are data sufficient to determine the adaption process unambiguously. It has little relevance to the challenges around choice or

---

[20] W. Ross Ashby (1956) *An Introduction to Cybernetics.* New York: John Wiley & Sons.

action under uncertainty. More interesting is organizational learning that is "proactive," for this is clearly strategic, implying that the learning results from some projection of strategic inputs into situations otherwise under-determined. There is not much literature here because it is not easy to theorize the nature of an entity that can both know and generate strategic inputs. The archetype here, of course, is Man himself and his "human agency," his evident capacity to change the world as well as learn about it. But we do not yet know how such agentic acts of imagination and intention work. So we make assumptions. Rational Man is fine and can "know" in his particular way—how to compute— but he cannot be "agentic" and generate change. He may not be able to learn either; he simply computes the data supplied. So I axiomatize "proactive Man" with capacities of both reasoning and judging. This problematizes the nature of learning since it carries the analysis beyond the learning that reduces our ignorance of a knowable world. It specifically embraces imagination, the capacity to go beyond what is known.

Any discussion of people or firms as knowing and learning entities requires clarification about who or what learns, and how, and the nature of what is learned. Much of the organizational literature presumes firms can know and learn. I find this curious. One version arises when the firm is seen as a "program," a set of instructions for transforming inputs (factors of production) into outputs (goods and services). A bureaucracy is similar to a computer program, an organized set of processing instructions. In some cases these can be built into an expert system, and much business process re-engineering and ERP design follows this line. The firm's knowledge is the program generated and "firm learning" can be measured by its change. Note this places the system's designer outside the organization—which is her/his "artifact" just as a program is the programmer's artifact. By keeping the alert designer in mind, the agent who is observing what is happening, assessing organizational performance, and adapting the program accordingly, the analysis can be made reasonably dynamic.

Unfortunately this stylization has some fundamental flaws, especially those associated with the term "group think"; the point being that the program also sets specific boundaries to the data that it can admit, so it rejects data that do not match what was expected. This excises surprise. Human beings, in contrast, have a capacity to be surprised and aware of much that they cannot make sense of—leading some to conclude that machines will never be able to do the things we can do.[21] Programmed machines are vulnerable to surprise, to any unanticipated changes in the firm's environment or process that have not been anticipated by the programmer and built into the program as branch

---

[21] H. L. Dreyfus (1992) *What Computers Still Can't Do: A Critique of Artificial Reason*. Cambridge, MA: MIT Press.

points. The possibility of being surprised is the source of the strategists' doubt and anxiety and of the perennial businessperson's question, "What does it mean for us?" Maybe learning is something that firms (programs) cannot do, and it only happens to humans. Then the firm-as-program learns only as the programmer transforms her/his learning into new rules. In such circumstances the programmer becomes the strategist—but what programming rules or language should be adopted? In this sense, my book is a manual for those managers "programming" firms in contexts marked by Knightian uncertainty. The initial challenges—which my book addresses—are to choose (*a*) the program's parameters, and (*b*) the programming language.

## 3.7 Evolution and Self-Regulation

If the capacity for strategizing is to be brought within the firm rather than left beyond analysis, a different model or metaphor is required. Recall Simon's warning that there is nothing so crucial to the analysis as the choice of the model of the individual. The question is whether there is any model of the firm other than that of a system whose rules are changed by a programmer (or board)? Put differently, are there non-mechanical entities that might offer a workable metaphor for the firm? Since Herbert Spencer's popularization of Darwin's evolutionary notions and the attempts to apply them to social and economic affairs, the most widespread alternatives have relied on biological notions—the firm as an organic entity. Penrose famously cautioned against these on the grounds that biological analogies ignored the distinction between human beings, who had a degree of free will and made "real" choices, and systems, mechanical or biological, whose mechanisms were causally determining and so were not open to the human processes of judging.[22]

When the Darwinian model is used the change is intergenerational and general, at the species level because the environmental change impacts the species' reproductive mechanisms—in contrast to the Lamarckian view of "soft inheritance" that presumes a particular organism can change during its lifetime and pass the changes to its offspring. Given the view of the firm as an "unnatural" person who is not a prisoner of a biological life cycle (having no necessary death) the Lamarckian model seems more relevant, but it is not clear whether the "offspring" is the changed firm (what the specific firm changes into) or some new firm. No doubt that there is a great deal of imitation in business, indeed franchising exploits this directly by propagating a specific business model. But is it useful to put this idea into an evolutionary framework?

---

[22] E. T. Penrose (1952) 'Biological Analogies in the Theory of the Firm—I', *American Economic Review*, 42(5), 804–19.

Is anything added over presuming it to be a version of the EIF paradigm, change controlled by the strategist? The singular appeal of evolutionary approaches to business lies in the way they open up middle ground between the positions that have been explored so far in my book: determinism (causal theorizing) and entrepreneurial judging (because Knightian uncertainty makes causal approaches inconclusive and gives us a degree of agency). The strategist is the source of judgment—perhaps softened to "the strategist and the others who engaged in the strategic conversation that led the strategist to her/his conclusion." I have not yet focused on middle ground between the positions. The main reason to do so is that it points to what the strategist cannot control or theorize as determined—but may regard as strategically important nonetheless as s/he exercises judgment.

"Command and control" presumes things only happen because management has decided to make them happen. This is so obviously not the case in any real business situation that it is laughable (or tragic) that so many business people and academics still embrace it as an appropriate metaphor for what managers do. The problem, of course, is to identify an alternative that leaves management with a non-trivial role; if they are not in control, who is? Do they matter? A notable group of academics (population ecologists) suggest management's role is minimal; at best they are the instruments of market-driven evolutionary selection as the better companies drive their lesser brethren out of business. This puts the market, the law, or some other social institution "in control." The market suggestion is comfortable for neoclassical economists— and one of the reasons why economists have long flirted with evolutionary ideas—seeing the market as an economic version of Nature. But Nature has secrets, perfect markets do not. The market becomes transparent when it is perfect. It has no characteristics other than being perfectly competitive in that every buyer and every seller has full information and the market clears instantly. The market does not really exist analytically until it suffers imperfections. When a market "evolves" it is because of the impact of some unknown determining logic that shapes the only characteristics it has—its imperfections. For instance, fashion changes because many people are both self-conscious and fretful and easily bored by what they are wearing. Fashion evolves, but what is the evolving entity—society, individuals, the clothes-making industry, taste? The imperfection here is that this evolution cannot be predicted, an information or judgment asymmetry that hinders perfect competition, but provides imaginative designers an edge that can lead to rents. Likewise the law evolves, but is it its practice or its statutes? Few would argue its progression is predictable, whatever their hopes.

Evolutionary approaches enable the analyst to hand the strategic initiative to a non-human entity—something or someone other than the management or the strategist. But this move only works when the entity in question has definable characteristics—in fashion's case perhaps the speed with which the market evolves. It is essential to keep timing in mind. Clothes designers often work on an annual cycle reflecting the differences between the seasons—Nature's cycle. Apple has taken to releasing new iPhone models in autumn, perhaps with Christmas sales in mind. Evolutionary explanations are held in place by a specific notion of time. Darwinian time is set by the species' reproductive cycle. Lamarckian time is set by the organism's own change cycle and it is not clear how traits acquired are passed on—genetically, by instruction, by imitation (another mode of learning). If time is left unspecified the result of handing over the initiative remains puzzling—the commanding entity is going to do something, but when? Firms are often thought to have a life cycle, but how to measure progress along it?

Nelson and Winter offered an ambitious evolutionary treatment of firm evolution as opposed to market evolution, yet did not specify their model's time-base.[23] Their proposal presumed the organization was somewhat like a bureaucracy in being a rule-system, though they dubbed the rules "organizational routines." Their evolutionary model was somewhat Darwinian—variation, selection, and retention—but more Lamarckian in that the firm was able to change as its constituent parts evolved, without dying and reproducing. Again, there was no theory of the firm, how many or which organizational routines constituted a firm, which evolved and which did not, how they were translated into gain. The variation mechanism was that variations arise all over the firm as operatives intentionally or accidentally deviate from the previous routines. Management, paying attention to the market, then selected, indicating improvements, making them felt through competition, external, or managerially, internal. Management chooses which routines to retain. Aside from the lack of a time-base, though the firm's managers probably have a good intuition of how quickly the firm's routines can be changed, the analysis suffers from the problems Penrose pointed out. In as much as the market drives the selection process it looks as if the strategist's judgment has been excised. In practice, of course, the firm's performance derives from the interaction and integration of a large number (bundle) of routines—and contextual happenstances too. When performance is analyzed it is seldom possible—except when things go wildly out of kilter—to establish a particular organizational routine or contextual event as the cause. So the market cannot provide definitive information about which routines are improvements and which not without resolving the uncertainties around (*a*) how a specific routine impacts the firm's overall performance, and (*b*) how markets will change in the future. As Penrose pointed out, the most serious questions

---

[23] R. R. Nelson and S. G. Winter (1982) *An Evolutionary Theory of Economic Change*. Cambridge, MA: Belknap Press.

about evolutionary approaches are not only whether human judgment is required to deal with uncertainty and whether the strategist retains a pivotal role because of Knightian uncertainty. Rather it is with the notion of agency and the intentional activity that follows from pursuing a goal. There seems to be no place for agency in Nelson and Winter's evolutionary model.

Even without identifying the time-base of the entity considered "in control," working strategists can learn something useful from evolutionary approaches. First, even when their own control is supplemented by their judgment, they are never able to achieve full control and thus able to predict the outcome of the firm's practice. Full control is an inappropriate aesthetic for the strategist; husbandry, mediating and shaping the creative work of others, is a more appropriate metaphor. When our rationality and knowledge is bounded it is because we are not sole actors in the situation. Some other actors may work against us directly, inducing indeterminacy. Others may find the firm intruding into their space and push back—local resistance to gas drilling or Wall St resistance to operationalizing the Dodd-Frank Act. When the pushback is not part of a conscious plan but seems to be an unintended consequence it can be explored by analyzing the "self-organizing" properties of the entities reacting. Crowd psychology—and crowdsourcing—explores this; just as economists are interested in "externalities." More formal analyses arise through "small world" phenomena,[24] and the strategist can analyze the constraints to her/his options space more dynamically, not only those already present at time $T_1$ but also those that arise at $T_2$, after action has begun.

## 3.8 Entrepreneurship Theory

Business school students seem increasingly hungry for courses in entrepreneurship. Some schools have labeled themselves specialists, distinguishing themselves from schools that specialize in marketing, finance, industrial production, IT, and so on. The entrepreneur has become a modern folk hero, endlessly lauded in magazines such as *Inc.* and *Forbes*, and the subject of TV programs like *Apprentice*. Even countries claim to be entrepreneurial and innovative—such as Finland. But current entrepreneurship writing leaves us far from clear about the topic. Is it about goosing up the current employees' imagination, restructuring the firm to be more open, or choosing rapidly changing markets? Is entrepreneurship the same as strategic work, or leadership? Is it more than preparing a business plan? The oldest tradition in entrepreneurship writing focused on the entrepreneurial person's "traits" for

---

[24] D. J. Watts (2003) *Six Degrees: The Science of a Connected Age.* New York: W. W. Norton & Co.

risk-taking and handling ambiguity—is she is an entrepreneurial person?—or on the attributes of the entrepreneurial firm. Decades of research have failed to identify these characteristics or skills. At the same time a great deal of national and regional economic policy hangs on increasing the activity of private sector entrepreneurs. Today entrepreneurship research has moved away from the entrepreneur her/himself and towards the process of discovering or creating "opportunities" for entrepreneurial activity and seizing them. One assumption, associated with Kirzner,[25] is that entrepreneurs are more "aware" of these and better able to root them out. A complementary line of thought, associated with Schumpeter, is that these opportunities are "created" by the entrepreneur's activity.[26] Dealing with opportunities, discovered or created, is also a managed process that moves the opportunity towards implementation, to gathering the necessary people and resources and "putting them in motion." The resulting analysis focuses on interactions between entrepreneurial individuals or firms and their commercial contexts.

It is not clear whether this way of looking at entrepreneurship is much different from strategy as conventionally framed. The most recent developments have turned from people and firms and their interactions towards deeper consideration of research method—seeking a specific entrepreneurial method. Discovering opportunities that already exist is obviously different from creating them. As soon as we take Knightian uncertainty seriously—my book's premise—the differences do not lie in the opportunities themselves but in the way we think about them—as matters of ignorance of what already exists (data) or as matters of indeterminacy or incommensurability (meaning and/or practice) that await the entrepreneur's/strategist's input. It follows that this entire book stands as a theory or method of entrepreneurship as a practice. At the same time my next two chapters (4 and 5) deal with aspects of entrepreneurial practice that have only just begun to appear in the research literature, with a discussion of entrepreneurship narrative and its part in managing the collaboration of others' entrepreneurial judgment.

## 3.9 Strategy-as-Practice

The strategy-as-practice (s-a-p) initiative is the newest of the strategic models or paradigms considered here. It is a shade academic for this book but worth considering for the way it presents academics' concerns about the strategy

---

[25] Israel M. Kirzner (1999) 'Creativity and/or Alertness: A Reconsideration of the Schumpeterian Entrepreneur', *Review of Austrian Economics*, 11, 5–17.
[26] J. A. Schumpeter (2008) *Capitalism, Socialism, and Democracy* (3rd edn). New York: Harper Perennial.

field's current state. Though it relates to the older "strategy process" tradition, its originators were European academics writing from 1996 on.[27] They sought a more social and practical view of strategizing, and were especially frustrated with dominance of the US abstractions and their irrelevance to everyday managerial practice. S-a-p is marked by the writers' considerable consulting and research experience, as well as their poor opinion of the US literature. First they argued organizations do not "have" strategies, they "do" them, defining strategizing as a dynamic practice. Second, they argued the mainstream strategy literature overemphasized the firm as the object of research attention, with its implication that "strategic" applied only to the firm-level analysis. Individuals throughout the firm engage in strategy-making; firms are not strategizing entities. Getting into the "black box" of the firm, the s-a-p writers saw strategies as arising from the interaction between senior managers providing "organization-level" direction and others (the "organizational community") being directed. The approach is somewhat "micro-foundational" in that it makes individuals central to the analysis. The senior manager–organizational community interaction is also two-way rather than bureaucratically mechanical or subordinating, as in the SECI model (section 2.10). Third, both the organization-level and actor-level practice are constrained and shaped by external "institutional" structures and processes. Fourth, this three-level ontology—for institutions, organizations, and actors are all presumed to be identifiable and theorizable economic entities—is bisected by conceptual or methodological distinctions between content and process at each level.

The analysis is not based on straightforward causal models in the way that much institutional theory suggests organizations are embedded in an institutional "field" and must conform to its dictates—or die. For instance, French cars look very different from German cars for reasons that have little to do with engineering. Perhaps the different cultures and social institutions cause them to look different; perhaps German roads are better, pointing to two different institutional fields—culture and infrastructure. Institutional theorists have argued for four basic models of institutional impact on firms: (*a*) how the firm absorbs norms, values, and rules from its context, (*b*) the socially constructed nature of the firm's context rather than its mechanical or "objective" nature, and likewise the social construction of the firm's internal notions of its critical resources and reputation, (*c*) the emergence or structuration of those distinct and "relatively enduring" systems or patterns of social belief and practice that become increasingly rationalized over time, as our roads are

---

[27] P. Jarzabkowski and A. P. Spee (2009) 'Strategy-as-Practice: A Review and Future Directions for the Field', *International Journal of Management Reviews*, 11(1), 69–95.

increasingly marked with signs to encourage their more efficient and safer use, and (*d*) the emergence or structuration of patterns of social belief and practice whose originating function have more-or-less "passed into the mists of time," like Cape Town's Noon Gun (once a time-setting practice) or serving food from the left (thought to facilitate the right-handed majority).

The s-a-p approach can be distinguished from such institutional theorizing by its attention to three levels and to the bilateral processes between content and process, including the negotiation of systemic or overall order and coherence. It recognizes power relations between individuals, organizations, and institutions, an aspect mostly ignored in the strategy literature except, as in the 5-force model, when the power relations get framed in strategic terms (impacting the firm's rents). Within the organization there are non-economic power relations (organizational politics) that shape the strategizing process, as well as the processes of constructing the entities at all three levels. Notably, the approach is "open" in that it allows for the patterns of order and interaction to emerge rather than being wholly determined, introducing a sense of complementarity between what happens and what was intended, and by whom—the core notion behind the evolutionary approach. Many writers regard the organization's strategy as the emergent pattern of its activity, so shifting the emphasis onto the organization's self-organizing tendencies (section 3.7). Thus s-a-p embraces three distinctly different kinds of organizing—management's directions, the actors' negotiations, unbidden emergent or organic order. This complexity can translate into an aesthetic of impatience at management's inability to achieve complete control or into accepting that strategizing is an ongoing, long-run activity in which little goes precisely to plan.

In addition to being a critique of treating the isolated firm as the sole object of strategic attention and management as a directed top–down planning paradigm, s-a-p is informed by a variety of European ideas that stand against the positivism dominating the US literature—thus s-a-p is a discrete strategic method. Institutional theory derives directly from Max Weber's social and economic theorizing, just as the social and economic approach to power often draws on Karl Marx's work. But, more specifically, the s-a-p analysis of social construction processes reflects the work of Vygotsky and Bourdieu. The first has some connection with the idea that language shapes how we see the world, mentioned in Chapter 1 and the thrust of Chapter 4. Lev Vygotsky (1896–1934) was a Russian developmental theorist and educator who argued social practices (interactions broader than language alone) were the principal means of shaping the personalities of those who grow up in a given community. Education changes people—deeply—perhaps makes them into the social beings they are. The emphasis in Vygotsky's "activity theory" shifts from a society's structure and social institutions and onto social activity as the principal medium of formative influence.[28] Pierre Bourdieu (1930–2002) was a French philosopher and anthropologist interested in the social states or fields in which we live, and their impact on our behavior and thought. He borrowed a Latin word *habitus* to describe this "field." Actors shape and are shaped by their *habitus*, and developing or "doing" strategy implies shaping the *habitus* of others and so directing their activity towards organizational ends.

The language of the s-a-p approach embraces actors, organizations, and social institutions by referring to the distinctions between "practitioners, praxis, and practices." Here the classical distinction between praxis and practices is somewhat up-ended. In s-a-p language "praxis" is the actual doing or instantiation, while "practices" are the ongoing patterns, the inventory of potential praxes the interacting practitioners might draw on to actualize a "praxis" (what happened). A final influence from European philosophy is the s-a-p's attention to historical and strategic time. While the interactions between the entities flow onwards, the s-a-p analysis cuts the phenomena to be analyzed from the ongoing background as "episodes" of interaction. This temporally bounds the phenomena being analyzed. They must also be bounded, of course, by the analyst's choice of actors, organizations, and institutions since the ripples of involvement can reach out endlessly once history is admitted to the analysis—perhaps we need to know about Napoleon's parents in order to analyze Europe's nineteenth-century "praxis"?

From the reader's point of view the s-a-p approach can be used to examine the history of a particular strategy or way of looking at the business situation at three levels and in a particular episode. It enables the analyst to evaluate many influences as well as the idiosyncrasies of the actors involved. But to date s-a-p writers have made little of the essentially historical dimension of its method or of the implications of bringing time into the analysis. In Appendix A, which deals with researching, writing, and teaching cases, I touch on these issues; but we can intuit the compatibility of s-a-p and case analysis. It points to one of the differences between the strategy tools discussed here and in Chapter 2 versus the s-a-p approach. A strategic tool's usefulness lies in how it provides strategists with a way of identifying the opportunity space or *habitus* into which their strategic judgment gets "thrown" as they confront and resolve the uncertainties that the firm has met in the pursuit of its chosen goals. In itself the historical method is not a strategic tool, rather it is a general methodology for creating an illuminating and judgment-shaping narrative. The method is universal, whereas the firm's opportunity space and strategic dilemmas are always particular. Surely Chrysler's history illuminates the firm's strategic problems. Do these grow out of design weakness, turned around

---

[28] R. G. Tharp and R. Gallimore (1988) *Rousing Minds to Life: Teaching, Learning, and Schooling in Social Context.* Cambridge: Cambridge University Press.

under Iacocca, or their inability to achieve the same economies of scale as Ford and GM, or simply misdirected management? History can be revealing, which is why cases are interesting and useful, especially as ways to investigate the language adopted by those engaged in or analyzing Chrysler's strategizing. But the historical narrative is laid onto the events in the narrative, and so can never determine them. However it can highlight the kinds of strategic judgments made in the past and possibly required in the future.

This section is included for the sake of completeness, for this chapter is about the academic contributions to understanding the nature of strategic work and s-a-p is one of our field's most recent "new academic paradigms." Being new, its goals, uses, and weaknesses are not yet quite clear. It may hold interesting possibilities, especially for analyzing differences between the concepts of practice and language that have yet to be clarified. The function of academic work is to chase down these possibilities by looking at a paradigm's methods, assumptions, and range of applicability, to see how they interact with the actor's choices and responsibilities in alternative paradigms. At this point the s-a-p literature has not established its differences, if any, from the conventional case-writing methodologies built up over the past century or more. In Appendix A I emphasize how the mechanics of case-writing require the researcher to adopt a model of the target situation. A case is not a mere recitation of "historical facts," it implies uncovering a historical pattern with a strategic meaning that is "transported" into the present situation.

The debates about how to evaluate and justify the historical approach are ancient challenges for historians, especially as they locate the locus of the historical "impulse" or change.[29] Is history the artifact of "great men" such as Napoleon, or driven by an emerging social structure, just as France transitioned from Empire into Revolution and has now become inured to its post-colonial role in the world? The s-a-p approach admits both kinds of impulse and many others besides. History also provides mechanisms for passing control to another as discussed in section 3.7, becoming something against whom, perhaps, the strategist struggles. The choice of historical impulse, such as the cultural changes that lead German cars to be different from French ones, or the impact of rising literacy on a nation's economic possibilities, becomes the strategic issue around the choice of tool. Our histories tend to overemphasize "great men" (people are interesting) and underemphasize demographics or changes of climate (facts are dull) even though their long-run impact may be greater. Throughout Chapters 2 and 3 I emphasize that the

---

[29] R. G. Collingwood (1994) *The Idea of History* (rev. edn). Oxford: Oxford University Press. J. L. Gaddis (2002) *The Landscape of History: How Historians Map the Past.* Oxford: Oxford University Press. M. MacMillan (2009) *Dangerous Games: The Uses and Abuses of History.* New York: Modern Library.

main reason to list the various tools currently available is to point up the essentially strategic nature of the strategist's choice to use one tool rather than another when there is no rigorous justification for their choice, "no right answer." This is precisely the same choice as faces a historian or case writer: what drives the story they choose to tell?

## 3.10 Summary

This chapter reviews some academic theories of the firm, ways of answering, or beginning to answer, Coase's questions. As yet there are no complete or compelling answers and in this sense the theories offered "fail"—clearly a comment on the state of microeconomics. In spite of this the strategist can learn a great deal from the ways in which these theories fail for they indicate the kind of strategic judgment called for. My method is to turn the theories upside down. Instead of seeing what they prescribe we look for what they leave open. Methodologically I emphasize practice over theory. The academics' objective is proof. The working strategist believes proof is probably unattainable and anyway irrelevant. S/he looks for sufficient confidence to act. Surprise—action's equivalent to doubt—cannot be denied. At the same time action makes no sense unless the situation has time dimensions that also bring the undesirability of inaction into the analysis. Real strategic situations press in on the strategist. Inaction has strategic implications; no pressure, no action.

This chapter's two main lines of academic theorizing turn on (*a*) people or (*b*) resources. Real firms and their strategic challenges embrace and synthesize them. The academic works considered have opened up the firm as an apparatus (black box) of (*a*) interacting people, and (*b*) interacting resources. Even without synthesizing these, no definitive or deterministic models have emerged. A well-developed approach to (*a*) is principal-agent theory (PAT—not "agency theory") and to (*b*) transaction cost economics (TCE). PAT axiomatizes divergence of interest between interacting/collaborating individuals. While monitoring and incentives can shape the consequences for both, not simply the principal, there is no rigorous solution. Time must pass, when strategist's judgments then play into interpreting the actors' experience of working together, developing mutual learning and, maybe, trust. The TCE analysis disaggregates the firm into transactions. It begins with the make-or-buy decisions that relocate the firm's boundaries—one transaction at a time. Given Knightian uncertainty, cost comparisons cannot determine their correct location rigorously. TCE also goes into managing the contracts made to implement make-or-buy decisions. Bridging two problems, TCE stands on mutually incompatible axioms and is riven with uncertainties that threaten its coherence.

**Table 3.1** Summary of terms suggested by the models in Chapters 2 and 3

| Section | Label | Strategic Terms |
|---|---|---|
| 2.1 | SWOT | resources, context, strengths, weaknesses, opportunities, threats |
| 2.2 | Learning & Experience Curve | scale, cumulative output, unit cost, productivity, human capital, project-time, context change |
| 2.3 | Life Cycle | internal evolution, context evolution, firm-time, reinvention, self-organization |
| 2.5 | Break-Even | investment, return, project-time, risk |
| 2.6 | Chandler's theory, Porter's 5 Forces, LCAG | strategy, structure, fit, efficiency, EIF, multi-divisional, multi-market, general managers, functional specialists, centralization economic rents, rivalry, suppliers, customers, new entrants, substitute products, firm-time, cost leadership, differentiation what the firm might do, can do, wants to do, should do |
| 2.7 | Ansoff matrix | current products, current customers, new products, new customers, risk |
| 2.8 | BCG, Bartlett and Ghoshal | investment portfolio, cash cows, question marks, stars, dogs, funds flow globalization, international, multinational, global scale, transnational, local responsiveness |
| 2.9 | Organizational Change | adaptation, single loop learning, double loop learning, unfreezing-refreezing, resistance, inertia, intermittent, episodic |
| 2.10 | Knowledge and K-flow | explicit, tacit, skill, organizational capital, strategic timing |
| 2.11 | Scenario Planning | relevant environment, planning, game theory |
| 2.12 | Culture and Stakeholders | prospector–analyzer–defender–reactor organizational boundary, values, social responsibility |
| 2.13 | Triple Bottom Line | sustainability, ecological responsibility |
| 2.14 | Balanced Scorecard | financial performance, customer response, internal process improvement, learning and growth initiatives |
| 2.15 | Goldratt's Theory of Constraints | goal, focusing, cause, effect, evaporating clouds, consensus |
| 3.1 | Value-Chain | division of labor, decomposition, modularization, coordination, administration, technology |
| 3.2 | Principal-Agent Theory | market failure, principal, agent, monitoring, incentive, mutual learning, trust, bonding, residual loss |
| 3.3 | Transaction Cost Economics | transaction, make-or-buy, comparative costs, modes of governance, hierarchy, fundamental transformation, bounded rationality, uncertainty, information impactedness, small numbers, information cost, holdup, property rights |
| 3.4 | Horizontal and Vertical Integration | horizontal, vertical, integration, cost minimization, risk management, cluster, network |
| 3.5 | Penrose on the Growth of the Firm | resources, services, management team, learning, knowledge, surplus knowledge, firm-time periods, non-rivalrous resources |
| 3.6 | Resource- and Capabilities-Based Views | resource-based view (RBV), VRIO, inimitability, factor markets, heterogeneity, dynamic capabilities, organizational learning |
| 3.7 | Evolution and Self-Regulation | organic, evolutionary economics, biological models, organizational routines, firm-time |
| 3.8 | Entrepreneurship | traits, opportunities, awareness, interaction, process, dynamism, methodology |
| 3.9 | Strategy-as-Practice | historical methods, case methods, institutionalization, process, episode, power relation, emergent order |

Going beyond PAT and TCE the chapter reviews various other academic contributions, notably Penrose's "theory of the growth of the firm," that promise a more dynamic approach to strategizing. Sometimes the dynamic comes from the entrepreneur (strategist), sometimes from the market. Evolutionary theories relocate the source of the dynamic from the market entrepreneurs make towards some other controlling process. Nelson and Winter's theory of evolving organizational routines is a major achievement. Strategy-as-practice, a recent European initiative, loosens the discussion up to include institutions, organizations, and individuals—but may be little more than an argument that strategic analysts should reconsider the historical method. The combination of Chapters 2 and 3 provides managers, consultants, and teachers with a comprehensive set of ways to consider what strategizing means when it is defined as the process of projecting judgment into the knowledge absences chosen (see Table 3.1). But the list is finite and there will be situations in which none of the approaches considered in these chapters seems adequate to grasp the strategist's situation and its possibilities. What then? The next two chapters outline a more general approach to (a) setting up the opportunity space into which the strategist's judgment must be "thrown" (Chapter 4), and (b) engaging the support of those others whose judgment complements the strategist's, making up for her/his judgment-absences (Chapter 5).

# 4

# Building Language and the Business Model

## 4.0 On This Chapter's Method

This chapter crosses the bridge from where most of us begin, lulled into thinking of strategizing as collecting and analyzing the facts of the situation—the approach implied by the previous chapters' models—and heads towards the task of imagining, creating, and occupying the unique space/time situation the firm must inhabit if it is to create added value. At first, adopting one of the models listed in Table 3.1 seems an attractive short cut. But it presumes the facts are (*a*) knowable, (*b*) relevant, and (*c*) available. Yet when relevant facts are available, the added value gets competed away unless the process is structured as both rent-yielding and sustained by non-economic forces. In which event the added value is perhaps more due to those political, cultural, or institutional forces rather than to economic ones; political shenanigans often lead to someone's profit, which is why lobbying is so prevalent. But this book is about the private sector, the market economy, and the economic value that springs from (*p*) occupying a unique knowledge absence and (*q*) demarcating, operationalizing, and "owning" it via the exercise of entrepreneurial judgment.

Democratic capitalism is remarkable for the market-based freedoms it offers entrepreneurs. Twitter's founders sought no political help but intuited an absence, something others eventually realized they wanted, and set about operationalizing and owning the result. Once a firm (more precisely a business model) is transformed into ongoing practice, enacted, and inhabited, it becomes visible to others and may need protection along the lines of Porter's thinking (section 2.6). But there is nothing to protect until value has been created and exposed to the market. Perhaps the practices that created the firm are beyond analysis, pure happenstance. I write a novel without thinking about my reader and it becomes a best-seller, or I mix an energy cola and the rest is history. Accidents happen in business, a chance meeting, finding a new demand. But accidents are seldom beneficial unless anticipated—chance favors the prepared mind. Preparation demands a language in which to think about the context's possibilities, practices, and outcomes. Chapters 2 and 3 present a variety of applicable languages. But adopting another strategist's language means the firm's uniqueness is limited, perhaps no more than a variation on a theme, like a barbershop, rather than something radically innovative, as Facebook was. Imitation limits "scalability."

My method, to study the firm's language as a way of probing its BM's uniqueness and potential, is set against the common idea that all businesses are basically similar and open to being analyzed with some general overarching theory (and rigorous language) of "the firm" or "organizations." To the contrary, the BM's value-creating potential lies precisely in what is not shared or common. Firms are often similar in many respects—implemented under common corporate law or embedded in a single socio-economy. They may share technology or administrative structure. But as Penrose argued (section 3.5) it is not the firm's resources that matter; rather it is the management team's knowledge about how to use them—and this knowledge is the source of firm's idiosyncrasy, profit, and growth.[1] My core proposition is that the firm is a unique human artifact, a particular act of the entrepreneurial imagination, partially reflecting the entrepreneur's cognitive sense of the opportunity but ultimately her/his deeply practical and tacit knowledge, so resistant to rigorous analysis but able to occupy the instant of practice. It is most obviously so when we focus on its operating language, how those in the firm talk about what they are up to. But the BM's value-creating potential is always beyond being fully articulated, especially its capacity for responding opportunistically to the dynamics of knowledge absences. The entrepreneur's creative capabilities lie hidden behind the instantiation of the business model. We can look at Jackson Pollock's paintings for hours without identifying the creativity that flourished in their making. There can be no "explanation" of creativity beyond its arising. Entrepreneurs—and painters—spend a great deal of time and energy thinking and searching out the unique questions (knowledge absences) they want to address with their different practices. They need, first, to create a language capable of grasping the elements they wish to bring into fruitful collision—their identity, intentions, and context. There is nothing mystical about this. It is down-to-earth practical stuff because our

---

[1] E. T. Penrose (1995) *The Theory of the Growth of the Firm* (3rd edn). New York: Oxford University Press.

language is ultimately grounded in our lived situation and its dynamism. We understand things through the impact they have on our practice. We discuss football strategy using language grounded in what we think can be done in practice with players, pitch, ball, and rules.

The first few sections of this chapter extend the previous discussion about the nature of the strategic task. After section 4.4 the attention moves to framing the strategic task as the construction and use of a firm-specific language. Overall this chapter encourages the reader/researcher to pay attention to how business talk is constructed and how business people's talk is the closest we get to understanding their practice—instead of trying to fit their actions into a rigorous model of our construction.

## 4.1 The Strategic Task

In previous chapters I suggested the point of strategic work is to generate a business model (BM) well suited to the firm's particular circumstances. The choices of identity, intention, and context coalesce as the BM is synthesized from the data, meanings, and skilled practices available to the strategist—which is to say that the BM is not merely a "mental map" or "cognitive frame." It is also infused with the relevant practice-based skills, with knowing how to generate purposive action in a particular context, not merely to think about it. Every firm needs—is—its own BM because there is no general theory or universal model to adopt, there is no overarching theory of "the firm" or "how profitable business is done." As soon as strategy theorists admit to a plurality of possibly relevant models, the analysis switches from filling out the prescriptions of a favored model and towards the different task of choosing whichever seems the most useful from among those available—and to adapting it to the specifics of the situation. So teaching strategy should be a two-step process; first (*a*) introduce students to a variety of useful models and then (*b*) help them develop the choosing and construction skills necessary to select, adapt, integrate, articulate, implement—and justify—their choice. The second step may seem unfamiliar because the steps merge as we look at the situation, make a judgment, and then "plunge in with both feet," plus we often have to convince others to help or join us. This is the reality of strategic practice and there is nothing peculiar about it. We build an actionable sense of the situation—and commit. It is construction work of a special and important type, fundamental to managing and value creation—hard and stressful. Talking about it is a form of philosophizing, practical and down-to earth in intent, but philosophizing nonetheless. But the talk never takes precedence over the practice. Practice rules, to be seized and analyzed as best we can with language.

So this chapter explores a more fundamental approach as it abandons the comforting contours and language of the models in Chapters 2 and 3 and heads into the uncharted task of "rolling our own" BM. The final parts of the chapter outline a methodology or practical philosophy for selecting and engaging the knowledge absences on which value creation, profit, and growth depend. As a whole the chapter outlines a way of thinking that may help practicing strategists deal with trying to act mindfully and intentionally with less-than-complete knowledge. Even though the work is not philosophizing in the strict academic sense, its unusual flavor will require some readers to shift gears. There are no silver bullets, simple explanations, formulae, or if–then causal models, no acceptance that things are merely what they seem to be. The world, of course, is not a simple place, we have to work hard to engage it with our minds, and reduce its complexity to the point we can think logically about it and commit to action with some confidence. Actually the philosophizing is not complicated, it is an everyday practice. Doubt is key—we must remain open to the possibility that things are not what they seem, that we have been misinformed, that things will not turn out as expected, that we have to act afresh to keep things headed in the right direction. Behind this is the recognition that the possibility of profit hinges entirely on the interplay of doubt and surprise. The entrepreneur must ultimately find value in a resource its seller does not, just as the natural sciences are driven by dissatisfaction with the current state of knowledge. Information asymmetries feed doubt and make surprise possible. This chapter's methodology takes the reader into the "heart of doubt" whereat the strategic imagination discovers and draws out new value and profit. An analogy might help—through the multidimensioned window framed by our knowledge presences, our imagination reaches into the darkness of our knowledge absences and draws back something profoundly novel that changes our world. Value, profit, and growth are the imagination's artifacts as it engages a framed unknown; they are not the product of rational analysis. Neither are they the product of resources, designs, or logical mechanisms that transform resources into products and services.

Life (and managing) is a situation of persistent doubt and uncertainty—hence the acronym FUD (fear, uncertainty, and doubt). Fear may seem excessive when it comes to business affairs, but if I was wholly invested in a single enterprise I might get the jitters too. U and D are essential states of mind for any strategist with something at stake, with skin in the game. Living with U and D is not easy, so while Chapter 5 is mainly about how the strategist persuades others to jump into her/his pool, I shall also comment on personal preparation for the strategizing task, persuading oneself. Incidentally, this never comes to an end and is as perpetual as the business's life. There is no knowing what surprises lie in wait for us tomorrow—but it can make getting into the office fun too. Strategic work can be draining, for the strategist cannot

147

ever take her/his hands off the wheel. There are no arrow-straight freeways in the business world and the driver's responsibilities for negotiating the bends and bumps cannot be delegated. It is tough for entrepreneurs to take a vacation. Strategizing is more than simply inhabiting the socio-economy. It is a profoundly human, social, political, and mental activity that changes our world. Talking about it presumes the strategist can create some "distance" between the practice and experience of being and the mental activity of "planning" action. Planning presupposes, as noted before, that the lived world is rationally constructed and fact-filled—that the facts relevant and necessary to modeling the actor's clearly known objective can be gathered unambiguously, and a logical and controllable model or path discovered that connects the present situation with the end desired. This is all very well, but it shuts out the strategist's judgment or, more precisely, treats her/him as no more than a passive computer, crunching discovered facts. Strategic work is like this only when we have full information about the situation and our objective—which we never have. As we appreciate the situation is not rationally constructed, not fully describable, and not "computable," we see the strategist's role is active and creative. But this also means there will always be unresolved doubts about what is going on.

This is all rather vague, so how to proceed? Chapter 2 reviewed a number of the non-economic "managerial" models that strategy consultants might use to guide analysis of the particular challenges facing firms. Active judgment is required if one is to select one model rather than another. Whoever is doing the judging considers the situation and determines, for example, whether it is a problem of managing the flow of internal funds—when the BCG matrix might be helpful—or that the risks of the different lines of business comprising the firm's portfolio are what seem most significant and the GE or Ansoff matrices might get closer to the situation's options. Chapter 3 reviewed some of the models suggested by microeconomists and other academics. Perhaps the problem is managing the firm's boundary via make-or-buy decisions, in which case transaction cost analysis might seem appropriate. Or perhaps the moral hazards in the relations between managers and employees are the primary concern, in which case principal-agent theory might be more informative. Or perhaps the political context of the firm is changing and the stakeholder model is useful. These different models call for different kinds of judgment but all offer an opportunity-space that awaits the strategist's judgment input. Which leads to the possibility that there is something general about the models in Chapters 2 and 3 that we might make the basis of a general approach to building BMs—beyond offering the strategist a "space" for her/his judgment? The answer is "yes, there is," but surfacing it is not so easy because it lies in the realm of method. Strategic work is interesting and difficult precisely because it is so demanding of our methodologies for constructing and applying knowledge. It dictates a move from thinking about method as no more than rigorous analysis, the process of fact-gathering, data reduction, and knowledge discovery, towards embracing the different methods of knowledge construction that have non-rigorous imaginative and creative dimensions. This goes beyond the bounds of analysis based on "causal theory" or "model," the conventional idea into which so many of us have been trained—and gets into human creativity as the unpredictable process of adding value to the world, precisely because the collision of identity, intention, and context is not fully determined, is changeable, and concedes our ideas are capable of changing the world. It goes beyond thinking of the reality we inhabit as fixed, unchangeable, and so knowable, the universe of physics as non-physicists understand it (real physics is much more complicated). The constructive aspects of strategic work go beyond what some might call the Newtonian mode of thought, the causal or billiard-ball model of everything that logical analysis presumes.

Strategic work innovates, creating something new that did not exist before, a new fabric perhaps, or an opera or, most importantly, new economic value. New value is not simply the result of better allocation of our scarce resources, moving them to where their value is higher, but results from a transformative act of human imagination, the silk purse made from a sow's ear, a practical demonstration of humans' limitless ingenuity, our universe's limitless transformability, and, most importantly, that our lives are not bounded by Nature's physics. Of course we are within the physical universe and limited by its laws. But what we value is not bounded in this way. We inhabit imaginary universes of our own creation that offer their own kinds of value; art, for instance, where the power of an image or a sequence of sounds cannot be understood as a fact of Nature open to scientific analysis. Likewise economic value cannot be grounded in a logical analysis of our physical needs. Economics is about how we attach value to the products of our imagination, be that a tune, a patent, or a fashion statement. Given our bounded rationality or other "shortcomings" there is no point in trying to find an overarching rigorous theory of strategizing. I cannot prove this, of course; it is just a conjecture. But proof or disproof is not the point. My focus is on the strategic practitioner, not the academic journals. Perhaps somewhere sometime research will uncover the universal always-relevant theory of how to deal with and exploit a situation's economic uncertainties. But current management practice is not covered by theory and has strategic dimensions that lie beyond the grasp of theory. Strategic work is about how to create value in theory's absence or equally about how to avoid being trapped into inconclusiveness and inaction by our knowledge absences, by what we do not know—especially when the situation seems urgent.

The BM eventually chosen or built is a product of the strategist's personal judgment, supported by rigorous analysis as far as is possible, but ultimately more like a painting or a song than a QED or a "scientific result." Artistic judgment is not a matter of chance; you have to learn how to paint or compose music before you can break through what others have done and create something fresh and valuable, or properly judge the innovative work of others. Art is hard work, not accident. Before the strategist can bring judgment to bear s/he must have the intellectual and practical competence to engage the situation without being overwhelmed by or oblivious to its particularities. Then, to extend the artistic metaphor a bit further, we know the BM must be dynamic rather than static, more like a dance or an opera than a painting. Today the term theory generally means a rigorous intellectual construction that can be tested experimentally and unambiguously. Generally we think theory is about "reality," whatever exists that lies beyond and is independent of the theorist's mind. A BM is not at all like this. It is more a small world constructed and then inhabited by the strategist and everyone else having a part to play in an entrepreneurial opera that has no prescribed plot, no known ending, no knowing for sure what is going on, no knowing whether some *deus ex machina* temporarily hidden from the participants will upset everything and fill the situation with surprise. Doubt is probably the best attitude to adopt when inhabiting this scene, taking nothing for granted, with whiskers twitching for the first sign of trouble.

## 4.2 Mise en Place

Chefs learn to prepare for action, collecting pots, sharpening their knives, setting out the recipe's ingredients, heating the oven, and so on. Strategic work is similar—and the tools inventoried in Chapters 2 and 3 can be seen as recipe book entries. But when cooking, process is everything. The result is dominated by the chef's strategic judgments. Just so for the strategist, for a situation never presents as complete and coherent, more as a buzzing booming confusion of experiences, impressions, possibilities, relationships, etc. The first part of strategic work is labeling, distinguishing, and selecting what matters from what does not. There is a chicken and egg problem. When the BM is in place it labels and indicates what matters and what does not—but without it how is the strategist to know for sure? Experience might suggest what matters; that the past shows the appropriate way into the present task. But what about doubt? Maybe this time is different and if we remain bound by experience we cannot cut ourselves free of the past and move forward into a new world changed to make it our own. Sometimes experience is a crutch to be tossed aside if something truly innovative is to happen. Research suggests, for instance, that people who have been entrepreneurs before are more likely to succeed than those trying for the first time. Rather than know what to pay attention to in the new situation, perhaps they know how to cut themselves loose from their assumptions and overcome doubt. Then again, sometimes the old hands get it wrong and youth and inexperience gets its turn. But note also that the strategist is never concerned with averages or statistics but is always focused on succeeding in a particular situation.

Each of the BMs discussed in Chapters 2 and 3—SWOT, BCG, TCE, principal-agent, and so on—has usable components or elements. What do components look like? Can some be used again? Instead of looking for a completely novel BM, "rolling our own," some of these might be recycled as components or axioms with which to construct the new BM. Axioms are the ideas that underpin a discourse. SWOT's axioms are both subtle and flexible—which is why it remains so useful and popular. First, there is the concept of the firm as something that exists, distinct and separable from its environment. While this seems a self-evident truth, a real firm's boundaries are not so obvious, indeed some now talk of the "boundary-less" firm or an "open source network" of value-adding relationships. But note that when the firm is a discrete economic unit, it can possess "things," less clear when it is a network that stretches out to stakeholders and the public affected by the firm's operations. In a capitalist system resource possession is crucial to capturing the value created. We presume the things possessed include assets of tangible and intangible types, such as a factory with some defined production capacity plus the skills hired to work it, or a patent, or a market share, or a reputation. Second, beyond the firm's boundaries lies an "environment" of customers with desires that the firm must engage if it is to do business. It also comprises other firms with capacity similar to the firm's but competitive. Evoking a firm and its environment suggests a complete socio-economy comprised of suppliers, customers, competitors, regulators, corporate lawyers, local communities, and so on. Those in the environment are outside the firm, and thus not under the immediate control of the firm's managers, whereas the firm's resources are—so the firm's boundaries are of at least two types, those of control as well of possession. The components to be drawn into the BM may be both possessed and controlled—but what of those possessed but not controlled, or vice versa? The strategist has to decide what can be usefully drawn into the firm, and what is better left outside, more trouble than it is worth. The task becomes vastly more complicated when the resources in question are people's skills and knowledge. A machine is of no obvious strategic value if there is no one who knows how to operate it. But is an operator's skill a strength the strategist can count on, or a threat precipitated by its withdrawal in a strike? Obviously most BMs presume willing operators, but the strategist's role is to doubt, and to think through the risks of depending on them or on any other resource. Silicon Valley firms are famous for saying their assets "go home in the evening," so the strategist's doubts demand exploring these risks and finding ways of coping. Should the firm introduce an ESOP? Will it lead to confidence that the employees will not leave to set up a rival firm? The component being considered is not merely having an employee on the payroll with a resume that indicates the skills appropriate to the BM, but the full character of engagement that gives the doubting strategist reasonable confidence that the commitment of funds will lead to a satisfactory result.

The richness of democratic capitalism is that there are many hundreds of possible axioms to viable BMs. Chapters 2 and 3 have surfaced a few. Listening to those who make a comfortable living theorizing about business in the security of the classroom, it is easy to forget that business is done in the real world, a place of rampant complexity, competition, and ferocious change, with its own history far different from the theorists'. Few of us really understand enough about the history of capitalism to know how today's situation came to be. Indeed the financial events of 2008 show we do not know enough about how the private sector firm works. It can generate value, yes, but also horrendous social damage. We do know, though, that our capitalism is remarkable for the variety of ways in which business can be done; currency trading, making refrigerators, auto insurance, cruise liners, dogs' homes, haircutting, and on and on—and, no less important, we see business can be done under a wide variety of political systems whose axioms or principles must also enter into the strategists' thinking. Competition is not a necessary condition for value creation. When present it will add indeterminacy and more constraints, but any kind of purposive action under uncertainty calls for judgment and may generate value. Monopolistic firms have their own incentives to innovate. A complete list of possible BM axioms would be a strategist's description of the entire socio-economy, which would still not nail down the dynamism that depends on the entrepreneur's judgment and desire. The strategist puts the firm-level BM creation process into motion just as, as Schumpeter remarked, the entrepreneur puts the capitalist economy into motion.

Strategy researchers are not entrepreneurs, of course, and could usefully begin classifying all the axioms that might seem important to entrepreneurs, chapter headings in the Great Book of Business Knowledge like the *Encyclopédie*, Diderot's 1751 attempt to map the entirety of human knowledge. This way forward presupposes the possibility of understanding everything, that the Great Book can be completed and indexed (Google-able). Business schools put together a mini-version as a "function-oriented" syllabus, presuming a little accounting, together with a touch of organization behavior, human relations, production, and a few finance courses, equips the student to understand how a firm is able to create value. Of course it does not. This way of thinking is the antithesis of the strategist's for the situation's particularities are carefully submerged under the professor's generalities. The strategist focuses on productive value-adding action in a particular situation rather than knowledge *per se*. S/he is more of a *bricoleur*, making use of whatever lies to hand to actualize a personal vision of a changed world—often novel in the idiosyncratic manner of Rube Goldberg or Heath Robinson machines. In the end we only know those aspects of the world that have been brought into our world through practice—instantiations. Our limited ways of knowing (data, meaning, and practice) are always practice-grounded. We never know anything for sure as something "out there" independent of us. Rather, whatever we know is grounded in our doing, what we or others have done or failed to do in the past. The imagination and judgment necessary to constructing the BM begins with what has been learned from experience, with looking around at assets, ideas, research, *objets trouvés*, chance remarks in bars, news items, mold in a petri dish, or the effect of adding sulfur to rubber fluid, people's hunger for interaction, and so on. There is dynamic interplay between the entrepreneur's chosen goal and the activity of collecting the means to reaching it. Sometimes the entrepreneur has to revise or re-vision the objective when the necessary means are not available. It is said the start-ups that survive are those who learned quickest from their experience to let go of the ideas and axioms that attracted them into business in the first place. Amazon began with the intention of selling stuff not for profit but to gather information about its customers, which would then be sold as its real product—then discovered it could monopolize on-line book buying. Rolls-Royce was in autos, forced into aero-engines and then jet engines by UK governments engaging in war, just as it now provides nuclear submarine reactors (on which I worked). Schlumberger began with an electrical well-logging invention, which led to experience with drilling mud, which led to a broader portfolio of oil field services. One thing leads to another as one BM leads to another because all are inherently dynamic and inhabit a changing world populated by other BMs.

There cannot be any universal rules about how to search for and select a BM's axioms. There can be good advice, of course, but that would be based on experience gained in some other situation and it might actually be counterproductive in a new one. But a general knowledge-absence-based method seems imaginable, even if we cannot generalize about the BM's content and process. In the absence of general rules the analysis must begin part-way in at the point at which the entrepreneur/strategist already has a chosen or imagined vision (Q) in mind and has begun gathering up bits and pieces (axioms or elements A through N) that make it possible to define Q. In some instances the entrepreneur can identify some "causes" of the vision, seeing poverty while in the Peace Corps or the effects of resource mismanagement. But the lines are never direct or determining. With Q in mind s/he begins to build the BM as some function of Q and the axioms A–N. She may know about these elements from prior practice, even if that was someone else's practice formalized into some theories or heuristics. They can be understood as constraints to the strategist's agency, ways in which the range of actualize-able possibilities is bounded by forces and circumstances beyond the strategist's control—such as necessary resources not being available. Necessity is often the mother of invention, as problems with the supply of natural rubber led to research in synthetic rubber that eventually succeeded and made natural rubber a sideshow. Concerns about the ozone layer led to a ban on CFC and HCFC refrigerants, and the refrigeration industry was forced to turn to alternatives such as FCs and HFCs, though those too are now suspect. At this stage the aspiring strategist's best preparation may be to look around and observe the elements of the BMs in place for like businesses. This will help him/her grasp the categories to look for, though doubt remains essential. Perhaps there is a quite different way of doing business waiting to be realized, as Freddie Laker reinvented tourist air travel on the basis of his experiences flying the 1948 Berlin Airlift, or as Bezos reimagined book retailing. Every potentially viable BM's elements are already present in the existing situation, even if ignored by most. But their obscurity means the entrepreneur's mind must often "rest on" the challenge if the imagination is to be attracted into action. Imagination is more important than awareness.

The BM is at the point of convergence of the many constraints that arise in the firm's different universes of activity and knowing. Technological changes seem to drive much of business today, though to think that technology ever acts on its own as an innovating "force" is an error. There will always be several constraints acting in concert, plus the imagination or judgment needed to synthesize them into a viable BM. For example, to drive successfully from point X to point Y requires the road be clear, not washed out by floods or rock slides, the auto have sufficient gas, the tires not punctured, the driver to pay sufficient attention to stay on the road, other vehicles avoiding crashing into it, and so on. These are some different constraints to the trip and the strategy for getting to Y must address all those that are relevant. Typically many are ignored, taken for granted, and excluded from strategic consideration. The time of departure may be irrelevant, just as whether or not the driver has a mobile phone. In real business situations there might be legal constraints or technological constraints to the entrepreneur's vision while many infrastructural factors can be taken for granted, noted only when absent as dependable electrical supplies are absent in India. There are almost certainly strategically important customer constraints, defining what they are prepared to buy, likewise supply constraints, and so on.

The list seems endless—but is not. Perhaps five is enough. The 5-force model articulates five categories of strategic constraint relatively clearly—the "force" that suppliers, customers, competitors, and so on can apply, though those from new entrants and substitutes are less clear. The BCG matrix's constraints remain more implicit—for instance the model's presumption of a fixed basket of cash, denying the obvious alternative of borrowing further funds from investors and so breaking out of the model's funds-flow cycle. These categories are illuminating, but the strategist must identify the constraints and knowing the category is only part-way to doing that for a category is general, not specific; a metric, not the thing being measured. How is this synthesizing of elements into a business model to be done? Again we are more or less in the dark. Just as there is no telling an artist how many colors to put on his palette, or how to bring them together to best effect, so there is no telling the entrepreneur how to select and stitch together the items s/he thinks relevant to the BM in order to produce surprise and profit. Just as biologists remain unsure about the nature and components of Nature's most primitive cells, there is a deep mystery about what constitutes the minimal form of a BM and thus the minimum number of elements. Three seems a likely lowest number— land, capital, and labor, perhaps—and there was a mysterious medieval "rule of three." For example, microeconomics presumes a production function (their notion of a BM) synthesized from an integrated demand element, an integrated supply element, and some kind of manageable technology or value- adding process to connect them. The sense of three also comes through in SWOT; external elements, internal elements, and the judgment to fit them together. The number of elements increases as the BM moves closer to being practical. The 5-force model has more than three elements, obviously, just as there are six or more in the BCG matrix—four investment possibilities, the cash that flows between them, and the judgment to integrate the portfolio.

In empirical research twenty years ago I found real-world BMs seem to comprise around a dozen elements or axioms.[2] This raises a question about whether it is useful to talk about three, four, five, or six elements if there are a dozen in "real life." But strategic work is always about steps, first the discovery of the elements followed by synthesizing their interaction. The possible inter- actions between the elements multiply exponentially with the number of elements, so real BMs with around twelve elements can be hugely complex. Yet strategists are able to grasp them. Turning this point around; if real BMs are complex and strategists must have the ability to grasp them, is there anything to be learned from "classroom exemplars" with only a handful of elements? The answer is "yes" because the classroom learning experience is about the interactions with the BM's constraints, not their particular specification or nature. The classroom is a place for massive simplification—from a dozen or so

[2] J.-C. Spender (1989) *Industry Recipes: The Nature and Sources of Managerial Judgement.* Oxford: Blackwell.

elements to four or five. Then the student can see how these interact. The teacher hopes the simplification does not wipe out what students might learn about interaction and synthesis, that enough of the real strategic task remains to make it a useful learning experience. Using case-work and simplified classroom BMs the student can discover something of the nature of the synthesizing task—even if that does not equip the student to do it in any real-world situation. But it can be the seed to getting a feel for it, just as negotiating the nursery slopes give us a feel for skiing and role-playing provides a feeling for real negotiation.

The remainder of this chapter is a classroom simplification, offered to help prepare and aid those embarking on synthesizing strategic practice. Earlier I used the metaphor of "plunging in with both feet," pointing to the sense or act of commitment that synthesis demands. There is no halfway place between thought and action. One can toy with some ideas and possibilities but these cannot ever grasp a real situation in its entirety. So the essence of strategizing is always the situated practice, "plunging in," committing, not standing back and observing. Technically (philosophically) this illustrates the difference between generalization, standing back from the specifics, and practical engagement, tangling with the situation's specifics and uniqueness and exposing the strategist to surprise. "Plunging in" is one of the special dimensions of case teaching—the student must commit with a statement and to the implications others can see in it. So the student must also practice persuasion, justifying his/her act of synthesis to the classroom audience. Since there is "no right answer" the student's peers must judge. Thinking about this moment, of course, is not the same as experiencing it.

## 4.3 Data Collection

The strategic discovery process, looking for the constraints to her/his judgment that seem most relevant to the strategist, is initially a data collection process. But not all the data sought are alike. As noted in section 1.4, in the real world data problems arise because of three different kinds of knowledge absence that the data is intended to "fill"—ignorance, indeterminacy, and incommensurability. Ignorance is a lack of knowledge about what is presumed given (real) and knowable. Natural science strives to correct our ignorance of Nature, which we presume there and discoverable irrespective of what we think and do. Indeterminacy is a lack of knowledge about what other actors will do in response to our actions, when the others' actions have the capacity to impact our own. Incommensurability arises because what we know is often in fragments that stand on divergent axiomatic bases and so cannot be fitted together into a picture coherent enough for us to reason about it. The BM's multiple parts are likewise incommensurable and must be fitted together in an act of synthesis that leads to the firm's coherent language and provide an approach to the plunging-in practice itself. The synthesis must also fit together knowledge that addresses other types of knowledge absence, the responses to ignorance and indeterminacy.

For example, SWOT presents the strategist with addressing ignorance about the value of the firm's assets and liabilities. These may be knowable as firm-subjective estimates rather than objective measure, as discussed earlier. The 5-force model is not the same. The strategist has little trouble identifying customers and suppliers. The challenge is to deal with, perhaps anticipate, how these actors are going to respond to actions designed to increase or protect the firm's rent-stream. This considers indeterminacy so a different kind of judgment is implied. We deal with ignorance by doing more research, focusing on one mode of inquiry or methodology. Indeterminacy suggests taking out "insurance" against the other party's actions, or negotiating with that party, perhaps ending up with a contract that specifies moves and counter-moves, as well as remedies if either parties fail to stick to the contract. This is yet another kind of inquiry and judgment. We might define ignorance as the condition of dealing with another party when no negotiation is possible and what is there to be known is static, fixed, awaiting its discovery. When it comes to indeterminacy, recall that whenever we have complete knowledge of the other's responses to our actions that transforms an indeterminate situation into one of ignorance because strategy/gt (see section 1.4 again) then applies—it becomes a matter of fact about which we may be ignorant.

These distinctions between incommensurability, ignorance, and indeterminacy help illuminate the various ways in which the strategist can "understand" the firm's context by operationalizing its uncertainty. They show the nature of the strategic work to be done when developing a coherent and actionable sense of the firm's context. But the notion of understanding anything presents strategic challenges of its own, and these help us grasp how language works, or fails. Language is sometimes considered our species' most significant accomplishment, what most sharply distinguishes humans from other forms of life. It makes society and economy—and almost everything else about the human condition—possible. Language enables "communication," which implies knowledge transfer between people. Data resolves ignorance. Ask Google a question and you get an answer. Dictionary definitions of communication speak of conveying "information." The definitions of information might lead you right back to data, but some definitions are sensitive to the notion that information is data "interpreted" and so has "meaning" for the recipient—which is especially notable when it "disturbs" what the recipient understands already. Data imply "facts" of a static reality that lies beyond our minds, independent of what we think about it, in which case "meaning" is what we add to data to bring it into contact with the fluidity and uncertainty of our lives and practices. Meaning is how we possess data and make them part of our lives—hence the archetypal business person's question "What does it mean to us?"

Attaching meaning to data is an act of imagination quite distinct from perceiving the facts (sense-data perhaps). It points to a separation between the real lying beyond us and our interpretation of it as the basis for our reasoning about our actions. Put differently, despite what we often hear, facts are never self-evident. If they were there would be no call for strategic work. Because we are only boundedly rational and do not understand everything, or indeed understand anything for sure, we proceed through life by in a reasoned manner only by constructing a world of meaning that structures our life-world, meanings that we project onto our situation to make it comprehensible and actionable. We make a practice-based map. The facts of our situation must be brought into it if they are to shape our practice; the map is symbolic, constructed from what we think, it is not an objective or factual representation of the real. Another way to think of this is that since the facts cannot ever be self-evident, we have to know something already before we can see, hear, or recognize anything as something known. We have to know how to choose what to attend to. Our "knowledge pump" has to be "primed" with meaning before we can make anything of data about our world. Human beings are "meaning makers" precisely because facts cannot stand on their own if we are to know, think, and communicate about them. Alternatively, if facts refer to the world beyond us, meaning indicates that there is a different world of our knowing and acting, and the two are distinct because of our bounded rationality. It is what we know that matters, not what is real (maybe!). One practical implication is that the "meaning" of a message-load of data cannot be treated as we treat data. It cannot be contained within the message and communicated as data—a point made obvious when we consider the problems of encryption and decryption keys. The decryption key cannot be sent encrypted. But without the decryption key, the message is meaningless mush. Sense-data are likewise meaningless until we select from and transform them by adding or merging them with meanings that we construct with our imagination. Science is about testing meanings, not about accumulating data to reveal reality. Strategizing is meaning-making for ambiguous contexts not wholly determined by "facts." It is about changing the meanings others attach to a constrained context.

The problems of changing the meanings people attach to data are significant because we cannot tell someone else what things must mean to them. There is a gulf between what I tell you and what you think as a result, because you construct and synthesize what you think from many things besides what I tell you—the earlier point about why computers are not like us. Which brings us to the processes of persuasion tackled head-on in the next chapter. In the meantime note the difference between data and meaning as alternative and irreconcilable modes of understanding. The notion of "understand" only arises because data and meaning differ. If facts were self-evident that would leave no place for our understanding of them. "Understand" is only worth noting because you and I might disagree about the meaning of a fact. I give you data—"87"—but what is its meaning? While factual data help resolve instances of ignorance, meaning is especially relevant to dealing with indeterminacy, for that arises from the different meanings the parties attach to data they have in common. Negotiation is intended to shape the meanings the parties attach to the facts of their interaction. For instance when Firm A lowers its prices all the relevant players get to know this. But what is Firm B going to do? Do they take Firm A's move as an attack on Firm B's market share, and lower their own prices, so engaging in the "rivalry" that erodes the rent streams of both firms? Or do they see it as a signal of the coming commodification of that market segment and respond by doing something different, such as introducing a new breakthrough model that opens up a new market segment and leads them to a different rent-stream? When airlines watch each other and match pricing are they negotiating, colluding, or following market forces—three different "meanings" for the same data?

In the Preface I reported that I segued from writing on corporate strategy and into knowledge management (KM).[3] This turned out to be important because KM "problematizes" knowledge (or should) just as strategy writers problematize strategy by seeing it as not obvious, worthy of examination, as worthy of some theory or process. Much of KM problematizes knowledge by presuming it is in the wrong place. IT is especially handy for fixing this. Another branch of KM studies begins by presuming knowledge is a notion that cannot be defined—what would be the knowledge status of a definition of knowledge? Would it be meta-knowledge? Obviously the definition cannot be included in or be part of what is being defined. One way out of this conundrum is to agree that while knowledge cannot be defined as if we could ever stand outside it and observe it, it can be defined as a "state" of human knowing. We are forever trapped "inside" whatever we mean by knowledge. We cannot step outside it. The differences between data and meaning suggest our states of knowing differ. At which point we can borrow from the Greek epistemologists and contrast the different states of knowing that we experience. Data and meaning are contrasting modes of knowing. While neither can be defined "objectively" their difference illuminates what we mean by knowing. Data are how we know something when we take sense-data's meaning for

[3] C. W. Choo and N. Bontis (eds) (2002) *The Strategic Management of Intellectual Capital and Organizational Knowledge*. New York: Oxford University Press.

granted; the flight's arrival time, the number of players on the football team. Our focus moves from data onto meaning when meaning cannot be taken for granted—when data are problematized. As above, the data are "87"—but is the number a bus route, a code, or a stock price?

The strategist is vitally concerned with different ways of knowing. The constraints to which her/his judgment may be attached might be fixed data—here is a house. Or they might be changeable through acting on them—pulling the house down. Or a mix of data and meaning, the house might be re-zoned as a factory, indicating what might be renegotiated by persuading the other actor (the authority) to accept a new meaning. To illustrate differently; we decide to get into the coffee packing and distribution business. Here international market prices rule, and we know them as a strategic constraint on the supply dimension of our BM. But perhaps we can find a grower prepared to negotiate directly and so get an advantage over our competitors. Even though there are various "options" available in the coffee market, perhaps this grower might be interested in a special multi-year agreement that gives him a "hedge" against the vagaries of the spot market. Knowing his willingness to negotiate transforms our sense of the supply constraint to assembling our own BM. Or we might focus on labor as a constraint. We need TIG welders (a special skill), we advertise locally at $X/hr and may negotiate wage-rates with the few applicants who are TIG-proficient. But then the relevant Local of the United Association gets into the act and sets the wage minimum at $Y. What was negotiable with the individual welders has become fixed, and this impacts the process of building our BM. A fact's basis is often changeable and this brings meaning and meaning management to the center of the analysis.

To summarize the last few paragraphs; the constraint discovery process is to get to "know" those matters that bound the strategist's judgments—whether or not they are subject to the strategist's capacity to control and change. Such constraints are not mere facts but are elements of what the strategist knows that differ (a) because one fact differs from another but also (b) because they can be known differently, as data or as meaning, as fixed (all there is to be known about this constraint) or changeable, when in knowing the constraint we also know how to change/shift it (something more to be known beyond the data that treats them as fact). The practical implications of these different ways of knowing differ and the knowledge gained must be communicated in different ways. The distinction between data and meaning is commonsense and everyone knows it, even if it is seldom discussed. But there is a further complication. As we explored in section 2.1 the firm's knowledge assets may well include people's tacit knowledge, such as the TIG welder's special skill. Recall Polanyi described tacit knowing by saying "we know more than we can say" and writing about bike-riding as a skill that seems beyond language-based explanation. Tacit knowing lies outside data and meaning (information) as language-captured ways of knowing. So language has limits and it is clear that we can know in ways that go beyond language. Data and meaning point towards two modes of human knowing but we have to admit a third, tacit knowing—skilled practice. Our lived world cannot be fully captured by language, by what we can say. The trilogy of data, meaning, and (skilled) practice (DMP) are three types of knowing (knowledge presence) that complement the three types of knowledge absence. Data relate most closely to ignorance, as meaning does to indeterminacy. But practice relates to incommensurability, or rather, to be able to practice in a skilled way is to be able to deal with the incommensurability of what is known as data or meaning. This follows because practice is never one-dimensional, multiple issues are always present in the situation's specifics.

Practice is never the simple implementation or enactment of a logical idea. An explanation includes initial conditions and *ceteris paribus* clauses. The TIG welder does not do good work by slavishly following a one-dimensional formula. Even though theories, formulae, and heuristics can be useful they cannot ever be completely determining of practice—simply because situations can never be completely comprehended or categorized, there is always something unique and something unknown about them. The practitioner has to apply her/his judgment, choosing what to pay attention to in a situation that cannot ever be grasped in its entirety. The irreducible skill element of situated practice points to what cannot be generalized, to how the practitioner judges to resolve the gap between the prescriptions of theory and the uniqueness of the context of practice. Tacit skill points to a third type of constraint—skills that cannot be described, theorized, or otherwise captured in language. Practice is always specific, situated, instants of action and experience whose uniqueness lies beyond being fully captured in language, for language always relies on generalities and is helpless when dealing with the totality of a single instance. We can never capture the entirety of an experience. Even if our BM and strategizing indicates the action to be taken, can the individuals involved actually do it at the instant they must? The idea of the business model as a situation- (and actor-) specific language that goes some way to embrace three modes of knowing is useful so long as we also keep in mind the axiom that the firm is an apparatus that adds value by channeling people's imagination in ways that bring something new into the world. It is a creature of practice not theory. Adding value or innovating is a matter of practice, not talk, so the concept of value necessarily takes us beyond the limits of language. Value-adding is always a surprise, the practice-driven revelation of something hidden from what can be said and anticipated. Value is added only by doing and by opening ourselves to surprise, not merely by saying. Surprise is the corollary of strategic doubt.

This brief discussion of the nature of our knowing (properly called epistemology) helps shift the chapter's methodological focus from thinking that what we know is about a reality beyond us (those facts again) to highlight that our knowing is always internal, constructed by us, and about what we make of our experience of the things beyond us. The discussion is simply a lever to shift from "objective" strategizing towards a "subjective" approach—on the grounds that under Knightian uncertainty rigorous analysis cannot work. This book offers a subjective (practical) approach to strategizing and to creating the BM. I believe such subjectivity is commonsense and all of us do it all the time, even if the academics of it are a struggle. My knowledge-presence and knowledge-absence distinctions are hopelessly artificial, simply axioms to my method, just as the distinctions between cash cows, stars, and dogs are axiomatic to the BCG matrix's method. This chapter's objective is to move beyond the constraints and axioms noted in Chapters 2 and 3, those we find in the strategic literature, and towards a more general level that allows the reader a greater degree of freedom. At the same time I argue that data, meaning, and practice are fundamental modes of human knowing. They are not the only ones, for faith and emotion, for instance, are others. But, at the same time, I must presume the healthy human mind is a device powerful enough to be able to grasp all three and bring them into an actionable relationship. So they must have something in common and be interrelatable. We know meaning, especially, is tied up with practice. The pragmatists suggested they were almost the same, that the meaning of things is revealed in practice, the way we use them to further our projects—interesting philosophical matters that are not part of my book. But some engagement with these philosophical issues is necessary (*a*) to surface the nature of the constraint discovery process that leads to the strategist's selection of constraints and their subsequent synthesis into a BM, and (*b*) to dig into why, if the firm is to be understood as a value-adding apparatus, it must also be seen as a practice, not merely as a statement like a computer program, or a design, or a machine, or a culture, or in the other ways we sometimes regard it. It follows that strategic work must likewise be seen as an artistic endeavor that cannot be completely grasped with language, especially not as a theory stated in a formal or rigorous language. The next section examines language more deeply.

## 4.4 BM as Language

There is an old story that Eskimos have a dozen or more different words for snow. In spite of it being something of a hoax the story lives on because it seems a useful insight into the complexities of polar snow-practice. People in the Kalahari Desert are probably not interested, but snow skiers quickly learn the differences between corn, crud, and crust. Everyday Greenland life is surely tied up with the peculiarities of snow (though I do not know), just as people who live in the North African deserts learn the subtleties of sand and sailors learn about wind and currents. Language helps us categorize our thinking on these matters. It facilitates the connection of thinking to practice and experience and thereby both opens up and delimits the options we consider. If we cannot say it we probably cannot see it—even when it is there—or notice our experiencing it. Education makes us different by providing us with languages that help us see more and differently. The US anthropologists Sapir (1884–1939) and Whorf (1897–1941) argued a person's language determines the way they see the world; being brought up in one language leads a person to see their world in a way other-language speakers do not. We need not agree with the extreme "linguistic relativism" of the Sapir-Whorf hypothesis to see strategy as a field that offers managers several alternative languages they might use to (a) discover and (b) grasp their firm's situation. Is the situation a financial one to be untangled by following the money, or a technical problem that turns on better science? Is the problem a political one, or legal?

Strategy authors seldom pay much attention to business language and its capacity to frame the problems strategizing addresses. Terms like organizational goal, strategic objective, profit, and market share—in spite of the difficulties in defining them and the problems the terms create for accountants or shareholders—are presumed meaningful and adequate to discuss the firm's strategy. The financial press, practitioners' magazines, and news tickers keep up their endless chatter in these terms. The language is also global, as is the trade being reported and analyzed. But there are smaller universes of discussion. Accounting conventions differ between countries because of different tax legislation, and between industries. Industries have their own terminology, notable in finance, app-building, or surgery. Firms too have their own terminology; micro-universes of discourse. While some of their language may be based on borrowing terms from others, their industry perhaps, it also reflects the firm's particular context of activity and meaning, and this is where we must focus attention if we are to understand strategic work. Strategists strategize about specific firms, not industries, national economies, or professions. The firm is the strategist's locus of practice, even if much of the language adopted comes from elsewhere.

We see some business strategy languages are more widely adopted than others. Appendix C provides a list of contemporary strategy textbooks and their implicit languages. Teaching in our field is dominated by SWOT language and external and internal analysis. The "strategic" choice is to bring the firm and its "relevant environment" together with a good "fit." We can question the popularity of this EIF language, whether it derives from the ease with which it can be taught or its relevance to real business practice.

Interestingly it neglects everything that motivated von Clausewitz and ignores the vast bulk of English-language academic research into strategy since Chandler proposed EIF in 1962. Recall that Porter's 1980 5-forces model led to a reformulation of strategy theorizing and research—yet this transformation is scarcely visible in these strategy textbooks, beyond an uncritical recitation of it as an industry analysis—which it is not. Likewise, the RBV and its language of rare, valuable, and inimitable (VRIO) resources dominate academic theorizing, but remains invisible in these texts. Given these textbooks' continuing embrace of a fifty-year-old language, their authors seem to be from a completely different community, neither practitioner nor academic, selling their retro-wares to uncritical consumers (MBA and BBA teachers, and their unwitting students) on the basis of its teachability—without considering its utility, theoretical or practical, or the internal logic of its arguments, or whether it helps students to cope with working in real firms.

Even if it were possible to rehabilitate the EIF theorizing that more or less died along with "formal strategic planning" in the 1970s, these textbooks raise serious questions about the concept of strategy being presented. First, the EIF analysis is clearly not relevant to firms operating in inefficient markets or pursuing "economic rents" or "above average returns on their investment." Against the idea that firms operate in competitively efficient environments there are strong intuitions that every firm has to be a "quasi-monopoly" and exploit the particularities of its products, processes, people, and engagements. No two firms can occupy exactly the same economic opportunity space. Second, as we know, the EIF approach presumes that computably adequate knowledge about the firm's external and internal environments is available to the strategists at no strategically significant cost. These doubts—about the principle of equilibrium and the cost and computability of information—are connected because, if the market was efficient, then full information would be freely available, and vice versa—a tautology again. But if complete data were available what precisely would be the nature of the strategic decision being made? Plus why would firms exist? Under such circumstances the conclusions would be wholly driven by the "freely available facts of the situation" and not by the strategist. Neither judgment, nor surprise, nor profit would enter into the discussion. An appropriately programmed computer could do the job.

This has at least three implications for authors adopting the EIF approach: (a) their recommendations stand on the assumption of complete information, (b) they do not consider "satisficing" as a strategy for dealing with information that is incomplete but costly to acquire, (c) they dismissed the strategist's judgment as irrelevant, which means the strategist-as-human-being is also irrelevant. They presume the strategist is a Rational Man cipher. All of which leads one to wonder who is being taught strategy this way and why—for if these assumptions were correct, whatever the students learned would be irrelevant to their eventual work amidst Knightian uncertainty. Such doubts notwithstanding, the EIF approach is a popular strategic language—comfortable and familiar, with its shortcomings well hidden. Digging into its assumptions, we see the existence of the firm as an analyzable entity is also presumed—IBM or Alcatel or Siemens simply exist—and these firms have strategies that are determined by their management. The implication is that a firm can be distinguished from its strategy. But as we understand strategic work better it is clear the firm (from the strategist's point of view), its strategy, and its BM are all one and the same. As the strategy-as-practice authors insist, firms do not have strategies, they are strategies—for maximizing profit, employment, market share, risk-reducing investment, producing low-emission automobiles, or whatever. Second, since the EIF presumes firms exist, boundaries are also implied. Outside these lie competitors, regulators, suppliers, and so on—that also exist. There are also markets, both differentiated, as supply markets differ from demand markets, and immune to being impacted by the firm's actions. When the strategist's language assumes firms exist, it also assumes markets exist.

In a similar way each of the strategic tools considered in Chapters 2 and 3 invokes an entire economic universe, and in each we can ask, "Where does strategic work fit in?" As noted above, if the markets invoked are defined as discoverable with their relevant dimensions measurable, differing, perhaps, in return, risk, growth, competitiveness, and so on, there will be little for the strategist to do—and no prospect of surprise or profit. Inside the firm's boundaries there is a like differentiation, appeals to the divisions of labor, horizontal and vertical, that underpin bureaucratic theory as the most familiar theory of the firm. If the firm has been defined as a machine, predictable and discoverable, there is no possibility of surprise, no place for the employee's imagination to act and generate innovation. The firm's external market engagements are chosen, as it were, from a fixed menu of possibilities, and the firm's internal arrangements are fully controlled, for instance, by reorganizing the firm along divisional lines or abandoning a product line. Together these options help illustrate the boundaries not only to the firm but to the management options implicit in the EIF language. The language chosen inescapably delimits the strategist's options. If the language also determines the conclusion, as I suggested EIF does when full information is available, there is little strategic work left to do because no judgment inputs are necessary to set the firm in motion. At most, there is some need to collect the relevant data and compute the conclusion buried therein. The employees who do this are often labeled "strategic analysts" to differentiate them from the "real" strategists or "deciders" who are responsible for dealing with knowledge absences and providing judgment. Thus there is little overlap between real strategic work and what these analysts do.

The strategist is the imaginative person (or team) that "fills in" the knowledge absences with a language that, when absent, makes it impossible for the analyst to arrive at a conclusion. Notice that planners and strategic analysts must be given a language (goals, ends, means, boundaries, timescales, etc.) before they can get to work. It is often thought that rigorous analysis precedes any strategizing, but it is the other way around. Strategic work is the unavoidable preamble because real situations are never computable—which is precisely why they are of interest and can lead to value, and profit. A degree of non-computability is a fact of everyday life—organizational as well as political and personal—and the daily business of exercising judgment is the source of its value and our feelings about it. While many things are computable, the price of a 17 gallon tankful of gas when the pump shows $3.40 a gallon or the return on a 2% bond, these matters do not actually determine peoples' practices and feelings. A machine can do this computation. But as soon as we bring human beings into the loop things tend to get less computable, for data get measured against subjective expectations. This is especially relevant to entrepreneurs, for management is getting things done through others who have expectations and act on the meanings they construct, so the strategist confronts a person-filled reality and deals with its non-computability by borrowing or creating a language that carries some acceptable action options.

So long as we think or talk in terms of causality and rigorous scientific language we cannot see the strategic task. But how does a practical language leave space for strategic judgment? What kind of language can avoid being fully determinate? The majority of strategy text authors adopt EIF in ways that leave little room for judgment. They write as if the action recommended is rigorously dictated by the facts. In contrast, there is a surprising amount of evidence confirming SWOT as the practitioners' favorite "strategic language." As Chapter 2 showed, there are no objective or proven empirical measures of strengths, weaknesses, opportunities, and threats, no "rigorous" closure. How the strategist arrives at a SWOT portrayal of the firm's situation is not built into the analysis, nor is there a conclusion to be drawn. These are matters of judgment the SWOT language leaves open. SWOT leaves a great deal for the strategist to do or, more specifically, it calls for the exercise of a considerable degree of strategic judgment in how meaning is attached to the data available. The terms in SWOT language are beyond objective definition and so useless and objectionable to the academic theorist. In contrast, for practitioners SWOT's openness comes across as being useful simply because it provides a central role for strategic work that is very different from analysis—suggesting a powerful division of executive labor. The textbook authors who adopt EIF make no distinction between analysis and strategic work. It is unfortunate that the widespread use of SWOT by real-world managers is almost completely disregarded by strategy text authors. It is even odder as many writers and teachers fudge their espoused commitment to rigorous analysis by saying "there is no right answer" when it comes to the case-work they use to lighten up the text. All of which is deeply unsatisfactory for students—for they are left completely in the dark about what to do with an analytic approach that even its authors concede cannot work. Ironically, there may well be situations the EIF approach captures adequately, perhaps when internal structural adjustments to external change seem to be the only option. When Chandler's theorizing seems compelling, there may be little to debate. If the company is getting into multiple products nationwide it may make sense to adopt a divisional structure. But that would be a matter of strategic judgment for there is no logical compulsion.

Earlier I noted the paradox of talking about practice, of struggling with the disjunction between generalizations of language and the unique particularities of practice. Strategic work is ultimately about specifics and so more about practice than the analysis of generalizations captured with language. But talk is all we have until we plunge into practice and its different world. The hope is that, with a situation-specific language that articulates the entrepreneur's judgments, the strategist can approach the moment of commitment more closely than s/he can with an abstract but rigorous theory. The rest of this chapter deals with strategic work as the process of selecting and drawing in a number of generalizations to help the strategist engage her/his judgment and so shape specific practice. We might say "After-sales service is needed to sustain our product line" and we might also say "This service technician overcharged and pocketed the difference"—two incommensurable comments about a single context. The question, as always for strategists, is "What should we do now?" Those that respond from principle and assert that "Any malfeasance must be punished, so we must fire this technician" ensure the general overrides the specific and sacrifices the complexity of life to the simplicity of principle. But perhaps a "public warning" would do the trick and keep a potentially good employee on board. As soon as we abandon isolated principles and engage the situation in a way that admits the multidimensioned complexity of the human condition, options open up and we can pay more attention to the situation's specifics. These are innumerable; perhaps the technician's wife is sick and he has many dependents, and so on, a plethora of special pleadings. Real strategic work is about finding a way through the thicket of principles and particulars, hoping for the wisdom of Solomon and resisting the cop-out of raising one principle over all other aspects—for human situations always mingle both. The principles and abstractions on which numbers stand can never determine real-world strategic choice in the way presumed in the classroom. At the same time the particulars are being carried along in ongoing strategic time, as inaction quickly becomes a strategic choice of moment. There is no possibility of taking everything into account or analyzing forever. Sooner or later plunging in means action must take precedence over discovery and debate.

The remainder of this chapter explores what remained hidden in Chapters 2 and 3. As each tool was examined, it was presented as if it could define and structure the strategic work without further complication, whereas, of course, "the devil is in the details" and the specifics rule. The strategist needs a language that embraces all the constraints judged to matter, and when the models offered in Chapters 2 and 3 fail the strategist must "roll her/his own." How many constraints can be handled? I suggest around a dozen. We can only go so far towards capturing the specificities of real situations before we get overwhelmed and lose all sense of method or "structured practice." In this chapter and the following chapter I move closer to freeing up the notion of strategic work beyond the four, five, or six dimensions of Chapters 2 and 3, but not so far as to lose everything in the swamp of "it all depends." I expand the idea of the BM as a language in order to show how it is assembled following the process of constraint discovery. I also introduce a graphic, hoping readers will find it clarifying, just as the BCG or 5-force diagrams are helpful even if they lose some of the essentials, such as the multiple strategic times in Porter's analysis.

## 4.5 Exploring Language

Language theorists distinguish "syntax" from "semantics." The first deals with how words and terms are arranged to convey a message—nouns, verbs, adjectives, and so on. "The cat sat on the mat" works while "The cat mat on the sat" does not. Semantics deals with the meaning conveyed. "The cat sat on the mat" does not provide the same meaning as "the mat sat on the cat." If the BM is to be a viable firm-specific or "local" language, a "jargon," it must have (a) a syntax that links the terms, axioms, elements, etc. into patterns and (b) a semantics that enables managers and employees—the jargon's insiders—to debate and reason about the meaning of their experience of the firm and its situation. Terms linked by the language must have practical and situationally relevant meanings that give the language semantic substance. Technically this is called "indexicality," the sense that the term's users are pointing to something in the lived context—using their index fingers—such as "that cat" or "sitting now." For example, firms often talk about "customers." But in real situations the meaning or "indexicality" of that term will vary between firms who define their "customers" as those who have actually placed orders with us versus those firms who think of their customers as those who have received their goods and services, or even those who are likely to buy but have yet to be contacted and sold to, and so on. To illustrate the point differently, accountants have to decide whether an order booked is an asset or is so only when the invoice has been paid. There may be a national accounting standard to resolve the accountants' ambiguity, but there are no management-language standards that set what employees mean by "customers." In the classroom it seems easy to use the term, but in real business situations it is more troublesome. Ask ten business people what they mean by "customer" and we shall probably get more than a dozen answers.

The jargon gets even more subtle when employees speak about "good customers" as a way of expressing the salesman's expectations of future business that cannot be deduced from that customer's past behavior, or those that pay on time. All the BM's terms must be "indexical," practical, embedded in the firm's view of its situation and practices. For employees the term "customer" is not the abstract theoretical term used in the classroom but is indexed and so generally means something rather different in different firms. Creating a BM means settling on or indexing the meanings to be attached to such everyday terms. Only then will those engaged with the firm know what meaning is to apply in any particular case. Outsiders are typically baffled by a firm's jargon because they do not take part in its indexing practices and so do not understand the terms' contextualized meaning. But the firm is only managed through language (in which I include the rather complex notion of nonverbal language, to be elaborated later) and it will not be possible to create the firm until a strategic language has been established, promulgated, and absorbed by those whose practices then bring the firm to life. Herein lies the essence of creating a BM. The strategic work is to create, seize, or shape a local language that enables the firm's people to comprehend or operationalize the entrepreneur's strategic judgments about its situation and goals, and so deal with the inevitable unintended and unexpected results. "People" here includes many others besides the employees, as stakeholder theory suggests. Thus stakeholders can be defined as those people and entities whose views and actions can be shaped by the BM's universe of discourse—and those who have the power (as in Porter's model) to pressure and change the BM.

Each BM-language engages and addresses different strategic issues. SWOT implies a language whose terms and frame-able questions differ from those of the BCG matrix—so different issues are being addressed and different practice options implied. The strategist must first make an assessment of the issues and then devise a language to address them. Echoed here is Fayol's "all-round look" or "general survey" that must precede strategic planning.[4] But he

---

[4] H. Fayol (1949) *General and Industrial Management.* London: Pitman.

presumed the categories of things to be observed were given and not problematic when, in real situations, they are not "given" and must be selected or constructed. So Fayol paid no attention to the strategic work involved in selecting terminology and meanings, what must precede the debate and choice, for instance, of whether internal funds-flow or the protection of the firm's rent-stream is "more important." The strategist must construct or find a language suited to the choice of BM as synthesis of identity, intention, and context so that s/he can explain it to others and thereby secure their judgment in collaboration. Everything about the firm's value-adding follows. With the 5-force model in mind we might say auto-tire manufacturers have little clout in the auto industry, because there are so many tire makers that perhaps it is close to perfect competition. Which might lead incautious strategists to ignore how Ford and Firestone got into major difficulties in the 1990s when tire failure seem to be involved in Ford Explorer roll-overs. Ford and Firestone blamed each other. Contracts for future tires became part of their fight. What to do with tires already supplied and fitted became quite another. How were the companies to resolve the issues and get back to their traditionally fruitful collaboration? The 5-force model does not have a strategic time dimension for negotiating the indeterminacies covered. Multi-period principal-agent theory implies an appropriate notion of strategic time. So to analyze the Ford–Firestone situation it might make sense to bring principal-agent ideas together with those in the 5-force model, and that is not so easily done. A new strategic language must be constructed.

The value of introducing language as a metaphor, and saying strategic work creates the firm as a situated language, is that it emphasizes the BM is not like a blueprint for a machine or a computer program, it is as ephemeral and insubstantial as discourse—yet powerful nonetheless. It presents the BM as an influential idea expressed, operationalized, and contextualized and, as Victor Hugo noted, "nothing is as powerful as an idea whose time has come." While accountants and economists might see the firm as a bundle of price-able assets, this is not helpful to the strategist who is seeking to add value, to transform a pig's ear into a silk purse, to surprise all involved and bring something innovative into the world that was not there previously. But if neither the cost of an asset nor its market price gives the strategist a good sense of a resource's potential to add new value, where is s/he to turn? I say "the imaginative judgments articulated into the BM." Both cost and market price imply language that can be used to grasp a resource, but both are "backwards looking." Neither helps the strategist understand the potential value the resource might have when the strategist has imagined some different future use for the resource. The intuition at the core of Penrose's theory of the growth of the firm is that the management team imagines an innovative future use for a resource and then sets about translating their imagining into economic value. The BM as language allows the strategist to engage her/his imagination and so look to the future, just as some mission statements embrace aspirations, aspects yet to be realized—to be the industry leader or establish a global presence.

The BM is an art form, perhaps democratic capitalist society's most important. Few writers dare to engage art, though Frank Knight had the courage to write about business as an art form.[5] Art is neither simple nor transparent. It is easier to understand language and discourse as something constructed than to "understand" a painting because we can see the discourse's parts and there is a clear sequence through speech act time. A painting seems frozen into the instant of seeing it. It is not as easy to talk about a painting's parts or the painters' approach to the painting or its gestation, though there are established rubrics around teaching people how to make paintings, such as the "rule of thirds"—place the horizon two-thirds down. But this clearly does not apply to non-representational abstract art and raises questions about when a painting is not an abstraction. Similarly it is not easy to uncover how a particular painting might have been otherwise, the alternative possibilities the painter dismissed as s/he choose to represent the ideas in a particular way. The BM as a local language is more open to analysis and to separating its parts. As an example, the history of Xerox, we know, was that the first machine model was too expensive for most potential users, so Xerox chose to lease it, charging on a per-page basis. That change made it possible for departmental managers to contract for a copier without having to get head office's sign-off on it as a capital expense. The rest is history. The Xerox BM turned on this distinction between lease and buy, but one that had to be contextualized into their customers' administrative procedures before its strategic impact was revealed, an impact that could only be found in the BM, not in a financial analysis. But leased machines also had to work and have a backup and paper supply service. Analyzing the strategic constraints means uncovering and identifying the options that can be rejected in favor of those chosen, focusing as much on what not to do as on what to do. For instance, to choose the BCG language is to reject the SWOT or 5-forces language. Xerox rejected a conventional sale contract, just as IBM did when it chose to lease its tabulating machines in the 1950s. Appreciating the BM as a language helps analyze the separation of the way we want things to be from how they might have been otherwise.

The point of the language-building process—settling on a BM—is to give the strategist the confidence necessary to overcome her/his doubts, to offer enough of a conceptual grip on the situation to enable her/him to step back and consider alternative possibilities. At the same time, to anticipate

---

[5] F. H. Knight (1923) 'Business Management: Science or Art?', *Journal of Business*, 2(4), 5–24.

Chapter 5, the language generated can be used to convey the essence of the BM to those others whose efforts will be crucial to bringing the firm into being as a practice. Thinking of the BM as a tentative language, shared with others, enables them to debate and collaborate in the strategizing process, to suggest modifications to the BM as a vehicle for judgment that is open to being transformed through discourse. The creation of new language is seldom one of inventing completely new terms that have no attachment to previous terms. "Television" brings together two ideas—vision and distance, from the Greek *tele* or "far off." "Credit default swap" brings three ideas together into a new term of art.

Making new language is typically a process of recycling old language into new uses without getting completely bogged down in discovering the bounds and possibilities of old meanings. The good news is that recycled words sound familiar and seem ready-to-hand. The bad news, of course, is that they are not as available as they seem—for they now carry the new BM's different meaning. The new meanings get set or excavated as hearers take part in the firm's indexical practices. Thus jargon presents irritating problems—one of the reasons many react against it, presuming there can be non-jargon. On the one hand the words are familiar, on other their uses or semantics are not, so shutting out the uninitiated or unsocialized. But to the extent the words are familiar this makes discourse in the jargon curiously invisible, seeming to merge with the background conversation. You are in the office and people are talking, obviously in English (or whatever) and not in Swahili. But when you attend and try to make sense of what they are saying you cannot. BMs thus sound familiar, but you have to pass through the indexing process to penetrate or comprehend them to the point that you are able to relate the firm's talk to its practices.

There is a good understanding of "metaphor" as a mode of recycling words.[6] Today the term "bailout" has no connection with being granted bail, or even with a crime. The 2008 US bailouts were actually of a wide variety of types and mechanisms—but they shared the politics that made them happen. Today bailout is a political term that captures a political idea, an attitude towards dealing with some financial circumstances. Metaphor is defined as a figure of speech that can be used to attach one thing's qualities to another thing—"Her eyes were shining jewels." Recycling into new language involves moving a term from one semantic context to another by attaching new qualities— which is precisely what is happening as the new BM is being constructed using borrowed terms. The result is a local language associated with a small group of people who share a common interest, especially those who work

---

[6] G. Lakoff and M. Johnson (1980) *Metaphors We Live By*. Chicago: University of Chicago Press.

together. Bird-watchers' jargon "economizes" their conversation, conveying facts and opinions quickly and precisely, but in ways that others need to be socialized into; just as the new salesman who joins the insurance company's Chicago office will have to learn to detect attitudes and issues to which his New York colleagues pay no attention. The BM is workplace "slang," an economizing language focused on getting things done in the particular way that actualizes the strategist's vision. At the same time unanticipated consequences penetrate all human affairs, and irrelevances and history sometimes leave traces in the BM like scale in a kettle, terminology that no one can explain. Most workplaces are sullied with terminology that is no longer strategically relevant or even meaningful.

Earlier I made comments about the number of elements necessary to construct a BM. The answer will depend on the terms' new meanings and not on the meanings the words had previously. Human language is complicated, but central to our lives—and to business. Our fondness for Occam's razor—boiling ideas down to simple models and mechanical explanations—makes us aware of the usefulness of clear definitions but often leads us to overlook the subtleties of language. Yet language is at the core of doing business. Customers must be persuaded of the merits of the goods and services we sell. Advertising is a project to change terms' meaning, as when physicians' statements were used to advertise the healthful effects of smoking. Suppliers must be persuaded to sell, pay on time, not reverse engineer and enter into competition, not sell to those who would damage the company or the nation, and so on. Most importantly language is essential to creating the collaboration necessary to initiate and sustain the firm's value-adding processes, and this is where the special jargon leads to highly efficient discussion. Meetings, often pilloried as a waste of time, are absolutely essential to the effective control and exercise of the firm's own language, the mechanism for collaboratively adjusting the firm's jargon to reflect its changing circumstances or goals. The BM is a local language, dynamically dependent on giving old terms new meanings and implications. When we talk of "bailout" we do not start looking for a bail-office; rather we look to the political debate and try to find out which side of the political divide we are supposed to be on.

Surprise drives profit and growth, so the firm's managers must be able to capture experience that lies beyond and is not implied by the axioms underpinning its language. To help understand how language can do this, imagine a two-by-two matrix constructed specifically to facilitate discussion of bailouts. Two existing languages form the matrix's axes, each comprising the only two possible statements derivable from their axioms. Thinking of bailout situations, Language A comprises hold management responsible (A) or not (~A). Language B comprises apply taxpayer funds (B) or not (~B). These are the only statements possible in the languages chosen. I leave the reader to draw the matrix. The political idea embedded in the semantics of bailout today lies in only one of the four quadrants (~A and B)—use taxpayers' funds and do not hold management responsible. This political judgment cannot be justified or derived logically from the axioms of the A and B languages—so long as the two languages are axiomatically independent, not covariant. The choice about which quadrant is to be judged legitimate, and which not, is itself a matter of changing political judgment. It might be based on experience, or an expression of what it is hoped to experience—aspiration. The essence is not the synthetic statement "We are going to apply taxpayers' funds and not hold management responsible." Those are just words. The real meaning, political and semantic, is the view that judges this statement acceptable rather than either meaningless or unacceptable in preference to, say, A and ~B—"We are not going to spend taxpayers' funds and we are going to hold management responsible." Because the A and B languages are independent, orthogonal, the matrix illustrates how two (or more) dissimilar languages can be synthesized to capture our judgments, experience, and intentions. It also illustrates how we might set about persuading others to this political view by making contrasting statements of this type. I can try and persuade you that ~A/B is better for the economy than A/~B. You might disagree. Note again that it is strategic judgment (politics) that prefers one quadrant over the others—not logic, the words do not do it. Note too that the minimum complexity to allow this discourse to work is three languages; two framing languages (A and B), generalized theories perhaps, and one new, private, particularized "observation language" attached to experience and/or judgment—the BM.

Strategic work is hard. The labor of constraint identification, judgment, and idiosyncratic language construction is demanding. It seems so much easier to take terms for granted and fall back on the familiar, as most financial commentators and strategy authors do. But the price of this ease is that the logical and mechanical aspects of the firm come to the fore and the value-adding aspects get pushed into the background. The nature of the entrepreneurial judgment—and why the firm exists—gets ignored. Yet the point of strategizing is to create a value-adding BM, not a logical model. The BM comes to life in the middle of a tangle of constraint-specific languages (perhaps a dozen or so) or, more precisely, the languages in which specific constraints are described and analyzed. These indicate what to pay attention to and they also indicate the attitude to be taken towards the constraint indicated, its indexicality. The BM's real content lies in its many-dimensional impact on the participants' attitudes and thus on how to make the trade-offs necessary to sustain practice. To illustrate: expert systems are assembled from a series of IF–THEN rules; such as IF speed is over 50 mph AND road signs show the driver is in a restricted speed area THEN s/he should slow down. The system is silent on justifying the rule—that is embedded in the social decision to adopt the system. The rule is incorporated into the system's logic and this must be coherent and unambiguous if the expert system is to compute and generate answers. A BM is different because it has not been reduced to a coherent computable logic but remains open to interpretations that demand strategic inputs to resolve.[7] In addition to indicating how to resolve conflict between incompatible rules, the BM deals with the rules' interrelations and meanings. Thus, in addition to the above rule, perhaps there is another one about IF the driver's wife is in labor THEN he can proceed at above speed limit but at no more than 50 mph (because it gets too bumpy). But then again, IF there is a puncture in one of the tires, THEN pull off at a gas station that offers to repair the flat, even if the road is clear.

Just as—in theory—the US Supreme Court functions as a judicial practice to resolve conflicts of meaning that appear between established laws—and not to make new law, a function reserved to Congress—so the BM indicates how the conflicts of rules, knowledge, instructions, commitments, and so on that arise get resolved through the firm's value-adding practice. Clearly the BMs of many financial institutions need to be reconstructed to eliminate not merely the desire to brag about stiffing clients with junk but also the language that made that practice seem legitimate. The internal emails are very revealing of the language traders used to sell their "instruments." Even as the desire to maximize trading profits and the resulting bonuses is part and parcel of the finance industry, just as supermarkets are tempted to sell the past-sell-by-date products they still have in the store, the firms' BMs indicate legitimate boundaries to behavior. There should be no legitimate language for selling junk credit-default swaps or Ninja Loans—which means that the entrepreneur's most fundamental task is both to construct the firm's language but also control how it evolves through practice so that it does not evolve sub-jargons that legitimate behaviors beyond the pale. The strategist's (or CEO's) most fundamental task is to control the firm's language, for that shapes the behavior of those who bring it to life. At issue is the strategic attitude to the practices embedded in and enabled by the firm's language, not the adoption of some holier-than-thou principle that outlaws malfeasance, an attempt to import ethical language that cannot be attached to the firm's practices.

We can see two types of language—"formal" and "natural"—and the distinction is crucial to grasping the BM as natural language rather than as a theory or "formal" language—a distinction associated with this chapter's switch from objective to subjective methods. We can contrast some simple languages. The implications can be carried back into the more complex multidimensioned languages of real BMs. From a purely logical point of view, the

---

[7] E. M. Goldratt helps illuminate the differences here: (1990) *What is This Thing Called Theory of Constraints and How Should it Be Implemented?* Great Barrington, MA: North River Press.

meanings possible in a formal language are delimited to the implications of the axioms adopted to underpin the discourse. Each set of axioms can be elaborated into a finite number of possible statements as permutations and combinations. For instance, three axioms (assertions D, E, and F) can be arranged into factorial three or six permutations expressing statements of simple inter-axiom interactions—D.E, E.D, E.F, F.E, D.F, and F.D. The discourse is bounded and finite, so negations to any of these statements implies the rest in the set. To illustrate, if D.E is a valid statement, then it implies ~D.~E, F.E, and so on as valid statements too. The six statements form a logically complete constellation. Nothing else can be said, so there is no way of expressing surprise or capturing an experience that falls outside this set. However the matrix discussed several paragraphs above conjoined incommensurate A and B languages and makes a space allowing us to do this. The DEF language is "formal," rigorous, and fully structured. Mathematics is a formal language most of us are familiar with. Statements are either logically true or false, a condition that can be deduced from the premises or axioms adopted. There can be no surprises. The AB matrix allows four statements, all synthetic, none logically necessary. So the one judged true (~A and B) is not so because of logic but because of our politics—a different kind of truth, socially embedded or constructed. Natural language truths arise from our *habitus*, the circumstances of our lives, not from logic.

Everyday language is not "formal." We use "natural" language day to day. It is ambiguous, stuffed with contradictions and breaks and marvelously open to capturing our experience and surprise. Natural talk is full of non-logical syntheses, made especially obvious in poetry, which often uses the structure and meter of a poem to collide or hold incommensurate notions together in ways that convey feelings and ideas that lie beyond the explicit grasp of the words used. More formally, consider the differences between syllogisms (statements in a formal language) and synthetic statements. A syllogism comprises three parts; (1) a major premise, (2) a minor premise, and (3) a conclusion. Most know of the syllogism "(1) All men are mortal, (2) Socrates is a man—therefore (3) Socrates will die." Statement (2) is an instantiation of (1), so is logically covered by it. The conclusion is logically entailed in the major and minor premises; adopt them and you are bound to agree with it. A syllogism presents a closed system of thought that turns on the precise definitions of the terms adopted; it excludes judgments. In contrast, as the AB matrix above illustrates, synthetic statements are open and relate to judgments behind the words, leaving us open to doubting our judgments and to our surprise at being wrong. Natural language shifts the semantic emphasis from definition to judgment, allowing space for a judged-legitimated statement "If A then ~B." We use natural language precisely because it enables us to use our judgment to capture the experiences, surprises, and intentions formal statements cannot capture. Whereas formal language stands on a single set of axioms and logical entailment, natural language stands on multiple incommensurate axiom sets and thereby remains open to experience and contrary judgment. All of which is why two-by-two matrices are so popular. They are handy ways to present new thoughts—expectations or experiences. Strategy consultants have found them immensely useful for grasping intuitions that cannot be expressed in formal theoretical format. For instance, one of the more compelling research findings relating to Chandler's strategy and structure ideas was Burns and Stalker's[8] assertion that in stable market conditions strategists should focus on administrative efficiency, but in dynamic market conditions on loosening up the structure and allowing "organic" responses. This is a synthetic statement that perhaps anticipates a theory.

Academics tend to dismiss matrices, preferring rigorous deductions, proofs, and carefully defined generalities that suggest theories. They are less interested in synthetic statements because they apply to particulars. But strategists are always working with particulars and so have limited interest in theoretical statements. The two can be linked when, for example, matrices are used to frame hypotheses. The language of the AB matrix allows "If A then B," a statement that is open to experience. So it can also be deployed as a test; perhaps empirical test suggests "If A then ~B" would show better judgment. But when experience does not confirm this, perhaps the statement should be delegitimated, marked as "bad" judgment. In this way synthetic statements can be seen precursors to formal statements. "If A then B" can be turned into an empirically validated theoretical statement. Then "If A then ~B" is delegitimated and can be eliminated from the matrix, that quadrant is "disallowed" and the language is reshaped to leave no space to say it. The complex of judgments behind legitimation, illustrated as the judgments that would legitimate "If A then ~B," is eliminated on the grounds that no empirical tests support it. In this way theorizing can be understood as the academic practice of formalizing language by eliminating the language necessary to capture surprise. The process of silencing surprise and ending up with theory or formal language is the scientific method and purpose of hypothesis testing.[9] Hypotheses are open to empirical test but by dismissal (falsification or silencing) rather than by capturing surprises. It is not always appreciated that hypotheses imply joining mutually exclusive or incommensurate languages—most obviously that of the proposition and that of observation, for if the observation is entailed in the proposition the test is empty. More precisely, recalling the "rule of three" mentioned previously, we need three languages to intersect

---

[8] T. Burns and G. M. Stalker (1961) *The Management of Innovation*. London: Tavistock Publications.

[9] N. Goodman (1978) *Ways of Worldmaking*. Indianapolis: Hackett Publishing Co.

in the context of interest. First, the languages A and B, with which the hypothesis—"If A then B"—can be stated, and then a third language, the observation language O of experience and experiment, that bears on our judgment about the validity of the hypothesis. As experimental evidence is taken to reveal the truth and eliminate judgment, so the A and B languages are formalized into the causal theory, "If A then B." B becomes logically entailed in A and O is dismissed as impotent to inform us.

Language is central to our lives and practice—even as we take it for granted and pay little attention to its construction and limitations. Business depends utterly on the effective use of language in pursuit of chosen objectives. It is the essential instrument for creating collaboration and working through others. But language is complicated and bears a lot of thinking about. The point of this section's short exploration of the differences between formal and natural language is less to present a philosophy of language (beyond the scope of this book)[10] and more to underscore the BM as an open bundle of practices expressed and shaped by natural language. The openness is essential in that it enables the strategist to research the constraints that delimit the BM as a pattern of judgment. This option is closed off in formal language. The next section reviews what this openness can produce beyond merely identifying and itemizing the constraints. It goes into discovering the constraints' nature, in particular the degree to which the firm is able to shift, change, or manipulate them. Seeing the BM as a complex natural language makes it possible to speak about both what has been experienced and, much more importantly, what the strategist intends and anticipates. The analysis can be pointed towards the future, towards innovation and added value, by shifting the language's semantic content. Synthesizing axiomatically distinct or incompatible languages leverages us into an entirely different language game that captures something previously unexpressed lying in the space between statements and experience.

## 4.6 BM as Diagram

The discussion above about the BM as a synthesized natural language, the product of a process of attaching new meanings that appropriate old terms, may help some readers get a sense of the proactive and constructive nature of strategic work. Perhaps a diagram is helpful. The constraint labels (Figure 4.1) are mere suggestions. The constraint identification process finds those judged relevant to a real situation, probably with around a dozen terms that strike

---

[10] M. Morris (2007) *Introduction to the Philosophy of Language*. Cambridge: Cambridge University Press.

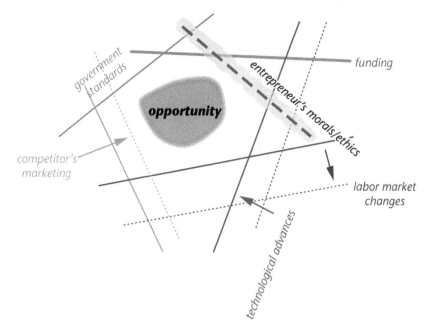

**Figure 4.1** An Example of a Possible BM

outsiders as local and "jargonistic." The different patterns of the lines in the graphic are intended to convey the constraints' multidimensionality, the parallel dotted lines their malleability. The BM occupies or operationalizes some of the space framed.

At first sight this seems to be treating the BM as an exercise in constrained maximization, and this is not completely wrong. But constrained maximization is mathematically rigorous and so not a matter for strategists, whose work is defined as an exercise of judgment that, because of Knightian uncertainty, lies beyond the bounds of rigorous analysis. Crucially, illustrating the BM this way, as lying in a flat plane of two dimensions, hides the many-dimensioned complexity of the opportunity space to be filled by the strategizing process. The dozen or so constraints of a real BM are axiomatically distinct and their being in different dimensions transforms the task from a rigorous analytic one, like working through a syllogism, into synthesizing new language.[11] In the previous section's example, the constraints of speed restriction, urgency to get to the hospital, and the risk of driving on a leaking tire lie in three different dimensions. This is the fundamental difference between classroom and real life. In the classroom awkward complexities get excluded from the

[11] J.-C. Spender (1989) *Industry Recipes: The Nature and Sources of Managerial Judgement.* Oxford: Blackwell.

analysis with *ceteris paribus* clauses. The real world cannot be so simplified. All things being equal it is wise to conform to the speed limit. Most of the added rules that might interfere with that (hurrying my laboring wife to hospital) are not likely to be upheld by the courts, the instrument for applying the law. But if the police officer who stops you is local and knows you and your wife, and accepts your being able to handle the leaking tire, s/he is likely to say "OK, let's go!" and will lead you on with lights and sirens blazing because doing so lies within their discretion.

This illustrates the general idea behind Figure 4.1, in this case suggesting three constraints to the driver's judgment or opportunity space. Absent the police officer's intervention, the strategist (driver) has to decide on his own how best to negotiate the space. The space seems equally valued and homogeneous. So long as the driver stays within it he can expect things to work out OK because the relevant constraints have been articulated into the BM's boundary. The intervention of the officer pushes the speed limit constraint part of the boundary outwards, expanding the opportunity space. There is an allusion here to what engineers call a system's "operating envelope" defined by, for instance, an airplane's maximum and minimum airspeed, altitude, and load. As the BM diagram becomes more realistic and complex with more constraints, the interdimensional trade-offs become more difficult to understand and manage and the opportunity space becomes more heterogeneous. Some options are going to be preferred, especially if they are less exposed to risk. But the profit prospects might also vary in a contrary direction, increasing with risk. The strategist must find or develop ideas or metrics that give the BM an internal geography that grasps the idiosyncrasies of time and place. As noted already, this begins by determining appropriate situational elements or axioms that can be construed into a coherent natural language for engaging strategic judgments about the situation, considering its options, evaluating activity towards the goals, dealing with trade-offs, and, especially important, persuading others to collaborate.

The diagram illustrates two features of the strategist's task better than the discussion of language above. First, the notion of "closure," the point at which the strategist has "covered the situation" or "done his homework," or the opportunity space has been fully framed with knowledge presences. The term "satisficing," due to Simon, has become popular. The idea is that we search, discover the relevant facts, and eventually come to the point at which we judge it OK to stop searching and gathering more evidence, and that it is time to plunge in. Enough already! We satisfice all the time. But there are problems. We convince ourselves that our search has caught the major issues and that further search will not reveal anything more as significant. We mistakenly associate significance with discoverability, that the major issues will stand out because they are major. Unfortunately, under conditions of uncertainty, this logic is false. In Rumsfeld's memorable terminology the idea that issues can be sorted into those we know we know about, those we know we do not know about, and those we do not know that we do not know about (the unk-unks) is simply an error and a misunderstanding of the nature of uncertainty, whether in business or war. There is no justification whatsoever for presuming that what is not known at the moment of satisficing or commitment is less significant than what has been established by the strategist's previous search and analysis. This is the nature of satisficing, it is an act of judgment not analysis and it can prove totally inappropriate. Under uncertainty, we often act anyway even though we have no logical or justifiable basis for ignoring or considering any particular facts, or for transitioning from fact gathering and analysis to plunging into action.

The models in Chapters 2 and 3 suggested closure would occur after four, five, or six constraints had been brought into the analysis. Classroom simplification again! Earlier I suggested empirical evidence for around a dozen constraints to real-world BMs—but can I justify this number rather than some other number? For me it was a judgment based on the empirical evidence generated by my research.[12] At best satisficing would be a form of behavioral economics, of surveying real strategists' behavior and generalizing. Or it might be a form of decision-making psychology, observing that human decision-makers are limited in terms of the complexity they can handle, that there is a relationship between strategic value and the number of variables engaged, diminishing to zero when there are too many to "get one's head around." Perhaps we can devise a test or a metric. The closure illustrated in the diagram is a simply a function of the strategist's judging. It is neither theorized nor determined by the data gathered.

The transition from natural language and synthetic statements to rigorous theoretical statements can be illustrated by shrinking the opportunity space to the point it disappears. All that is left is a set of formally stated causal relations between the constraints considered and their impact. They become the theory's variables. Judgment is neither required nor admitted. So long as uncertainty and doubt prevail there is a finite opportunity space indicating the need for strategic judgment to effect closure and the confidence to act—like a third dimension orthogonal to Figure 4.1's two dimensions. It illustrates a second point, that discovering the pertinent constraints requires probing their nature, their history, their origins, and, in particular, whether they can be moved, changed, or transformed. Perhaps the police officer in the example above agrees to turn a blind eye to speeding if the driver hands him a $50 bill. In real business situations many of

---

[12] J.-C. Spender (1989) *Industry Recipes: The Nature and Sources of Managerial Judgement*. Oxford: Blackwell.

the constraints the strategist must bring into the BM are regulation or law-based, created and administered by real people who are never entirely beyond acting in their own interests rather than those of their office—as PAT presumes. Even if bribery does not seem to be a viable part of the BM, lobbying Congress to change the rules in the firm's favor is an accepted, indeed necessary, business practice. There are local versions; giving to a politician's re-election fund may ensure a favorable business decision later. New York's Emigrant Bank was able to get a waiver on a Dodd-Frank regulation and save its shareholders around $300 million—fund donor Howard Milstein holding a majority of the bank's stock. Perhaps customer opinion is a constraint. Apple Inc. entered the MP3 market with the iPod, priced well above its rivals, but successfully persuaded customers to pay more than they would have needed to had the competition been "perfect." They leveraged that "loyalty" into the iPhone. A clearer example might be Doc Martens, a boot designed during WW2, eventually made in the UK and sold there cheaply. It became a punk skinhead fashion item and the rest is history. Note how the advertising industry transitioned from a pre-WW2 emphasis on "informing" the public about the characteristics and qualities of goods, into the post-WW2 emphasis on "educating" the public or "transform-ing" their sense of the goods' value. The change was much informed by WW2 theories, experiments, and investments in "propaganda." In general, we see that many of the constraints are individually or socially constructed, and therefore open to be further changed by the strategist's actions, and time is always of the essence.

A constraint indicates the kinds of uncertainty or knowledge absence that must be met by the judgments articulated into the BM. As noted previously, knowledge absences fall into three categories—ignorance, indeterminacy, and incommensurability. The strategist does not "understand" a constraint— through the prism of the BM—until its malleability has been explored. Some seem fixed and factual, not open to be changed, such as physical laws. Chief among these are technological constraints. Moore's Law successfully predicted the rate of chip development for many decades. It seems more or less a "fact of the situation," not open to being greatly molded. Yet there are many anomalies. Likewise, given specific weather, the yield for various types of corn is something farmers take to be a fact. But the weather is not a fact, so they can gamble on or against it with their planting strategies—a gamble that has become significantly more rigorous with the arrival of GPS location devices and a better grasp of their farm's various "micro-climates." This shows how even fixed facts seldom determine practice. In general, the closer we get to the relevant "hard science" constraints the more Mother Nature rather than our intentions and strategies seems to be in charge. Sometimes the constraint can become the subject of a research program, and be pushed back by the growth in scientific knowledge. The increasing storage density on hard drives outpaced Moore's Law, making terabyte drives widely available—even as DRAM capacity increased to the point laptops use chip storage rather than mechanical drives; all driven by science. Hybrid vehicles are a similar example, transforming fleet mileages and making new clean-air legislation possible. Much of the "green" program turns on moving technological constraints.

Because business is done in a heterogeneous socio-economy comprised of highly diverse people and social entities, the BM is seldom constrained by ignorance alone. Indeed ignorance may be the smaller part when compared with the uncertainties brought in by indeterminacy and incommensurability. Enquiring into the constraints that arise from indeterminacy means identifying the other party or parties who are generating the specific indeterminacies as well as the state of the firm's relationship with them. Sometimes these others are related only indirectly, such as mass-market customers. Their opinions are probably malleable and so become targets for advertising campaigns or open to discount promotions. At other times the others can be identified directly, such as the firm's suppliers, who might be persuaded to lower their prices. The 5-force model focuses on those whose relationships bring indeterminacy into the BM. Up to this point the primary source of the uncertainty arising from incommensurability lies in the space of the constraints' interaction (recall the Supreme Court's role). A more specific example is when regulators demand one thing while customers quite another and judgment is required to trade off the implications into the BM. But the firm's relations with others are also likely to be many-dimensioned, especially when risk is involved. Collaborative judgments apportion risk between the parties. Moral hazards may be introduced. Judgment is required to act between constraints as well as within them.

Finally there is the judgment required to close the gap between what can be framed in language, or presented as a graphic, and the tacit skills needed to translate that into action in the opportunity space—and so into value. This points to what neither language nor diagrams can capture—and to what the strategist must learn through personal practice because no tool or theory can fully clarify the judgment/s necessary. We should not forget that strategic tools and management education are intended to help managers who have not come up through the business and thereby learned it well enough to get insight into the strategic judgment necessary to run the business. It focuses on managerial knowledge absence that did not exist a century ago. But tools, theories, and classroom education can go only so far to fill such a gap. Doubts must remain, surprises are inevitable and the skilled strategist needs the ability to respond imaginatively. So to summarize this section, strategic work constructs or builds the confidence necessary to plunge in. The process begins with considering how the interplay of identity, intention, and context is grounded in some fact/s of the situation—perhaps a specific goal chosen, or some specific resource available, or some specific customer to be served. It moves on to deal with indeterminacies and incommensurabilities. The process of developing the BM as a natural language for grasping the situation is obviously iterative. As it emerges the operational significance of the strategic choices of identity, intention, and context become clearer—and substantial revision may be necessary. Eventually the interplay can be grasped well enough to bring practical detail into the language. The process outlined above is (1) identify the constraints to the entrepreneur's strategic judgments (including identity and intention), (2) identify the nature of the knowledge absences the constraints indicate, (3) assess the potential to change, move, or transform the constraints that matter, (4) create closure on a functional language, and then (5) act.

## 4.7 Von Clausewitz's Methodology

Surprisingly little has been written specifically about the nature and application of business judgment, even though it is widely discussed and its importance recognized. Its impact is the stuff of business history and much financial journalism. Psychologists and behavioral economists have done analyses such as "prospect theory" that use empirical evidence to distinguish bias and decision-making practice from fully rational decision-making, and offer generalizations about human choosing that do not bear directly on the specifics of strategic work as discussed in this book. But one or two authors deserve comment. Mary Parker Follett noted incommensurability as she wrote of the difficulty of reconciling (a) principles, (b) precedents, and (c) particulars in legal and business contexts, somewhat along the lines of the present book. Strategic judgment has been considered specifically by the military, especially by Carl von Clausewitz (1780–1831).[13] This section considers some aspects of his work to help clarify and buttress the sections above. It pays special attention to his methodology. At the same time there are fundamental differences between business and military activity, so caution is in order. The purpose of the next section is to help the aspiring strategist sense something useful that might be judged worth applying in the strategist's context. Recall my book's methodology: two switches are (a) from generalizations to specifics, and (b) from an objective standpoint to a constructivist or subjective standpoint, arguing the strategist has to look out at the world through the prism of the

---

[13] T. von Ghyczy, B. von Oetinger, and C. Bassford (eds) (2001) *Clausewitz on Strategy: Inspiration and Insight from a Master Strategist*. New York: John Wiley & Sons. J. T. Sumida (2008) *Decoding Clausewitz: A New Approach to 'On War'*. Lawrence, KS: University Press of Kansas. H. P. Willmott and M. B. Barrett (2010) *Clausewitz Reconsidered*. Santa Barbara, CA: ABC-CLIO LLC. W. Duggan (2007) *Strategic Intuition: The Creative Spark in Human Achievement*. New York: Columbia Business School.

BM s/he has created. Even though tacit knowing and non-verbal intuitions loom large, the analytic challenge is to get as close as possible to the specifics of the strategic work and practices through which value is created. My (*a*) and (*b*) switches led to the previous section's discussion about the relationship between theoretical (formal) statements versus synthetic or natural language statements. Ultimately the strategist must close off the natural language discussion the BM makes possible, draw in some final tacit judgments, and plunge into practice. Debate is fine but practice is what matters. The particularization or localization discussion above gets closer to practice than a purely theoretical discussion allows. Practice is often presumed to be the implementation of theory. But theories are always constructed with simplifications, excluding some features while attending to others. Thus no theory can embrace all the issues a practice engages. Several complementing theories or constraints are always necessary to grasp practice's in-the-world nature. No practice can be adequately evaluated in a single dimension. Put differently, real practice must be evaluated in the world of experience that is never of a single dimension or embraced in the abstract world invoked by a theory. Judgment is always necessary to reasoned practice, a view theorizing tries to deny.

A book on strategy must avoid the cop-out of presuming practice is no more than rigorous theory actualized. Von Clausewitz's notion of practice was not one of implementing a theory, so his thinking remains important to business strategists on methodological grounds alone. He saw the gap between theory and practice—like the gap between generalizations and specifics—as the locus of strategic work. Having studied the scientific work and the theory generated the strategist must work to attach it to the context of practice, at the same time recognizing practice as a distinct analytic category that differs from theory and is not subsumed under it. Anyone who thinks implementing a plan is no more than describing it has missed the immediacy and riskiness of practice—the way it exposes us to surprise. One approach to the theory–practice gap is through Polanyi's idea of the inexpressible aspects of tacit knowledge, what separates an explicit description of practice from the practice itself. The distinction between generalities and specifics is helpful because practice is always specific. The idea of strategic time and practice as in the present connects expectations with experience, bridging the separation between the universe of thinking and the real world. Thus the experience of practice differs fundamentally from any statement about practice.

Historians struggle with the same issues, how to describe an event without judging it from their own point of view—being "judgmental" in spite of the fact that no language is neutral. There is a great deal to be said about the relationship between theory and practice in warfare, a matter of life and death rather than academic squabbling. Without getting bogged down in the historical details, von Clausewitz, a fascinating and courageous man with personal experience of the battlefield's chaos, horror, and brutality, was vitally concerned with educating young officers in ways that would be efficacious when they were confronting battle's realities rather than war-gaming in the classroom. In von Clausewitz's time military thinking had tilted towards excessive rigor in theories of formation, lines of fire, general rules about the center of battle gravity, and so on. The assumption was that a proper application of the scientific method would lead to theories about surefire ways to win, changing the face of war and international diplomacy forever. War would no longer be a matter of chance; it would be a science. These notions were central to the training in the French military schools. Von Clausewitz, who fought the French and feared they would overrun Europe, thought thinking of war as a science a grave error, a misunderstanding of its indeterminate (foggy and chancy) human nature, and that the real issue was not whether any of the available theories were valid or not, but rather how they might be best applied under battle conditions. He did not dismiss theory, far from it. A well-substantiated theory could be regarded as a "fact," but maybe not about this particular battle situation. Newton's laws of force, mass, and acceleration are scientific facts and, we presume, true everywhere and always—but should they be considered when getting a posse of cavalry across a river or dueling?

The key to von Clausewitz's thinking lay in his "dialectical" method, his sense that in the real world there were always at least two opposing or mutually exclusive ways of thinking about something—perhaps two theories or heuristics. He thought of strategizing in terms of natural language and its openness to surprise and creativity rather than formal language and deterministic theory. The Clausewitzian world is one of trade-offs—matters of practice inevitably involving judgments supported by, but never dictated by, analysis. In business this might appear as the tussle between canceling the R&D budget on the grounds that it was not certain to produce something of value and could be a waste (not expected to deliver a suitable internal rate of return), versus doubling down in the hope of scoring a home run against the competition (through some currently unanticipated technological innovation)—the glass half empty or half full issue. Von Clausewitz argued no theory should be presumed relevant without first identifying its antitheses, the opposing ideas or critique, and then second, appreciating that choosing between the opposing ideas was the very essence of strategic work, a judgment-call that lay outside any of the theories being judged. In other more philosophical terms, until we have the long-sought theory of everything (and no uncertainty remains), there can be no theory of applying theory. There is no theory about when to adopt or reject a theory—a point made by both Gödel and Wittgenstein. To adopt any theory blindly (without justification) is unstrategic, especially if you are anticipating a practice with major downside risks. But no justification can be rigorous. The choice should be based on evaluating both the theory's supporting ideas and those opposing, and appreciating the choice between them as a matter of judgment. This is a familiar characterization of human knowing and acting. As the writer F. Scott Fitzgerald argued, a sure sign of intelligence was "the ability to hold two contrary ideas in the mind at the same time, and still function".[14] The difference between knowledge, having information, and wisdom, knowing when it is appropriate to use it, runs along similar lines. Thus von Clausewitz was not at all opposed to theory, only to the neglect of the judgment inevitably involved in its application. The educational implications were that students should learn all the theories available and then be taught to factor them into the strategizing process—but, most of all, taught never to subordinate their judgment to any particular theory.

If the strategist cannot ever take a theory for granted as indicating the way things must be analyzed, there are immediate practical implications. First, there can be no theory of strategizing. Indeed strategizing is about dealing with situations that cannot be theorized. I presume business situations are shot-through and fraught with uncertainty and knowledge absences to the point that no theory can be applied without considerable doubt and danger that things are not what they seem. Second, theory comes into the strategizing process as a constraint on the strategist's choices, never more or less significant than another kind of constraint. It carries no special authority and von Clausewitz's main critique of academics was their assumption that theory was a superior form of human knowing. To the contrary, it stands *pari passu* with facts, intentions, heuristics, emotions, and intuitions, not above them. Anticipating human action, the strategist must deal with constraints of many types—legal, normative, cultural, financial, technological, historical, motivational, and so on—but the emphasis is always on the synthesizing. Practice is what matters, not theory.

Von Clausewitz showed how a theory might be fitted into the inventory of chosen constraints without debating whether it differs from, say, local government regulation, the entrepreneur's personal preferences, or the workforce's cultural norms. Constraints are always defined contextually, in terms of those features of the situation that seem to constrain the strategist's choices at that time—seen through the prism of the BM. Some constraints are expressed in the language of the situation's politics, others as psychology or history. Theories are simply statements in the peculiar language of science. Under Knightian uncertainty this is never more than a choice of rhetoric. Nonetheless some theories are excellent candidates for many BMs. The

---

[14] F. Scott Fitzgerald (1936 ) 'The Crack-up': http://www.esquire.com/features/the-crack-up.

interplay of supply and demand, for instance. Decrease prices and demand goes up. It certainly seems wise to bear this in mind when getting a new product out into a competitive marketplace. But even here things may be not as straightforward as they might be and price theory may prove irrelevant. Price might be an indicator of quality instead, as with those strange Giffen goods that we consume more of as their price increases—alternative theories about the relationship between price and demand. Rather than presume any of the strategic field's many theories and tools useful, they should all be learned, yet regarded with a doubting eye and inspected through the prism of the firm's BM. Von Clausewitz regarded detail as no less important than theory. One of his definitions of strategy is "choosing the time and place of engagement," to maximize strategic advantage, exploit surprise, information asymmetries, and so on. But notice both "time" and "place" are indexical not general or theoretical. Von Clausewitz was very cognizant of the various geographies of the multidimensioned opportunity space, placing strong emphasis on detailed knowledge of the terrain of the engagement, and on the value of local knowledge.

Third, with this view of theory von Clausewitz resolved or avoided entirely what academics call the rigor–relevance problem, the frequent criticism that business school curricula, for example, fail to deal with matters relevant to business people. Academics say theorizing is always what we aspire to, our mistake is that we theorize the wrong things. Their reforming proposal is that business schools and economics departments be reoriented towards research-ing and theorizing matters of greater relevance to business. Von Clausewitz saw no point in chasing after relevance the way many business academics do. He regarded this as a "category error," confusing apples with oranges or dog sleds. The rigor–relevance gap is the unavoidable result of the positivist assumption that business activity can be wholly grasped by a single theory's statement. Yet theory, by definition, is an artifact of the human mind, a generalization only tenuously related to practice, which is about singular—but total—engagement with the world. Thus theory cannot have any logical relation to practice. Von Clausewitz saw that theorizing and practice were in entirely different domains of experiencing and knowing. If a theory seems to relate to and inform a practice, that is a matter of judgment, not logic, to be contested before being accepted. For instance, from the general public's point of view, the tussle between Keynesian and non-Keynesian economic policies ("quantitative easing" versus "austerity") is not about whether one theory is more logical or scientific than the other. While economists certainly debate this—debate being their livelihood—the practical consequences for ordinary people are more serious. The public is not going to charge politicians with adopting poor theory. Politicians stand or fall on their policies and their impact on the voting public's experience. Policy decisions made the Precariat or Occupy Wall St movements visible, just as they made the 1932 US Bonus Army and the 1936 Jarrow March to London visible. The theories that shaped the debates that led to these policies remain unremarked in the literature, to be dug up by historically inclined economists.

Fourth, von Clausewitz showed the practical relevance of historical analysis. If scientific theory can never fully grasp practice, how can a better understanding be gained? Our overenthusiasm for the scientific method has led to an unbalanced theory of understanding. We have been trained to think it is about facts, leaving judgment and practice unconsidered—along with much else such as ethics and faith. As a major chemist Polanyi pushed back with the term tacit, pointing out that successful laboratory research required skills that were impossible to theorize or explicate. Von Clausewitz's dialectical method, seeking the opposite so that something can be held up to the mind's eye and examined critically, can be applied directly to thinking about human understanding—"Is there a way of thinking that balances or complements the scientific method?" The question goes to the heart of philosophy, of course. Von Clausewitz believed history matters; important to strategists because theorizing is not the same as "doing" or "making history." Much history debates facts such as dates and scores. But historical thought reaches beyond facts in two ways. First, historical generalizations are implied as we move back from particulars towards generalities—for instance, history may teach that rulers generally have enemies who try to depose them, or that firms that take on excessive risks generally go bankrupt. Thus historical thinking may lead inductively to "general laws," perhaps probabilistic, like the laws of Newtonian science, and so lead on to predicting and explaining what happens in society in a rigorous scientific manner. For instance, history might suggest high taxes lead to civil unrest or increasing workers' benefits increases their productivity. But second, and very different, history goes beyond accumulations of fact by focusing on human intervention. The Nature science probes is predictable but human beings cannot (yet) be completely predicted. Instead of history being the search for general laws it also works the other way around. The result of human interventions into others' lives can seldom be predicted. In which case general laws are not applicable to human affairs. This is the difference between ignorance and indeterminacy in different clothing.

Human interventions are practices, singular and specific, and transform history into a story of how specific human beings acted in specific situations. How can we explain Napoleon's decision to attack Russia? History is more about interventions than generalizations, about specific actors not knowing situations completely enough to predict the responses correctly. Then it also becomes a story of revealing mistakes, a bit like the market failures that make value-adding and profit possible or, more importantly, about how individuals act on the belief the situation is malleable and can lead to profit and growth. The historical analysis can bring together evidence about the degree to which the situation is (*a*) predictable or (*b*) changeable by the specific actor whose history is being examined. History can inform the strategist evaluating the malleability of each constraint. So von Clausewitz regarded historical studies as crucial to educating young officers about how they might make things happen by studying how specific others—generals, platoon leaders, rulers, prisoners, rebels—had acted and changed situations in the past. Thus history helps complement the notion that circumstances determine correct action— the irony in the NRA's slogan that "guns don't kill, people do." Studying history brings complementary ways of thinking into the analysis. Von Clausewitz's objective was dialectical as always, to present the strategist with alternatives of both fact and method within which to frame and then exercise her/his unique judgment. Historical facts are gathered up, ordered, and presented as grist to the mill of the strategist's judgment, to illuminate the dialectic between external causes and creative human action.

Finally, fifth, von Clausewitz regarded the study of theory and history as essential to supplying actors with the language they need to grasp and do their strategic work, both individually and collectively. Historical analysis helps uncover the languages actors used in the past to frame what they saw as their strategic options. For instance, the search is still on to find the documents authorizing the "Final Solution." Not only to establish who drew them up and signed them, but most of all the language that was used to frame genocide as discussable. Likewise, study of the Cuban Missile Crisis reveals a great deal about the practice of politics, and continues to do so years after the first analyses were done. Theory is a powerful way of compacting what others have thought in ways that make it accessible to others trained into its language. But theory can never stand alone as a guide to reasoned human action. Overall, we can see that von Clausewitz's methodology resolves the tension between theory and practice by treating theory as no more than a constraint to the practice that follows the application of judgment, a constraint like any other—a goal chosen, legal rule, ethical norm, resource constraint, etc.

## 4.8 Changing the BM

This chapter provides some guidance to those undertaking the construction of the firm's BM. The sequence is simple enough; the work is difficult and demanding. First, the strategist senses the interplay of choices about identity, intention, context, and strategic time. Then, second, s/he thinks through operationalizing the firm's practice, bringing ideas into contact with the context by (1) discovering the relevant constraints to her/his imagination,

(2) probing the nature of these constraints—whether they spring from ignorance, indeterminacy, or incommensurability—and so looking into the actions that might reveal (i) more of their given nature, a matter of ignorance, or (ii) the interactions that might improve the entrepreneur's position or power, a matter of indeterminacy, or (iii) new conceptualizations, a matter of incommensurability, then (3) creating closure on the BM, (4) propagating the BM as a workable characterization of identity, intention, and context to those whose further imaginative inputs are necessary to create the value-adding processes that bring the firm to life, and (5) putting everything in motion. This is a long sentence of some complexity—but the firm's fundamental value-adding capabilities are neither logical nor simple.

This chapter section offers some practical illustrations, mini-cases. These lead towards case analysis, and Appendix A covers this in more detail. At the same time these illustrations cannot fully identify the BM of the firms considered; they focus on instances of BM change. The nature of the BM is often clearest at times of breakdown and change. Much of sociology works this way too, noting the aspects of a complex social process that surface during breakdown. We are forcibly reminded of the infrastructure of our lives when it fails, otherwise it remains in the background, taken-for-granted. Recall complete understanding of the BM is unattainable. First, its tacit dimensions and its jargon are only open to those inhabiting its activities. Second, even then, the judgments on which the BM stands may not be obvious because many individuals contribute their differing judgment in the course of bringing the firm to life and sustaining it dynamically. Many of these individuals do quite different things, part of the division of labor, which makes getting a sense of the whole very difficult. Even though the entirety of the BM is not available, a discussion of what comes to the surface during breakdown can be helpful because breakdown is seldom total. Typically one of the constraints changes to the point the BM's viability is threatened. The strategic work of fixing it almost certainly goes beyond that one troublesome constraint, for constraints interact, so changing or fixing one generally means adjusting or changing others. Analyzing this interaction reveals more of the BM.

At this point some readers might wonder if I am ignorant of the substantial academic literature on business models or am simply ignoring it. Indeed I know some of it but shall respectfully put it to one side on the grounds that it does not address the strategic work that is my focus. The business models these academics have in mind are not much like what I propose. Rather they offer another strategic tool, a way of presenting the strategist with an objective framework rather than a *habitus* to be grasped from inside. In this chapter, leveraging from its discussion of creating language, we leave Chapter 2 far behind, probing the strategist's construction of her/his own BM, to be inhabited, not borrowing language from others. The academics writing about BMs seem unsure of their audience, who they are helping with their analysis—beyond themselves and their resumes. I believe the way managers talk about BMs is consistent with my view; they do not talk about their firm as the implementation of a tool. When managers use or borrow a tool they adapt it to the firm's own language, identity, intention, and context. No doubt I risk confusing the reader when I use the term BM differently—but I appeal to managers for support. There is a categorical difference between a tool and a BM. The analysis in Chapters 2 and 3 shows how, at best, a tool can only imply a BM by helping the strategist generate one as other constraints and judgments are melded into it.

The academic literature on BMs urges managers to (*a*) pay attention to and analyze the business model, and (*b*) change it when circumstances suggest, presuming that closer attention to the BM leads to improved performance. The majority of authors begin at (*a*) by proposing a definition of the BM, following the objectivist methodology that begins with "define your terms" and then moves on to offering testable theories. With that definition in hand the strategist is directed to collect data about the categories or elements that make it up. Yet there is little agreement about these categories—just a list. Some authors see their BM's categories as derived directly from organization theory—the BM as an assembly of customer relations, value-chain propositions, distribution channels, key resources, key activities, key partnerships, and a cost structure. Or with customer value propositions, key resources, key processes, and a profit formula. Or as an integration of mission, structure, processes, revenues, technology, and legal issues. Or the value-creating insight on which the firm turns. Or with the business idea that has been put into practice. Or as the generation of novelties, customer lock-ins, complementary activities, and operational efficiency. Or as an innovation process, an organizational innovation together with organizational implementation and organizational anchoring. Or as a reflection of the firm's realized strategy. Or as integrated activities operating at three levels: market, organization, resources. At the same time, bearing Porter's distinction between cost leadership and differentiation strategies in mind, many analysts simply changed the language of his nostrums and wrote about cost leadership BMs versus differentiation BMs.

All of this sounds reasonable but does not advance the analysis beyond Chapter 2's tool concept. Who is to define the BM-as-tool categories when they are not self-evident—under conditions of knowledge absence? As in Chapter 2, judgment is always called for and remains the demarcating essence of constructing a BM. Few authors make mention of judgment or strategic work, drawing their terminology uncritically from the academic literature of generalities and causal relations researched with large samples and statistical analysis—and published in the A-journals—forgetting that the BM's categories are only valuable (relevant) when they are grounded in the firm's own people and the language that sights them through the prism of the firm's BM. But, as ever, the academics chase after the mirage of a theory of value-adding in situations presumed fully knowable, an apparatus that is designable and capturable within an objective analysis. Drawing on von Clausewitz and others I argue to the contrary, believing the possibility of value-adding and profit comes from knowledge absences engaged successfully through skilled and imaginative practice. For me the BM is a human artifact, capturing how a world looks to those with imagination enough to grasp it subjectively with their practice, precisely what is denied by the academic literature mentioned and which they intend their tool to replace. Since a viable BM cannot be grasped in its entirety, one opportunity to analyze it is to see what needs to be repaired when it breaks. Doing this helps reveal its components and something of the interplay that yields value, profit, and growth.

### 4.8.1 *Hilti*

A relatively simple example often discussed in business schools was Hilti's switch from equipment sale to a service arrangement. At that time Hilti sold high-end power tools into the construction industry. Just as Xerox did, Hilti thought it would be good to switch to leasing rather than forcing customers to purchase. While the cost of a power tool was not a capital purchase that would have to be authorized at the highest level of the customer company, one of the reasons the Xerox BM worked so well, having the equipment around only when it was being used, and having it maintained or replaced if it malfunctioned, added considerable convenience. Hilti decided to sell tool-use rather than tool-ownership. This drew Hilti into additional capital expenditure and restructuring their balance sheet, for they had to carry the tool inventory. It also required they transform their selling techniques, develop efficient IT, warehousing, inventory management, maintenance management, and financial controls for their senior managers, and new web-based contract management tools for their customers. In this way Hilti changed their BM to absorb the capital cost and the risk of breakdown by building an effective sales and service support system.

### 4.8.2 *Intel*

Another example. Because the BM is known only to insiders, empirical research on BMs has generally been cursory and journalistic, often driven by the academic's prior judgments about what managers should be paying attention to rather than getting at what the firm's strategists actually paid attention to. An interesting exception is Intel. Due to Robert Burgelman's long personal relationship with co-founder Andrew Grove, and their various joint publications, more than usual is known about the Intel Corp and its strategic changes. Intel's initial business was in DRAMs. But by the late 1970s the rapidly expanding DRAM market was increasingly dominated by Japanese manufacturers. Over a period of about five years up to 1984 Intel moved progressively into microprocessors and finally abandoned their DRAM business. Burgelman tells the story of Grove meeting co-founder Gordon Moore and reviewing the decline of their DRAM business.[15] They wondered what would happen if Intel was bought out by new owners. Moore said the owners would fire the co-founders, exit the DRAM business, and get into microprocessors—so they decided they would more or less fire and rehire themselves to do just that (p. 20).

These facts are widely known. But the reinvention of Intel's BM was neither simple nor quick. Prior to 1984 Intel had become progressively more diversified—DRAMs, EPROMs, other microprocessors, and so on. Each group worked alone. Increasing diversification made the firm complicated and difficult to manage or change. Eventually the 1984 exit from DRAMs precipitated an entirely new organizational concept and form; the focus moved onto carefully managed experimentation in order to keep pushing the boundaries in both design and manufacturing. At the same time IBM was introducing the PC and standardized on an Intel microprocessor and Microsoft operating system. The resulting explosion of demand generated a "virtuous circle" of lock-in for Intel and Microsoft. The new Intel BM put heavy priority on development to drive a steady stream of improving cost-performance that became the exemplar of Moore's Law. The notion became key to Intel's jargon and BM, indicating its strategic intention. Intel shifted from DRAMs as a commoditized product and towards securing an economic rent-stream by generating such a pace of development that PC builders had to agree to be locked in if they were to protect their own business. But, inevitably, the vigor of Intel's strategy of experimentation led to an internal split between the mainstream CISC technology (the 386 and 486 microprocessors) and a contesting RISC (reduced instruction set) technology developed in a "skunk works" operation hidden within their labs. The hugely successful 1980s BM was increasingly threatened and chaos developed. In the 1990s Intel was forced to choose, picked CISC, and re-established monopolistic control of the PC manufacturers' chip supply, with attendant rent-streams that were only disturbed as the PC business itself went off the boil. This set Intel looking at strategic alternatives once more, whether they should diversify away from their BM's singular focus on microprocessors. Intel's core achievement was to see how strategically prioritizing

---

[15] R. A. Burgelman and A. S. Grove (1996) 'Strategic Dissonance', *California Management Review*, 38(2), 8–28.

scientific and manufacturing development in two different periods could be translated into sustained profit and growth. As each new chip was designed, itself dependent on a step forward in the science and manufacturing technique, Intel was able to standardize, specifying the chip's manufacturing plant as a complete turn-key operation repeatable, green field, at various locations around the world. Rather than the switch from ownership to use that marked the revamped Hilti, Xerox, and IBM BMs, Intel's BM and strategic timing depended on the virtuous interplay of market evolution and technological progress.

### 4.8.3 *IBM*

Equally well known is IBM's 1993 strategic switch away from prioritizing hardware development after it reported what was then the largest corporate loss in US business history. A new CEO (Lou Gerstner), without any computer industry experience, redirected the firm towards providing computer services—computer use rather than ownership. By 2006 more than half IBM's revenue came from services. The shift involved a reconceptualization of the firm's identity, along with a change in the company's culture and the types of people needed. Engineers and hardware salespeople gave way to service providers as the computing power of mini-computers and then micro-computers became more widely available, eroding the value of IBM's continued dominance in mainframes.

### 4.8.4 *Airbus*

The pace of technological innovation disturbing a firm's BM is illustrated in aircraft manufacturing. The basics here are known around the world even though, as the slow evolution of the Brazilian and Chinese aircraft industries shows, it all takes a while (now Japan is joining in too). Airbus (EADS), the European aircraft manufacturing alliance, has grown to rival Boeing and the other US manufacturers in every respect and secure around 50 percent of business worldwide. They know whatever there is to know about building world-class airplanes. But the strategic implications of its wide-body, double-deck A380—its UHCA (Ultra High Capacity Airliner)—disturbed its own BM. The A380 is the world's largest commercial jet and a huge business gamble. Its maximum capacity in "all-economy" configuration is around 850 passengers. The first prototype flew in April 2005. There were immediate problems with engineering the wings. Further problems with the electrical wiring forced Airbus into substantial redesign. Several difficulties interacted to present the engineers with massive technical and production challenges and the firm with serious strategic threats. The A380's construction logistics are unlike those of Airbus's other airplanes. EADS is a government-supported European consortium created as part of a multinational political strategy to ensure sustained design-and-build capacity in Europe, to avoid strategic dependence on the US capacity at Boeing, Lockheed Martin, Sikorsky, etc. The early EADS aircraft, such as the A320, had parts manufactured all over Europe with the final assembly and interior fit-out done in Toulouse, in the south of France. A320s are now also assembled in Tianjin, China, with many parts made in China, and will soon be assembled in Alabama as well. Because of its size the A380 had entirely different logistics. The airframes are assembled in Toulouse, then flown to Hamburg where the interiors are wired and fitted out. All the design, assembly planning, and customization is done using CATIA, a complex, expensive, and widely used software product developed in 1977 by the French military aircraft manufacturer Dassault. But there are several different versions—and the German plants were using CATIA v4 while the French and British plants (which manufactured the wings) had migrated to v5. The result was a disastrous mismatch when it came to the wiring harnesses. Together with many other difficulties Airbus was forced to delay delivery of orders already received, first by six months, then longer. The EADS share price fell over 25 percent, the EADS CEO, Airbus CEO, and the A380 program manager all left or were reassigned, though there were other issues including insider share dealing. The new CEO resigned after three months, unable to implement his strategy. EADS board member Louis Gallois took over in July 2006. What was he to do?

Ensuring knowledge sharing and software compatibility across the A380's vast multi-site logistical network remains a monstrous task, and clearly essential. This is easy to say but it is only the tip of an iceberg of problems that challenge engineering operations everywhere. Designers are hard at work changing the specifications for almost everything most of the time, because that way lies continuous improvement, sometimes to catch up with commitments already made (as in the A380's case), sometimes to push the design envelopes forward to improve efficiency and reduce operating costs, sometimes to recover strategic advantage in the marketplace. The result is a sustained torrent of design changes that have to be promulgated to those they affect. Part of the A380 build problem was that the allocation of work between Toulouse and Hamburg made it impossible to overlap inside and outside work in the same way the A320s are built. If that could be done it would shorten the build cycle—and pull back some of the delivery delays. But reallocating work was complicated by the interplay of labor commitments to the governments that supported EADS financing, commitments to the heavily unionized workforce, contract commitments to the thousands of subcontractors, and commitment to EADS customers. The complexity of the widespread logistics network also exposed it to the consequences of the Japanese tsunami in

2011. Aircraft purchase contracts are complex, with money upfront, perhaps, but also penalties for late delivery and underperformance that Boeing faced over the Dreamliner 787 grounding. There was also the task of managing EADS's reputation, not only with the airlines, the airport operators, and the various unions, but also with the same governments who had created the firm for their own strategic reasons. Politics being changeable, the relationships between EADS and its host governments are constantly changing and made much more vulnerable when EADS is losing money (as in 2009). Given the breadth and complexity of EADS's operations, the financial analysts tend to focus on products and projects—hence the continuing speculation about whether the A380 project can ever turn a profit, and how this impacts the marketplace, the workforce, the unions, the airlines, and the competition. It also affects those planning airport development, for disembarking or embarking a fully loaded A380 is a very demanding event to handle. If the A380 is going to fail, there will be no need for double-level access-ways.

### 4.8.5 *Arsenal Football Club*

A final different example highlights the subtle interplay between technology and government regulators rather than between technological change and customers' demands, as for IBM and Intel, or technological change and production, as in the EADS case. Arsenal Football Club (AFC), one of London's principal teams, needs a BM very different from those of the firms above. They have no possibility of changing ownership to use and the technological developments are indirect—TV coverage, crowd management, security, etc. Football has become big business worldwide—both legal and illegal—and presents strategic challenges. Demil and Lecocq analyzed the recent history of AFC.[16] The authors hesitated over the mainstream literature's categories but still adopted an objectivist framework (resources and competencies, organization, and value proposition—RCOV) that presumed an outside analyst can properly identify these three types of BM component. They justified this through the club's history. UK football clubs were always involved with local business interests because a successful soccer team made for a more competitive local workforce. The club's costs were players' and staff salaries and the upkeep of the stadium and grounds. At first gate-receipts were the only revenues. In the 1980s TV fees came into the picture and grew to become a significant revenue source. As the TV-hype around sports teams grew, so the sports franchise and branded products grew into a major source of revenue. Commercial sponsorship became common. Thatcher-era loosening of

---

[16] B. Demil and X. Lecocq (2010) 'Business Model Evolution: In Search of Dynamic Consistency', *Long Range Planning*, 43, 227–46.

UK real estate development regulations transformed property values and many clubs found their grounds had become hugely valuable.

Demil and Lecocq argued that in the 1990s three external events transformed the soccer business. TV revenues climbed further. But players' salaries sky-rocketed too after a European Court of Justice ruling freed players from their traditionally restrictive contracts and allowed international transfers, vastly increasing the size of the market for players and accelerating the income of the top players. New UK government regulations came in after almost 100 spectators died in a panic at the Hillsborough stadium. The resulting 1990 Taylor Report required all-seating stadiums, eliminating the traditional standing areas behind the goals. This significantly reduced stadium capacities and, with that, gate-receipts. AFC's Highbury stadium had been built in 1914 and little changed. It was clearly inadequate as post-Taylor its capacity fell from around 60,000 to 38,400. Indeed AFC had to move their most important international matches to other larger stadiums, a major inconvenience to the club's supporters. The club regrouped by securing major new sponsorship from Emirates Airline and, with local authority help, purchased new ground 500 meters from the old stadium and built a modern stadium seating 60,300. They also brought in a highly talented Frenchman, Arsène Wenger, as manager and, as a result, were able to attract some of the world's best players. AFC became one of the world's most prominent teams and financially successful clubs. Clearly AFC's strategizing was around a quite unique constellation of constraints.

## 4.9 Summary

Readers may find these illustrations interesting, especially after the abstraction of my earlier philosophizing. But they are also a puzzle. What is to be made of them? The academic researcher's impulse is to look for what the examples have in common in the hope of coming up with some generalities, and most of the BM literature moves in this direction. They show firms occupy the space between supply and demand and must have processes that transform resources—but what else? This is trivial, at best, and simply leads the analysis back to whatever unproblematic concept of the firm the writer adopted at the outset. Many writers also assume, without explanation or justification, that clarifying the BM leads to improved performance. If that was the case alert firms would surely hire these academics to do more of their strategic work. But one important generality is that stuff happens and the firms' strategists have to do something about it. Another is that actions are always complicated by interactions. Plus firms like IBM—even AFC—are generally complex with multiple types of activity and location. There is a gap between the enterprise as a portfolio of rather distinct BMs (the BCG model) and what most writers mean by a BM. Yet another is that the vast majority of private sector firms are SMEs, family firms, or sole-entrepreneurships, and not much like the Top 500 firms that typically appear in the BM literature. Most small firms are not required to file the results publicly held firms must and are very opaque. Their BMs are even tougher to puzzle out, even though they are more important to the economy and to job creation than their bigger brethren. So, even more importantly, without some understanding of these BMs how can governments take appropriate measures to "stimulate" the private sector?

My view is that there are no strategic generalizations—it is a contradiction in terms—and that the whole point of building the BM is to escape the uniformity or homogeneity that nullifies the possibility of profit and growth. But if each BM is unique what can be said about these examples? The commonalities here are in method. Note how each BM carries the seed of its own destruction. There is perpetual change as each BM changes the situation and then leads on to further strategizing. Managerial hubris and over-reach is only one kind of risk. The dynamic nature of the elements of identity, intention, and context, and of their interplay, ensures that risking surprise and failure is an unavoidable corollary of seeking value. Method is key. Just as intelligence means being able to carry two or more contrary ideas, so a strategic understanding of each BM implies knowing the counter-story, what economists envisage as the context of "opportunity cost." Strategizing is a matter of judgment, so it can never be fully grasped by what is chosen, it must also deal with what was both discussed and dismissed, the next best alternative. For example, in spite of IBM's continuing research efforts, consistently successful, their 1980s commitment to "heavy metal" was vulnerable to the advance of mini- and microcomputers, a business in which IBM participated but was never able to establish a dominant rent-yielding presence. But few of the discussions of IBM's strategic shift from hardware to services make much of the fact that there was already a brisk business in computer services and facilities management, so IBM's switch into this well-developed market was risky. They were "new entrants." But in the background, too, was IBM's history of risky strategic shifts. One was the firm's plunging into System 360 in the 1960s.[17] At the time the financial press was well aware that IBM was "betting the company" on this new product line, which entailed a massive reorganization and cannibalization of its existing profitable lines of business. No one knew if the promised gains would materialize. History shows the decision paid off handsomely and System 360 quickly set the standards for all future mainframe business. But as with all BMs, IBM's success bred its own

[17] E. W. Pugh, L. R. Johnson, and J. H. Palmer (1991) *IBM's 360 and Early 370 Systems.* Cambridge, MA: MIT Press.

problems. In 1969 the US Department of Justice filed a claim against the firm for monopolizing the industry. The case dragged on for thirteen years and was eventually dropped, but as one of their concessions to the pressure, IBM closed their service bureau. So when Gerstner argued for switching strategic emphasis from hardware to services he was proposing reversing this history, moving back into a field now dominated by other players. What was the counter-story? What proposals did Gerstner dismiss when he settled on the service strategy? What was the language of the strategizing debate inside IBM? As far as I know the internal debate has never been adequately reported. Yet this is where the strategizing took place.

As with Intel, the way to get a better handle on the specifics of a BM is not by cross-comparison with other firms' BMs, but by getting a longitudinal sense of the firm's own history and unique interplay of strategic crisis and response, the interplay of what were considered viable alternative BMs. What is going on in the context matters, but it never determines the alternative chosen. This reinforces that the BM is a creature of the synthesis of identity, intention, and context that has a specific strategic-time character. Historical research methods are vastly more fruitful for looking at this than the cross-sectional methods that chase after generalities. The BM's history is highly episodic—as the strategy-as-practice authors suggest. Carrying the seeds of its own destruction, every BM eventually loses vitality or collapses under an impulse that might be external or internal. Then strategic work is required to reinvent and create a new BM able to handle the new situation, reinforcing the fundamental difference between calendar time and strategic time. Again, the strategic work to be done is simple to characterize but difficult to do. If it is to be the pathway to value-creation it must capture the situation's uniqueness. Each constraint, whether theoretical, physical, conceptual, normative, or skill-based, must be explored to discover how, when and where it can be worked on to expand the BM's opportunity space or offer greater resistance to the change efforts of others that would shrink the BM's space. To illustrate, strategizing's difficulty is demonstrated by the difference between the principles politicians proclaim during election and the practice they engage in when they are in office and no longer have the luxury of ignoring the situation's constraints.

This chapter suggests the most fruitful way to think of BMs is as local natural languages that outline opportunity spaces entrepreneurs and their colleagues must inhabit. A firm's terminology points to the constraints that are important—services and use versus hardware and ownership, or multiple coordinated franchise-based rent-streams versus gate-receipts. The strategist's problem is always "What to do?"—and the answers begin with creating the language that enables them to characterize and talk about their situation. Abstract generalities may provide a start, but as von Clausewitz argued, are poor guides to practice because that belongs in an epistemological space that allows strategic judgment. This demands a natural language rather than a formal scientific one. With the BM in hand, the next chapter deals with promulgating it among those whose further judgment inputs are crucial to approaching the point of commitment. Action—not thought—brings the firm to life and sustains it as it responds to external and internal shocks and breakdowns, and to the emergence of new opportunities.

# 5

# Persuading Supporters

## 5.1 Talk

Chapter 4 explored an approach to constructing the special language that carries the firm's unique business model. The constraints to the strategist's judgment are the terms in this language. Judging the relationships between these terms becomes its syntax. The relationships between the language and the practices the language shapes become its semantics. The BM-as-language identifies what the strategist should pay attention to and how to articulate what s/he finds into the firm's practices. It is a "local rationality." It is idiosyncratic, a firm-specific jargon understood by those who take part in the firm's indexical practices, but obscure or meaningless to outsiders who do not. The language is "natural" rather than rigorous and "formal." It is able to carry emotion and tacit meaning. It is open and incomplete, unable to grasp the entirety of the experience or history of those in the firm. But it approaches an understanding of the synthesis of its identity, intentions, and context more closely than a universal or formal language can. Theory has its place but only as a component of the firm's natural language.

Chapter 5 moves beyond the isolated strategist or entrepreneur to treat the firm as a process of active collaboration between those whose judgment is necessary to the firm's existence and value-adding practices. It reaches behind Coase's questions to consider why a freely choosing person would ever contribute her/his judgment and creativity to the firm and so to the profit of others. This points to the fundamentally paradoxical nature of the private sector firm. Firms exist because they have proven to be effective apparatuses for harnessing the judgment and creativity of others to an entrepreneur's goals. A firm can only exist because people have been persuaded to act in the interest of others rather than solely in their own interest. Rhetoric is the ancient study of persuasion. So Chapter 5 redefines the firm as a rhetorical artifact that, engaging Knightian uncertainty through effective practice, is democratic capitalism's principal instrument of economic value creation. Talk (including sign-language, symbols, and non-verbal communication) is more than mere information movement. Talk creates the fabric of the lived life. Communication theory has drifted towards mechanistic models, a move accelerated by the amazing developments in IT. But human communication has aspects and dimensions that cannot be computerized. Defining strategic work as the application of human judgment to non-computable business situations means human communication goes well beyond what can modeled, simulated, or otherwise rendered computable.

Chapter 5 focuses on why talk is so central to value-adding practice. To deal with its subtler aspects I turn to rhetoric, often called the "art of persuasion." The best-known text is Aristotle's, so rhetoric is an ancient art.[1] Unfortunately rhetoric is not well appreciated today; indeed it is widely maligned. There are good reasons for this. Rhetoric is not only the study of persuading others to a particular point of view; its end point is persuading others to specific directed action under uncertain circumstances, when the action intended changes the world. It is an instrument for communicating intentions, exerting social power, as powerful for bad ends as for good. The point of business strategizing is action towards the strategist's chosen ends; it is not merely for declaring or constructing a goal, a plan, or a framing. Businesses exist because others (such as employees) have been persuaded to act towards the goals established by the entrepreneur—goals that are not the employees'. Acting on others, strategizing is demanding and stressful, and calls for a certain personal talent. Preparation is essential. The reader can sample the extensive modern literature on self-management without my guidance, so I do not review it. It is largely psychological. I take my cue from von Clausewitz who, as a military man, was less psychologically inclined and more interested in the training and study regimes that intending military strategists should adopt. History is especially important to understanding effective military practice. Exemplars for Americans might be Patton, or for British readers, Montgomery; both were lifelong students of military history with deep understanding of von Clausewitz's methods. Von Clausewitz argued the study of military history was useful in part because it helped give those participating in the strategizing process a shared language with which to exchange their personal ideas. Entrepreneurship in business is inevitably collaborative. No person or entrepreneur is an island and strategy comes into being via discourse between the different

---

[1] Aristotle (1991) *The Art of Rhetoric*. London: Penguin Books.

actors, just as the sole proprietor must deal with banks, suppliers, and regulators, and so on.

Note I reject the commonplace that subordinates act towards the firm's goals because they reason it is in their interest to do so—get paid, keep a job, make a career, and so on. One of the puzzles about private sector operations is that the beneficial results of its activity are not uniformly or equitably distributed. If everyone involved got fully recompensed for his or her contribution— assuming that could be calculated—there would be no "surplus" left over to call profit. For employees in particular, the value they create for the firm must exceed what they get out of it. Such questions around why free individuals might act in others' interests are central to this discussion. Strategizing is the practice of persuading others to accept less than "full compensation" for what they are doing for the firm or entrepreneur. Whenever this happens we know people have been persuaded, just as advertising has often persuaded us to buy what we may well not need. The study of rhetoric helps unpack means from ends. No question, management is a talking and persuading game, not simply one of making choices, rational or otherwise. Its objective is collaborative action under the realistic conditions of fragmented knowledge, under circumstances in which simple instructions fail because their sender did not and could not fully anticipate what the employee finds in her/his practice. Management's rhetoric deploys the strategic language constructed in Chapter 4. After a long hiatus, academic study of the rhetorical practices of contemporary organizations is emerging and it is clear that practicing managers can benefit greatly from this effort. Management is primarily rhetorical, as Mintzberg's early studies suggested.[2] Several consulting products and recent how-to books reconstruct classical rhetoric for modern managers. The military also have much to teach us about how this works or does not.

The central thought here is that strategizing, as von Clausewitz saw it, is part and parcel with having to act collaboratively in a timely and reasoned manner when full information is not available, when there are complications, subtleties, and knowledge absences the strategist has neither the time nor the money, nor even the technological capability, to fill—but must act anyway. Nowadays academics are pretty committed to theorizing managers' decisions as if there is always enough information to support rigorous analysis, especially when aided by "big data," analytics, probability theory, agent-based modeling, fuzzy set math, and so on. They pay little attention to knowledge absences, or to time's passing, or to the press of the situation. This is curious given thinking about choice when confronting knowledge absences has a long history going back, especially, to Enlightenment philosophers like

---

[2] H. Mintzberg (1973) *The Nature of Managerial Work*. New York: Harper & Row.

Hume and Locke, whom I follow directly. Ironically, as we advance into the Information Age, with our rising ability to collect, analyze, and share huge quantities of data, academics seem less interested in the everyday-ness of our not-knowing, of not being able to "connect the dots." Yet this is where we so visibly fail.

There are important discussions by writers such as Herbert Simon, Frank Knight, George Shackle, and Edith Penrose. I borrow much from their work (see Appendix D: Further Reading). But my claim that practitioners and students can gather something useful from such high-level scholarship needs justification too. I hope to show that practitioners and students who have neither the time nor the inclination to debate these authors on their academic ground can still gain enormously from learning how they viewed business situations. John Maynard Keynes (1883–1946) was the British economist whose name was much bandied about as the theorist behind the recent US and Eurozone "bailouts." He remarked practical business people are often unwitting intellectual slaves to dead economists. This applies whenever managers think strategic decisions can be rigorously data-driven. Perhaps there was a time when strategy theorists really believed in the relevance of rational decision-making. I urge readers away from the idea of strategizing as a dehumanized numbers-driven quasi-science and towards a practical economic humanism, an urgent task for many reasons, professional, social, and political. Real people have limited capabilities, as Simon's notion of "bounded rationality" captured. Numbers-driven thinkers have gotten us into a fair amount of trouble of late but social reform is not my objective. My focus is on helping the private sector entrepreneur. I see strategizing as the practice of synthesizing as many of the available facts as possible, together with personal judgments when facts are not available. It is not an implementation of scientific theory and rigorous analysis. It is an active creative process, pushed forward by the application of personal judgment, not by sitting back and presuming the facts or theory can drive a solution. The academic tendency is to write personal judgment out of the story and claim theorizing as a superior mode of thought, to presume theory lords it over practice, that a theory of strategy would be more real or valuable than effective strategic practice. Fortunately several books, such as Schön's well-regarded *Reflective Practitioner*,[3] show the best academic thinking about the development and application of professional judgment is entirely accessible to managers and students alike—so long as the writing is reasonable. There is absolutely no need to "dumb-down" theory for managers; indeed to imagine so is deeply insulting to those who actually create value in our socio-economy. Plus it is a grave misconception of how

---

[3]  D. A. Schön (1983) *The Reflective Practitioner: How Professionals Think in Action*. New York: Basic Books.

managers think and act, and of the consequences. Equally it is a misconception of the academics' role in society.

Academics sometimes patronize managers because they understand things in ways that managers do not. But managers know a great deal about what they are doing even though they seldom write about it in great depth. Academics tend to write more but understand less. Along with the work of the authors mentioned already, Chester Barnard's *Functions of the Executive* and *Education for Executives*[4] remain the most penetrating examinations of private sector managing in the English language, and I draw on his ideas extensively. Barnard did not have a strong academic background, being largely self-taught after dropping out from Harvard and running a dance band. Nonetheless he rose through the ranks at AT&T to become CEO of New Jersey Bell Telephone and led the USO (United Services Organization) during WW2. After retiring, he became President of the Rockefeller Foundation and Chairman of the NSF (National Science Foundation). He knew a lot about generating economic value and the practice of science, and he applied highly original thinking to the analysis of management practice. Our literature would be better if more authors had significant experience of the personal judgment necessary to being an effective manager before they begin to write about it, especially if that "management experience" was as a responsibility-bearing insider rather than as a consulting outsider (an example of authority without responsibility, perhaps). Consultants have done more than academics to produce the ideas and techniques managers find useful. Yet both consultants and academics tend to miss the moral and ethical dimensions that managerial responsibility brings with it. Nonetheless while there are many weaknesses and problems with academic work on management, much of it is useful to practitioners. Some of it is awfully good and fully deserving of a busy practitioner's time even if most of it has little immediate managerial relevance.

Being focused on strategizing as a practice I eventually deal with cases, one of the strategy professor's handiest academic "tools" (Appendix A). Case-writing is a form of theorizing using historians' methods. These are not as widely understood as the basic hypothesis–sampling–analysis methods that dominate the research literature today. So part of my agenda is to explain why historical methods are worth rehabilitating for they often provide important insights into the human condition that might otherwise be missed. In Chapter 1, for example, I used the history of post-WW2 strategy theorizing to contrast efficiency-seeking against rent-seeking. The contrast does not require rigorous definition of either, rather it helps highlight the context of

---

[4] C. I. Barnard (1945) 'Education for Executives', *Journal of Business of the University of Chicago*, 18(4), 175–82. C. I. Barnard (1968) *The Functions of the Executive* (30th anniversary edn). Cambridge, MA: Harvard University Press.

the change and the different needs being met. Historical methods are central to strategizing, so I review teaching strategy and the use of casework in Appendix B. There has been a welcome degree of strategy text specialization and attention to local matters as the MBA market has expanded globally. Business situations vary greatly so there is little point in using the Continental Can case, a classic US manufacturing industry case, for students headed into tourism or financial services, or for students in Brazil. Much strategy theorizing implies nostalgia towards manufacturing even as there is little of it left in the developed nations and it is seldom the students' main interest. Most business schools have transformed themselves to meet the growth of the financial services sector, yet there is surprisingly little understanding of what students actually do when hired or how the industry's instruments are generated and sold. Nonetheless cases are drawn from an increasing variety of industries, though few detail financial operations even as the majority of MBA students are headed there. In Appendix B, I presume the instructor will choose cases that work best for his/her students and I comment on selecting and using these. Case-writing has become a specialism among academics and today there are many fine on-line libraries of cases available to suit every strategy teacher's need and taste.

Strategizing practice is using our given capabilities to make judgments in under-determined situations. In the background is the realization that strategizing is not simply about coming up with an action plan to be presented to the world as something complete but also about being able to persuade others into collaborating or supporting that choice. It is always about collaborating with others, fellow workers, and, through markets, customers and suppliers. As Porter's analysis emphasized, it is also about signaling and deterring others (section 2.6). All interact through a language that persuades. Strategizing is most obvious when innovating, as the entrepreneur imagines a new world that must be communicated to others if it is to be realized. Everyday language changes all the time, new terms, nuances, and meanings come in, old ones go out. Developing a new language is almost always achieved by recycling familiar terms, giving them new meanings in the specific context of the firm's situation. The firm uses borrowed terms in new ways, often puzzling to outsiders. As most people who have worked know, the first step towards being productive and engaging your capabilities is to understand what your colleagues are talking about, what they mean by the terms they use. You cannot make a contribution until you have learned the situation's language.

## 5.2 OK, We Have Strategy, Now What?

The previous chapters covered the ground from using the models in the strategy literature—both organizational and economic—to define strategizing as the process of framing a business situation so that the strategist's judgment can be applied to it. I present this as an art form, perhaps the most important art in our capitalist democracy, for without it nothing much else could happen. Economic value-adding makes universities, scientific labs, and art museums possible—and most everything else. The value that business produces is our civilization's driver, its "horn of plenty." There are other civilizations and ways of organizing society, but ours is marked by the central place of economic "enterprise." Our social and political system is capitalist; business strategizing is at its core. In Chapter 4 the strategizing processes of Chapters 2 and 3 were generalized to (a) the discovery of the specific constraints that limit how the strategist's judgment can be applied, and (b) the construction of idiosyncratic language or jargon that enables the strategist to grasp the situation and its possibilities, bring them into the mind, and so envisage the business model as an apparatus to translate imaginings into added value. Natural language embraces the tacit knowledge embedded in effective practices and bridges between the strategist's chosen goals—imagined—and the business practices that realize added value.

Now I finally turn my back on defining people—employees, customers, managers—as self-maximizing economic agents, presuming they do things only because they believe it is going to benefit them. This is almost irresistibly tempting because it so easily leads on to powerful rigorous models and strategic formulae that answer pseudo-questions like "In which business should I invest?" or "How can our firm secure a competitive advantage?" The answers are publishable but, given the uncertainties of the real world, such pseudo-questions cannot ever be answered definitively. They relate to questions strategists have no interest in answering. Rather, strategists work to select and embrace the real uncertainties of a particular situation and, by engaging human creativity, transform them into opportunities to develop innovative value-adding processes that would not otherwise have come into existence. People seldom know what they need or will consume until after they have been persuaded. Who knew they needed an iPod in 1991, ten years before it appeared? Who knew they needed bottled water—which today costs more than gas? Via innovation firms often achieve a measure of quasi-monopoly, each being unique, different, and able to generate enough "economic rent" to open up the possibility of profit and growth by creating needs (Coke rather than Pepsi) and then monopolizing the means of meeting them—Big Macs, airport landing slots, elite sports cars, etc. In practice the supply of something novel often creates its own demand, an entrepreneurial act that shapes the market rather than the other way around, with demand driving supply. It comes down to people and their desires, not perfectly designed products. Sustained competitive advantage is often the result of creating demands that did not previously exist and "owning them," ensuring others cannot meet them as well as you can.

A handy definition of management is "getting things done through others." This chapter switches from imagining people being commanded or incentivized into place to realizing how you can persuade others to help you do something you cannot do alone. Instead of envisaging a team of economic agents built into the purposive mechanical apparatus—as on a Fordist production line—the firm is a collaborative social context in which every individual is contributing their judgment towards the creation of a value imagined by the strategist. But the strategist cannot build and breathe life into the collaborative situation or business model on his/her own. Even the sole proprietor must work out how to get others involved (customers, suppliers, and a landlord, perhaps). In the modern situation employees cannot normally be drawn into the value-adding process simply by offering them economic incentives or by terrorizing them into obeying orders, but by the processes of seeking and securing their help, especially by securing their creative judgment.

The switch to persuasion takes us into the heart of the "trick" the previous chapters have been moving towards. Here it is. It is one thing to engage others in an exchange relationship—you do this, I pay you that—quite another to say: "I do not know how to do X, please do it for me. And I'll pay you Y even though you realize that Y is less than X." People work for income, of course, but the firm only exists when it gets the better part of the deal, making more out of the employee than s/he is being paid. Getting sensible people to go along with this arrangement is the puzzle at the core of the firm. Strategizing boils down to being able to make this happen and this goes beyond having judgment. The source of the value added by the firm's activities does not lie in the firm—its structure, funding, design, tangible or intangible resources, or production or value-chain processes—but in the buzz of fruitful and uncertainty-absorbing relationships with creative people, employees, customers, investors, etc.—and in how these get harnessed to the entrepreneur's vision. Note it is not possible to understand this trick in the abstract; a business model is always something specific that follows from a creative interpretation of the specifics. There can be no theory of how to do this. Clearly there are situations in which people are compelled to seek whatever work opportunities are available—hunger, the one-company town, taking over the family business—all ideas about forcing otherwise free individuals into specific work. But these are not explanations of how the value-adding and work-providing apparatus comes into being or how collaboration produces economic value. Earlier I noted but dithered about whether strategizing is a collaborative or individual process. My intuitions are towards the individual end but there is some slipperiness. Irrespective of whether strategizing is collaborative or individual, interpersonal communication is central. When the strategizing process is collaborative, it is because people interact with each other, perhaps by talking and texting. When the strategizing process is concentrated in a few hands, the strategy resulting has to be communicated to those others whose work brings the firm to life. Talk is the practice at the core of the firm. Talk is what gets people working together to create the firm as a value-adding process.

This chapter focuses on talk, defined widely so as to include "signaling" and non-verbal communication—your frown, the competitor's ad, who gets the corner office. Not all talk is the same. Strategizing makes it essential to distinguish "persuasion talk" from "instruction talk." Plans lead to the instructions given to those whose actions bring them to life or "implement" them. But action in the real world is always colored by faulty anticipations and bumping into knowledge absences. Things get missed out when plans are being made—Murphy's Law prevails (anything that can go wrong, will). All of which is perfectly obvious to everyone outside the classroom. The question is "How can we shape practice enough to achieve what we intend?" Plans are often less effective than they might be because communication systems do not work efficiently. Most readers will recall playing the parlor game "post-man's knock" or "post office." You see messages get seriously mangled as they are passed from one player to another. A paperback I bought years ago (before the UK adopted decimal coinage) had a cover that was hilarious—or tragic. It showed the initial message "send reinforcements, we're going to advance" being transformed into "send three and fourpence, we're going to a dance." So this chapter will look at various notions of communicating and, with those in mind, what the strategizing group can do to minimize information corruption or loss—a topic familiar to communication engineers. In other words, when we have chosen what we want to communicate, how can we do that efficiently?

A different problem arises when managers do not know what message to send. Managers seldom have the ability, as a communication engineer has, to be completely certain about the message being sent. "This guest is a VIP, make sure his needs are met" is pretty loose even if important—or "order 200 flange gaskets," only to discover the flange design has been changed. We think we make things clear, only to discover we misunderstand, or have been misunderstood, perhaps accidentally, perhaps intentionally, as some hearers work hard to find ways to exploit our communication inadequacies. Emails or tweets about sensitive matters are especially open to being misinterpreted. Smileys may help but are not well suited to precise communication. Some things are best said face to face. We generally have more comfort with face-to-face communication because we feel we have more control of nuance and body language. We say something critical and soften the hurt with a smile. We show incomprehension or surprise. One of the sharpest American quips is "What didn't you understand about what I just told you?" which combines a rhetorical question with an insult—and a statement of power. Instructions are fine in theory but less so in practice. Indeed the idea of a manager instructing a subordinate may be misleading. Instruction presumes the instructor has so complete a grasp of the recipient's situation that the recipient is no more than a passive cog in the instructor's scheme of things. The thing to be done is preconceived in the instructor's mind. "Take the second left, then the third right, and it's in front of you." That is fine, but maybe there is a passage between two office buildings the instructor has always disregarded, that catches out the stranger anxiously counting his way to the train station. How much does the recipient have to know in order to understand the instruction? In principle, everything; so the situation gets more complicated when the speaker does not have a full grasp of the situation. "It is on the other side of the river, but not as far up as the cathedral" or "I'm told there are good restaurants on 31st Street." Here the recipient has to supplement the instruction with her/his own search skills—judgment. The action becomes a creative collaborative effort with speaker and listener working together towards an ill-specified end goal, and "instruction" becomes an inappropriate term for describing the communication.

Instruction presupposes at least three things about the relationship between instruction and action. First, the instructor has a thorough grasp of the resulting action and its consequences; second, the hearer has the ability to relate the instruction to her/his understanding of the action options; third, the hearer has the capacity to act in the way instructed. These capacities become constraints when absent. Thus even when the hearer can connect the instruction received to the action options perceived—a communication constraint—s/he may not have the resources necessary to execute the action—a different kind of constraint. All this seems so obvious it is scarcely worth remarking. We issue instructions all the time; I take my shirts to the laundry confident the people there know what to do with them, and have the appropriate resources. The firm orders desktop computers of a reputable make and expects them to work when delivered. When circumstances are clear instructions may trigger market transactions with the terms of trade known, both parties undertaking to deliver their part of the deal. You do that and I pay you this. The law stands in the background to remind the parties what instruction means and to settle any argument about the parties' liabilities and remedies. In a bureaucratic organization there are similar non-market transactions that take place within an authority structure that gives instructions their meaning. The market's logic is absorbed into the administrative apparatus. You get a job with defined terms of engagement and a defined quasi-market system of incentives and punishments stands in the background (the administration). Subordinates are hired to execute specific tasks on the basis of their capability to execute the instructions associated with the role. Train drivers are to respond correctly to the signals, schedule, and speed restrictions or will be held accountable and at fault. The context of practice is well understood, it is plan-able and instruction seems an appropriate metaphor.

This way of looking at the situation suits those who regard a strategy as a plan to be communicated to others to execute. Unfortunately, as the reader knows already, real situations are riddled with knowledge absences arising from misinformation, bounded rationality, or whatever. Thus whenever strategizing is necessary the communications that lead towards implementation cannot be instruction-like. We must shift gear from instruction to persuasion. The second part of this chapter deals with how persuasion works. It takes us from mechanical communication towards people with feelings, doubts, fears, and so on. It is all very well for consultants to trumpet the simplicity of it all—get clear about your goals, lay out a logical plan, measure progress, etc.—but this is more their ideology than practical advice. Instruction implies those being instructed are little more than tools, as passive as a hammer or electric drill. As the instructors confront their inability to grasp the action situation and to choose and use the right tool, they put themselves in the hands of the other actors who know what they do not. I have toothache and put myself in the dentist's capable hands. We retain a local attorney to help us bid for a contract in a foreign city. We cannot manage these relationships by planning until these helpers have contributed what they know and so rendered the situation plan-able. We can only instruct them after they have agreed to fill in the gaps in our instructions. People are not available to be instructed until they have been persuaded to subject themselves to our instructions. When we start with individuals who are free to choose what they do, the PAT analysis (section 3.2) shows persuasion is the first step towards creating a fruitful relationship. Others have to be persuaded to become tools to our project and this begins with recognizing they are neither passive nor mere tools. Instruction "disrespects" until those being instructed have been persuaded into accepting instruction, a point Barnard made central to his analysis of managing.

There are dozens of excellent books about how managers can set about persuading others, from how to make a good PowerPoint presentation to how to structure a conference speech to how to negotiate and close a sale. These books shift from logical language—as in "do this because it is scientific, right, or economically beneficial"—towards more personal and impassioned language. Instead of instruction, even the implicit instruction of acting with economic benefit in mind, they draw us in as human beings with more complex natures. The shift has an odd side effect—we get feelings about what we read. Sometimes these feelings are positive—wow, yes! I need to learn how to be persuasive like this—sometimes negative, give me a break, people are pretty cynical and will not fall for such poseur's talk. We resist propaganda. Mission statements are a case in point. They can be exhausting to produce, people arguing violently for months over every single word, yet utterly banal and predictable when done—respect our customers, seek excellence, praise not blame, etc. This is the bad news aspect of persuasion, it is tricky and can go wrong. But the good news is (*a*) it is absolutely central to human activity, whether in firms, markets, parliaments, or elsewhere, and (*b*) we know a great deal about it.

Persuasion is one of the most important, comprehensive, and ancient of studies. The contemporary material is invariably grounded in the study of rhetoric going back to the Ancient Greeks and their interest in, among other things, political debate (the central feature of democracy, versus the instructions that are the tools of dictators) and legal argument (finding someone guilty beyond reasonable doubt when no one can be certain of the facts of the case).[5] It is useful to hear what rhetoric has to say about how the strategizing group might set about persuading others to implement the strategy chosen. The history of rhetoric illuminates. First, it has always attracted scathing criticism. If someone says "that's just rhetoric" or "more campaign rhetoric" it is to imply the facts do not support the statement or the facts are being hidden. Rhetoric is open to this charge precisely because of the loose fit between the facts and the speaker's intentions—persuasion comes into play precisely because the facts are not compelling or definitive on their own. Rhetoric is about situations in which no proof is available, and seems to be opinion and false for that reason alone. But the converse applies, that when you cannot marshal compelling facts you are forced to rely on persuasion—"I cannot be certain we'll make money doing this, but I need your investment before I can show you it works!" Rhetoric embraces the non-factual or non-objective aspects of human communication—around us everywhere all the time. The guys at the bar arguing about their sports teams, or the ladies at the beauty salon exchanging rumors, even the professor in the classroom, all are deeply engaged in persuasion. Over the centuries the study of rhetoric has produced powerful and effective heuristics about how to set about being persuasive, and these are essential to understanding and mastering the effective communication that strategizing demands. Sports fans and professors can make good use of them too.

Later this chapter steps beyond this system of talk preparation and looks into practical aspects of persuasion in business situations that are seldom noted in the "how-to" books. My earlier chapters turned on the presumption that strategizing is about the application of judgment. Key is getting to grips with the specific knowledge absences and constraints that make the situation unique and so shape the judgments to be applied. It follows the practice of communicating the results of the strategizing process must turn on these details too. There are no generalities. Persuading always turns on specifics. Later I explore how to be specific and shape the communication's content and

---

[5] T. M. Conley (1990) *Rhetoric in the European Tradition*. Chicago: University of Chicago Press.

process. There is no need to propose anything new here, analyzing content has always been a part of rhetoric—technically known as "question or stasis theory"—but it has seldom made its way into the management literature.

One way to think about this is in terms of what subordinates need from managers. They need many things but chief among them they need managers to help them deal with the knowledge absences that arise in and impede their work. When things do not work as anticipated managers need to be on hand to redirect or "fix" the practice. Instructions are good, they tell people what to do and can be important if one's income and promotion depend on following them. But when circumstances are uncertain, when the surprises of practice throw the instructions into question and the managers do not know enough to issue clear ones, and when one's fate turns on things that cannot be easily measured, subordinates have serious knowledge absences and anxieties. Most real work, if not all, requires subordinates to contribute personal judgment because managers are never able to deal with the full range of knowledge absences that arise in the execution of the instructions they give. Managers might issue them but subordinates have to adjust them to the particularities of the action situation through the exercise of their own professional judgment. Thus all managed activity is collaboration between people with incomplete understanding. In which case managers have to try and balance between (*a*) leaving subordinates free to apply their own judgment and (*b*) ensuring they act in the firm's interests rather than their own—the PAT problem. To achieve this balance, managers need to speak to the specifics even when these cannot be defined, and this is the severest test of their capacity to persuade. Choosing and controlling language is crucial here, which is why Chapter 4 focused on the construction of language as the core of constructing the firm's business model. At the same time rhetoric pays insufficient attention to the two-way interchange between speaker and audience. These days business takes place in non-authoritarian contexts that require managers to be persuasive within strategic conversations. The dictator/owner-manager of yesteryear has passed into history—perhaps. When subordinates can "talk back" and the managers are "open to suggestions," proper handling of content is crucial to keeping the conversation fruitful. Conversely overgeneral (bland) content can kill the communication process—as we know from political campaigns and their vacuous promises.

At the conclusion of this chapter we see again what has been obvious all along, the process of strategizing is intimately tied up with creating the organization and it is counter-productive to try to separate them, they are different facets of the purposive activity that is as close as we can get to defining a firm. Ultimately a firm is only what it is capable of doing—not what it has, owns, or did. If we applied this definition to ourselves we might say we are how we live—revealing our capabilities and values in our actions, not only in what we say. We make a place in society in the same way, though actions not proclamations. Likewise business is a pattern or system of practices involving actors whose judgments are fundamental to what happens—everything a logically designed machine is incapable of. Managers are challenged to shape this by melding their powers of analysis and judgment. Strategizing is the continuous reinvention of collaborative activity. The business's purpose, of course, goes beyond creating collaboration, however interesting that seems. Its real purpose is to ensure the activity results in added value measured in the multiple ways that impel our desire—economic gain, social progress, competitive power, etc. Private sector effectiveness leads to success, to profit perhaps. In the public sector it leads to good policy, the enemy's defeat, or social betterment. All of which take us on to the Chapter 6, my final chapter, and its discussion of the challenges contemporary strategists face.

## 5.3 Communication

Talk is just one of several modes of human communication. Interpersonal communication is more varied and puzzling than many care to admit. Indeed it is probably as puzzling as human nature itself for we are clearly a communication-dependent species. Given that we can never know ourselves for certain or fully, it follows that we are not likely to get to the bottom of our talk or fully understand it. So talking about talk will always be difficult. This section is difficult too—perhaps my toughest. But it is essential to lay out some concepts of human communication—for managers need a workable way of communicating their strategizing to others. If a strategy was simply a logical plan to reach a known objective, and many think of strategy of this way, communicating it would be easy. But the preceding chapters show strategizing as an ongoing process of selecting and dealing creatively with the situation's uncertainties. Even when this has been done and the firm's BM has been constructed, resourced, and its implementers trained up, and there is an appropriate idiosyncratic language with which to express and control it, those implementing will get further surprises and meet further uncertainties as they transform thought into action. It follows the strategizing process is not complete until it has been translated into irrevocable action, until all the actors identified have committed, "plunged in with both feet." We cannot depend on a simple gap between thinking and doing; they always merge. In military terms, strategy cannot ever lift its hand from the plow of battle. So strategizing managers need a communications approach that engages the implementers and others in the strategizing process actively and draws them into it, rather than an approach that treats their hearers as dumb cogs in a mechanical system designed to achieve their plans. Indeed it is not possible to build a human organization as if it was a machine, irrespective of the moral and dehumanizing aspects of trying this. Strategists need to know how to engage their subordinates in a process that continues up to the very moment of commitment.

Pointing to two limiting conditions can sharpen this up. First, everyone implementing might be made party to the strategizing process from its start. Extensive participation has many merits, plus it implies the result does not need to be communicated; it already has been, during the construction process. But this approach is more complicated and difficult to manage than it seems. It also runs up against the benefits of the division of labor and specialization that Adam Smith recognized as fundamental to the concept of the firm and its profit potential. A firm evolves because different people do different things and thereby bring a unique mix of differentiated knowledge and skills to bear on a situation more complex than any one person can grasp and handle on their own. So different implementers know, say, and do different things. Second, those strategizing might try to finalize their work in all its details, treating the result as a comprehensive strategy that others should implement faithfully. As we know, strategists cannot do this without anticipating every possible possibility, much as those sending an unmanned lander to Mars (14 radio minutes away) must anticipate every likelihood because it does not carry a human pilot who can respond on the fly (the issue in Tom Wolfe's *The Right Stuff*), nor can it be flown from Earth as a pilot in California flies a drone over Waziristan. Even if it were technically possible to generate so complete a strategy the cost-benefits would almost certainly be greater if there was an effective division of labor between the senior managers, who know about the "big picture," and those working closer to the place of value-adding action, who know different things because they do different kinds of work. Thus the opportunity space has two dimensions: (*a*) uncertainty about how to bring identity, intention, and context together and (*b*) dealing with the consequences of the division of labor. The communication model must explain how subordinates are (*c*) informed and persuaded rather than directed and (*d*) brought into dealing creatively with what remains unspecified and incomplete. The communication process creates collaboration and orients its activities, even as none of these can be fully anticipated. The remainder of section 5.3 probes this double-acting notion of interpersonal communication, and its implications, distinguishing it from conventional ideas about communication.

### 5.3.1 *Fidelity*

Communication has been studied extensively and the simplest notion to follow is that of the communications engineers who treat a message as a coherent "knowledge object" to be moved from A to B, the transfer of something definable, unambiguous. Knowing what it should be they are interested in "fidelity," the way the signal gets diminished and corrupted as it travels. Their focus is on the degradation of the signal. Computerized communications systems clearly depend on the faithful transfer of data packets as objects, and on the packets not being opened or changed during transmission—a sealed letter in a secure postal system. Among IT specialists there is much discussion about how to set up corporate communications so that messages can be created, moved, and received in a secure, timely, and efficient manner, but little of this analysis bears on the communications challenges above. We need to understand why.

First, interpersonal communications is not simply about sending and receiving signals. Of course, the receiver needs to understand the signal, just as the American Continental Army soldiers needed to know that a lit beacon on a far hill meant the impending arrival of the British troops rather than a celebration. There is a fundamental difference between the signal and its meaning. The problems with communicating meaning may not be obvious. You are on the beach and someone halfway up the cliff above you waves. Is it a cheerful greeting, a warning about something approaching that you have not seen, a call for help? As noted earlier, a message's meaning cannot be part of the message—just as an encrypted message cannot be read without its decryption key, which cannot be part of the encrypted message. Messages do not contain their own meaning, yet we cannot get at the knowledge contained in a message without knowing what it means. Hence the business person's frequent response to news—"What does it mean for us?" The communication engineer's analogy conflates the object (signal/letter/data packet) with its knowledge content, ignoring the distinction between message and meaning.

### 5.3.2 Meaning

At first sight communicating meaning seems simple—you talk and the hearer knows what you mean. But, alas, how to do this? It depends on having a means of explaining the meaning—"the British are coming" rather than "it's a celebration." But how can you be sure your explanation of the message's meaning is understood, that the hearer will understand the meaning you intend? There is a risk of infinite regression as the explanation of one meaning depends on another meaning, and then another. Interpersonal communication implies being able to communicate both data and their meaning, the combination many call "information." It is the teacher's challenge as well and things get complicated when your students are not able to follow what you are telling them. You give them data and no information results. There are two kinds of problem; (a) your hearers do not "get" your meaning—there is communication failure—or (*b*) they presume a meaning you did not anticipate—there is miscommunication. Students may well think you mean X when you actually mean Y. Likewise A can communicate some information, thinking it slight, while B, receiving it, sees it as momentous—because B knows something A does not. The reverse also; B can tell A something B thinks momentous that A sees as trivial. The separation of data and meaning means that the same data can be seen to have a variety of meanings, depending on what the hearer knows already. Interpersonal communication turns as much on controlling meaning as it turns on data.

How to proceed? Many think communication an IT matter. No question, computers are increasingly important. But IT cannot do everything that needs to be done. We can discover more about how humans communicate by exploring what computers cannot do. Computers have their own way of distinguishing between a message's data and its meaning, the first deals with a transmissible bit-coded statement such as "0087" in binary. The second deals with managing data categories; the data structure that knows "0087" is a flight number while "1507" is the EST takeoff time. Before there are data there must be data structures, and these set the data's meaning. Human communicators say they "understand" something when they get the categories right. Then they can merge data with meaning and into information. Take causal explanation, many academics' model of "understanding." A specific event is subsumed under a covering law; the event being described by the initial and final condition data, the law being the meaning that relates initial and final states. Theorizing a phenomenon "explains" the connection between initial and final states, demonstrating an understanding—P happened because of Q. At first sight, computers do not have to understand to be able to communicate effectively. They just take in and put out a stream of bits without knowing what it all means so long as they are able to route the stream or packet to the correct recipient—just as the post office has no problems with a letter's content so long as the address is readable. But correct routing depends on the data structure as well as the data's presence. The element to be communicated must "fit" the medium of transfer—postal systems handle letters, not jelly-beans, computer systems only handle data that fits into the data structures the programmers have chosen. In this sense both computers and postal systems must "understand" their addressing protocols and data categories, and know them prior to receiving whatever is to be transmitted. Both have to "know" or understand something, such as the categories, before they can process anything. In short, communication only works when the active agents knows something already.

Meaning is bounded. Computers handle data by representing it in ways that match an associated set of "bit switches" that constitute a "register." In our present computers a single switch can represent only two "states," 1 or 0.

A four-switch register can represent sixteen different states (perm 2 to power 4) and so represent sixteen characters such as the numbers 2 (0010) or 13 (1101). Today there are computer codes such as ASCII or UTC-8 that presume registers with seven or eight switches respectively, able to represent all the numbers and letters in the alphabet plus a few non-printing or "control" characters too. The computer engineer's data object is a value—number 5 or letter p, say— "encoded" as a statement about the state of the switches in a register. To the extent that a data object is encoded in a way the software can handle, the computer "understands" the data—in its own curious way. Note this understanding is contingent on the machine—more specifically its registers— placing what is known—the letter "K"—in relation to what can be represented or known. The four-switch register can only know sixteen different states. It cannot "know" our full twenty-six-character alphabet. Its universe of meaning is bounded—0 through 9 plus A, B, and C—in ways that are completely understood, and the converse is also true. Only when we know the boundaries of what is knowable (in a specific language or symbolic system, for instance) can we claim to know something "for certain"—logically. Knowing is the interplay of state and possibility—and therein lies the notion of meaning. The computer's understanding is contingent on its programming, its knowing how to handle the data object and its knowing the limits to what it can know. Humans know differently. How does this matter? A computer system—or a mobile phone—helps interpersonal communication when the sender's encoded SMS letter "B" gets communicated to the recipient's mobile, which is then able to "decode" or "recode" it back into the letter B, which the recipient can understand. The way the computer encodes, decodes, and "understands" is irrelevant to human users so long as the recipient is able to get back faithfully to the language the sender used to articulate her/his utterance (a technical term for human signal). We do not care as long as we can get back to a human way of knowing.

### 5.3.3 *Natural Language*

There are many different encoding or symbolizing systems other than our computing and talking languages. These include architectural drawing, DNA, and Laban dance notation. Some of these systems are like the computer register above—to know their language is to know both how to represent a state and the limits to what can be stated. In formal systems the range of what can be said in the language is bounded. Their syntax functions logically. In contrast, as we know from Chapter 4, human communication is "natural" and often open-ended. Note natural languages can include symbols. I can send you an engineering drawing of something I want you to make. The conventions of engineering and architectural drawing are intended to be such that whatever can be drawn correctly can be made. The formality we imagine of three-dimensional space is articulated into the formality of the drawing. But, as Escher's drawings show, this does not always work properly and we can draw things in two dimensions that cannot exist in three, showing us that our drawing languages turn out to be more ambiguous—and natural—than we realize. *Ceci n'est pas une pipe.* The point about natural languages is that we cannot know their boundaries for certain. A computer's language is formal, while human languages are natural. This makes it much more difficult to know what we mean by "meaning." The limits to a formal language tell us what a statement means. Natural languages do not do this.

As natural language users we do not care how computers talk (formally) to each other so long as they can translate faithfully back into our languages. But note that computers still have to "understand" in their own way if they are to talk, to know what a communication means in terms of what they can and cannot do with it. Note the lack of ambiguity. The computer knows precisely—it can know in no other way—as it relates the data to what it already knows—its program. Most readers know that most computers "know" two different kinds of thing—data and instruction or, more precisely, they can treat the contents of a register as an "operand" or as an "operator." An operand is a character, 5 for example, while an operator is an instruction to calculate, such "cubing." Receiving both, the computer calculates the cube of 5—the result 125. A conventional "von Neumann" computer cycles at "clock speed" between the operand and operator modes of understanding, between its data and meaning modes of knowing. The point being that the computer is able to know both kinds of information without ambiguity because the range of possible operands and operators are both bounded. Each computer has a specific range of operands, data it can process, and a specific range of operators, computations it can make. At all times the significance of a new piece of information is determined by what the computer already knows, so long as the input properly separates operands and operators—on the one hand "5," on the other "cube." We humans handle many kinds of data the computer cannot process. To the computer much of what we know is meaningless, outside its universe of meaning. Thus it cannot calculate, discover, or "create" anything that lies outside the universe already built into its inventory of operators and operands. It cannot be surprised. It has no capability that corresponds to the human imagination, able to bring something novel into its world.

### 5.3.4 *Saying*

Human communication is different because judgment and imagination always penetrate our "natural" knowing. The way we draw on imagination and memory to interpret a signal or sense data is indeterminate because there are no known bounds to the meanings we might attach to the data. Consequently it is unlikely a sender can predict the impact of a message on a recipient because (*a*) the sender does not know for sure what the recipient already knows that could shape the meaning s/he attaches to the message, plus (*b*) the recipient, having imperfect imagination and memory, cannot know for sure what s/he knows either. Do any of us really know how we are going to respond to (give meaning to) some surprising news, especially news that is strategic and might affect our lives? While the computer's knowledge universe is rigorously structured and bounded, ours is not. It follows that (*a*) we can never understand anything completely, beyond a shadow of doubt, and (*b*) we cannot ever relate it unambiguously to what we think or know already.

The ambiguity and uncertainty in our knowledge universe is extended by the gap between what we think and what we say. Natural language can only imperfectly encode what we think, even presuming (*a*) our coding is unambiguous and our statement has content, (*b*) we know what we think, and (*c*) we are managing to say what we think, as in Weick's memorable quip—"How do I know what I think until I see what I say?" A computer—HAL excepted—has no private "inner language" with which it thinks while not speaking, so no thinking–speaking gap is present. We may have private language—a contested idea that cannot ever be tested unequivocally one way or the other. So the computer has it easy, it can only say what it knows. Our thinking and talking cannot be related with certainty. So the idea that human communication is an attempt to create in the recipient's mind something that corresponds to what is in the sender's mind is hopelessly flawed. The suggestion is a crude attempt to apply an engineer's model to a situation that is very different.

### 5.3.5 *Knowing Already*

At this point I know I am testing the reader's patience, but we cannot proceed without a workable concept of interpersonal communication that is consistent with the context of uncertainty in which strategic work makes sense. There must be a match of medium and message. If strategizing is to shape the collaborative practices of others, by negotiating, pursuing, or creating added value in an uncertain context—my basic assumption—we must get clear about what communication means in that context. The engineer's model fails completely. After a couple more steps we shall move directly to the practicalities of everyday talk—to communicating strategy to those who must implement it, and thence to my conclusions.

Going back to the computer analogy, its program tells it the meaning of everything it is hearing and saying—limited by its set of operators and operands and programmed data structures. The computer knows what to do with the messages it receives and can work out their impact. Now the puzzle: to make the impact of human communication analyzable we have to tell people likewise, explain the meaning of the message, to shut down or at least seriously limit the ambiguity of natural language. When I say "47" I have to explain I mean a bus number not the lady's age. The recipient must have a "program" appropriate to the data we are going to communicate. This program is (a) what the recipient must "know already" to attach meaning to the data correctly and (b) to shut out everything else s/he may already know that would lead to a different meaning—thinking 47 a speed limit. Human communications problems begin because we are not "blank slates." We have no trouble attaching meaning to a signal, we do it all the time and find it is almost impossible to prevent, except when we are surprised or shocked. "What was that bang?" "What did he say?" So the message sender's problem is to ensure that a specific meaning is attached rather than some other. The computer analogy is that the machine has to be reprogrammed. How is this done? When we update our version of Microsoft Office we rely on operators available in the operating system. One level behind this, our machine is able to update its operating system by relying on operators buried deep in the "firmware," hard coded into the chips that control the machine's "boot." Every layer of software has another behind it until we reach those the hardware designer chose and built into the chip. These cannot be changed—as we noted in the Intel story, RISC is different. The crucial point is the designer makes these instructions available by anticipating them. The machine is always in a universe whose capabilities have been anticipated and laid down precisely—and forever constrained by them. There is no way to tell the machine something that has not already been anticipated as a message within its universe of possibility. It cannot make sense of or handle anything that lies outside this universe. The only way to tell a CISC machine something truly novel is to equip it with a different chip, such as a RISC chip, making it into it a machine that occupies the RISC universe.

### 5.3.6 Natural or Formal

The puzzle of human communication is that we presume we can learn new stuff that we did not know already, that our knowledge advances, in particular that we can learn new meanings. But can we? The core challenge of strategizing practice lies in communicating a completely new meaning or new interpretation of the firm's situation to those whose actions and judgment are to bring it to life. Computers cannot arrive at a meaning that was not already encoded into them; strategy makes no sense to them. It seems we humans can arrive at new meaning and thereby advance our knowledge. Paradoxically, it is our inability to know anything for certain that lies at the core of our ability to learn new things. Conversely, because a computer always and only knows things for certain, it cannot learn anything truly novel or go beyond the boundaries its designers built into it.

How it is possible to tell someone something that they do not already know at some fundamental level? Along the lines of the computing analogy, the Greek philosopher Plato argued that human learning was a matter of clearing away misunderstandings about what we knew already at some intuitive level. Doing this we emerged from the shadows in our cave of ignorance and into the blinding light of the real and true. He saw learning as the process of helping someone understand what they knew already, coded into human firmware, the nature or DNA of our species. The Platonist/engineer's analogy is not easily dismissed, especially if the alternatives imply that all communications between people must be understood in the context of what the parties know already—leading us towards the impossible, for how can one person ever know everything someone else knows? The engineer's materialist model is attractive because it is clear and workable while the proposition that communication depends on its impact on our lives seems hopelessly indeterminate. Many contemporary writers, especially psychologists exploring the function of mind with MRI machines, are probing for what they presume is encoded in our hardware.[6] I presume instead the unboundedness of imagination and judgment—and thus of natural language and knowing. I deny the possibility of a coherent theory of interpersonal communication. While Plato is revered and important, Aristotle and those who disagreed with him more directly influence our thinking. The way Aristotle and his colleagues found through the impasse described above was, and remains, intellectually breathtaking. There is nothing strange or difficult here; at worst we have simply forgotten it. The point of dragging the reader through the previous parts of this section (5.3) was to help her/him into position to appreciate the implications of the Greeks' insight, for it opened up an entirely different approach to interpersonal communication. We need it if we are to achieve an understanding of strategizing.

The difference between formal and natural language, one closed, the other open, is not the only difference between computers and people. The Greeks concluded that, while perfect knowing and total knowledge was not available to them, it was productive to presume people know things in several different and partial ways—a reminder of the ancient tale of the seven blind men discovering an elephant. The Greek epistemologists argued for several fundamentally different types of knowledge or modes of human knowing. They distinguished between, for instance, *episteme* (true justified belief), *techne*

---

[6] T. W. Deacon (2012) *Incomplete Nature: How Mind Emerged from Matter*. New York: W. W. Norton.

(knowing how to do something—technology), *phronesis* (appropriateness), and *metis* (street smarts). *Phronesis* enabled you to see that just because you could do something it may not be socially, politically, or ethically appropriate to do it. *Techne* is fine so long as you do not confuse it with certainty about reality (*episteme*); we use aspirin and know it works and has many positive side effects, yet we are still ignorant of the mechanisms. The philosophical technique here is to see human knowing as grounded in the human condition, in the fragmented life we live, rather than in the way we moderns have become accustomed to, which is to say that all real knowledge is scientific and a representation of the seamless interconnected and logically constructed reality of the natural universe that lies beyond our minds and lives. In other words, these Greeks presupposed the uncertainty of our condition rather than the certainty of our context, and saw human knowing as our attempt to negotiate our lived situation towards freely chosen goals. Chapter 4's story is no more than my retelling of the Aristotelian story that lives on in Polanyi's explicit/tacit distinction or Ryle's "knowing that"/"knowing how" distinction.

### 5.3.7 Entrepreneurial Idea

Whatever we know of a particular situation is clearly bounded by the manner in which we know it. As in Figure 4.1, I argue we cannot know everything about a situation, so have to make a selection of fragments and synthesize them into actionable language. But note how *episteme*, *techne*, and *phronesis* imply different constrained modes of knowing. The difference between the previous chapter's discussion and here is that, while Chapter 4 identified the different things strategists might choose to take into account—as also explored in the mini-cases—we are now pointing to the different ways in which those things might be known. This adds another degree of freedom—and complexity—into the opportunity space the strategizing process fills—impossible to draw of course but not beyond thinking about. The constraints reflect different things to know about but also the different modes in which they might be known. Some knowing might be purely scientific, other knowing moral or ethical, yet other knowing might be political. Other knowing might be more psychological or emotional—she loves me, she loves me not. Again, we are able to synthesize our fragmented knowing because we have imagination and an actionable intention towards our chosen objective. Intention is complemented by identity, by what we know (aided by memory) or imagine when memory fails. This is where humans are utterly different from anything that can be said about computers. The point being that strategizing is a quintessentially human activity of imagining a new lived world that has no analogy in the computer's universe of possibilities.

Two final points and we are ready to roll! First, the categories of human knowing that interested the Greeks were grounded in the way they lived and in what they regarded as the essence or purpose of life. Those familiar with Greek tragedies, such as those of Euripides, know that concepts surrounding "honor" were a central concern for the period's intellectuals and, we can presume, for the audiences for whom they wrote. Our lives and values in the developed West are, however, very different, and the Greeks' categories do not reveal much about how we think in the modern context. They are principally of interest to historians and philosophers. But, for us, the firm's purpose is value-adding. The popular and business press shows many feel commercial advantage and personal greed have overwhelmed "our better angels," and I shall deal with this in Chapter 6. But here we are working on how to communicate the strategizing that takes place in the pursuit of value-adding, how to fill the opportunity spaces democratic capitalism offers via collaborative communication. Rather than look to the Greeks (who did not share our view of democracy either) we can look to Barnard as a managerial philosopher and skilled articulator of today's commercial situation. Recall he distinguished three "primary sub-systems"—physical, personal, and social. He pointed to ways of knowing familiar to us—physical (scientific), personal (at the level of the executive's personal psychology), and social at the level of the society in which the firm was embedded. This trinity of modes of executive knowing is the foundation to his managerial theorizing. The implication is that strategizing and the communication of strategizing can both be analyzed in Barnard's rather general three-way framework. Barnard's opportunity space—mine is simply an elaboration—is constrained by the executive's capacity to synthesize her/his knowledge of the firm's situation when viewed from these incommensurate physical, psychological, and social angles. Barnard termed this synthesizing capacity "leadership" and argued it was the limiting factor in business, the organizational/human capability in shortest supply. We can turn Barnard's analysis on its head and say that when the leader wants to communicate the results of her/his synthesizing to others s/he should use the same framework as s/he used to generate it. Then the strategy is not communicated as a "fait accompli" but as a leader-shaped context in which subordinates do their own strategizing as they bump into their own unforeseen knowledge absences.

So now for the last trick. The essence of the Barnardian synthesis is not that the executive discovers, uncovers, or gets to some new scientific knowledge, or novel psychological or social insight. The executive task is to find something new and entrepreneurial in what, in principle, is available to everyone else—and seize it as the firm's entrepreneurial idea. Such novelty drives a capitalist democracy. Barnard's entrepreneurial novelty lies in the synthesis, the democratic and imaginative application of judgment, not in any special insight into the three universes of human knowing. It follows that communicating the entrepreneurial idea can be grounded in what the entrepreneur (strategist) and the hearers know already. The novelty lies in their interplay, their synthesis with the actor's goals. Perhaps the entrepreneurial idea is "a better mouse-trap," an advance on something familiar. But when the idea is tied too closely to what we know we cannot escape the constraints of the familiar. Entrepreneurship, innovation, undertaking, and Defoe's "projecting" are economically and politically important and important precisely because they reach beyond the familiar and into the future that gets constructed thereby; the lived world beyond what can be forecast. But, conversely, the result must still be attachable to the present if it is to be a source of economic profit and social progress. The entrepreneurial idea must be framed by what people already know—but had not fully realized—about their situation. If the concept is scientific, the hearer must know the science—and likewise the psychological and social universes. They must know enough about them to get the gist of the entrepreneur's novel idea. If someone says, I have this great idea for a new food (crushed bugs, for instance) we may have an immediate psychological response—yuk. Yet it turns out the science is compelling, so compelling that it is pretty clear that farmed and crushed bugs will be a major source of food within a few decades. But today?

### 5.3.8 *Leveraging Uncertainties*

So, the way to communicate strategizing lies in appeals to what the hearers know already but remain uncertain about—what remains open to be re-synthesized into a new view of the lived world. What we know is (*a*) always bounded and incomplete, and (*b*) multifaceted according to the different ways of human knowing that characterize our age's intellectualizing—physical, psychological, and social. The creative novelty of strategic work lies in choosing how to interplay the things already known, make new music on an old piano. As in the kitchen, the recipe's ingredients can stay the same while the chef plays with the quantities and process. Clearly science is a powerful mode of human knowing, the rigorous distillation of our empirical experience of the physical. But it is not the only mode of our knowing. We know psychologically about what it means to be alive, have a private life, and deal with an uncertain existence. We also have social knowledge of what it means to be in a community of others—with their own private lives and objectives, even as both the psychological and social are embedded in and penetrated by the physical (technological). Because computers do not live our lives they cannot ever "think" or "imagine" as humans do—they will probably never "feel" as we do, but that is peripheral. Our ability to deal with uncertainty comes from our imagination. Communicating the result of strategic work means engaging our three modes of knowing, and there is nothing complicated about it. It is perfectly familiar. It turns out there is no need to invent a new process or methodology for strategic communication. It is well studied and has a huge literature—which we shall now plunder. It is rhetoric.

## 5.4 Rhetoric

Rhetoric is sometimes called the art of persuasion, moving people towards new meanings. Specifically, it is defined as "the art of selecting the best available means of persuasion to suit a particular situation." It deals with talk-practice and with how human beings act on each other's lives through talk. Managerial rhetoric is central to every aspect of business in the circumstances in which logical plans and instructions fail—deal-making, selling, inspiring, leading, and creating value-adding collaboration (how I view the firm). Unfortunately, while rhetoric is ancient and much studied, it has also suffered centuries of criticism—from Plato on. Today the term "rhetoric" is mostly used pejoratively. The implication is that the statement being commented on is untrue, biased, or in some other way deficient and less honest, factual, or objective than we might hope. Rhetoric does not seek proof. The conclusions (*pisteis*) of the rhetorical process are merely "reasonable," as the speaker successfully captures the hearer's under-articulated and under-formed thoughts and feelings, refashioning them into the speaker's own intentions and expectations. Reasonable is to proof as everyday life is to classroom analysis. Law courts are part of the real world and the hope is that the rhetorical practice that goes on between the judge, prosecution, defense, and jury leads to a finding "beyond reasonable doubt"—but not proof. In the business world reasonable is to proof as strategizing is to planning, or as persuasion is to instruction, or as equilibrium is to value-adding.

Rhetoric is an art rather than a theory because it is a natural language concept—not a scientific concept. The context of management's rhetorical practice is organizational life with all its knowledge absences, tensions, and doubts. As we saw in the preceding section, rhetoric does not try to provide an audience with knowledge it does not possess already. Its method is to provoke listeners to resynthesize what they know in a way the speaker desires and thereby to new practice. Effective rhetoric persuades an audience to look again at what they already know—at some level, perhaps tacitly or intuitively—and so construct a new sense of their situation to guide new practice. To make a compelling case the speaker must combine a selection of the facts the audience accepts as relevant to the situation, together with an amelioration of the hearers' fears and doubts about what might happen (the downside), especially when these doubts interfere with their practice. Thus the strategist's ever-present doubts must encompass those of the audience and perhaps others too that the strategist chooses to keep to her/himself. Effective leaders sense every feeling or reason why others hesitate to follow and help their hearers deal with them.

Interpersonal persuasion is hugely important to our lives. It need not be left to chance or mere amateurs. It has been theorized and professionalized over the thousands of years people have been trying to persuade each other to do things both good and bad: storm fortifications, set up hospitals, eject immigrants, save for a rainy day. Managing is a profession precisely because it is one of the principal applications or "genres" of professionalized rhetoric in contemporary life. The professional rhetoric of law is called "forensic" or "judicial" and is still taught in law schools. The professional rhetoric of politics is called "deliberative" and is typically taught first in debating societies and clubs like the Oxford Union, but is generally learned the hard way at the grassroots level of local politics by being, for instance, a union or community organizer. The Greeks also recognized laudatory rhetoric (*epideictic*), for praising war heroes and citizens such as the pilot Chesley Sullenberger who landed his crowded plane in the Hudson River in 2009. There is also the religious rhetoric learned in seminaries, rabbinical schools, and madrassas. These rhetorical genres underpin the "talking professions" as they stand alongside the "analytic professions" such as actuarying, or the "creative professions" such as engineering or architecture, or the "doing professions" such as dentistry or piloting airplanes.

Managerial rhetoric is an essential component to the private sector. Note that it is not like public sector rhetoric for that turns on social or political purposes and personal duty. Managerial rhetoric is the precursor to the pursuit of economic value. Many doubt management is a profession because it seems to lack the definable body of professional knowledge needed to underpin its practices. But this is their error, for they are presuming management's knowledge should be "scientific" like the knowledge they imagine (incorrectly as it turns out) physicists and engineers use. The accepted professions like accounting, medicine, and architecture leaven their science (*techne*) with a large measure of practical wisdom (*phronesis*) as well as with moral and ethical "attitude" and content. So long as the private sector remains a legitimate aspect of modern life (a political matter) it will involve a distinct kind of talk. In which case private sector management is a profession with an identifiable body of knowledge—one of the modern rhetorical genres.

Rhetoric was at the core of education for military, political, and religious leaders from before the time of Plato up until the late nineteenth century. Adam Smith was a professor of rhetoric—there was no economics in his day. John Quincy Adams (the sixth US President) was Harvard's first professor of rhetoric. Rhetoric was pushed out of its central place in education by several trends, the most significant being the rise of the scientific attitude. Yet rhetoric's power and relevance remain as evident today as ever, especially in those areas where the sciences seem weak. In the political sphere we might note Reagan's or Obama's ability to stir people to action. Churchill and Hitler are often cited as historically significant orators or "rhetors," individuals with a strong grasp of how to persuade others. In the business arena Lee Iacocca, Jack Welch, and Steve Jobs had strong rhetorical skills, albeit very different. In Chapter 6 I shall explore the history of the private sector and argue that Western private sector managerial talk goes back to the time of the Dutch Republic around 1600—sometimes called the first modern economy.[7] Prior to that time businesses were largely family affairs, or religious or feudally structured with a very different rhetoric. The Dutch Republic's entrepreneurs evolved a new class of business models that were able to draw the newly enfranchised labor into their commercial affairs, people of varied religious inclinations who immigrated into the religion-free Holland that had just escaped the Spanish colonial system. This new labor pool opened up the possibility of modern capitalism—a novel mode of managing—and a new managerial rhetoric made it happen. Without getting into the details, it is worth noting that there were at least two types of gentlemen's clubs in Holland's main cities—Amsterdam and Rotterdam—that were like the Lions or Rotary Clubs today. There was the local militia—memorialized in Rembrandt's *Night Watch* painting (1642)—probably more drinking clubs than anything to do with protecting the city—but also rhetorical clubs, forerunners of today's debating clubs and, incidentally, the UK's Royal Society. As people began to appreciate political freedom they also began to see how managed talk could replace coercion as society's glue.

Rhetoric's centrality to business has been recognized for centuries and a substantial proportion of business how-to books are manuals of rhetoric. We might look to these for guidance on how managers should communicate their strategizing to those who must implement it, and conclude there is no pressing reason to complicate things by delving into rhetoric's arcana. Unfortunately most authors shortcut into rhetoric's familiar principles or "canons" as if they are simply "good things to know about," without ever really identifying the special challenges rhetoric can address. They see rhetoric as a solution searching for a problem they feel they already know about. In contrast, section 5.1 sharpened up the problem–solution relationship for those who understand managing as a talking game that turns on engaging the synthesizing capacities of others. The key distinction lies between reporting facts and telling an engaging story, or between instructing and persuading, or between

---

[7] J. de Vries and A. van der Woude (1997) *The First Modern Economy: Success, Failure, and Perseverance of the Dutch Economy 1500–1815*. Cambridge: Cambridge University Press.

delivering a finished strategy to be implemented mechanically versus harnessing others to fill the strategy's gaps to the point of commitment and action. Thus many authors recite rhetoric's canons or list of to-dos without revealing them as part of a fully articulated communicative tradition. Others flip back to Aristotle's triad of *logos*, *ethos*, and *pathos* without addressing "Why three?" or "Why do we need rhetoric?" or "So what?"

The analysis of interpersonal communication in 5.1 implies a rhetor (or strategist) cannot really tell her/his audience anything they do not know already at some level. This sounds like nonsense at first, but it bears consideration. Yes, we do learn things, but what is the nature of this learning? Learning is not merely hearing—receiving a message—it gathers up appreciating something's meaning and impact on our behavior, leveraging our previous understanding. There is little point in telling people things they do not understand. Should we communicate to those who seem not to understand by shouting louder, repeating the message? Consider innovations. We are so used to talking about innovation that we miss how innovations must be understandable to be taken seriously and generate value. We reach for this by distinguishing innovation from invention. Innovation must be attached to some preceding understanding, often at a deep level. We know a better mousetrap only because we know what mousetraps do, likewise hybrid autos or a healthier diet. More fundamental innovations, like electric light or new breeds of corn, diffuse slowly simply because they are inventions and it is so difficult to grasp their impact on our lives. The theory of innovation diffusion suggests five stages: knowledge, persuasion, decision, implementation, and confirmation. Some prior knowledge is always essential—but what knowledge, and how far can it carry us?

Academic innovations diffuse slowly too, as teachers know all too well. But the mechanisms are clearer. Theories derive from axioms. Academics adopt axioms and thereby define their field of discourse and research interest, and define themselves professionally. This sets up three modes of learning: first, an exploration of the discourse derivable from a specific set of axioms, a number of testable hypotheses perhaps; second, exploring the disciplinary relevance or practical impact of the theory; third, and most fundamental, exploring how the theory's axiom set might be adjusted. When this works the result is truly novel, such as the shift from a Ptolemaic view of the universe to a Copernican one, along the lines of Kuhn's work on "paradigm shifts".[8] This is "real" life-changing innovation. There was a similar shift in the concept of motion— from the Aristotelian one that presumed all motion required a steady force to sustain it—as when plowing—to the one Newton articulated for inter-galactic

---

[8] T. S. Kuhn (1970) *The Structure of Scientific Revolutions* (2nd edn). Chicago: University of Chicago Press.

space, that everything with mass keeps right on moving until stopped or slowed by something else. In the social sciences similar axiomatic shifts are from models of the individual that presume people are shaped by their culture to the different view that people are independent actors motivated by personal gain or a sense of social duty. Explaining new theory begins with identifying the axioms from which the theory is derived. But where do new axioms come from? There is a temptation to point to experience as if we are able to learn directly without intermediate analysis or categories. But we are no more able to make sense of an experience that has no relationship to anything that has gone before than we are able to make sense of something we do not understand. Axioms are the fruits of academic entrepreneurship, acts of imagination.

We are aware of our own existence and of being embedded in a social situation and in a reality that transcends our thinking and practice, an awareness of something "bigger than us." Rhetoric is grounded on the assumption that everyone in the community shares some understanding of these aspects of being alive. Each person is a member of a functioning social or family entity that has structure, from which people draw their identity. There are no wolf-children. We are also aware of ourselves as psychological entities with private feelings, desires, fears, emotions, and so on. The triad of *logos*, *ethos*, and *pathos* brings these three ways of knowing, and three kinds of thing that could be known, into a single narrative shaped to a particular situation and collaborative intention. Or, more precisely, it restructures what the rhetor believes her/his audience already knows. When Aristotle argued the rhetor should base his argument on *ethos*, it was because s/he knows everyone in the audience has some sense of his or her community's structure, where they fit in the scheme of things. Each listener would also know where the speaker was situated and be aware of why they should listen—or not. If the audience does not know the speaker then s/he needs—first of all—to establish a relationship to the audience and answer "Why should I be listening to you?" Once the speaker has the audience's attention, the next step is Aristotle's appeal to *logos*. This is based on the listener's ability to follow his selected meaning—if we fail to resist the enemy then they will be victorious or if we fail to invest in the next line of products then we shall lose our market position. The Greeks also believed emotion rather than logic was the spur to action. We may install solar panels to slow global warming, but carry on smoking, as in "the road to hell is paved with good intentions." People only act when they get "stirred up." The rhetor or leader's objective is not agreement but action; strategizing must carry through to action.

I feel a connection between Barnard's executive thinking and classical rhetoric's rhetorical practice. Barnard's three modes of human knowing are those of Aristotle's modes re-expressed in modern language. *Ethos* is the domain of the social, the recognition that there is something beyond the Self that counter-balances the Self's goals against communitarian goals. *Logos* is the domain of physics and mathematics (formal language), the belief that things are constructed logically, that cause and effect can be related rigorously. *Pathos* is the domain of psychology, of feelings, emotion, and ultimately action. Barnard argued the executive had to develop a good understanding of the social, physical, and psychological subsystems to prepare for the synthesizing act that would bring the organizational system into being. There are parallels to developmental theory or learning theory. The social construction of human knowledge, the "from outside to inside" sense of the individual's learning, is explicit in the work of Lev Vygotsky, the view that our first learning is shaped by our family situation. A person from a "deprived background" or "bad home" may have serious learning deficits. The internal or psychological construction of knowledge, "from the inside to out," is associated with Jean Piaget and the unfolding of our genetically given capacity to learn. With some capacity under development a person can begin to acquire useful knowledge "by doing" and by reading and taking part in educational processes. Vygotsky's and Piaget's theories of learning and development dominate current educational research and practice, but note both argue learning is leveraged from knowing something, not from perfect ignorance. There has to be a "boot program"—Piaget looks to the genes, Vygotsky to society. Learned knowledge is leveraged from some prior form of understanding, and this is fundamental to understanding rhetorical practice.

One common way to look at learning is as "aggregation"—add more stuff, like more shoes to the closet. The closet remains the same, unchanged by the shoes added. Human beings are clearly not like this; they are changed by what they learn. What are we if not what we have learned (and eaten)? The modern tendency to see the individual as something fixed—genetically perhaps—underplays our plasticity, the extent to which we are forever changeable, a "work in progress." For instance the project to map the brain implies it is something relatively static that can be mapped as we might map Mexico, noting where the different brain functions take place. Yet neurological researchers know that if one part of the brain is damaged other parts may pick up the damaged part's function. The deeper we get into rhetoric the more we appreciate it is the process of re-forming individuals through interpersonal communication. The individual is presumed malleable. Indeed the older notions of the human being were quite unlike "rational" or "self-maximizing man." *Homo sapiens* is not fixed but evolving, both phylogenetically (between generations) but also within generation, through learning. The notion of knowing in rhetorical theory is likewise embracing as people learn and become different. There is no stable "genotype," no viable definition of the human being, at least not one that we yet know of. In the same way we can never fully know ourselves and discover our unchanging "fundamental" nature. There are no such fundamentals. A Greek definition of the human being was "one who could persuade, and could be persuaded," thus change-able. Herbert Simon's word for this was "docility," responsiveness to external and internal influences and over time. The object of rhetorical practice is not simply to persuade people of something, as if they could abandon one opin-ion and take on another, like changing hats. Rather it is to recreate the audience into the people envisaged by the rhetor, literally to create the people with the capacity to actualize the strategy. In the US we say "get with the program." There is a story about George Balanchine, one of the twentieth century's most influential choreographers, who trained in Russia, the world's leading country for ballet. When invited to the US to start its first major ballet company he said "First, a school!" knowing he could not choreograph any-thing on the material (dancers) then available and that he had train a new cohort who could dance his way. Leadership is changing people into those who can then bring new things about. The strategist's fundamental task is not to simply to create the BM and thus the firm, but to create the people who can bring it to life.

### 5.4.1 Ethos

Having "read the audience" (assessed what they already know about the three fundamental aspects of its human situation—and are therefore able to hear about) the rhetor proceeds to persuade them to rearrange what they know already into some novel synthesis. This is the final phase of strategizing and is straightforward for those who know what they are doing. But how is the strategizing in Chapter 4 to be connected to such rhetorical practice? Chapter 4 presents the constraints as the discovered axioms to the strategist's chosen language for capturing the firm's situation, not simply as a description but in ways that point to the possibilities for change and reorientation. The process selects the constraints and evaluates if and how they might be changed. In this section we turn to the "canons" of rhetoric and what they have to say about how to construct a persuasive bridge between what every-one in the firm knows and the particular constraints that are made the basis of the firm's idiosyncratic language and business model. When a firm exists it provides a social structure that allows the speaker to move directly to the *ethos* aspect, to establish his/her right to speak. S/he may be the managing director, and well accepted by the audience, playing to the home crowd. The relevant logical arguments may also be broadly familiar to the audience. For instance, the firm's past experience, well known to the audience, may underline the risks of their trying to introduce products in "beta" form, before they are fully tested. Plus the firm will have a culture, articulated in the dress, office style and layout, and communication modes that interface between individuals' feelings and their organizational actions. The BM offers a sense of "right action," what some regard as the moral or intangible laws of personal behavior.

The rhetor represents these fragments of the audience's current understanding in a new synthesis. Of course there will be some desirable sequence to this, perhaps beginning with selection of constraints, then working out a story about how they relate and then learning how to tell it convincingly, and even practicing it in front of a mirror. The sequence forms rhetoric's five canons or body of rules: (1) invention (*inventio*), (2) arrangement (*dispositio*), (3) style (*elocutio* and *pronuntiatio*), (4) memory (*memoria*), and (5) delivery (*actio*). Or, to borrow a great deal from Sam Leith's delightful discussion of contemporary rhetoric—you think up what there is to say; you devise an order in which to say it; you get this into your head; and then you get up and do it.[9] If this seems obvious, it is less so that rhetoric has much more to say on the process. The whole of Chapter 4 deals with "invention"—coming up with appropriate axioms or basics to the firm's discourse; discovering how to speak about the firm's strategic situation. With *inventio* done, arrangement is not as simple as it might seem to those who have never composed a speech or a substantial written document. We learn in school that every story has three parts, a beginning, middle, and end, but this triple is not much help with the task of bringing ideas together in a way that builds rather than confuses. Should one begin telling of the past or the vision for the future? Aristotle argued that a good speech has two parts, the narration, where you lay out the points you want to make, and the proof, where you back up your points. Cicero, the great Roman rhetorician, suggested a more complex arrangement—*exordium* (establish your role as speaker), narration (lay out your case), division (discuss what others agree or disagree with), proof (demonstrate the force of your case), refutation (demolish your opponents' arguments), and peroration (wrap up and conclude).

The conventional story of rhetoric points to Aristotle's three kinds of appeal—*logos* (logical argument), *ethos* (respect for the speaker's character), and *pathos* (appeal to the listener's emotions). This obscures what Cicero makes clear, and Leith confirms. *Ethos* is the leading issue, every speaker's first challenge is *exordium*, establishing the right to speak and be taken seriously by the audience, get their attention. This is where the speaker's *ethos* can come into play. Managers may have it easy, they speak from a known position; sales director, global supply chain manager, etc. A position may work against the speaker. To be prominent by reason of office, family, age, degrees, etc. is no guarantee of the audience's attention or respect. Take the sales

---

[9] S. Leith (2012) *Words Like Pistols: Rhetoric from Aristotle to Obama*. New York: Basic Books.

director, if our sales are down again this quarter, what then? Sometimes an audience empowers the speaker—to her/his surprise—by public acclamation, like Yeltsin on the tank in Red Square. Presuming the strategizing work has been handled by a small group that has a positive reputation, the audience is likely to be interested in what they have to say—for a variety of reasons beginning with "What does it mean for me?" perhaps reaching as far as "What does it mean for the firm?" But none of this can be assumed; it is always about the situation's particulars. The impact of *ethos* on the speaker's ability to engage the audience is so massive that it mediates everything else. Even the most characterful and prestigious rhetor may be severely challenged. Rhetorical theory suggests four alternative strategies to bring the audience around to accepting you: describing oneself, attacking those the audience accepts are opponents, discussing the audience themselves, or stating pertinent facts that all in the audience accept.

### 5.4.2 Arrangement and Proof

The communication process can only begin when the speaker has gained the audience's attention and its preparedness to listen. The speaker's *inventio* (1) has identified what is to be said, with particular attention to what the audience is able to hear and understand. Then arrangement (2) begins with "narration," stating the proposition, and is followed by "division," the pros and cons and what others might think. The story might be along the lines: "Our present BM and recent new products are no longer competitive, given recent technology developments. PQR Inc., our strongest competitor, has already responded with several new models. Their responses were made possible by their recent acquisition of ABC Inc., the start-up that developed and patented a technology that takes their products ahead of ours. We shall take another path. Plus we also do not want to appear to be mere followers. Many of you know we have been working on an alternative technology, part of our ongoing research program. It is now time for us to incorporate the results into a line of products that will move the market away from PQR and towards our vision of products that offer customers an even greater experience and value for money." Rhetoricians point to the many duties served by the "rule of three"— as in, beginning, middle and end, or, more notably, the use of the "tricolon" or rising triple as in "friends, Romans and countrymen" or "I came, I saw, I conquered." A more mundane tricolon might be along the lines: "We created and owned this market for over 20 years. In the last five we fell asleep while new entrants transformed it. Now we are going to remake and own it once again."

After narration and division comes "proof"—*pisteis*, discursive not mathematical—statements offered in support. Up comes a PowerPoint graph showing market growth has been slowing over the last two years, that the competitive pressure has been rising. "This is no situation for a me-too strategy, it is crucial we carve out a niche we can own. We shall defend this with an alliance with this niche's primary retailer. That could cost us some margin, though it is worthwhile insurance on the marketing side. It means we have to lower our production costs. As we break these costs down—next slide please—see this item here, tariff charges on the components coming in from MN Corp. We have been looking at these for some time, knowing they are unacceptable. So today I can tell you we have signed a deal to transfer all of this work to the ST Corp, with a substantial capital commitment on their part. The move will produce the savings we need to hold our margins—satisfying the Wall St analysts who have been following and recommending our stock for the last five years." Note that this does not work well enough—the niche proposed has not been adequately defined in terms of the constraints with which the audience is already familiar. The audience is left to assume the niche is defined in terms of production costs, a pretty me-too strategy, and while the proposal may well be viable, it lacks emotional (*pathos*) force.

Rhetoric theory has useful things to say about proof. Aristotle distinguished technical from non-technical proofs—nothing to do with our use of the term "technical." Technical proofs are arguments the speaker contrives, such as those above. Non-technical proofs are those advanced by others. A technical proof might seem to follow logically from the facts; in situation A one should do B. But notice the facts of a business situation are never given, even if they are presented as self-evident and incontrovertible. They are the result of the selection process discussed in Chapter 4, the *inventio* stage of rhetorical practice. Every business situation is packed with facts, opinions, and contraries. There are no certainties, no facts independent of our strategic intention; everything is viewed through the prism of the BM. Even the most compelling of facts may turn out to hide strategic weakness. Perhaps the ST Corp is about to be bought by PQR? Or our new technology is about to be (*a*) disputed by another provider who has related patents or (*b*) overtaken by a new entrant into the industry that has developed a radically different technology we have never seen before—5-forces again. In the real world there are always at least two stories to be told, the glass half full or the glass half empty—the counter-story. Every seasoned manager knows to listen for both before showing his/her hand. *Inventio* is not merely the selection of the facts to underpin an argument, but also an articulation of the entrepreneur's aesthetic, style, and spirit. "We know the two previous attempts with this product failed, but our competition did not even try! From our failure we already know what they have yet to begin learning, and now we are ready to roll all over them!"

Non-technical proofs are the warrants or evidence judged relevant and available to others. Aristotle identified five types: laws, witnesses, contracts, tortures, and oaths (of allegiance, for example). Laws and regulations appear prominently in Chapter 4 because they are surprisingly often overlooked in academic discussions about business strategy. In part this is sloppy homework, leading to omissions of great importance. But it also recognizes two aspects of legal practice. First, there are a great many laws and regulations and it is a professional lawyer's task to decide which apply and which do not. Second, the law of the land is not like a law of the universe. The legal system is a human contrivance riddled with our weaknesses and shortcomings. Even if a law is judged applicable to a situation, that conclusion is always open to interpretation by a skilled lawyer/rhetor able to argue a contrary case to the judge, so moving the legal constraints in their favor. Aristotle argued that, if law A seems contrary to one's position, the argument should be generalized towards B, the broader accepted notions of equity and justice, from which position the imaginative lawyer can then argue law A is actually against the wider public interest as articulated by B. Witnesses are equally slippery. Expert witnesses are those with an *ethos* grounded in some milieu other than the firm. They stand on authority that differs from the strategist's. As a result experts may be extremely dangerous to the strategist's cause and have little to lose by turning against the case being made. Expert witnesses need to be managed with care. The fact they speak to only one side of the case diminishes their *ethos*. Paradoxically, dead witnesses are more reliable, though they too are open to reinterpretation by others. Notions of "commonsense" are especially powerful, but can be tricky to position; widespread acceptance does not make a view correct. Likewise contracts are arrangements between people not mechanical devices. There are always ways of reinterpreting, reshaping, and renegotiating contracts.

Torture has been much in the news during the last decade and should not be presumed something that belongs in the past, such as the Inquisition, or nothing to do with business. There are many non-physical forms of torture: bribery and blackmail, for instance, or threats to one's family or career. These pressures are widespread, especially where there is corruption, something also more widespread than many assume. Transparency is difficult to achieve or maintain in business, especially if the accountants who do the auditing are easily bought. At the same time the BM chosen may hinge on oaths, secrecies, technology, financing, advancement, and so on. Oaths of allegiance are not necessarily formal, as they are with Masons or the military. They may be implicit in the selection and preferment of a particular religious group. Their rightness or wrongness in the wider context, morally, ethically or legally, is not the issue, so the strategist must consider their presence in the opportunity space. When they impinge on the opportunity space strategizing must take them into account. This can prove tricky—as some find under the Foreign Corrupt Practices Act (FCPA 1988). The speaker may also be drawn into oaths of commitment to future action—a common predicament for politicians, but equally relevant in business when, for instance, opening a new plant or location and committing to keep it open even when financial logic suggests it should be closed. Many businesses make commitments to governments, state or local, as part of their pleading for tax-breaks, subsidies, and other assistances that reduce their costs and facilitate their operations. Firms often renege on these commitments, normally without remedies being demanded by the governments concerned. The strategist, ever doubtful, must test the movability of all such constraints, along with all the others surfaced in the invention process.

After narration, division, and proof comes "refutation," the case against the proposition. If there is no refutation the proposition may sound like special pleading or mere dogma, as if the proposition has never been exposed to falsification. As arguments against are marshaled and the proposition survives them, they take on strength and maturity. This often works by reasonable misrepresentation of the case against. Rhetoricians sometimes advise switching refutation and proof, especially if one's case is weak. Sometimes refutation clears an opportunity space that can be more easily filled than starting with a positive proposition. Then comes the wrap-up or "peroration." Some rhetoricians use the rule of three to partition the story: start by telling them what you are going to say, say it, and conclude by reminding them of what you have said. As stressed throughout this chapter, the rhetor must restrict her/his *inventio* to stay close to what the audience already knows. Our most frequent and tempting error is to think we can tell an audience something they do not know, especially if that is couched as something they should have known—so carrying a double load of surprise and insult. The three-fold partition pays no attention to the way a wrap-up can be played against the bulk of the story. The peroration is an opportunity to step off the story and excite the audience directly, bring the story home to the situation. For instance, the speaker might say "I know you all expected I would avoid talking about X (horse-meat in our burgers). Well, we are going to talk about it, and what is more, we now see how it shows how great we are, that we could take that on the chin, fix it, and get up from the mat ready to compete. That shows who we are."

### 5.4.3 *Style, Memory, and Delivery*

After (1) invention and (2) arrangement comes (3) style. Again rhetoricians play the threes—high, middle, and low or "plain" style. On the US political scene, Bush 43 (George W.) had a notable gift for the plain style, coming across as a "guy to have a beer with." Obama's style was at the high end. In the UK, Cameron struggled against being labeled a "toff" with high style. Churchill's style was high, but history gave him an unusual window of access to his compatriots that disappeared quickly at the war's end. Steve Jobs's style was high, Silicon Valley high, carried by his *ethos*, of course, but primarily by his *pathos*, infectious authenticity, and total commitment. Rhetoric's complexity and subtlety is especially evident in style. Or rather, rhetoric's closeness to the human condition and its complexities becomes evident. It is clear that almost any style can be made to work if something else is grasped—the chosen style's relevance to the relationship between speaker and audience's strategic situation. Invention's purpose is to plug the speaker into the audience and vice versa. Authenticity is the measure of whether this feels right and real. The thing we recall most easily about a speaker is her/his authenticity. Often we recall little of the message, but still recall how we felt as we listened. Authenticity is what reaches directly into *pathos*, our sense of ourselves. It turns out a high-authenticity speaker can make us pay sympathetic attention to ideas we strongly reject, getting us to "think it through again." Authenticity points directly at how one person can pull on another's heartstrings. Great actors are those who can repeat lines already familiar to us, but still make us cry by projecting their authenticity. When authenticity is absent the speech situation is not simply neutral, other feelings come in because we feel we are being used, or abused, perhaps manipulated.[10]

In Chapter 4 I suggested style appears as the gap between language (what can be said) and the situation's practice, the inevitable gap between the generalities on which all languages stand, and the instantiation and particularities of practice. The issue is whether the bridge between generalities and specifics is made or not. Does the talk "fit" the situation? Rhetorical theory treats this as a matter of "decorum," of "right action." This is sometimes called "accommodation." For instance, there is the matter of idiom. Young people are constantly revitalizing language with new terms and tonalities—"Valley speak," parody, or injecting "like." It serves to point out that all adult and professional language is equally idiosyncratic in term and tonality and has its place and time. Teen-speak would seem indecorous in a speech—or even private conversation—at the Lord Mayor's Banquet. Style indicates that no matter how thoroughly rhetoric theory is structured there will always be aspects of rhetorical practice that lie beyond the reach of its rules. Style refers to the unstructured region of practice that, arising out of uncertainty, highlights the speaker's strategy in ways different from her/his use of rhetoric's rules. Two speakers can adopt almost identical approaches to dealing with the various steps of invention and arrangement but end up in sharply different odor as a result of having a decorous or indecorous style.

The invention activity analyzed in Chapter 4 also implies an exploration of the firm's jargon and style; not only what is discussed and what is ignored, but

---

[10] Authenticity is a core concept for Heidegger, see M. Inwood (1997) *Heidegger: A Very Short Introduction*. Oxford: Oxford University Press. S. J. McGrath (2008) *Heidegger: A (Very) Critical Introduction*. Grand Rapids, MI: William B. Eerdmans.

how it is said, how labels are used and how the non-explicit aspects are deployed, the firm's own "body language," such as its buildings, uniforms (both formal and informal), and logo. Are the terms ironic, used to convey the very opposite of the term with hearers knowing they are not being used in a conventional way? IBM standing for "I have been moved" or someone saying "He's being a baby!" Many of the emails surfaced during investigations of the financial disasters of 2008 show the financial community's endless capacity to exploit metaphor, irony, and the other rhetorical devices or "figures of speech" such as simile, metonymy, and synecdoche. It is sometimes said that all jokes originate at the Stock Exchange. Some style dimensions are humor, gravity, steadiness, hesitation, and other aspects that shade off into delivery (5). Ironic, satirical, and self-deprecating styles seem those most accepted today. If tinkering with style is dangerous, risking non-authenticity, jokes are even more so. A joke is dangerous, at risk of going off at the wrong time or place. Timing is everything, precision, and rhythm not far behind. Some jokes exploit a particular figure of speech—called the "paraprosdo-kian"—a sentence or phrase with a surprise ending—such as Will Rogers's "Where there's a will, I want to be in it," an added value.

The problems with jokes are two-fold—speaker and audience. Some people tell a good joke, but this is generally because they can adapt or shade the joke to the audience—in some mysterious way reading each different night's different audiences. A joke is never in an abstract formal space like a computer program. Most spin on a contextualized juxtaposition or reversal—things have their usual relationship changed, you slip on the banana-skin, find a fly in your soup. The rhetor must sense the opportunity space the audience offers for the joke; no space, no joke. Jokes can be a powerful tool to jar the audience's attention and open it up to new connections between the discovered constraints they already know. A talented strategist may be able illuminate the business model as a joke. There is also tense, whether to speak passively or actively, of the past or the future—or the present. Memory (4) might seem outdated in our universe of computers, on-line access, and mobile devices—to say nothing of the teleprompter—but is glaringly obvious when the speaker turns to the PowerPoint screen and seems astonished by the slide brought up—reading it verbatim. Memorization is important because it shapes style. But it is more than facility and familiarity with the material. Memory is one of the trinity of "faculties of the soul"—memory, understanding, and will—as St Augustine called them. I focus on the interplay of understanding and will, i.e. where understanding is absent because of uncertainty, there is an opportunity for our will to act. Memory puts flesh on the bones of our words, for in memory we find what we understand and thereby the opportunity space for our will. Memory implies more than remembering a speech, it also ensures authentic connection between the thoughts expressed and the world the audience inhabits, the connections to their memory. The "art of memory" or of memorizing has popped back into the public eye lately, in part because of Foer's *Moonwalking with Einstein*.[11] Memorizing used to be central to rhetorical education.

## 5.5 Question Theory

As strategists face the challenge of communicating the results of their strategic work to those who must (*a*) bring the strategizing to closure and (*b*) act, using their judgment, to bring the new or reinvented firm into existence, rhetoric theory helps unpack the task into identifiable and do-able modules and illuminate how to string them together. There is no doubt that business people can benefit from some understanding of rhetoric. My intent in the previous section (section 5.4) is to distinguish between thinking of interpersonal communication as (p) telling hearers something they did not know and (q) persuading them to resynthesize what they already know into some new appreciation of their situation. The switch makes the communication of strategy into a very different task, not at all what most communication theory suggests. More important, it defines it as the communication of an incomplete task (like an incomplete contract) to be taken up and finished by the hearer, thus a matter of persuasion, rather than a finished plan or instruction to be implemented passively.

Pointing to what the audience knows, even if only intuitively in their awareness of living in a physical, social, and psychological situation, and using that as the basis for the communication, inevitably points towards what the audience does not know. Donald Rumsfeld, perhaps the least able Defense Secretary in the history of the US, had a remarkable facility with language and is remembered for his quip distilling the differences between what we do know and what we do not. Military-speak already included the term "unks-unks"—the things we do not know that we do not know—but Rumsfeld's distillation also drew attention to the known unknowns, the things we know that we do not know. We presume these knowable, of course. The philosopher Slavoj Žižek topped Rumsfeld by pointing towards the "unknown knowns," the things we know but deny knowing. The audience knows that what it does not know is associated with or derives from what it does know, of course. You have to know something before you can realize there is something you do not know. We "know" uncertainty (ignorance, indeterminacy, or incommensurability) as the result of knowing data,

[11] J. Foer (2011) *Moonwalking with Einstein: The Art and Science of Remembering Everything*. New York: Penguin Press.

meaning, or practice—biting into the apple of knowledge, attempting to engage the world purposively. What we do not know is the source of our "anxieties," what I earlier labeled strategic doubts. Thus we know we die, but do not know when, or about that experience, or if any things happen later— all sources of anxiety to many. Knowing leads directly to anxieties about what is known to be unknown, the future, what others really think of us, what is going to happen to our children, and so on. These anxieties are part of being alive, often exacerbated in organizational life because most serve at the pleasure of others and can be dismissed "at will." This mode of employment is a particular feature of US labor law where the employment relationship can be broken freely on either side unless there is a specific employment contract in place with a definite term. There are anxieties about the consequences of setbacks and disagreements, and other anxieties around the firm and its future. Over the past decades many of US business history's most prominent firms have been closed or merged into other firms, for reasons that are often obscure to the workforce and the public and sometimes to their managers and shareholders as well.

Reading the audience's anxieties, what they know they do not know, is as crucial to the strategizing process as reading the things they know. The current literature on rhetoric, especially the managerial literature, pays little attention to these already-in-place anxieties. They imply the audience is a "blank slate," waiting to be marked by what the manager tells them. This does not work. In fact rhetoric theory has another layer, beyond those noted in the sections above, called "question theory" or "*stasis* theory." It deals with the questions that the rhetorical process addresses. Earlier in this chapter I skipped around this as I framed the rhetorical task as that of communicating the results of *inventio*—the process outlined in Chapter 4. Too often writers on rhetoric leave the audience's questions unaddressed. Putting rhetoric in the framework of the interplay of the audience's knowing and not knowing clarifies the interplay between rhetoric's canons (answers) and its *stases* (questions). Given rhetorical processes are synthesizing rather than analytic, the validity and rigorousness of the answers being produced cannot be established rigorously. They must always be evaluated in terms of their space/time-framed consequences, their impact on the real practice situation. Thus rhetoric is incomplete until both answers and questions are addressed.

*Stasis* theory complements and completes the canonical approach to rhetoric. The classical *stases* typology emerged over several centuries and was summarized by Hermagoras of Temnos as four-fold: the terms (in English) being (1) conjecture, (2) definition, (3) quality, and (4) policy. There is considerable scholarly disagreement about *stasis* theory but we can get the general idea from the following illustration:

1. Conjecture, Fact, or Act—Jim murdered Mary
2. Definition—not every killing is murder. Was this murder?
3. Quality—even if this was murder, are there exonerating circumstances, such as Jim's sanity or Mary's provocation?
4. Policy—even if we conclude Jim murdered Mary, and stands exposed to the full weight of the law, is it socially beneficial or ethically sound for us to deny him lenience?

One of the modern interpretations of *stasis* theory is the 5Ws (who, what, when, where, and why), a questioning scheme popular in journalism, education, and criminal investigation. At stake is the contextualization of the questions being resolved by the judicial rhetoric and the commitments and actions that follow a reasonable conclusion. The questions bear on the society's processes as well as on the lives of the individuals involved (including the court, police, jury, etc.) and so carry implications beyond the particular case (precedent). They embed the process in its context.

But strategizing's questions are not in the judicial context. To the contrary, they are in the private sector's realm of value-adding economic activity where quite different values hold. I am not aware of any literature that addresses *stasis* theory in management research, so my suggestions are preliminary. At the end of Chapter 4 I implied that, as business model (BM) or firm-specific language is established, the strategizing process passes beyond the strategizing group to those to whom it must be communicated. Thus their first *stasis* question is "Does this BM have value-adding potential in our particular situation?" The second question follows directly: "Do we have a means of measuring this potential—other than by trying it out?" It is easy to forget the objective is to fill in the knowledge absences between, at one extreme, those entrepreneurs who have such natural charisma and communicative ability that they do not need to explain their BM, we just follow, and, at the other extreme, such complete knowledge of how the market operates that the analysis can be rigorous and judgment rendered irrelevant (when *logos* alone will do). Trying out the BM may well seem viable—punting into the future—but it underplays the possibilities of managing the learning from what happens. The third question is wonderfully illustrated in Porter's five-forces model: "What threatens this BM's viability—competition, technological change, labor legislation, etc.?" The fourth question reflects the point made towards the end of Chapter 4, that strategizing turns on the constraints discovered, but that these are seldom fixed and can be moved or replaced. So Question 4 is "What about this BM is malleable and how can it be changed?" A fifth question is the inverse to Question 4: "How robust is this BM against unexpected shocks—the unk-unks of the firm's situation?" A sixth question places the BM into real-time: "How long do we expect this BM to remain viable?" Finally, a seventh question brings us back to the firm's specific people: "How exposed is this BM to losing the people whose judgments comprise the firm?" We might call this the Jobs question, given it will be a while before we, or Apple Inc., can comprehend the strategic significance of Jobs's death.

## 5.6 Strategic Change

Much of the academic strategy literature presumes the executives' principal challenge is overcoming others' "resistance" to the new. I see it as more about the challenge of bringing the reimagined firm into existence by persuasion. As discussed above, attention must always be paid to what the audience knows already. They are never "blank slates," so change entails forgetting as well as learning. This is especially difficult when what is known is highly tacit and is at the level of habituated practice not cognition. Changing your golf swing is not so easy when you have one that serves you well, but not well enough to meet your competitive goals. It may seem simple to change a person's opinion with new facts but, as Wittgenstein taught us, they are embedded in their practices, not merely in their memory. As mentioned earlier, much of the meaning of the terms in the firm's language will be grounded in peoples' experience of the terms' associated practices and little of the "strategic change" literature deals with tacit-level "anchoring." Much written about organizational change seems to blame the employees for their reluctance to take up unproved practices and risk abandoning practices that work well enough for them.

One promising approach to real strategic change is to model or pilot the new in ways that people can experience, so they can report back to their colleagues "You know what, this new thing could work!"[12] The implication is that strategic change can be incremental, begun in a small way, just as incoming CEOs are advised to achieve a few quick wins before engaging the less tractable issues. But what if the new entails wholesale rejection of the old? Then incrementalism is not likely to work and the rhetoric must be more revolutionary.

## 5.7 Summary

This chapter brings the insights of the previous chapters together with Adam Smith's insight into the place of the division of labor in value creation—and

---

[12] L. DiBello and J.-C. Spender (1996) 'Constructive Learning: A New Approach to Deploying Technological Systems into the Workplace', *International Journal of Technology Management*, 11 (7/8), 747.

thence into the place of the private firm in a capitalist democracy. I combine Knight's and Penrose's ideas to focus on the relationship between uncertainty and economic value or, more specifically, between the entrepreneur's freedom to engage a commercial knowledge absence with practical imagination and so bring identity, intention, and context into actionable synthesis. The division of labor arises in part when the entrepreneur does not have the time to do everything her/himself. The image of the firm in Dickens's time was more like this. The founder/owner knew how to do everything, but did not have the time. Today the division of labor is driven less by time limitations than by capability limitations, the entrepreneur's desire to reach a goal that goes beyond what s/he knows how to do. Delegation is fundamental.

Today's work is specialized and separated into many different professions, all knowledge-intensive that require years to master—product design, marketing, accounting, architecture, engineering, and so on—plus managing. Strategizing pulls this professional expertise together. But Chapter 4 shows this explanation does not quite work as often presented. These capabilities do not easily cross disciplinary boundaries and come together in effective practice. Bland exhortations to communicate and collaborate cannot work. Managing collaboration and value creation demands getting into the details and specifics. The strategist must specify the knowledge and skills—which are those implied by the constraints that underpin the firm's BM. These indicate the knowledge presences and absences the collaborators must deal with—which may or may not relate to the professions listed above. Someone may know a lot about marketing, as did John Scully, but not how to market Apple's products, or Ron Johnson JC Penny's. Given that most people's skills cover only part of the modern firm's BM, collaborative imagination is crucial if the strategist's intentions are to be translated into effective practice. This cannot be achieved through instruction alone. The essence of the employment relation that Coase implied in his 1937 paper[13] is a type of "subordination" that leaves the relationship open to the employee's enterprise and judgment. So the PAT framing is more pertinent than the mechanical one that underpins most organization theory. The key to the modern firm is that it goes beyond the coordination of what can be explicated, so defining the firm as a logically designable machine. Strategic leadership engages what remains uncertain and can only be achieved through collaborative acts of imagination. Thus managerial rhetoric has little to do with superior modes of instruction or more effective communication of what the senior executives know. Senior managers do not and cannot know everything essential about their firm.

---

[13] R. H. Coase (1991) 'The Nature of the Firm' (1937), in O. E. Williamson and S. G. Winter (eds), *The Nature of the Firm: Origins, Evolution and Development*. New York: Oxford University Press, pp. 18–33.

The rhetorical practice that shapes the creative actions of others is precisely what makes the modern firm possible.

In the final chapter I consider the historical background of this type of rhetoric-based entrepreneurship, its power but also its limitations. It provides some insight into the broader challenges facing today's private sector firms and their strategists.

# 6

# The Business Strategist's World

## 6.1 Making Management's Knowledge

This final chapter looks at private sector business strategizing and its history in the modern context. I consider where today's strategists might look for added value, profit, and growth, and how they might think about responding to what they discover. Clearly the strategist's world is complicated and it is not easy to make sense of what is going on. Managing is neither simple nor clear; it cannot be so along as our world is complicated and fuzzy. Most who write about the value of clear goals, logical plans, and tight controls do so from the comfort of the classroom, seldom able to attach their pronouncements to the real world. In part strategizing is the intensely practical process of making the complicated world clear enough to generate confidence and justify practical action to all involved. It leads on to thinking of managing as creating and using knowledge to shape human practice. It is a practical form of philosophizing so managing is applied philosophy. Second, the strategist is surprisingly free to take her/his own position on thinking about the world, the corollary to the freedoms created by the practice of capitalist democracy. The business model is freely chosen.

Too often strategy writers deploy a pseudo-scientific reading of a firm's context that transfers the initiative from the firm's entrepreneurs and their judgments to elsewhere, suggesting strategic change is driven by external change—competition, technological advance, new regulations, etc. This presumes an analyzable universe of economic possibilities beyond the firm, in its market-places, structures, technologies, or governance, and focuses on discovering how to access and own or control these and to compete against others pursuing the same objectives. For the aspiring strategist this gives away the store—for the initiative is always with the firm and those whose judgments bring it to life. Strategists are free to respond—or not—to competition or any other external changes. Competition is simply one of the constraints to strategizing. A firm's strategists may obsess about outperforming some other firm, being "number one" or "best in class," but these are odd blinkers to choose to wear, for a firm's primary business opportunities always lie in the pursuit of its own intentions by generating changes in its products and services or its markets. But far and away the most important changes are in people—by changing those already engaged or by engaging others.

People bring firms to life, so managing them is strategic work's true target. Resources, technology, and market demand are secondary to knowing how to exploit them. But what are "people"? Chapter 5 defined people as rational, skilled, and so on, but also with "enterprise" that is persuadable, transform-able, "docile." It follows this chapter's focus is not, as the reader might initially assume, about forecasting social, economic, and technological changes in the world "out there" that might drive a firm's strategic changes in the future. Rather it is focused on the firm's people and the reality they choose to create—as Apple Inc. chose to create a world that needed the iPad, and then set about making it theirs, or the Wrigley Company inadvertently created a world that needed chewing gum. Of course the success of these products ultimately depended on the entrepreneurs connecting with some deep human desire to work with information or to chew because, at bottom, all commerce is driven by human desires. But the full range of these is forever unknown, and the strategic and economic implications of such basic needs are normally impos-sible to determine *ex ante*. *Ex post* we can say "Aha, of course!" but who could have imagined the hunger for communication revealed by the mobile phone, now carried by half the world's entire population? Who, suspecting this, would not have invested everything and more in mobile communications? The real world is always being transformed—Schumpeter said "set in motion"—by entrepreneurs who look future-wards, directly into the face of uncertainty, and, overcoming doubts and fears, reach into the void to seize unanticipated opportunity. This calls for imagination, judgment, and confidence, not "heightened awareness" or rational analysis. As Chapters 4 and 5 show, stra-tegic work creates the new knowledge that can fill a chosen knowledge absence and transform it into a window into the void.

This first section (section 6.1) considers connections between the know-ledge-making process and the uncertain situations that make what is created valuable. Ideas that have been running underneath the discussion are surfaced. Many of the common metaphors for managing—designing, direct-ing, measuring, controlling, and commanding—must be abandoned on the grounds they do not work in uncertain circumstances. Strategic work brings imagining and judging to the fore. New knowledge is generated and then transformed into added value through skilled practice. Entrepreneurship is seen as applied philosophizing, creating new language to make sense of particular aspects of the world in ways that can be (*a*) discussed and so opened to debate and (*b*) transformed into economic value. There is no reason to think, as many academics do, that philosophizing is too complicated to be part of managing; the contrary is the case. The deeply philosophic nature of managerial work is meat and potatoes to those with responsibilities for the actions of others, as Barnard showed. Ironically, even with the best of intentions, the academics' pursuit of rigorous models becomes their chosen way to get out of philosophizing management. They attempt to pack it into *logos* alone. This entails assumptions of certainty about the world that real managers would see as hilarious were they kept locked in the classroom—instead of impacting the lives of others, such as students or consulting clients. The philosophic disposition embraces persistent doubt and criticism; able to capture knowledge absences in language that exposes them to contrary views. Doubt stands opposed to dogma, the belief that you know something for certain, beyond reasonable doubt. Criticism stands opposed to passive listening, blindly accepting what you hear. The effective strategists' most crucial capabilities are philosophic, the doubting and critical faculties that enable them to bring imagination and judgment into contact with the world of action and persuade others. *Logos* is always part of persuasion, of course, but as Chapter 5 showed, in uncertain circumstances it must be complemented by a different grasp of the situation's social and psychological dimensions before it becomes relevant to the firm.

Throughout my focus is on the strategizing managers' knowledge; (*a*) what they know about how value can be added through the firm's practices and then (*b*), in dynamic and uncertain circumstances, how that knowledge can be extended, reimagined, and adapted to suit new circumstances and engage newly imagined business possibilities. Finally (*c*) how the resulting body of knowledge might be communicated to those employees and others whose imagination and judgment is instrumental to filling out the business model to the point of commitment and effective practice. Value is added only by practice, not analysis. Analysis may shape but can never determine human practice. At the same time my notion of knowledge is subjective, mirroring the question "What does it mean to us?" rather than implying any objective or "scientific" representation of the physical or social or economic reality "out there." Recall Barnard's position as presented in Chapter 5. He argued the executive's core function was to synthesize the organization's idiosyncratic reality from what was known of its three "sub-economies"—its physical, social, and psychological situation. The firm's business model becomes unique and particular, and transforms whatever seem to be relevant facts into meanings in its own universe of being and language. Everything is viewed through the prism of the BM and judged relevant or not on that basis. Contrary to the conventional approach to strategic analysis in which "object-ive reality" drives or determines the BM, in an uncertain world it is always the BM created that determines what is meant by the firm's "reality" or relevance—what anything means to the business.

Philosophically this is a switch in methodology from an "etic," outsider or uninvolved observer's view to an "emic," insider or engaged and contributing actor's view. The terms "etic" and "emic" come from cultural anthropology, created by researchers trying to make sense of another society's social behav-ior. Even though we might observe, objectively, the rituals of Trobriand Islanders in the Pacific and compare them to our own rituals, such as getting married, serving dinner, or giving a gift, we shall never understand their lives in the same way those born onto the islands do. This is the point; the rituals' meanings and practices relate to a specific way of life and how its participants live, understand, and construct that. The way that life is lived will ground all meaning, sense-making, and practice. A firm is somewhat similar in that it is a social event or living process that inhabits its own constructed space, history, and sense of possibility. You are reminded sharply of this when you move from one firm to another. The new firm feels like a different universe and way of being, not only with a different jargon but also different values and orien-tation. This is not as complicated as it might seem. Strategizing determines the firm's way of being, selected in the pursuit of its freely chosen goals. The goal (intention) is relatively certain because the strategists have chosen it and so know it well, as their identity is known approximately. The context in which the firm's goal is pursued, and the outcomes of its actions, seem less certain. Ultimately the BM connects the firm to external politics and the processes creating and sustaining social stability. A capitalist democracy stands on the political processes of legitimating the creation and occupation of a socio-economic space in which private sector entrepreneurs are left free to choose their own goals, bet their own funds and property, and engage others in their pursuit. This view of strategizing stands against the literature that presumes strategy decision-making is a deterministic analysis of a knowable economic situation. It takes place within a real political system. Capitalist democracy offers us places in which to make our own choices and succeed or fail thereby. It leaves us free to have our own view, to make our own knowledge and then check it out against what we do not know about our situation until we act and discover it. This constrained freedom is the essence of private sector business.

Some strategic writers look at firms as if they were machines for producing goods and services that can be designed to maximize efficiency and control. But democracy does not function under certainty. Democracy and the firm's value-adding processes are intertwined. Democracy is the politics of freedom precisely because things are not known for sure. People's views and judgments differ legitimately so the political situation turns on the language and debates that resolve the uncertainties involved—whether they are matters of ignorance, indeterminacy, or incommensurability. If peoples' views were "correct" or known with certainty there would be no markets, no differences in valuation to drive them, no need for entrepreneurship to set them in motion, no democracy to shape the process. Other strategy writers might think the firm an apparatus for seizing economic rents, which is fine until we ponder how these arise in a democracy. Governments can certainly use their military, legislative, and political powers to create monopolies and economic rents—but in a capitalist democracy firms' power to create rents is limited and regulated (with patents, for instance). Absent monopoly a firm's rents are grounded in the freedom to hold to different views of the business situation, to be able to respond differently to the situation's uncertainties. The resulting economic rents, if any, arise from the different knowledge created, not properties acquired from others by chance. Note that patents are a relic of the pre-democratic mercantilist era, knowledge properties protected (for a time) by government against the market and knowledge transfer processes that compete quasi-rents away. A firm might well adopt an innovation-oriented strategy and set about doing the research and development intended to generate patents or rents. But while this is deliberate engagement with uncertainty, the outcome cannot be forecast: perhaps no rents are created or seized.

These comments help show that two common metaphors or "images" of firms—as a machine or an arm of government—pay no attention to the uncertainties that characterize a capitalist democracy. Thus the metaphors are not appropriate to the value-creating firm. The strategy literature offers a third metaphor, the firm as a "system." This is equally inconsistent with a democratic political context, but in a different way. The origins of "systems thinking" in business go back to Herbert Spencer and his popularization of "Social Darwinism" in the nineteenth century, considerably reinforced during WW2. The assumption is that a system has its own nature, like that a thunderstorm or geyser displays. We can model and simulate these with computers. Likewise a pendulum is a simple system and easy to simulate. Ecosystems, as competing species rise and fall in a constrained habitat, are more complicated but are still modelable so long as they are presumed bounded. Many think of firms as systems and it is clear that a great deal of research has gone into discovering their essential nature. Jay Forrester's "systems dynamics" has been influential here.[1]

---

[1] Jay Forrester (1961) *Industrial Dynamics*. Waltham, MA: Pegasus Communications.

Without getting too deep, this view is not helpful to understanding management's role and contribution under conditions of Knightian uncertainty. Even if an organization system's fundamental characteristics were known they would do no more than expand the bureaucratic rule-set used to design the firm as a mechanical system. Exceptions might arise if we discovered firms had self-organizing capabilities that mechanical systems do not. This is being vigorously researched, but no such capabilities have yet been established.[2] Even if they were found, it is not clear how managers would respond to them, for at the extreme they render managers' choices irrelevant. The critical questions concern the firm's capacity for dealing with non-computability. No innate judging capability has been found other than that of the creative individuals engaged in the firm. Dismissing the three metaphors noted above—the firm as money-making machine, or arm of government, or system—my conclusion is that a firm's strategic capabilities are always grounded in and limited to the capabilities of the particular individuals who participate in it, who bring it to life and sustain it. A firm has no form of existence (ontology) beyond its participants. Its assets are perfectly balanced by its liabilities so the firm cannot own anything that is not owed to its shareholders. There is no system-like entity. Even the firm's tangible and financial resources are irrelevant to adding value without the human capability to put them to use. In short, a firm cannot have capabilities that are not brought to it by its participants. Its capabilities are limited to those these individuals have, which include their capacity to imagine and reason logically and to remember. They also provide its moral, ethical, and aesthetic judgment, additional capabilities real strategists work to bring to bear on the firm's practices.

At the same time we are not isolated or atomistic individuals, rather we are social beings and often operate in collective and collaborative modes. There are four principal modes of collective action; calculation, coercion, culture, and communication.[3] Calculation and rational choice fail under uncertainty. People will not enter into employment for purely rational reasons so long as they cannot calculate the outcome. Plus the rewards must always be less than their economic value to the firm's shareholders—else there would be no return for them. So a rational choice approach cannot explain employment, a major impediment to a rational theory of managing and one of the reasons to distinguish explicit and implicit incentives, the latter adding value beyond their cost. But even this theory of incentives fails under uncertainty. The

---

[2] S. Kauffman (1995) *At Home in the Universe: The Search for the Laws of Self-Organization and Complexity*. New York: Oxford University Press.

[3] R. Collins (1994) *Four Sociological Traditions: Revised and Expanded Edition of Three Sociological Traditions*. New York: Oxford University Press.

notion of reward-determined behavior must be transformed into a constraint on judgment. Coercion, such as indentured service and slavery, has an important place in the history of commerce (see section 6.4), but retains no such place in a theory of managing in a capitalist democracy.

Chapter 5 suggests the firm is an entity whose fundamental nature is more cultural than system-like, a statement in natural language or a body of practical knowledge the participants share in part and generate through their inter-individual communication. This metaphor works in an uncertain context, so for me the firm is best seen as a knowledge-creating and learning apparatus that shapes and thereby harnesses value-creating activity. This image permeates the book but is no more than a reflection of the private sector firm's political situation, embedded in the uncertainties of a capitalist democracy and the politically managed distinctions between firms and markets. The firm is bounded by what is legitimate in that specific situation. Turning this around we see the private sector firm is a child of the political and cultural processes that open up and demarcate an opportunity space lying within socially legitimated constraints. Entrepreneurs are given the freedom to inhabit this space as they attempt to generate economic value by engaging its uncertainties. In a capitalist democracy, the economic value created, especially the taxes generated and the spillovers that occur, helps legitimate the apparatus that is also, of course, impelled by private gain and the entrepreneur's desire. Note the other metaphors for the firm—machine, rent-seeking apparatus, or self-contained system—do nothing to help us understand why the private sector came into existence or the nature of the entrepreneur's contribution. Capitalist democracy and the private sector firm are intertwined with uncertainty, mutually defining and supporting their value-adding. The planning, design, or machine models belong in a centrally controlled politics. The rent-seeking apparatus belongs in a feudal system. Conversely, an appreciation for the political context of private sector business is germane to effective strategizing.

## 6.2 Practical Philosophizing, or How Managers Do Not Think Like Academics

Today's academics are trained into logical rigor and its objectivity as their *modus operandi*. Their project is the development of objective knowledge. This was not always academics' goal. Managers, of course, have a different focus. I justified the methodological switch from an etic (objective) view to an emic (subjective) view by focusing on judgment rather than on analyses of external causes some might think determining forces. Even though "forces" exist as constraints, uncertainties remain for we are never mere mindless billiard balls being banged about by others. Because of uncertainty we are active and imaginative agents who form (construct) our own views (and hunches) and it is these that shape our practice. Sometimes we seem well informed by careful experiment, good science, and rigorous analysis—to the point we think we can picture reality objectively. Taken to this extreme we can imagine developing a complete picture of reality and its causes and effects—and so see ourselves as victims of a situation beyond our control. But we are never in this position. One of the most remarkable aspects of Primo Levi's writings about being an inmate at Auschwitz, the Nazi death camp,[4] was how, even under those appalling circumstances, some managed to operationalize choosing how they lived. Indeed this was called "getting organized." While some aspects of a situation may seem general enough to warrant applying some rule, there will always be other aspects that are unique—the impulse behind the business person's perennial question "What does it mean to us?" Identity is unique, chosen, and central—hence my switch to a subjective view.

Managerial knowledge is at the core of strategizing, but there are subtle philosophical twists here. The strategist's fundamental sense of doubt is a reflection or realization that we can never know the world (or future) for certain because (*a*) some of its nature and detail will always elude us, but most importantly (*b*) because it is constantly being constructed and reconstructed by us and by others. Strategic doubt is the complement to our appreciation of the world's malleability, our realization that we can act on the world and change it to our advantage. Echoing Marx, the point of strategizing is less to understand the world than to change it. There is a further corollary. As we saw in Chapter 5, rhetoric presumes we are docile and persuadable, as well as being persuaders. As we change the firm and its world, we change all involved in the process. Training, education, information, good IT systems, incentives, humanistic management, and so on are all crucial. But they are peripheral to the entrepreneurial challenge, which is to change others so their imaginations and emotions "align" with or are harnessed to the firm's goals. Effective rhetorical practice acts on people by changing them into what they were not before—aligned. They become informed, of course, but also inspired, not merely to think, imagine, create, and act enthusiastically and energetically, but with passion and commitment towards the entrepreneur's goals rather than their own. To a significant extent they put aside their own personalities and ambitions and adopt and articulate a different personality, shaped by the firm. They become "de-personalized," "organization men"— and women.[5]

---

[4] P. Levi (1986) *If This is a Man: Remembering Auschwitz.* New York: Summit Books.

[5] W. H. Whyte (1956) *The Organization Man.* New York: Doubleday & Co.

There is no running away from the fact that rhetorical practice is a form of "propaganda," even as firms and our capitalist way of living depend on it. Without some form of subordination, as the rhetor subordinates the audience to her/his will, there cannot be firms. It follows there are moral questions about how and why people choose to give up their socially and legally legitimated citizenship and freedom as they are moved by the leader's charisma or the rhetor's rhetoric to become someone else aligned with someone else's form of life. For those readers that presume individuals have inalienable natural rights, this is the ultimate conundrum of our value-creating entrepreneurial system. We are caught between how we value the results of subordination and collaboration, without which our lives would be unrecognizable— no electric power, cures for AIDS, education, or even social order—and our belief in the given-ness and integrity of our identity. All men are born equal but some, it seems, must be subordinated in the interests of advancing capitalist democracy. We are loath to admit that all forms of social, economic, and political collaboration require that we allow ourselves to be changed into more efficient collaborators by those who lead. In the military this is obvious and necessary. Recruits are "broken down" and transformed into "aligned" and replaceable instruments to be commanded, no matter how skilled or creative. Effective collaboration in an uncertain world entails giving up some freedoms.[6]

Leaders transform those they lead and thereby they take on grave moral, ethical, political, and psychological responsibilities as they strategize. The mainstream approach presumes strategies are driven solely by the objective facts of the situation, enabling managers to ignore the ethical and moral dimensions, to hide behind the idea that the numbers or some "invisible hand" rules, to ignore the entailments of synthesizing and constructing others' lives. This is false and unhelpful, preventing proper understanding of the embedded social nature of strategizing. It is also morally unacceptable and socially corrosive to teach as if strategizing were neutral, data-driven. I argue managers cannot ever escape moral and ethical responsibility for the choices they make in the uncertain situations that are the defining characteristic of capitalist democracy.

## 6.3 History and the Private Sector Firm

The private sector is a remarkable socio-political "invention" that is integral to Western democratic capitalism.[7] Private sector firms enable us to pursue our

---

[6] For a superb in-depth discussion on these matters see D. N. McCloskey (2006) *The Bourgeois Virtues: Ethics for an Age of Commerce*. Chicago: University of Chicago Press. D. N. McCloskey (2010) *Bourgeois Dignity: Why Economics Can't Explain the Modern World* (vol. ii of *The Bourgeois Era*). Chicago: University of Chicago Press.

[7] J. S. Coleman (1974) *Power and the Structure of Society*. New York: W. W. Norton.

strategic intents within the broader sweep of the socio-economy's activity. It is one of the key modes of economic freedom, allowing us to commit our own funds and effort in the pursuit of added value and profit as managers, employees, or investors. Private sector firms produce goods and services, employment, taxes, and opportunities for the ambitious. They transform locales and nations. They are crucial to policies designed to help the economy recover and create jobs. We are transformed by engaging in them. All this is bound up with our social, legal, educational, and political commitment to our particular version of capitalism and to Western society as it has evolved over the last 400 years. No doubt public agencies and public sector social institutions are capable of generating value, but in a capitalist democracy the private sector becomes the primary source of new value, leaving the public sector to set boundaries to the private sector's opportunity spaces in the interest of the public good. As the post-WW2 welfare movements have got into fiscal and political difficulties there have been moves to privatize more and more of the public sector's activities—health care, education, even aspects of the military. I take no view on this, except to point out that all strategizing is within boundaries shaped by the political and legislative processes—just as von Clausewitz argued war is politics by other means. Whether or not entrepreneurs agree or disagree with the private sector's boundaries, they are political facts to be brought into the strategizing process.

Many are suggesting capitalism has been "broken" by an excess of asocial individualism, deregulation, or political corruption, or is finally succumbing to its internal contradictions or, more optimistically, is once again adapting and reinventing itself in the face of new circumstances. Again I take no position on this for I cannot see "the future," that imagined point in time when the truth or falsity of any of these diagnoses is revealed—that lies "out there" somewhere beyond the present, waiting to be discovered or predicted. To the contrary, I see "the future" as no more than a way of talking about our expectations, the world we hope to create through our strategizing and practice. Democracy is a situation in which people with differing expectations are constantly trying to create different futures and are given the freedom to try. The present is what emerges from these many tangled, fragmented, contradictory, and incommensurate attempts to advance private interests and, maybe, the social goals we also adopt for non-economic reasons. Being doubting creatures in an uncertain universe we have an unquenchable thirst for prediction nonetheless and imagine there is a future to be discovered—by futurologists, soothsayers, stockmarket analysts, or whoever. All of which de-emphasizes our ability to shape "the future." We appreciate our value-adding processes are collaborative and perhaps there is a self-organizing "invisible hand" that determines our future irrespective of what we think and do. Ironically, if this was powerful it would lessen our ability to create added value.

It is easy to imagine how events might conspire to bring our democratic capitalism to an end. The private sector would cease to exist and strategizing process would be very different. Note the extent to which this occurred during both World Wars, when the US and UK economies—as well as the Soviet and German economies—were more or less "nationalized." The entrepreneurial choices remaining were very different, mostly about serving the government's various arms rather than public markets. The absence of private sector competition as a means to control economic behavior led to the frequent charges of war profiteering, as it does today when so much of national defense has been privatized. There is a surprising implication here, another aspect of the radical difference between conventional approaches to corporate strategy and additional insights that might follow from my view. Most strategy authors simply assume firms "exist," along with their assuming the nature of the individual as rational and self-optimizing—thereby overlooking strategizing as the process of bringing a specific firm into existence; in other words, ignoring the key question strategizing should answer— "how does this entrepreneur create this firm?" Chapters 4 and 5 clarify what entrepreneurs might do—but they do not, of course, prescribe or present managers with a rigorous determining model that denies their freedom of choice. Rather Chapters 4 and 5 offer a guide to their strategizing that remains left to their judgment, just as a recipe might guide the chef facing a collection of ingredients (and diners) or a score the musician. It follows that if entrepreneurs create (and continuously recreate) their firms then they reconstruct the history of the firm too.

Instead of the history being of the firm as an ongoing defined entity, as a business historian of General Motors or IBM might tell it, or the chart of the firm's stock price over many years implies, it becomes a history of management's strategizing processes, a history of how the firm's *in situ* managers reimagined its identity, intention, and context at a particular moment in calendar time—but, most of all, how they acted on and changed the people (employees, researchers, strategists, and investors) engaged in bringing the firm to life. So along with the switch of method outlined in section 6.1, there is a switch in the phenomena about which strategic history is written. Instead of focusing on the evolving firm as a coherent story of asset acquisition and deployment, or relationship restructuring, it switches onto (*a*) the strategists' changing circumstances, both given and created, and (*b*) their strategic choices. The management history of IBM, for example, is best revealed in their strategizing around the service bureau, System 360, the PC, their involvements with foreign governments, and today's hardware manufacturing and facilities management—rather than in the company's stock price or financial record. That deals with what investors want to know, not with what managers can learn from.

The private sector is a label for a set of political circumstances that provide legitimated business opportunity spaces for entrepreneurs to plunge into. To analyze the strategists' world we cannot look at the history of the firm as an entity with its own nature and characteristics, such as implied by the life-cycle theory of the firm or any biology-based evolutionary theory, but must look at the only aspect that is vital—management's strategizing processes. Barnard probably provided the best model we have. Note his world is a capitalist democracy, offering private sector opportunity spaces to occupy, and comprising both private and public sectors. My approach derives directly from Barnard's but brings the analysis closer to the typical manager's work. Likewise Porter's 5-force model shows strategizing as the executive synthesis of managed relations with several classes of economic agent—customers, suppliers, competitors, etc.—who might choose to work against the firm's synthesis and use their economic power to pull it apart or reduce its rent-streams. Porter's model is not the same as in Barnard's. Porter's is specifically within the private sector, presuming a universe of free economic agents described in economic terms and each pursuing their own economic interests without collaborating with others. There is no recognition of the public sector and there are no non-economic dimensions to Porter's socio-economy. His firm has no social obligation; it is not constrained by corporate laws or regulators. Barnard's model is richer, encompassing many of the concerns being explored today in "stakeholder" models. His model informs entrepreneurs who choose to pay attention to the political, legislative, and cultural aspects of the firm's context left out of Porter's analysis. It also explores the dynamic interplay of public and private sectors, thus of government's role in capitalist society. This is the subject of great debate today as capitalist democracies pull back from the rising burdens of defense, welfare, and other "entitlements." But Barnard's model is way too philosophical to be practical. The model I propose is closer to the managers concerned but, in consequence, is less universal. The three-part generalities of Barnard's democratic model have been abandoned in favor of multiple firm-level constraints—perhaps a dozen or so—with which the analyst can grasp the uniqueness of her/his firm's BM. This illuminates the entrepreneur's opportunity space or region of the private sector while also indicating its structure and limits from the legal, regulatory, political, and cultural points of view. The BM emerging in Chapter 4 will always be relative—relating to that part of the socio-economy the firm's strategists choose to engage.

Even so there are some useful things to be said about the private sector and its place in the broader socio-economy. There is probably no greater difference between the USA and Europe than the differing place private sector firms occupy. President Coolidge's oft cited quip "The business of America is business"—which actually misquotes "The chief business of the American people is business"—captures something fundamental about the US that cannot be said of any European country. "Old Europe's" balance between public and private is different from that in "New America." In the US the idea that private sector firms have a foundational duty to serve society (beyond paying taxes) is largely wishful thinking, not evident in American history nor, more importantly, supported by American corporate law. The private sector is not an arm of US government policy. In contrast European firms are closer to being an arm of government, articulated through a specific industrial policy. Thus Boeing complains that EADS benefits from huge government subsidies. Yet, through their own government contracts, Boeing and firms in many US industries, especially agricultural and defense, benefit also. The situation in Europe varies greatly between countries, but there is plenty of evidence that firms exist at the pleasure of the government to an extent that would be politically unacceptable in the US. Relative to Europe, US corporate law is "business friendly," less a matter of tax loopholes and subsidies than of leaving firms to their own devices, constraining them less. From the time of the Constitution forward American business has been able to influence the political process in its favor and has developed considerable political "clout." It is not just the money given to lobbyists and others, or the venality of Washington insiders, or the impact of the recent *Citizens' United* case, or the power of funding to shape the political process. The entire US political and legal system is more aligned to private sector business interests, and it has been so since the start of the Revolutionary era.[8] America's social institutions have been developed with business in mind, rather than the citizens or social welfare. As a result the private sector is significantly more powerful politically and culturally, and this greatly shapes every US firm's opportunity space.

Earlier I identified a few of the common metaphors for the firm—machine, monopolistic power nexus, system, or culture and language. But what is the firm from the legal point of view? The private sector firm is often dubbed a "legal fiction." From the entrepreneur's point of view the firm does not exist until it has been created at law with articles of association and, in the UK, a charter. Legal existence is a prerequisite to the firm's value-adding process. The fiction outlines a socio-economic opportunity space created by the political and legal process. Governments had to create and legitimate that space before entrepreneurs could fill it with their strategizing processes. The fiction arose as English and American lawyers struggled to give private sector firms legal substance that differentiated them from (a) legally constituted public sector, government, or religious agencies and (b) private citizens whose property included business assets, resources, and obligations. Partnerships, for instance, are an

---

[8] M. J. Horwitz (1992) *The Transformation of American Law, 1780–1860*. New York: Oxford University Press.

example of the second, the Navy of the first. Private firms differ from both to occupy a subtle legal and political space between the citizens and the state that is the hallmark of capitalist democracy. This space expanded, first, as non-governmental associations of citizens were permitted and no longer judged a threat to the state, and second, as the state let individual merchants, inventors, and entrepreneurs own and freely deploy their assets, embrace business risks, and generate economic activity on their own behalf—while eagerly accepting the tax revenue it produced.[9]

These ideas go back to Babylonian times and while they inform strategizing today, modern firms are importantly different. They evolved slowly through frequent experimentation. Some consider the London or Hudson Bay companies established by the British Crown to colonize and exploit the North American colonies as precursors. Yet these were really public sector agencies, owned by the Crown and granted rights to operate politically and commercially throughout geographically defined territories. Others cite the Dutch Vereenigde Oost-Indische Compagnie (VOC), founded in 1602 to exploit the Southeast Asian trade. The VOC was a mercenary organization to which the Dutch government's colonial military, trading, and occupation activities had been outsourced. In essence it was a colonial navy and army granted rights to manage, exploit, and guard a region being contested by the British, French, and others. Other historians of commerce see the "invention" of the joint-stock company as the point at which the private firm began to be distinguished legally from those citizens who owned it. Note the VOC's initial arrangements were that no shareholder could withdraw the funds invested for at least a decade. The modern firm achieves much more than these earlier models because ownership is out of the government's hands and entirely in the hands of its shareholders. Many companies are quoted on stock exchanges that allow their investors to exit at will. At the same time the invention of "limited liability" enabled private shareholders to take part in such businesses without exposing all of their assets in the event the firm failed.

The history of corporate law, especially in the US, shows the firm's legal identity was not based on any public sector economic institution—such as a joint-stock agency—but on the concept of a citizen's identity and rights. Thus today firms are sometimes called "unnatural persons," in part because they can live forever, in part because they come into existence in a very different way than human beings do. But they are close to being people at law, in spite of much protest. They can own, and be held accountable, in the same way people can. While a lawyer might be needed to spell the relevant legal constraints out in any particular business context, the legal fiction is always

---

[9] J. S. Coleman (1974) *Power and the Structure of Society*. New York: W. W. Norton.

present and defines constraints specific to every firm. Note the Crown joint-stock companies had no need of this fiction since they dealt only with what feudal or government authority already claimed to own and command. They were monopolies that brooked no competition. Conversely family businesses had no need of the fiction because there was no separation between the firm's resources and the family's property and rights. The family's people were fully liable and were not separated by limited liability. The business's identity was the same as that of the owner or partners. There was no separation of owner and firm. No doubt the "invention" of the modern firm as a socio-economic institution accelerated economic growth and the social improvements made possible through the jobs, products, and services provided, and taxes raised, but there were many negatives. The legal device of limited liability also accelerated growth because it enabled firms to access the new capital markets of private citizens' savings that lay beyond the business's retained profits or the funds of professional investors (money lenders) and commercial traders. The firm's person-like nature remains, though its freedoms are bounded and contested through changes in the corporate law that is always a work in progress at the boundary between the public and private sectors, part of the ongoing political process. Specifically, the modern firm is an unnatural socio-economic legal person independent of both the state and its participating shareholders who can (*a*) own resources as citizens do, (*b*) enter into contracts with governments, firms, and citizens, and (*c*) be held legally accountable under those contracts and be sued by any firm or citizen who feels wronged by the firm's activities.

Our form of democratic capitalism evolved as this new socio-economic institution moved to the center of the political system—with rights and obligations that balanced those of the state or its citizens. The converse was also true, that the opportunity space for private sector firms expanded as the social and political institutions of capitalism came into existence and matured. In the US a major impulse behind the growth of the private sector's opportunity space was the state's choice to allow private firms to compete with and so curb the inefficiency and corruption that arose in the post-Revolutionary state-owned enterprises. The legal constraints to the private firm are always germane to strategizing (and lobbying) and new legal formats are constantly appearing, especially in the financial sector—often to lessen taxes. The struggles over Glass-Steagall and Dodd-Frank are mostly about the permitted constitutions of firms in the banking and investment sectors. But hedge funds, holding companies, not-for-profit 501(c)(3)s, S corporations, and so on all illustrate the undimmed legal inventiveness that is often, though not invariably, applied to protect the private firm's freedom of choice and man-euver from government or labor interests, or inhibit competition, or exploit loopholes in the state's taxation regime.

The boundary between the public and private sectors is shaped by state regulation and control of private sector competition. Just as there is no complete monopoly in the real economy, so there is no pure competition—outside of the classroom. Every real enterprise is unique in some strategically important way, and absent a degree of idiosyncrasy would be unable to generate the rent-stream that enables the firm to overcome the inevitable frictions and inefficiencies that attend all human activity. Firms are entities that can only survive and thrive in a universe of uncertainties, imperfect markets, and functional inefficiencies by creating added value. This may lead to profit and growth—but not necessarily. Uncertainty and added value are necessary but not sufficient conditions for profit and growth, but are necessary and sufficient to the firm's existence. In spite of what neoclassical economics teaches, economic exchanges always hinge on (a) producers' doubts about the results of their productive activities, and (b) buyers' uncertainties about the value of their purchases. The pursuit of rents is everywhere central to the political process. Most states have no interest in trying to eliminate the profit margin between a haircut at a Vidal Sassoon salon and at your corner barber, preferring to leave that to "market forces." But managing the price of products like corn and electricity may be different because that carries political implications. While the price and format of bread is not controlled in the US, it is tightly controlled in France, as is liquor in Canada. In general the state's attitude towards monopolistic rents waxes and wanes continually, being determined politically. Sometimes states acting against those private firms seen to be exerting monopoly power in the belief that they inevitably lessen social welfare, not the case for 'natural' monopolies.

## 6.4 Technology

Though the legal constraints on the firm are fundamental in how they indicate the state-set boundaries to the opportunity space within which the firm is permitted to become a legal fiction, file a charter, enter into contracts, and do business, much strategizing focuses on responding to and taking advantage of technological developments. Technology-driven innovation is the theme of the day. We certainly live technologically structured and penetrated lives and new technologies have created huge universes of opportunity for the private sector, even if they were initially opened up by military or publicly funded research. As Google and Facebook showed us, these spaces can be colonized at lightning speed, at least at first, just as eighteenth-century colonization moved fast. Then things settle down and the tough sledding of exploitation and protection begins. But science advances and a constant stream of new technological achievements keeps venture capitalists, existing firms, and entrepreneurs on their toes, looking for the "next big thing."

Technology is a puzzle, somewhat clarified by distinguishing it from science.[10] Science focuses on generalized knowledge. Technology is closer to tool. Its value lies in the particular, what emerges through practice, especially the novel practices of innovative private sector BMs. Strategists appreciate technology from within their context and intention rather than something defined objectively, through the prism of their BM. The insider's "What does it means to us?" view of technology opens up different dimensions of constraint and possibility. First, in production. For example, the industrialization of the Haber process of nitrogen fixation led to the bulk production of fertilizer and eventually transformed the world's agriculture and helped create the "green revolution." Today the fertilizer being produced is estimated to sustain a third of the world's population. The massive impact on crop production radically reshaped the agricultural opportunity space that previously depended on letting ground lie fallow to absorb nitrogen directly from the air, and on the labor-intensive process of spreading the dung of the farm's animals. Crop breeding and the diffusion of new planting techniques also contributed. In similar fashion productivity gains were won by reducing planting and food storage losses. The results are important, not the science that helped produce them. Likewise the early textile mills were built in approximately cubic form to minimize the energy losses involved in moving power around the building by belt and pulley from the central waterwheel or steam engine. Scrap and energy loss reduction became scientific management's agenda and framed strategizing as the pursuit of efficiency from the 1850s onwards, leading to "managerial capitalism." After WW2 innovation's emphasis shifted from production to demand creation as, for instance, residential homes became insulated, air-conditioned, and upgraded into their modern power-hungry mode. Formica replaced wood and metal kitchen counter-tops and now we have marble, granite, and synthetics like Corian and Silestone. But how could these technological changes be incorporated into a BM, how had the private firm's opportunity space been transformed? This is the strategist's question about technology. The scientists' answer, about the advance of scientific knowledge, is irrelevant. A technology's strategic relevance can only be viewed through the BM where it appears as a constraint, like a theory, but of the practical world rather than that of ideas.

Technology does more than impact production costs. It has a second dimension of great significance to strategizing, its capacity for control. In

---

[10] J.-C. Spender (2010) 'Technology: Discourse and Possibility', in V. K. Narayanan and G. C. O'Connor (eds), *Encyclopedia of Technology and Innovation Management*. Chichester: John Wiley & Sons, pp. 3–8.

addition to extending, improving, or transforming production, technologies provide means of controlling people's work and behavior. The "panopticon"—the prison cell block layout in which the guards at the center can see through the bars of every cell in the block that circles them—is a famous example, the building's design creating a "technology of surveillance." This is a passive technology, implemented at the prison design stage. A checkout clerk's programmed input register is more active—input errors can be minimized while the clerk's performance is being monitored. An auto's automatic braking system (ABS) is even more active, overriding the driver's brake-pedal push whenever the wheel loses grip. Finance is also technologically penetrated—obviously so in market-making and high-speed trading activities. Creating an options market in which farmers could hedge their planting bets and lay off some of the risks associated with weather and imports similarly transformed agriculture. Again the strategic question is not the existence of a technology but how it might be incorporated into the BM's interplay of constraint and control. For those seeking innovation new search and communication technologies have revolutionized the knowledge resources at their disposal. Likewise the development of computer models of drugs, nuclear warheads, or industrial accidents has changed the way regulators, scientists, and experimenters work. But technological developments have also transformed surveillance and the possibilities for employee control and monitoring discussed in principal-agent theory (section 3.2).

Perhaps the most significant changes in management theory over the past two centuries revolve around managers' use of technology to control work and workers. Chaplin's movie *Modern Times* presented a dramatic view of Fordism, the use of continuous production lines to control how a variety of labor inputs are coordinated and synthesized in the production process. Today's call center operators' responses are tightly controlled by artificial intelligence "scripts"—just as the center's computer system allocates calls to them, measures their throughput, and monitors their bathroom time. We are clearly plunging into an Orwellian society with surveillance at work, in public places, on public transport, and, increasingly, in our private lives. Mobiles chirp their locations to spy satellites and elsewhere. Salespeople carry machines that tell head office their location and activity, in addition to providing instant feedback on stock levels or delivery possibilities, or immediate pricing on insurance policies. Using technology to control the work of others highlights and separates the two modes of control considered in Chapter 5—instruction and persuasion. Control by instruction can be built into the work by adept use of technology. Control by persuasion can define the constraints the worker should consider, as the rhetor does. Thus technology as control is a form of silent rhetoric. But this raises questions about who is doing the talking, for technological choices often have strategic impact.

Spreadsheet software can be shaped to particular transactions, setting the sequence of data collection steps, controlling the calculations, checking for errors, and delivering a response that is consistent across the organization—for instance, a pension determination that will be the same whichever Social Security office you step into. On the other hand, the firm might adopt software, such as a word processor or intranet that allows employees and customers to enter their own views and data, with very different strategic implications.

Viewed through the prism of a BM, technology will have several different faces. It is useful to sort these out in terms of the different constraints they leverage into the opportunity space. At one extreme a technology may change our world in ways that cannot really be escaped. For instance, the last century's steady improvement in commercial fishing equipment and techniques led to many ocean areas being fished out. Irrespective of whether more effective fishing management can lead to stock rebounding, fish stocks are a "fact of Nature" that cannot be escaped without moving to a different form of life, in the case of the fishing industry, or an alternative food source for those previously dependent on fish. At the other extreme are aspects of the human condition less touched by technology—our feelings when we look out to sea or bump someone while crossing the street, or our feelings about those who struggled to control the Fukushima plant meltdown. Between these extremes lies a wide range of ways in which we might be impacted by technology as a tool-like extension to our capabilities—to watch a rock concert on TV and discover it bears little relation to the experience of being there, to cook a TV dinner in the microwave, or feel the ABS system kick in as we negotiate an icy road. In this mid-range we experience the technology's dual capacity for productivity and control. The control aspects are clear as we begin to learn some new software. But tools drop out of our "focal awareness" as we get comfortable using them. Our focus shifts onto what it can do and we begin to feel the productivity impact.

Strategizing technology is not simply about forecasting changes in its scientific foundation, where those exist, such as the discovery of a new way of manufacturing masers, or when a known procedure gets changed, such how a new version of Windows might change the computer industry. The strategist's focus is always on changes to their existing BM. When the impacts are radical it may be necessary to step back one level and completely retheorize the opportunity space along the lines of Chapter 5. For instance, the commercialization of quartz crystal timing precipitated a redefinition of the entire wristwatch industry. The Swatch Group was formed after a sequence of restructuring and recovery moves, with a new appreciation of the market. The name is a contraction of "second watch," leveraging a new distinction between a high-quality timepiece (the most acceptable form of male jewelry) and a handy timekeeper (increasingly threatened by the mobile). Two opportunity spaces were recreated. Through radical redesign of product and production Swatch was able to compete with the base-level timekeepers made in Asia. But the Swatch Group was also able to dominate the design and manufacture of precision parts for the increasingly sophisticated and profitable "male jewelry" market in which the Asian companies had little or no traction. The group was able to build a new BM with a new set of constraints, adding electronic technology to their existing mechanical knowledge-base, of course, but also new labor policies, new design, new marketing, all with significant help from new management, ownership, and financing policies. Now we see a wide variety of wristwatches priced in excess of $500,000.

The middle ground in a strategizing approach to technology as shaping both production and control is illustrated by how we use computers, what Turing showed us as a "universal machine," able to be turned into an infinite variety of tools made "ready to hand" to our projects. Their application may be productive or controlling, showing how technology has no implicit nature until it is attached to our lives through its use. It is not a "thing" or "know-ledge" that stands apart from its application. Computerized control of auto engines makes them hugely more fuel-efficient and responsive, with all manner of impacts on vehicles' use and their environment. Computerized control of the airline pilot's work is essential to safe operation and to air-traffic management. These impacts do not act directly; always through the BM. This tells the strategist how to categorize technology from a use or emic perspective when it appears as practice. The etic perspectives, the science or even the history and path dependency of development, are when we present technology as theory.

It may be useful to distinguish between technology that offers its user (*a*) no possibility of strategic choice or change, (*b*) some latitude, together with some constraints the user cannot alter, or (*c*) such universality that few strategic constraints arise. As an instance of (*a*), the bridge across a river has one purpose—to help traffic across the river. The (*a*) category is "infrastructure," a "fact of the situation" like the fish stock. The strategizing has to take into account infrastructure that is less physical but just as immovable—the local educational facilities on which the firm depends for its workforce or the capital markets it must use to access further funding. In (*b*) there is probably more latitude in the use of the employees' human capital, how what they learned can be applied to the business. Likewise most production equipment is not completely specialized, even if resetting it takes a while. The story of how Japanese auto firms were able to combine physical and human capital to reduce the downtimes involved in resetting their body presses illustrates how such technological changes can ricochet through the business model. This middle ground is what most managers mean by technology, where they have choices and can evaluate the strategic implications of changing from one technology to another. At the universal (c) level the strategists' emphasis is no longer on the tool or technology, but on the production and control objectives of using it. The firm's processes are then designed and controlled using non-technology-dependent means. For instance, while many beers are brewed by "brew-masters" slavishly following chemists' instructions, there are others who have their own ideas about what should go into the vat and when. Management may not wish to control this with a mechanical apparatus or metrics-fed AI device that replaces the brew-master, and may choose to control by more traditional means, including incentivizing or firing the brew-master.

Beyond the reach of technologies successfully integrated into the BM lies the region of craftwork. Craft is the imaginative practical response to situations that cannot be codified rigorously and unambiguously into a non-human practice—a machine's or a system's operating envelope. An automatic machine tool can be programmed to produce the same article over and over. While the programmer can control it to a certain degree the machine's human operator may be able to do still better. One of the great insights into engineering as craftwork lies in grasping how, in the hands of a skilled operator, a machine built to tolerance X can produce parts to a much tighter tolerance, a fraction of X, and so move fabrication forward. Professionalism is a white-collar term for what blue-collar workers see as craft. Ways in which professional work can be shaped parallel ways in which craftwork is shaped. Getting an architecture degree is much like the apprentice cabinet-maker's process of producing his "masterpiece."

We associate professionalization with absorbing an established body of knowledge, tested by examination. The link to professionalized practice is more complicated. My emphasis on language throws up additional ideas, that the language that members have to know to be guided by and contribute to its knowledge base marks the profession. In the same way that Penrose destabilized the economic notion of resource, so the profession's knowledge base is impotent without the judgments that bring it into the world of practice. A profession thereby shapes its knowledge and skills into a technology of production and control. The firm's use of professional knowledge always lies in the middle ground—as in (b) above—creating tensions between those processes fully aligned to the firm's objectives and those to which professionals hew by virtue of their membership of the profession. Qualified accountants may resist top management's desire to manipulate the firm's financial reports, just as a balky semiconductor chip design team might resist being brought under management control at Intel. When the firm relies on professionalized knowledge the imagination and judgment that drives craftwork and makes it valuable test the boundaries to its business model. Fully controllable and interchangeable labor might be considered a form of technology, bound to specific applications that require no judgment. But work is inevitably animated by imagination and influences that lie beyond the boundaries of the BM.

## 6.5 Labor and Work

My topic is people and work in the private sector. Strategizing's objective is the creation of economic value as they transform knowledge and resources into products and services that meet others' desires. The temptation is to focus the analysis on the inanimate resources involved, as neoclassical economics or value-chain analysis does. But there are no resources that can be detached strategically from peoples' abilities to transform them into value. These abilities bring resources into the BM. Thus the firm becomes defined as a tentative, dynamic, and managed pattern of value-adding practices, relating people with many and varied capabilities. Its coherence and identity is always tentative, present only in these practices, for added value arises from people's imagination, not from their obedience to instruction. The fact that the firm exists "at law" or as a set of accounts with their corresponding lists of assets and obligations, or as an organization chart, has little relevance to the firm's strategists or entrepreneurs. The lawyer, accountant, and bureaucratic manager are not considering the firm's capacity to add value. Their concern is the definition, measurement, ownership, allocation, and administration of the value already present. In contrast, entrepreneurs or strategists focus on the firm's value-creating potential beyond this, and on how to realize it. They alone are responsible for bringing the firm into existence and sustaining it. Thus the firm is a label for the institutionalized practices that link the entrepreneurial idea to the value-creating capabilities of those engaged, to the practices that harness their imagination to the entrepreneur's project. Note their non-creative talents and labor might be as readily accessed and coordinated through market relationships for they are forecastable and measurable. Thus the firm's nature hinges on the capacities that cannot be coordinated in this way, as Coase suggested. So in many respects the firm grows out of the strategic responses to and exploitation of both market and instruction failures.

In this section I focus on the issues raised by trying to harness the imagination and judgment of others to the entrepreneur's vision. Earlier I suggested the demarcating characteristics of the modern private sector firm might be (a) its democratic political circumstance, with its pervasive uncertainties, or (b) its particular legal constitution, such as limited liability, or (c) its strategic capacity to bring technologies into the business model. Until Chapter 5 I did not pay much attention to administration, the issue beloved of organization theorists who probe the differences between bureaucratic and more flexible modes, or between centralized or divisionalized structures. Administration makes little sense until we are clear about the people being administered or, more specifically, which of these people's nature-given or acquired capabilities are management's focus.[11] This gets to the kernel of the matter. In Chapter 5 I argued that the most fundamental aspect of the managerial process is rhetorical because that is how leaders persuade rather than instruct, and so get their audience to apply their imagination and judgment to the firm's uncertainties. I contrasted cultural communication to other methods of coordination—coercion and calculation. In this section (section 6.5) I suggest the essence of the modern firm lies in turning away from coercion and calculation as modes of administration, and turning towards persuasion. This puts strategizing into a context ultimately characterized by the specificity of its mode of persuasion, and we can make two points. First, to distinguish work from labor, second, to consider the history of the private sector.

A distinction between work and labor is germane to this book. It is also germane to the broader discussion about the place and nature of work in contemporary society, to the question "do we work to live, or live to work?" The earlier comments about propaganda and "de-personalization" apply, given the private sector firm depends on it. Work is purposive activity and when collaborative is tied up with subordination. But there are always two questions: (a) who or what determines the work's purpose, subordinating others, and (b) to what extent does it call for judgment as opposed to mere instruction-following? Labor might be characterized by being directed and controlled by some other person, a manager perhaps, determining the work's purpose. Much of what we do is shaped by others, customers, and regulators as well as bosses. So we are all intermediaries in the social power network and (a) is weakened. The more powerful notion is of labor as instruction following, when there is no call for the employee to exercise judgment. Employees are thereby "commoditized," rendered replaceable, perhaps fully depersonalized. The control dimension of a technology can be used to structure work in ways that "deskill" workers, turning them into laborers. In the extreme, labor becomes slavery while work is characterized by the judgment called forth to deal with the activity's uncertainties.[12] Employees then put something of themselves into the process. Yesteryear's presumption was that slaves (and women) had nothing worth putting into the work other than their labor. Many humanist writers take up an ethical position here, suggesting that work is more ethically defensible or psychologically satisfying than labor—that

---

[11] H. A. Simon (1997) *Administrative Behavior: A Study of Decision-Making Processes in Administrative Organization* (4th edn). New York: Free Press.
[12] John Paul II (1981) *Laborem Exercens* (On Human Work). Boston: Pauline Books.

work is "enriching" and can lead to human "flourishing." At the same time, because we are intermediaries, the question of who determines the work's objective remains analytically intractable. Is the manager choosing the work's objective freely, or is that institutionalized into the firm, or the industry, or set by the shareholders, or technologically determined? Every firm is a specific form of life with its own micro-politics, constraints, and patterns of power. Are its managers more than the owners' agents of a power derived from ownership? The separation of ownership and control hinges on knowledge asymmetries and uncertainties between the parties, in which case no one is really "in control" because each depends on the other to sustain an ongoing system of practices to which all are ultimately vulnerable.

Clearly we need an ethics of private sector management, but there might a more fruitful discussion if we appreciated more of the Western firm's history. Its demarcating characteristic is its rhetorically intensive mode of governance. The widespread switch from coercion to persuasion arose in the Dutch Republic around 1500. There it became the emerging private sector firm's dominant mode of collaboration, leading to what some economic historians label the "first modern economy".[13] Spain, which had occupied Holland, was eventually driven out, allowing the Dutch to adopt a non-sectarian approach to government that laid the groundwork for today's capitalist democracy. Though Church was not separated from State, commerce was separated from both. The religious freedom in Holland attracted immigrants from the other parts of Europe being roiled by religious conflict, also drawing in scholars, writers, and skilled workers of every type. These immigrants were often highly skilled in ways that could be translated into the collaborative creation of economic value quickly. They were also fully enfranchised, free to quit and go elsewhere. They became the first modern labor pool and presented Dutch entrepreneurs with management challenges that had never existed previously: how to stop the firm's assets from crossing the street and setting up in opposition? Entrepreneurs who wished to expand their enterprises beyond the constraints of their family's members looked to this labor pool and explored means to generate and manage collaboration.[14]

The Dutch government also prioritized and supported education, to the point the Netherlands became the most literate nation in the world, better equipped than any other to discuss science, politics, economics, and other complex ideas. The core of university education had been earlier institutionalized into, first, the "trivium" and then the "quadrivium." The trivium

---

[13] J. de Vries and A. van der Woude (1997) *The First Modern Economy: Success, Failure, and Perseverance of the Dutch Economy 1500–1815*. Cambridge: Cambridge University Press.

[14] In the UK and US context these matters are explored in R. J. Steinfeld (1991) *The Invention of Free Labor: The Employment Relations in English and American Law and Culture, 1350–1870*. Chapel Hill, NC: University of North Carolina Press.

curriculum comprised grammar, logic, and rhetoric, the quadrivium added geometry, arithmetic, astronomy, and music. Promoting education and literacy the Dutch political system evolved the manner of debate that drives our democratic politics. Scientific and artistic societies flourished and commerce along with them—so long as the extensive new human capital resources of non-family members' judgment could be brought into play. The resulting vigorous expansion of the Dutch economy made it the world's most powerful and it remained so until well into the 1700s when Britain and France began to dominate after their industrial revolutions had taken off. We have inherited the Dutch appreciation for "letting a thousand flowers bloom," bringing democratic governance and persuasion to the core of our economic activity. The story, then, is that the demarcating characteristic of the modern firm—what sets strategizing's true nature—is not the private sector's politics, nor the development of bureaucracy and rational administration, nor the firm's ability to absorb technology to enhance productivity and control, nor more scientific understanding of the market's demands, but the entrepreneur's ability to draw skilled, independent, free-thinking people into aligning their imaginative capacity with her/his freely chosen and then delegated uncertainties. Thereby the division of entrepreneurial (judgment) work becomes synthesized with the division of labor, made manageable through the rhetorical practices elaborated in Chapter 5.

## 6.6 Management Education

My hope is that reading this book proves a worthwhile educational experience—whether the reader is a manager, entrepreneur, consultant, teacher, or student. It is intended to offer a supermarket of ideas the imaginative private sector strategist might draw into their work. This objective intersects with management education, so this section considers its state in the light of my book's ideas about subjectivity and imagination. US management education's history goes back to the mid-nineteenth century, paralleling the accelerating growth of US commerce and the resulting increased demand for managers, elaborated commercial institutions such as the capital markets, and better education, medical care, transportation, and other infrastructure.[15] As in the Dutch Republic two centuries before, US family firms sought ways to expand beyond the constraints of the family's capacity to supply enough managers. Given Americans' high regard for commerce, contrasting with the

[15] R. Khurana (2007) *From Higher Aims to Hired Hands: The Social Transformation of American Business Schools and the Unfulfilled Promise of Management as a Profession*. Princeton: Princeton University Press.

Europeans' disdain for "trade," management was quickly accepted as an appropriate calling for young men as they sought a place in society. This applied to every social stratum, not simply the "well-born." In spite of being briefly a pastor himself, Horatio Alger memorialized business as key to social mobility in the nineteenth century—a legitimate alternative to a church or military career. But where were these young men to find relevant knowledge and training? Initially offered by small for-profit commercial schools right across the nation, college-level management education became a big business in its own right. It continues to expand rapidly, putting all kinds of pressure on the colleges and universities that host it. Now that almost one in every four US college students is taking some form of business studies there is a growing literature of criticism. Given the business schools' growth and self-image as centers of professional competence, the public ponders (*a*) their cost, given the growing problems of student loans, (*b*) their value beyond mere job-getting connections and credentials, (*c*) their aesthetics and ethics, as MBA graduates are criticized for their wealth-orientation and sense of entitlement, (*d*) their political posture and neglect of the public sector—and so on.

Over the last century management education's content and method has shifted substantially, with greater attention to quantitative analysis. The synthesizing aspects that were explored in case teaching before WW2 have been pushed to the sidelines, while data collection, statistical techniques, computer-based modeling, and rigorous theorizing have become the center of the curriculum. The shift has been accompanied by a growing sense that management education has become less able to inform management practice—leading to what academics label the "rigor–relevance problem." The change does not seem to have dimmed the students' or recruiters' enthusiasm. Among management education professionals there are repeated calls for a reorientation towards greater attention to management practice. For many this means moving away from classroom abstractions and changing the focus back to what it was around the 1900s, the practical realities of managing a business. For others it means observing the details of management life rather than applying grand theory, seeing management as a practice or process.[16]

An alternative view is that we need to change the methods educators impute to managers. Prior to WW2 managers were seen to exercise judgment, so management was seen as fulfilling work, morally and ethically penetrated, both a burden and a source of self-realization for those engaged in it. During the war the success of operations research (OR) and the development of computing machines able to handle huge amounts of statistical data led many to see management as a data-supported science rather than a craft,

---

[16] H. Mintzberg (2004) *Managers Not MBAs: A Hard Look at the Soft Practice of Managing and Management Development*. San Francisco: Berrett-Koehler Publishers.

a labor wherein managers were commoditized as "the numbers" began to drive their conclusions. Perhaps expert systems and AI would eventually ensure that computers could do everything a laboring manager did—more reliably, faster, without error, and without emotional entanglements. The business education curriculum evolved accordingly. In 1959 the Ford and Carnegie Foundations issued reports on the state of management education that transformed US business schools. Teachers whose only claim to expertise was their experience and judgment as "seasoned executives" were displaced by a new generation of young men (and increasingly after the 1990s young women), whose background was very different. Their skills were intellectual and analytic, their background was the academic research literature and the analytic competences displayed in their Ph.D.s. They were often strangers to the practicalities of life in firms, and so without experience or judgment. Since the Foundation report business schools teachers have been light on business experience and so not able to make much sense of the judgment managers need as they confront the uncertainties of their firms' situations. Most business schools—a notable exception being Harvard's—let managerial judgment drop out of the curriculum. The business educators' professional association is the AACSB, founded in 1916 as the American Assembly of Collegiate Schools of Business, but renamed in 2001 to match a new global strategy as the Association to Advance Collegiate Schools of Business. For some decades after the changes precipitated by the 1959 Foundation reports, the AACSB mandated the strategy course as the accredited MBA's "capstone" course— wherein the syllabus "came together" and was related to "general management's" strategizing practice. To the extent managerial judgment was taught at all, it was here, with strategic analysis as its vehicle and discipline. But as microeconomic methods and topics colonized the strategy field in the 1970s and 1980s things began to change, executive judgment was displaced by rigorous analysis, and case-work was marginalized. After 1994 the AACSB no longer mandated strategy as the capstone course—though many schools still consider it so. The AACSB shifted to emphasize cross-disciplinary, but still academic, teaching. They pushed schools to match the curriculum to the school's declared mission and to adapt their curriculum to embrace, for instance, social and political issues, globalization, ethics, and sustainability. The original pre-1979 accreditation objective was to police the curriculum, to ensure every accredited school taught a defined common body of knowledge (CBK). By 2000 the objective shifted towards examining each school's curriculum and educational resources to see if they appropriately supported its chosen academic mission. The shift freed accreditation-seeking schools to choose their own educational objectives rather than adhering to those implicit in the earlier CBK. Many moved from general management towards more specialized staff areas such as finance, accounting, innovation, or entrepreneurship.

The variety of issues considered in the generalist capstone strategy course was limited, but there was no doubt that the original pedagogical position saw strategizing as a creative process that melded analysis with synthesizing. Chapter 5 offers an explicit treatment of this, following von Clausewitz's thinking, and argues that as long as strategists view their inventory of theories through the prism of the BM they construct, the dichotomy of the rigor–relevance question does not arise. It is a consequence of moving the focus onto analysis alone, dismissing synthesis. The strategy course texts listed in Appendix C illustrate how this has played out. The texts are categorized according to their underlying model: (1) external–internal fit, (2) rent-management, (3) sense-making, (4) emergence, (5) socio-politics, (6) tool-kit, (7) microeconomics, (8) game theory, and (9) planning. Models 7–9 exclude the synthesizing found in models 1–6 and are explicitly "rigorous" and analytic. In the immediate post-WW2 years the planning metaphor dominated the management literature, adopted as a consequence of the perceived success of the war's military OR planning. It has now disappeared from most business school curricula. Appendix C also shows that, however one might assess the state of strategic theorizing by looking at the papers published in our top academic journals, strategy teaching is still dominated by pedagogical practices that call forth the students' judgments about what to take into account, when the options are uncertain. The emphasis is on how to evaluate the options' relative significance and impact on the firm, and that can seldom be calculated. At the same time the continuing shift of institutionalized research methodology towards quantitative methods erodes such pedagogy; especially when buttressed by requiring incoming strategy teachers to demonstrate proficiency with the quantitative methods evident in the research literature rather than with HBS-style case teaching. Research methodology has displaced business content. Case teaching also presents teachers without business experience with significant professional challenges. When trying to show students how judgment is key to making use of analysis—when there "is no right answer"—on what can they draw?

The continuing denial of the judgment-centered work of management, as opposed to the more lauded labor of data collection and reduction, has had many side effects. I see strategizing as a profoundly human practice, more akin to art (craft) than to science. There have been centuries of debate about craftwork. The dichotomy may be false and unproductive—though widely adopted. Management is neither art nor science, the distinction memorialized in C. P. Snow's 1959 lecture on "two cultures".[17] It is a creative practice that draws on both modes of knowing. Nonetheless the idea of the split is deeply

---

[17] C. P. Snow (1959) *The Two Cultures and the Scientific Revolution: The Rede Lecture 1959.* Cambridge: Cambridge University Press.

ingrained in our culture and language, and especially in the micro-culture of management education. Yet reason alone cannot ever be sufficient to determine professional action in the uncertain circumstances we inhabit. Inasmuch as management is a professional activity, all action analysis should bring together as much "scientifically established knowledge" as possible. We expect our doctors to be "up" on their professional literature, just as we expect realtors and train operators to know what is going on as their trade advances too. But, as von Clausewitz reminded us, it is a mistake to expect that theory can ever provide doubt-free answers. Judgment is always necessary. So the resulting choice is always unrigorous and "doubt-full." The moment we let go of doubt we cease strategizing and become dogmatists, pushing our view of the world without accommodation to intention and context. Case-work can inculcate and exercise this doubting or adjusting attitude, though it is often used in ways that have different results. I make some comments about case teaching and writing in Appendix A.

Those who want to teach management without attention to managerial judgment have many problems. Each discipline defines a universe of phenomena to be considered with theoretical models constructed in a formal language that stands on a specific set of axioms. Neoclassical economics deals with one formalized universe of phenomena, behavioral theories another. Under Knightian uncertainty not everything important to responsible action can be captured with a single language. The business schools' response to this is to put a variety of courses into the curriculum as one group of faculty grudgingly accepts the relevance of other disciplines (and departments). But the hapless student is left to make sense of the various offerings and "bring them together" on their own in ways the faculty members cannot, hence without professorial guidance. Interdisciplinary or "trans-disciplinary" courses are often proposed to address this gap in the curriculum. But this strategy has a troubled history. The dynamics of academic politics, and the reward systems, militate against it.

It follows that, if judgment should be an important component of management education, many business schools do their students a double disservice. First, when business schools fail to teach the development and application of managerial judgment, they abandon what used to be a key element of the pre-1959 curriculum. Second, students are being trained for analytic positions rather than executive ones, to be analysis-based staffers rather than strategists or entrepreneurs. If schools hope to restore strategizing or entrepreneurship to a central place in the curriculum (perhaps relabeled leadership) there is much to be done. While executive experience is plentiful, it is difficult for experienced business people to fit into the contemporary business school because the methodological climate has moved so far from their way of thinking. Quantitative methods have advanced hugely, impelled by computing. Social network analysis or enterprise resource planning (ERP) were beyond the reach of academic researchers twenty years ago. Now the better-resourced schools have access to "big data" and "analytics" techniques. Computerized qualitative analysis has likewise advanced rapidly, especially in marketing and managing the firm's identity, image, and market positioning. Senior executives are not likely to be entirely familiar with these methods, having delegated their deployment to their staffer MBAs, just as the development of "financial products" has been delegated from experienced bankers to "rocket scientists" or "quants".[18] Senior executives who move into management education cut themselves off from their data collection and decision-making support staff, and can do little more than puff bland generalizations at their students. Their core deal-making skills and work are not readily taught, being so entwined with the particularities of their firms' intentions and context, and their personal relationships. So it is not clear how to get beyond cases to improved methods of teaching managerial judgment.

There are some answers, perhaps through collaboration with other university departments, such as education, psychology, and engineering. Reaching out to other disciplines has always been one of the richer features of university life, so my emphasis on harnessing the judgment of others has one clear implication. Chapter 5 argued the processes of generating the BM differ from those of communicating it. If teaching toward judgment addresses the first, teaching students about rhetoric and persuasion addresses the second. Until the mid-nineteenth century all young men educated for leadership in society—whether in politics, religion, the military, or commerce—would be taught the principles of rhetoric in the parts of the syllabus that addressed the "trivium." Rhetoric virtually disappeared from this central place in university life as our culture veered towards science. The competitive internal politics of university life challenged all disciplines to adopt the new "scientific method" or be cast aside. Many of the liberal arts experienced "culture wars" over this and remain divided, sustaining the opposition of art and science. Management education, still unformed as rhetoric disappeared, drifted into disrepute during the years between the wars. Its post-WW2 rescue hinged on adopting science as its central metaphor, redefining management as a science that called for analysis rather than judgment. Rhetoric, even public speaking, disappeared, though it survives in the English department's courses on composition, and in college debating societies. We would do well to restore it to a central place in management education. There is a vast literature on how to teach rhetoric and there is no great problem adapting it to the special challenges that face private sector managers.

---

[18] S. Patterson (2010) *The Quants: How a New Breed of Maths Whizzes Conquered Wall Street and Nearly Destroyed it.* New York: Crown Business.

Summarizing, the implications of my book's approach for management education are (a) to be less adamant that data are everything and admit to the Knightian uncertainties that underpin democratic capitalism, firms' existence, and their value-creation potential, (b) to establish a more appropriate balance between teaching judgment and analysis, (c) to follow von Clausewitz and teach synthesizing as a practice, and (d) to restore rhetoric to the curriculum, for management is a talking game.


## 6.7 Self-Preparation

Strategizing is stressful, wearing work, especially when the lives of others are being affected. Experience reveals this quickly, the visible aging of Presidents. There are many books about stress management, elaborations of homilies such as "never take a major decision without sleeping on it," or "take a walk to clear your head." Von Clausewitz had much to say about preparing for the act of commitment. Extensive research on all of the constraints to judgment in the situation should be followed by a period of calm, freeing the strategist up to allow insights and "light bulb" ideas to come into the mind. He spoke of the *coup d'œil* as "the unanticipated but all encompassing answer" that reveals itself, but is not likely to do so to the mind cluttered and distracted by tactical minutiae.[19] The capability connects to a great executive gift, the ability to see into the heart of a complex problem quickly, to separate the essential from the peripheral. The process is imaginative rather than logical and makes for tremendous economy of time and effort. But like all art, whatever natural ability one is given is honed by and much extended through hard work. Sometimes this means bookish study, as von Clausewitz urged study of military history. Serious chess players invest enormous effort into studying others' games. Sometimes it is a matter of concentration and focus—quiet time. Both Newton and Einstein remarked on their ability to hold a specific problem in their "mind's eye" for months at a time before a solution emerged. Most artistic achievement is preceded by enormous work. Business achievement is clearly as important and not likely to be less demanding.

The work to be done here should be put in the context of engaging the imagination to change the world. My book's analysis is "micro-foundational," arguing strategizing begins with an individual or a very tight group—probably not more than three people—that collaborates to the point of merging their identities in respect to the work to be done, so they can almost predict how the

---

[19] W. Duggan (2007) *Strategic Intuition: The Creative Spark in Human Achievement*. New York: Columbia Business School.

others will respond.[20] Thus the self-preparation is sometimes collective, but always springs from change at the micro-foundational level, becoming a new person. This is hard work and is not about trying to manifest oneself by dominating and reshaping the situation. To the contrary, it hinges on the creative restructuring of interplay of identity and context. The creativity that leads to added value begins with personal growth, the Sophoclean struggle to get beyond the passive imperative to "know thyself" as a stable discoverable entity and to achieve a greater measure of one's potential. In our capitalist democracy business offers many of the leading opportunities to do this.

## 6.8 Summary

At the beginning of this chapter, the reader may have expected some predictions about how the world is changing—technologically, politically, ecologically, etc.—and be disappointed by my writing that I know no more about this than the reader, indeed I have the gravest doubts about the possibility of forecasting the world we shape through our work. But, as I have repeated *ad nauseam*, I do know that everything about the firm needs to be viewed through the prism of its business model. Of course there are always important things happening which matter to everyone, no matter where they are in the global economy. There is a long list. Given our bounded rationality and attention I would urge the reader to give the firm's and the political and legal constraints to strategizing more consideration rather than obsess on the financial, marketing, and technological commentaries that so often dominate the media and our literature. In-depth consideration of the changes in the firm's social, economic, political, and technological environment begins with identifying the firm's BM. That alone enables the strategist to break free of others' categorizations—such as the social, economic, political, and technological—and refashion her/his enquiry in ways that findings can be drawn directly into the firm's idiosyncratic discourse—to answer the ever-present "What does it mean to us?" question.

## 6.9 Concluding Remarks

Now we are at the end. Has anything been achieved? Should a book on business strategy be informing its readers about academics' work? If so,

---

[20] T. Kidder (1981) *The Soul of a New Machine*. New York: Avon.

I have failed completely. Everything I have done is to stand all available theory on its head to show what it does not do. My aim has been to help readers appreciate the nature of the judgment called for in creating and managing private sector firms—precisely because theory has nothing definitive or determining to say about strategizing practice. In the light of these theorists' failure to answer Coase's questions I believe business people can properly claim to "own" them on the grounds that they answer them as matters of everyday practice. Their answers are not theories, of course. Perhaps theory cannot provide answers precisely because, like democracy itself, the private sector firm is a creature of the uncertainties of modern life. Douglass North argued that a society's institutions reflect its principal anxieties, uncertainties that need to be addressed through collective practice. I see the firm in the same way. My intention is to help those who knowingly shoulder the burdens of strategizing and have no intention of giving up their responsibility for acting in their firm's uncertain circumstances to others. Rather they are seeking some Clausewitzian clarification to help them separate what they alone must attend to from the quotidian clutter that consumes their attention and hinders the application of their imagination to the creation of new value.

My book is seriously deficient in one important respect. In spite of various management-level tales and suggestions throughout, there is not one fleshed-out example of a business model, the object of the process covered in Chapter 4. Just as Balanchine said "First a school!" so I say "First a language!" Until we internalize the BM-as-language we cannot grasp how it captures the firm's strategic challenges and judgments. We can only access the managers' view of the firm through the language they use. It becomes meaningful only through participation in the indexical practices that are going on within the firm all the time. Hence there is no point is revealing the managers' talk to those who have not learnt the firm's language by inhabiting its space-time. The mainstream academic approach to strategic analysis is that it can be done in some general objective language. I think this a contradiction in terms, for strategy is only relevant to the particular, never to the general. As noted in Appendix A on case-work, because most cases are written by academics the language in which they are written is likely to be the same that they use to present theories to their students. In which circumstance, the case is being used to illustrate questions framed in those theories rather than being a historian's story that captures the insiders' (emic) view of the situation. The point of history is to tell a compelling story—so it is an exercise in rhetoric. Narrative theorists argue a story differs from data in the way poems differ from data. They carry meanings the author intended but that can never be made explicit. Because the firm is ultimately nothing but human activity, getting into the BM-as-language requires a longish human story, wonderfully illustrated in *The Soul of a New Machine*,[21] not a simple list of facts. In my earlier book probing the subjective approach to strategizing, each of the three "industry recipes" took a full chapter to flesh out.[22] Even then a huge gap remained between the managerial talk and the reader's understanding. The examples this book has omitted can be found in the business history literature—so, as von Clausewitz suggested, entrepreneurs and executives do well to prepare themselves for their creative work by reading the history relevant to the identities, intentions, and contexts or the BMs they intend to create. For some the history of technology will be crucial, for others the history of government regulation, or of fashion and consumers' fickle taste, or of labor movements, or . . . .

My book sketches a subjectivist or "constructivist" approach to managing economic value creation in the private sector. It follows from taking Knightian uncertainty "seriously." Thinking, as many strategy authors seem to, that there is a rigor–relevance gap between rigorous theory and effective practice implies managers should aspire to conform to theory, perfection neither they nor we can ever attain. I dismiss this impractical dream. Instead of dealing with data gathering in categories set by academic theories and rigorous analysis to surface the optimal answers buried therein, I argue an uncertainty-dismissing approach cannot work—on its own. Though my method contrasts with the certainty-assuming deterministic approach, it is not intended as a dismissal of rigorous analysis. To the contrary, it is to complement it. My borrowing of von Clausewitz's methodology embraces all forms of human knowing, and synthesizes them to raise the strategist's confidence to act under uncertainty. The analysis-alone approach is an academic artifact of little practical use to managers. The reasons for its popularity and place in the management education curriculum lie more in the history and machinations of the academy's institutional practices. They do not lie in the practical usefulness or value of the recent decades of academic research. Ironically, as we pay more attention to the history of the private sector firm we see the academic approach actually denies the ancient meaning of strategizing for it is a reflection of our believing we have choices whose choosing requires judgment and whose ultimate consequences can only be imagined. Thus strategizing is no more, or less, than the practice of reflecting on how we think about ourselves and our doings. Rather than presuming we are passive rational calculators I presume our unquenchable desire to look our expectations (future) in the eye in the process of creating new value. Our political system puts this freedom at its core, as should our concept of managing.

---

[21] T. Kidder (1981) *The Soul of a New Machine*. New York: Avon.
[22] J.-C. Spender (1989) *Industry Recipes: The Nature and Sources of Managerial Judgement*. Oxford: Blackwell.

# APPENDIX A

# On Case-Writing and Teaching

The Harvard Business School (HBS) is widely considered the main source of business school case teaching expertise. Its Christensen Center for Teaching and Learning (CCTL) offers a variety of valuable (and free) insights, resources, and tips for case teachers and writers.[1] For many years HBS was also the main source of business cases, but today many others also serve this growing market—such as CasePlace.org,[2] ecch,[3] EmeraldMangementFirst,[4] Ivey,[5] Globalens,[6] and NACRA,[7] plus a variety of on-line offerings, and in languages other than English. The CCTL guidelines for teaching a case successfully are important—thorough preparation, good planning, respectful listening to the students, leading the discussion to closure, etc. The teacher is urged to have two or three clear learning objectives in mind and plan a four-stage process: structure, opening, discussion leadership, and closure.

But in spite of HBS's enormous experience, few theories of case teaching and writing or explanations of how it works have emerged. Among the recent HBS-sourced books is *Education for Judgment: The Artistry of Discussion Leadership*—co-edited by Christensen.[8] Cases are part of a pedagogy that stands on HBS's view of how people learn. This is not made explicit but presumes students learn in several ways; "new knowledge is acquired by extending and revising prior knowledge, new ideas acquire meaning when they are presented in a coherent relationship to one another, and knowledge becomes usable when it is acquired in situations that entail applications to concrete problem-solving".[9] Elsewhere there are suggestions that learning implies personal change. Note this description does not distinguish case teaching from other pedagogical modes, for "participation" in the educational process goes back to Socrates and is not exclusive to case rooms. The "guide on the side" can displace the "sage on the stage" anywhere

---

[1] http://www.hbs.edu/teaching/    [2] http://caseplace.org/
[3] http://www.ecch.com/educators/
[4] http://first.emeraldinsight.com/browse.htm?PHPSESSID=t7h7c8t1064th52vpmq5p38tf4&subject=km&type=casestudies.
[5] https://www.iveycases.com/    [6] http://globalens.com/
[7] http://www.nacra.net/crj/index.php5.
[8] C. R. Christensen, D. A. Garvin, and A. Sweet (1991) *Education for Judgment: The Artistry of Discussion Leadership*. Boston: Harvard Business School Press.
[9] R. F. Elmore (1991) 'Foreword', in C. R. Christensen, D. A. Garvin and A. Sweet (eds), *Education for Judgment: The Artistry of Discussion Leadership*. Boston: Harvard Business School Press, pp. ix–xix.

there are teachers and students, being more a practical aesthetic of the teacher–student interaction than a theory of learning.

HBS's case teaching has two main parents—Christopher Columbus Langdell (Dean of the Harvard Law School from 1870 to 1895) and Edwin Gay, HBS's founding Dean in 1903. Langdell reacted against conventional law teaching that characterized legal rules as quasi-theoretical abstractions. He believed it important for students to immerse themselves in the particulars of the cases that were most influential in setting legal precedent. Law, he argued, was a socially embedded generative practice—not a theory—and could not be understood as the application of overarching formalized rules. Gay, an economist, learned the data-heavy Socratic or "seminar" method of teaching while doing his Ph.D. in Germany under Gustave von Schmoller, one of the fathers of the industrial organization (IO) economics that shaped HBS's approach to business.[10] Gay was able to introduce a version of business case-work at HBS's inception because the Harvard Law School's case-work had already legitimated case teaching within the university. Mintzberg's discussion of the history of case-work and its adoption is clarifying.[11]

But it is not easy to make sense of the literature on case-work until one decides which epistemology to adopt. As readers are aware, the mainstream view is that all valid knowledge is of a reality, logical and stable, that exists beyond our thinking. Facts are such learning's target. The only type of uncertainty admitted is ignorance of what is logically constructed and fully knowable. Within this epistemology cases are tentative explorations of objective knowledge. Yin's *Case Study Research*—perhaps the most highly cited work in our field—is a primer on this methodology.[12] Note that Yin sees Kidder's *Soul of a New Machine*,[13] mentioned earlier in this book, as an excellent case study, but of little use to researchers because the author does not keep control of the unit of analysis—is it the engineering team, its individual members, the mini-computer being developed, West (the project manager), or Data General (the firm)? Along the lines of Yin's approach, conventional research methodology courses view cases as useful for exploring the theory-based categories that can be used to describe and measure phenomena of interest. Case methods become the first step to more rigorous research that then uses these categories to address a larger sample and so fit well into Van de Ven's *Engaged Scholarship*.[14] Of course HBS's approach to and use of cases is nothing like this; its focus is on introducing students to the nature and burdens of executive judgment, not on teaching them how to do publishable research. But case research's problems inform us about teaching executive judgment.

Ethnographic researchers are interested in how a particular target population (often a native tribe) categorizes and dimensions their experience of their lived world. Interpretive or social constructivist case research can help. Its epistemology stands against the positivist one and has different strengths and weaknesses. This introduces a risk of

[10] H. Heaton (1968) *A Scholar in Action: Edwin F. Gay*. New York: Greenwood Press.

[11] H. Mintzberg (2004) *Managers Not MBAs: A Hard Look at the Soft Practice of Managing and Management Development*. San Francisco: Berrett-Koehler Publishers.

[12] R. K. Yin (1994) *Case Study Research: Design and Methods* (2nd edn). Thousand Oaks, CA: Sage.

[13] T. Kidder (1981) *The Soul of a New Machine*. New York: Avon.

[14] A. H. Van de Ven (2007) *Engaged Scholarship: A Guide for Organizational and Social Research*. Oxford: Oxford University Press.

fruitless relativism, that the tribe (senior management team, perhaps) develops a view of the world that is charmingly idiosyncratic but hopelessly out of touch with their situation's scientific facts and experience (group think). Particular thinkers (prophets) or charismatics (such as Andrew Carnegie or Steve Jobs) can make a historical impact and a culture unique and not immediately comprehensible to outsiders. For millennia scholars have debated the generalities–specifics distinction, whether something essential is missed from an understanding of the life lived as the specifics are lost when events are aggregated to highlight the generalities they share. The researcher's intent, of course, is to break through from "samples of one" to analyses that have the attributes of good statistical work—validity and reliability. Flyvberg's summary is useful.[15] He quotes Nietzsche on doing science—"one would not wish to divest existence of its rich ambiguity" and hints that modernist science promotes generalizations as the only valid knowledge while dismissing the particular and so "disenchanting" our knowing.

The distinction between what is general and what is particular is crucial to understanding case teaching's differing objectives because it can be used either to (*a*) exemplify generalities and generate theory, the mainstream academic objective, or (*b*) probe those aspects of events that reveal the actors as agents with idiosyncratic personal judgment, the historian's objective. If case-work is towards (*a*) it has no great potential to teach personal judgment. No doubt many teachers use cases to present students with data that are less than complete and may include contradictions. The student's task is to sort through the different options or logics that are present in the information, given the data is insufficient to dismiss all but one of the interpretations possible. A well-written case denies any one option's priority—"there is no right answer".[16] Chapter 1's concept of strategizing is of choosing from among several alternatives. For the most part HBS case teaching presumes this, so it is interesting to visit the CCTL website and hear faculty talk about their teaching. They emphasize extensive preparation for the process. The students learn choosing by being compelled (when "called on") to pick one or other of the options surfaced in their study team's intensive study of the materials. The student justifies that choice by deploying data that all share. The implication is that thorough homework, well argued, can tilt the evolving consensus in the classroom to any of the options embedded in the case material. The teacher provides good "discussion leadership" by being sensitive to the discussion's dynamics and resisting the temptation to foreclose on her/his own preferred conclusion. The outcome is a generative collaboration between students and teacher that all gain from. Thus CCTL advises the teacher to develop the "art" of asking the right question of the right student at the right time—and in the right way (rhetorical practice again). In an HBS class's packed eighty minutes, the section's ninety or more students will struggle to impress with their individual choices. The teacher must prepare thoroughly to stay on top of this process and must also remain remarkably alert if s/he is to provide good "discussion leadership." But what is being learned?

---

[15] B. Flyvbjerg (2006) 'Five Misunderstandings about Case-Study Research', *Qualitative Inquiry*, 12(2), 219–45.
[16] J.-C. Spender (1983) 'Crisis Casework for Policy Courses', *Journal of Management Education*, 8(4), 35–7.

Critics argue the package of case materials and the short time available to study them does not allow the student to get into the place the case-writer intends them to be in—that of a real executive facing an urgent situation that demands strategic action. Yet HBS's rhetoric seems tempting. There may be some surface validity in their claim that the case relates to a decision a real executive once faced. But the case's historical verisimilitude may do little beyond merely justifying its use—showing it is a case about business rather than law or war. Note the pedagogical objective does not turn on the historical correctness of the case content. The "facts of the case" are actually peripheral and it does not matter whether they are correct or not. They simply constrain a discursive context in which the student has to make strategic judgments. The class could equally well be asked to deal with a public policy situation—should marihuana be legalized in Cayuga County, or what sea defenses should New York build? Or even an engineering decision, should the Netherlands government subsidize electric cars and, if so, with what type of battery? The pedagogical challenge is identical; to unpack a mountain of incomplete data and arrive rapidly at an actionable conclusion, and then to make a case for it with the teacher and other students present. There is no right answer against which it can be tested; only against the equally limited information and opinions of the teacher and students.

This kind of constrained choosing is what the HBS approach trains MBA students to do—on the grounds that it simulates "real strategizing." The process can be very much like that outlined in Chapter 4. No question students learn something useful about data analysis and debate in the process but it certainly does not simulate managerial practice. It misses the essence Chapter 4 addresses—the nature of the firm as a historically particularized context of power, constraints, intention, ambition, and collaboration with specific people who have specific characteristics and history interacting in the firm's own strategic time. It also misses the tension between alternative possible BMs, the doubts and counter-stories the case-writer never picked up on, the ways the firm's identity might have been changed away from the line of business discussed in the case, the paths not taken. Case-based teaching also presents teachers with nagging questions about students' Googling to inform themselves about the real firm, perhaps finding strategically significant facts the case-writer missed or misunderstood. Should the students regard the firm being analyzed as the real one or the one presented in the case?

Business case-writers are not likely to be trained historians, so they will probably miss the "rich ambiguity" of the situation as the actors experienced it and revealed themselves through negotiating its uncertainties. What categories did these people use to construct their knowledge of the firm and its situation, and shape their practice? Where did these categories come from? The case seldom raises these questions because it is written "etically," by outsiders whose analytic categories are drawn from the theories they teach their students, categories set by their own academic training, or by professional accounting conventions, or by the atheoretical concepts of the consulting literature reviewed in Chapter 2—strengths and weaknesses, rivalry, core competencies, dynamic capabilities, etc., or by the somewhat theoretically structured ideas reviewed in Chapter 3, or even by business journalists—such as competitive advantage, market making, or open innovation. In short, the case is extremely unlikely to present the situation in the firm's idiosyncratic language. The point of Chapters 4 and 5 is to focus on the language used by those in the firm who shape its uncertainty-resolving and value-creating practices. If students are to learn only about analyzing and selecting between opaquely framed options the case-writer's choice of language does not matter greatly. But it leaves the student without experiencing confrontation with the emotionally, morally, and aesthetically demanding uncertainties of the real resource-consuming practices of creating economic value. As Mintzberg summarizes pithily: "management is a responsibility, not a game played in a classroom".[17] The process of strategic work outlined in Chapters 4 and 5 turns on and is held together by the strategists' responsibilities to the firm's "stakeholders" and to themselves.

HBS is curiously inward-looking and inattentive to the social sciences' broader experience of case research and teaching, an experience that is highly contested.[18] The "emic" tradition attempts to get as close as possible to the "protagonist's" lived experience to surface how social life works and how individuals shape it. Emic methods have powered much sociology and have led to new ways of framing and analyzing sociological phenomena. Their positivist critics protest, "What is the point is looking at the unique? We are scientists and want to know what can be generalized and used to clarify (even determine) other action situations." But we risk confusing emic and etic, different kinds of research. Etic methods look for generalities, presuming sociological phenomena are subject to universal laws somewhat similar to those of natural science—exploring a given-ness of social life the researchers presume logical and knowable. The emic project explores the nature of agentic choice and action, and presumes individuals differ and reveal their differences only through their actions in under-determined situations. People are what they do under uncertainty. The research focuses on the strategist as artist or architect of value creation. This is strategizing as I presume and present it in Chapter 4. The personal judgment that shapes agentic action is not merely about picking from one or other determining (logically constructed) course of action in a situation marked by ignorance alone, as in Chapter 1. Rather it is innovative and context-creating, a combination of categorizing, data collection, meaning-making, and synthesizing that is much more demanding. In the Clausewitzian manner, the emic draws in the etic, and vice versa, as well as the strategist's own judgment. Since our capabilities to do this stand on more than our logical capabilities, learning depends on experience and the tacit grasp developed. This points directly towards Dewey's extremely influential theories of learning, sometimes mentioned in the case literature but seldom unpacked.[19] Surprisingly—or revealingly—there seems no evidence of interaction between HBS and HGSE, Harvard's School of Education. Likewise and also apparently ignored at HBS, just across the Charles River MIT provides the same pedagogical challenges, teaching students to analyze case-type data and model problematic engineering situations.[20]

[17] H. Mintzberg (2004) *Managers Not MBAs: A Hard Look at the Soft Practice of Managing and Management Development*. San Francisco: Berrett-Koehler Publishers.

[18] J. R. Feagin, A. M. Orum, and G. Sjoberg (eds) (1991) *A Case for the Case Study*. Chapel Hill, NC: University of North Carolina Press.

[19] J. Dewey (1997) *Experience and Education*. New York: Touchstone. J. Dewey (2007). *Human Nature and Conduct: An Introduction to Social Psychology*. New York: Cosimo.

[20] P. White (1992) *The Idea Factory: Learning to Think at MIT*. New York: Plume Books.

Von Clausewitz argued studying history is useful precisely because it helps one understand how past notables revealed their identities, talents, and failings as they constructed their strategic contexts. It is especially important to see how they dealt with the situation's indeterminacies, for in war nothing is more important than being able to enter the mind of the enemy to assess his judgment. This goes far beyond picking from among pre-existing options (written into the case by its author/s) and contrasts passive and active (agentic) modes of judgment. Historians claim their research methods enable the reader to approach the uniqueness of the actor's context and creative process, even as they realize they cannot enter the actor's mind—but their aim is to get as near to this as they can. When achieved in some measure, it sets up a discussion between alternative stories about the past, the counter-story, reminding us that, since the facts of history are never determining, what did not happen is often as revealing as our story of what did happen—"the dog that did not bark" in the Sherlock Holmes story. In this way we use the history's methods to clarify our sense of the present. Business history has good resonance for students seeking insights into the nature of the strategizing challenges executives faced in the past. Good history, of course, is the opposite of theoretically justified determinism, it deploys specifics to complement generalities and create a compelling story.[21] It is also always open to new data and reinterpretation, and to the incommensurabilities generated by multiple research methods or "triangulation." It is infused with an appreciation of the indeterminacies of political, economic, and social life, both within the firm and without. History's methods are synthesizing and so illuminate the strategic synthesizing of others.

In practical terms the less the case data are structured by the author's theoretical predispositions the more the student is challenged to categorize, select, and synthesize, using her/his own judgment to develop a story. The balance between story-construction and story-telling—persuasion—can then be shifted in pedagogically beneficial ways. Non-trivial case-work has two distinct task aspects: (*a*) unraveling complex data and synthesizing a compelling story, and (*b*) telling that story to persuade others. Case-writers pay less attention to (*b*) than is warranted—given students probably find their rhetorical experiences of case learning more searing than their analytic and synthesizing experiences (as in *Paper Chase*). If the (*b*) aspect is to be taken seriously, case teachers should teach their students something about effective rhetorical practice before putting them on the spot to persuade the rest of their section. But the case material also needs to be rich enough to provide a rhetorical challenge, more than mere hard data to compute. Complex accounting or forecasting exercises present analytic challenges rather than rhetorical ones.

Chapter 5 showed the rhetor's first challenge is *ethos*, to establish the right to speak. The social situation of the classroom presents many challenges since the section's members have generally learned a lot about each other during their program. The case must also allow the speaker to consider the protagonist's *ethos* challenge. We know *pathos* is pivotal to generating human action and the student's ability to engage this rhetorical mode can become a crucial means to justify a choice that might lack *logos* when compared to other options, but still has the possibility to carry the audience.

---

[21] R. G. Collingwood (1994) *The Idea of History* (rev. edn). Oxford: Oxford University Press.

Treating case-work as a means to teach managerial rhetoric as well as analysis and synthesis brings the student closer to "real management" experience. Aside from framing management as a collaborative talking game, it reinforces the view that the firm—and its management—is fundamentally discursive in nature. In spite of the modernist disposition to prioritize facts (*logos*) over the other modes of rhetoric, the idea that strategizing language should comprise nothing but the facts, or be as close to the facts as possible, insults managers and the strategic work they do. There is a good case to be made that business schools are best thought of as temples of business talk that school students into the languages appropriate to their future managerial role, rather than schools of administrative, organizational, or financial engineering. Managers are not technicians; they are persuaders that need to walk and talk. Note how few of the deterministic theories taught in business schools have found their way into management practice, as opposed to the engineering of financial tools and derivatives. But we surely concede that the student's facility with business talk is crucial to their recruitment.

The pedagogical challenges of case teaching can be clarified with Chapter 5's brief review of rhetorical practice. Participation and discussion is pivotal to the Socratic method. Students often sit back and criticize wordlessly, but the practice of "speaking out" is fundamental to learning. The commitment involved calls for thought and rehearsal. Every speaker needs to develop a manner and technique that matches who he or she is, for authenticity is essential to rhetorical effectiveness. College debating societies, for example, are risk-free environments in which students can develop a style that works for them. Case rooms could provide something similar for students' business personae. Familiarity with managerial rhetoric helps the student develop (*a*) the courage to press forward into the uncertainties that make strategizing necessary, (*b*) a critical and doubting attitude that helps her/him to debate others and keep an open attitude on her/his own positions, and (*c*) some sensitivity to the "*stasis* issues"—the questions that need to be answered for this particular audience in this particular speech situation. There is no point in bombarding the audience with financial data if their concerns are on the ethical issues. Speakers have to learn to "read" their audience. Attention to rhetoric opens up the learning to "argumentation theory," a more contemporary and user-friendly framing of these matters.[22]

In summary, there are two modes of case-writing and teaching: one theory oriented, just as one did practical work in high-school labs to help one understand the materials being theorized, the other synthesis oriented. The second gets closer to the strategists' work, of course, though the majority of case teaching takes the first position.[23] The assertion that the second can simulate management strategizing in any but the most trivial manner is untenable, albeit often held by teachers who have never managed anyone. Notwithstanding, case-work can provide valuable training in both analyzing and synthesizing. But there is no need to sit in a case classroom; it can be done

---

[22] S. E. Toulmin (2003) *The Uses of Argument* (updated edn). Cambridge: Cambridge University Press.
[23] W. Ellet (2007) *The Case Study Handbook: How to Read, Discuss, and Write Persuasively about Cases*. Boston: Harvard Business School Press.

self-paced and on-line. Indeed, there is much to be said for business simulations and "virtual world" approaches.[24] At HBS and the other schools that use cases extensively for "option choosing" alone, the case room is generally no more than a technology for adding pedagogical pressure. Note that balancing synthesis-oriented teaching against theory and analysis-oriented teaching is extraordinarily difficult, so many business schools push synthesis aside and leave the student with no opportunity to develop executive judgment.[25]

The case classroom certainly provides a context for learning the rhetorical skills that are fundamental to effective managing. Indeed these may be the most important of managerial skills after, as Knight, Barnard, and others noted, learning how to surround yourself with good people and keep them loyal. To provide rhetorical learning cases must offer students the full range of rhetorical instruments, availing them of *ethos* and *pathos* as well as fact-driven *logos*. Case-writers need a correspondingly broad range of research methods at their disposal, aside from some facility with the written word—a stubborn medium. These days, business school faculty members seldom have the familiarity with the interpretive and constructivist methods that would enable them to capture some of a real firm's indeterminacies and incommensurabilities. Likewise an understanding of historical methods is essential. Unfortunately historical methods are threatened in most business schools. HBS is an exception, something that goes back to Gay's initial vision for the place, reinforced by Wallace Donham, a successor Dean.[26] But if rhetorical training is part of case-work's teaching objective, recalling the trivium, then in-class case debates are a grand means for helping the students acquire such crucial value-creating capabilities.

---

[24] http://en.wikipedia.org/wiki/Business_simulation.
[25] R. Khurana and J.-C. Spender (2012) 'Herbert A. Simon on What Ails Business Schools: More than "A Problem in Organizational Design"', *Journal of Management Studies*, 49(3), 619–39.
[26] http://www.hbs.edu/businesshistory.

# APPENDIX B

# Teaching From This Book

My book comprises three distinct stages—(a) looking at the strategic languages offered by others, (b) constructing your own language, and (c) deploying it to harness others' judgments. As the Preface states, it is intended for a wide audience—private sector managers, consultants, and teachers of corporate strategy. I hope the book is also reasonably global and not overly tied to US thinking. I intend it as a supermarket of strategic materials to be drawn on according to the user's interests and styles. For (a), Chapters 1, 2, and 3 move into strategizing as choosing between whatever options seem to be available. The options themselves are described using the languages offered by the various strategic tools and theories reviewed in Chapters 2 and 3. For (b) Chapter 4 moves beyond this inventory and presents strategizing as a creative synthesizing process that brings the firm's identity, intention, and context together into a firm-specific language that grasps the firm's history, time, and strategic expectations as well as its day-to-day experiences. For (c) Chapter 5 moves to see the enterprising strategist as using talk, communications, and rhetoric to create collaboration with those others whose skills and judgments are crucial to bringing the firm to life. Note that by "teaching from this book" I do not mean only formal teaching in a college setting. The entrepreneur's task revolves around "teaching" others her/his way of strategizing. The consultant's practice is a balanced process of learning from clients and teaching them a new approach.

Chapters 1, 2, and 3 can be used on their own by teachers who feel a review of the currently available (and used) strategic tools and theories is more than enough to fill their semester. In which event the teacher might wish to supplement my book's three chapters with (a) the tool graphics, such as the BCG and Ansoff matrices, readily found on the internet, and (b) managerial-style readings that fill out my brief discussion of each tool or theory. The history of the Balanced Scorecard is especially interesting.[1] I see the teacher as in charge here, selecting materials that properly reflect the expectations and experience of her/his body of students, as well as their own tastes and ideas about the phenomena being discussed. Appendix C lists a number of strategic texts. Not all support the approach I take, but I appreciate the feeling of reassurance students can gain from having a text to help them structure a course. At the same time I see no reason

---

[1] Kaplan, R. S. (2010) Conceptual Foundations of the Balanced Scorecard. *HBS Working Paper 10-074.*

why a confident teacher whose sights are set on (*a*) needs to offer her/his students more than my book's three chapters, fleshed out with graphics and supplementary readings.

Chapter 4 takes students into a more overtly subjective and creative world, a direct confrontation with Knightian uncertainty. The core of the strategizing process is then of balancing between identifying constraints and synthesizing a rich BM-as-language. This cannot be explained as theory. It is a practice and develops only with some experience. This is a major challenge to those (most of us) who got trained into positivist modes of thought somewhere along the line. Case-work seems essential to breaking us open. But there is a trade-off between using cases written by academics who have option-selection in mind (see Appendix A) rather than using understructured stories that leave the student more room to synthesize. Students might find it more interesting and valuable to write their own mini-case on a firm, drawing on whatever information they can glean from the internet, the financial press, or even the firm itself. This brings the student close to the strategist's own experience.

Chapter 5 puts the task characterized in Chapters 1, 2, and 3, and the synthesizing task of Chapter 4, into an entirely different light. It finally turns the strategist's challenge from "making a decision" to "persuading collaboration into existence," so creating the value-creating firm. It takes the student beyond the ideas behind strategizing and into its practice. This is hard. Rhetoric can seem a dry subject to be studied without the added dimension of exposure to a live audience, searching for one's own style. Yet a college course can do this and offer a relatively risk-free environment. In general the more students are exposed to the language the *in situ* managers use, the more valuable their learning experience will be. Thus there is real value in bringing the studied firm's executives into discussion with the students. But note that senior managers confront very different challenges from those the students are used to facing. Which leads to a different mind-set and way of talking, so facilitators might prove useful. But this also illustrates the importance of the firm's rhetorical practices, surfacing how crucial they are to the firm's strategizing.

# Some Strategy Texts and Their Implicit Theory

The point of this table, which captures only a fraction of the strategy texts in print and will obviously be out of date before it is printed, is to illustrate the variety of approaches adopted by strategy teachers. The classification scheme reflects my view of these texts—which are far richer than my crude schema suggests; nonetheless the table shows serious divergences about the subject and how it might be taught.

| Principal implicit theory of strategic work ☞ | external–internal fit | rent-management | sense-making | emergence | socio-politics & law | microeconomics | tool-kit | game theory & modeling | planning & decision-making |
|---|---|---|---|---|---|---|---|---|---|
| Abraham, S. C. (2012). *Strategic Planning: A Practical Guide for Competitive Success*. Bradford: Emerald. | | | | | | | | | X |
| Ackermann, Fran, & Eden, Colin (2011). *Making Strategy: Mapping Out Strategic Success*. London: Sage Publications. | | | X | | | | | | |
| Afuah, A. (2003). *Business Models: A Strategic Management Approach* (4th edn). New York: McGraw-Hill. | X | X | | | | | | | |
| Amason, Allen C. (2010). *Strategic Management: From Theory to Practice*. New York: Routledge. | X | | | | | | | | |
| Andersen, T. J. (2013). *Short Introduction to Strategic Management*. Cambridge: CUP. | X | | | | | | | | X |
| Andrews, R., Boyne, G. A., Law, J., & Walker, R. M. (2012). *Strategic Management and Public Service Performance*. Basingstoke: Palgrave Macmillan. | | | | | | | | | X |
| Angwin, Duncan, Cummings, Stephen, & Smith, Chris (2011). *The Strategy Pathfinder: Core Concepts and Live Cases*. Chichester: John Wiley & Sons. | | X | | | | | | | |

| Principal implicit theory of strategic work ☞ | external–internal fit | rent-management | sense-making | emergence | socio-politics & law | microeconomics | tool-kit | game theory & modeling | planning & decision-making |
|---|---|---|---|---|---|---|---|---|---|
| Barney, Jay B., & Hesterly, William S. (2012). *Strategic Management and Competitive Advantage* (4th edn). New York: Prentice-Hall. | X | | | | | X | | | |
| Baye, Michael (2009). *Managerial Economics and Business Strategy* (7th edn). New York: McGraw-Hill. | | | | | | X | | | |
| Besanko, David, Dranove, David, Shanley, Mark, & Schaefer, David Lewis (2010). *Economics of Strategy* (5th edn). Hoboken, NJ: John Wiley & Sons. | | X | | | | X | | | |
| Bilton, Chris, & Cummings, Stephen (2010). *Creative Strategy: Reconnecting Business and Innovation*. Chichester: John Wiley & Sons. | | | X | | | | | | |
| Bloomfield, S. (2013). *Theory and Practice of Corporate Governance*. Cambridge: CUP. | | | | | X | | | | |
| Bower, Joseph L., Bartlett, Christopher A., Christensen, C. Roland, Pearson, Andrall E., & Andrews, Kenneth R. (eds) (1991). *Business Policy: Text and Cases* (7th edn). Homewood, IL: Irwin. | X | X | | | | | | | |
| Carpenter, M. A., & Sanders, W. G. (2009). *Strategic Management: A Dynamic Perspective*. Upper Saddle River, NJ: Prentice Hall. | X | | | | | | | | |
| Carter, Chris, Clegg, Stewart R., & Kornberger, Martin (2008). *A Very Short, Fairly Interesting and Reasonably Cheap Book about Studying Strategy*. London: Sage. | X | | | | X | | | | |
| Chia, Robert C. H., & Holt, Robin (2009). *Strategy Without Design: The Silent Efficacy of Indirect Action*. Cambridge: CUP. | | | | X | | | | | |
| Clegg, Stewart R., Carter, Chris, Kornberger, Martin, & Schweitzer, Jochen (2011). *Strategy: Theory and Practice*. London: Sage. | | | | | X | | | | |
| Coulter, M. K. (1998). *Strategic Management in Action*. Upper Saddle River, NJ: Prentice-Hall. | X | | | | | | | | |
| Cunningham, J., & Harney, B. (2012). *Strategy and Strategists*. Oxford: OUP. | X | | | | | | | | |
| David, F. R. (2010). *Strategic Management: Concepts and Cases* (13th edn). Upper Saddle River, NJ: Prentice Hall. | X | | | | | | | | |
| de Kluyver, C. A. (2000). *Strategic Thinking: An Executive Perspective*. Upper Saddle River, NJ: Prentice Hall. | | | | | | | X | | |
| de Kluyver, C. A., & Pearce II, J. A. (2012). *Strategy: A View from the Top* (4th edn). Upper Saddle River, NJ: Prentice Hall. | X | | | | | | | | X |

| Reference | | | | | | | | | |
|---|---|---|---|---|---|---|---|---|---|
| De Wit, Bob, & Meyer, Ron (2010). *Strategy: Process, Content, Context, An International Perspective* (4th edn). Andover: South-Western Cengage Learning. | X | | | | | | | | |
| Dess, Gregory G., Lumpkin, G. T., & Eisner, Alan B. (2010). *Strategic Management: Text and Cases* (5th edn). New York: McGraw-Hill. | X | | | | | | | | |
| Fleisher, Craig S., & Bensoussan, Babette E. (2003). *Strategic and Competitive Analysis: Methods and Techniques for Analyzing Business Competition.* Upper Saddle River, NJ: Prentice Hall. | | | | | | X | | | |
| Foss, N. J., Pedersen, T., Pyndt, J., & Schultz, M. (2012). *Innovating Organization and Management.* Cambridge: CUP. | | | | X | | | | | |
| Freeman, R. E. (1984). *Strategic Management: A Stakeholder Approach.* Marshfield, MA: Pitman Publishing Co. | | | | X | | | | | |
| Frynas, J. G., & Mellahi, K. (2011). *Global Strategic Management* (2nd edn). Oxford: OUP. | X | | | X | | | | | |
| Furrer, Olivier. (2011). *Corporate Level Strategy: Theory and Applications.* Abingdon: Routledge. | | | | | X | | | | |
| Gamble, J. E., Thompson, A. A., & Peteraf, M. (2012). *Essentials of Strategic Management: The Quest for Competitive Advantage* (3rd edn). New York: McGraw-Hill/Irwin. | X | X | | | | | | | |
| Gandelli, G., Pezzi, A., & Venanzi, D. (2012). *Strategy for Action,* i. *The Logic and Content of Strategic Management.* New York: Springer. | | | | X | X | | | | |
| Gandelli, G., Pezzi, A., & Venanzi, D. (2013). *Strategy for Action,* ii. *Strategy Formulation, Development, and Control.* New York: Springer. | | | | X | X | | | | |
| Gimbert, X. (2011). *Think Strategically.* Basingstoke: Palgrave Macmillan. | | X | | X | | | | | |
| Grant, Robert M. (2010). *Contemporary Strategy Analysis and Cases: Text and Cases* (7th edn). Chichester: John Wiley & Sons. | X | X | | | | | | | |
| Grant, Robert M., & Jordan, Judith (2012). *Foundations of Strategy.* Chichester: John Wiley & Sons. | X | X | | | | | | | |
| Heesen, B. (2012). *Effective Strategy Execution: Improving Performance with Business Intelligence.* New York: Springer. | X | | | | | X | X | | |
| Heifetz, A. (2012). *Game Theory: Interactive Strategies in Economics and Management,* tr. J. Yalon-Fortus. Cambridge: CUP. | | | | | | X | | | |
| Henry, A. (2011). *Understanding Strategic Management* (2nd edn). Oxford: OUP. | X | | | | | | | | |
| Heracleous, L., & Jacobs, C. D. (2012). *Crafting Strategy: Embodied Metaphors in Practice.* Cambridge: CUP. | | X | | | | | | | |
| Hill, Charles W. L., & Jones, Gareth R. (2009). *Strategic Management Theory: An Integrated Approach.* Mason, OH: South-Western College Publishing. | X | | | | | | | | |

| Principal implicit theory of strategic work ☞ | external–internal fit | rent-management | sense-making | emergence | socio-politics & law | microeconomics | tool-kit | game theory & modeling | planning & decision-making |
|---|---|---|---|---|---|---|---|---|---|
| Hitt, Michael A., Ireland, R. Duane, & Hoskisson, Robert E. (2010). *Strategic Management: Concepts, Competitiveness, and Globalization* (9th edn). Mason, OH: South-Western College Publishing. | X | | | | | | | | |
| Huff, Anne Sigismund, Floyd, Steven W., Sherman, Hugh D., & Terjesen, Siri (eds) (2009). *Strategic Management: Logic and Action*. New York: John Wiley & Sons. | | X | X | | | | | | |
| Husted, B. W., & Allen, D. B. (2010). *Corporate Social Strategy: Stakeholder Engagement and Competitive Advantage*. Cambridge: CUP. | | | | | X | X | | | |
| Jenkins, M. and Ambrosini, V. with Collier, N. (eds) (2007). *Advanced Strategic Management: A Multi-Perspective Approach*. Basingstoke: Palgrave Macmillan. | | | | X | X | | | | |
| Jensen, Michael C. (1998). *Foundations of Organizational Strategy*. Cambridge, MA: Harvard University Press. | | | | | | X | | | |
| Johnson, G., Langley, A., Melin, L., & Whittington, R. (2007). *Strategy as Practice: Research Directions and Resources*. Cambridge: CUP. | X | | X | | | | | | |
| Johnson, G., Scholes, K., & Whittington, R. (2008). *Exploring Corporate Strategy* (8th edn). London: Prentice-Hall. | X | | | | | | | | |
| Kaplan, J. M., & Warren, A. C. (2012). *Patterns of Entrepreneurship Management* (4th edn). New York: John Wiley & Sons. | X | | | X | | | | | |
| Kay, John (1993). *The Foundations of Corporate Success*. Oxford: OUP. | | | | | | X | | | |
| Keidel, R. W. (2010). *The Geometry of Strategy: Concepts for Strategic Management*. London: Routledge. | | | | | | | | X | |
| Kotler, P., Berger, R., & Bickhoff, N. (2010). *The Quintessence of Strategic Management: What You Really Need to Know to Survive in Business*. Berlin: Springer-Verlag. | | | | | | | X | X | X |
| Kumar, D. (2010). *Enterprise Growth Strategy: Vision, Planning and Execution*. London: Gower. | | | | | | | | X | X |
| Lindgren, M., & Bandhold, H. (2003). *Scenario Planning: The Link between Future and Strategy*. Basingstoke: Palgrave Macmillan. | | | | | | | | X | |
| Lynch, Richard (2011). *Strategic Management* (6th edn). London: Pearson. | X | | | | | | | | |

| | | | | | | | | |
|---|---|---|---|---|---|---|---|---|
| MacLennan, A. (2011). *Strategy Execution: Translating Strategy into Action in Complex Organizations*. London: Routledge. | | | | | | X | | |
| Mahoney, Joseph T. (2005). *Economic Foundations of Strategy*. Thousand Oaks, CA: Sage. | | | | | X | | | |
| McNamee, Patrick B. (1987). *Tools and Techniques for Strategic Management*. Oxford: Pergamon Press. | | | | | | X | | |
| Montgomery, Cynthia A. (2012). *The Strategist: Become the Leader Your Business Needs*. New York: Harper Business. | X | | | | | | | |
| Nonaka, I., & Zhu, Z. (2012). *Pragmatic Strategy: Eastern Wisdom, Global Success*. Cambridge: CUP. | | X | | | | | | |
| Pearce II, John A., & Robinson, Richard B., Jr. (2010). *Strategic Management: Formulation, Implementation, and Control* (12th edn). New York: McGraw-Hill. | X | | | | | | | |
| Pitt, Martyn R., & Koufopoulos, Dimitrios (2012). *Essentials of Strategic Management*. London: Sage. | X | | | | | | | |
| Rainey, D. L. (2009). *Enterprise-Wide Strategic Management*. Cambridge: CUP. | X | | | | | | | |
| Robertson, Duncan A., & Caldart, Adrián (2009). *The Dynamics of Strategy: Mastering Strategic Landscapes of the Firm*. Oxford: OUP. | | | | | | | X | |
| Rothaermel, F. (2012). *Strategic Management: Concepts and Cases*. New York: McGraw-Hill/Irwin. | | X | | | X | | | |
| Segal-Horn, Susan, & Faulkner, David (2010). *Understanding Global Strategy*. Andover: Cengage Learning. | | | | | X | | | |
| Spulber, D. F. (2011). *Global Competitive Strategy*. Cambridge: CUP. | X | | | | X | | | |
| Stacey, Ralph D. (1993). *Strategic Management and Organizational Dynamics*. London: Pitman Publishing. | | | | X | | | | |
| Thompson, Arthur A., Peteraf, Margaret E., Gamble, John E., & Strickland III, A. J. (2011). *Crafting and Executing Strategy: The Quest for Competitive Advantage* (18th edn). New York: McGraw-Hill/Irwin. | X | | | | X | | | |
| Ungson, G. R., & Wong, Y.-Y. (2008). *Global Strategic Management*. Armonk, NY: M. E. Sharpe. | X | | | | | | | |
| Verbeke, A. (2013). *International Business Strategy*. Cambridge: CUP. | | | | | X | | | X |
| Viardot, E. (2011). *The Timeless Principles of Successful Business Strategy*. Heidelberg: Springer. | X | | | | | | X | X |
| Warren, Kim (2008). *Strategic Management Dynamics*. Chichester: John Wiley & Sons. | X | | | | | | | |
| Wheelen, T. L., & Hunger, J. D. (2006). *Strategic Management and Business Policy* (10th edn). Upper Saddle River, NJ: Prentice Hall. | X | | | | | | | |
| Whitehead, J. (2011). *What You Need to Know About Strategy*. Chichester: Capstone. | X | | | | | | | X |
| Zanoni, A. B. (2012). *Strategic Analysis: Processes and Tools*. New York: Routledge. | | | | | X | X | | |

# Further Reading

My chapters have some footnotes that can lead interested readers onwards. This appendix casts a wider net to catch some of the stuff I have personally found interesting and influential. The English-language management literature is huge and I must apologize for my ignorance of the important work in Japanese, Spanish, French, Russian, Chinese, or German. As well as the field's volume, its variety tempts authors to stuff their pages with citations and commentary that would take the reader years to wade through. I have resisted the urge, in part because some well-mannered books with extensive bibliographies already exist, such as R. M. Grant (2010) *Contemporary Strategic Analysis* (7th edn), Chichester: John Wiley & Sons, or N. J. Foss and P. G. Klein (2012) *Organizing Entrepreneurial Judgment: A New Approach to the Firm*, Cambridge: Cambridge University Press. They have done it more effectively and thoroughly than I can.

The choices below are intended to open up my book's genesis to those who find it intellectually interesting. First and foremost, a subjective or agentic approach is not part of mainstream management thought—however much it deserves to be—so putting together a case for it calls for some selectivity. Nor is language paid much attention. Hundreds of books crowd for attention, so my choice will seem haphazard to some who know the literature. Beyond our field's core canonical works (five), I have arranged my choices in disciplinary sections. This is simply a rhetorical device to emphasize that my principal departure from the mainstream is philosophical or, more specifically, epistemological. It goes back to my Ph.D. and *Industry Recipes: The Nature and Sources of Managerial Judgement*, Oxford: Blackwell.

Readers who do not wish to study epistemology directly—it is an entire branch of philosophy—might best get traction by getting a fix on mainstream positivism's epistemology and methodology. Positivism is a huge hydra, but Kolakowski is reliable. With some sense of positivism in hand the importance of Knight's work becomes clear as it tilts the analysis of value creation out of positivism's reach. So the philosophizing comes first and helps identify the need for some non-positivist approaches. There is the interpretive or sense-making approach and Weick is this field's giant. As the reader knows, positivist approaches tend to ignore time because their explanatory logics turn on equilibrium, determinism, and causal mechanisms. Perhaps the most fundamental feature of non-positivist approaches is the way "lived time" rather than clock time is made central, so that the future is unknown, something to be created through our agency. Much of the thinking here goes back to Bergson, a difficult read but adequately handled in some introductory texts, such as Kolakowski's. Note there have been major shifts in professional attitudes towards epistemology since WW2—Theodore Porter is good on this. Rationalism has permeated all manner of discourse, especially business and management education. The work of Backhouse and others is helping raise business scholars' awareness that the results may have been more destructive than productive—but that is for another book. Ironically, though, it helped squeeze rhetoric out of education—yet the reader knows that purely rational argument (*logos* alone) cannot work when confronting Knightian uncertainty. I have found McCumber's work particularly useful.

Once time and uncertainty are taken seriously, it becomes clear that history's methods can complement the time-free "scientific methods" of positivism. So the second section deals with history. The abstractions of mainstream economic theorizing have little to say to managers (as Coase and Ning note in my book's epigraph) so I merge the history of applied economics with the history of commerce. I focus on the private sector, the value-creating core of our democratic capitalism. The historical work here varies enormously. The reader can distinguish commentary that has little grounding in the data on which historians thrive, old files, letters, etc. versus that which has involved a lot of that, maybe more than the reader cares for. But this is what leaves good historians in a doubting mood, knowing they cannot ever know for certain what happened and that that goal is a positivist tic, peripheral to an exploration of the human condition and its boundless complexities. The reader also needs to be cautious about "history" that is written for the express purpose of packaging the author's ideology. Such contrived history can lead to truly poor work as, for instance, J. Appleby (2010) *The Relentless Revolution: A History of Capitalism*, New York: W. W. Norton. Scholarly work on the history of capitalism has been recently energized by history-based critiques of Weber's well-known tale of the Protestant ethic. A recent study, I. S. Akçomak, D. Webbink, and B. ter Weel, B. (2012) *Why Did the Netherlands Develop So Early? The Legacy of the Brethren of the Common Life*, The Hague: CPB Netherlands Bureau for Economic Policy Analysis, picks up on earlier suggestions that literacy rather than religion was the driver of European capitalism. The argument carries a strong message for us today as we ponder the impact of our declining educational infrastructure.

Over the years I have become convinced that management theorists should pay more attention to the period before the Venetian Empire (approximately 1000–1500) that gave us, *inter alia*, Pacioli's double-entry bookkeeping, merchant banking, and the other things we know about commerce from Shakespeare's *Merchant of Venice* or Marlowe's *Jew of Malta*. More scholarly work is being done on the emergence of capitalism during the Arab Empire (approximately 600–1500). Many of the financial instruments necessary to the evolution of modern capitalism's processes, such as letters of credit and pooled investment, were already in use during the Arab period. Europe was following rather than leading. I argue the most crucial period in European management history was the Dutch Republic (approximately 1500–1750). Here modern democratic modes of business governance displaced earlier coercive or feudal modes. The changes freed up capitalism's rapid development as Great Britain's and the United States' political situations evolved. Which brings us to Schumpeter and the Austrian economists. They are especially interesting to anyone thinking about value creation (or destruction) for their analyses hinge on peoples' prevailing expectations rather than on abstract equilibrium conditions. In many respects Penrose was a "closet-Austrian."

I have a particular fondness for Shackle's work, especially his last book, a truly valiant attempt to create a subjective economics.

The next section covers management directly. I see two historical backgrounds; one broad, from the time of the Dutch Republic, the other narrow, from the 1940s. The recent period is marked by significant change in the relationships between private sector capitalists, governments, the workforce, and the general public. Power and wealth disparity is the issue, not technology. Indeed our obsession with technological determinism muddies our sense of how capitalism really operates. The reader knows I see Coase's intuition that the nature of the firm is tied up with power and its exercise within the firm as key. It leads us towards the history of employment, the empirical facts of our labor markets, and to greater regard for the strategic place of corporate law—for instance in the work of Commons, Horwitz, and Steinfeld—albeit these are widely ignored in business schools. Modern management thinking rejects the dictatorial independence that characterized much nineteenth-century thought—a period dominated by owner-managers and robber barons. The interaction between the modern firm as a defined legal entity borrowing many citizens' rights and the broader society is being actively explored in major social debates. Many of today's ideas about corporate social responsibility and business ethics have been in circulation since before Shakespeare's time. But they have been re-energized, especially by Alasdair MacIntyre's critique, as well as the post-2008 financial catastrophes. MacIntyre's is a moral critique that stands apart from Marxism and the critiques that have fuelled "critical management studies." McCloskey's studies are superbly illuminating. All this work goes to the heart of the Coasian relationships within the firm and to the wider political discussion about the complex relationships between the private and public sectors. Thus critiques of the private sector from ecology and sustainability are now being added to those from politics and humanism.

The final section is on rhetoric. One of the curious aspects of rhetoric's history is that it tends to decline when times are stable—such as during the long period of economic growth since WW2—but re-emerge like a phoenix when things get shaky. It is re-emerging today to play in many venues, especially education. There is spreading regard for the narrative or discursive studies of organizational life, though little of this takes the view developed in this book. Rhetoric is a vast field of great subtlety—as broad as human communication—and no one should claim to understand it fully. Conley provides a fine overview of its history, Toulmin and McCloskey fine introductions to its everyday practice.

As noted in the Preface I think of the following five books as our essential canon, the "must reads" that have defined our field:

Barnard, C. I. (1968). *The Functions of the Executive* (30th anniversary edn). Cambridge, MA: Harvard University Press.
Knight, F. H. (1965). *Risk, Uncertainty and Profit*. New York: Harper & Row.
March, J. G., and Simon, H. A. (1958). *Organizations*. New York: John Wiley.
Penrose, E. T. (1995). *The Theory of the Growth of the Firm* (3rd edn). New York: Oxford University Press.
Simon, H. A. (1997). *Administrative Behavior: A Study of Decision-Making Processes in Administrative Organization* (4th edn). New York: Free Press.

## D.1 Philosophy

Ahearn, L. M. (2012). *Living Language: An Introduction to Linguistic Anthropology*. Chichester: John Wiley & Sons.

Ayer, A. J. (2000). *Hume: A Very Short Introduction*. Oxford: Oxford University Press.

Bronner, S. E. (2011). *Critical Theory: A Very Short Introduction*. Oxford: Oxford University Press.

Cowan, R., and Rizzo, M. J. (eds) (1995). *Profits and Morality*. Chicago: University of Chicago Press.

Critchley, S. (2001). *Continental Philosophy: A Very Short Introduction*. Oxford: Oxford University Press.

DeLanda, M. (2011). *Philosophy and Simulation: The Emergence of Synthetic Reason*. London: Continuum.

Dunn, J. (2003). *Locke: A Very Short Introduction*. Oxford: Oxford University Press.

Foucault, M. (1972). *The Archeology of Knowledge and the Discourse on Language*, tr. A. M. Sheridan Smith. New York: Pantheon.

Foucault, M. (1977). *Discipline and Punish: The Birth of the Prison*, tr. A. Sheridan. New York: Vintage Books.

Foucault, M. (1988). *Madness and Civilization: A History of Insanity in the Age of Reason*, tr. R. Howard. New York: Vintage Books.

Giddens, A. (1987). *Sociology: A Brief But Critical Introduction* (2nd edn). New York: Harcourt Brace Jovanovich.

Glaser, B. G., and Strauss, A. L. (1967). *The Discovery of Grounded Theory: Strategies for Qualitative Research*. Chicago: Aldine.

Kelly, G. A. (1955). *The Psychology of Personal Constructs*. New York: W. W. Norton.

Kolakowski, L. (1972). *Positivist Philosophy*. Harmondsworth: Penguin Books.

Kolakowski, L. (2001). *Bergson*. South Bend, IN: St Augustine's Press.

Kuhn, T. S. (1970). *The Structure of Scientific Revolutions* (2nd edn). Chicago: University of Chicago Press.

Lakatos, I., and Feyerabend, P. (1999). *For and Against Method*. Chicago: University of Chicago Press.

McCumber, J. (2011). *Time and Philosophy: A History of Continental Thought*. Montreal: McGill-Queen's University Press.

McCumber, J. (2013). *On Philosophy: Notes from a Crisis*. Stanford, CA: Stanford University Press.

Toennies, F. (1971). *On Sociology: Pure, Applied, and Empirical*. Chicago: University of Chicago Press.

Tsoukas, H. (2005). *Complex Knowledge: Studies in Organizational Epistemology*. Oxford: Oxford University Press.

Van de Ven, A. H. (2007). *Engaged Scholarship: A Guide for Organizational and Social Research*. Oxford: Oxford University Press.

von Glasersfeld, E. (2002). *Radical Constructivism*. London: Routledge/Falmer.

Weick, K. E. (1995). *Sensemaking in Organizations*. Thousand Oaks, CA: Sage.

## D.2 Economics and History

Andersen, E. S. (2012). *Schumpeter's Evolutionary Economics: A Theoretical, Historical and Statistical Analysis of the Engine of Capitalism*. London: Anthem Press.

Backhouse, R. E., and Fontaine, P. (eds) (2010). *The History of the Social Sciences since 1945*. Cambridge: Cambridge University Press.

Berle, A. A., and Means, G. C. (2003). *The Modern Corporation and Private Property*. New Brunswick, NJ: Transaction Publishers.

Braudel, F. (1967). *Capitalism and Material Life: 1400–1800*, tr. M. Kochan. New York: Harper & Row.

Burawoy, M. (1979). *Manufacturing Consent: Changes in the Labor Process under Monopoly Capitalism*. Chicago: University of Chicago Press.

Chaudhuri, K. N. (1985). *Trade and Civilisation in the Indian Ocean: An Economic History from the Rise of Islam to 1750*. Cambridge: Cambridge University Press.

Coad, A. (2009). *The Growth of Firms: A Survey of Theories and Empirical Evidence*. Cheltenham: Edward Elgar.

Commons, J. R. (1924). *The Legal Foundations of Capitalism*. New York: Macmillan.

Commons, J. R. (1931). *Institutional Economics*. Madison, WI: University of Wisconsin Press.

de Vries, J. (1974). *The Dutch Rural Economy in the Golden Age, 1500–1700*. New Haven: Yale University Press.

de Vries, J., and van der Woude, A. (1997). *The First Modern Economy: Success, Failure, and Perseverance of the Dutch Economy 1500–1815*. Cambridge: Cambridge University Press.

Drucker, P. F. (1972). *Concept of the Corporation* (rev. edn). New York: New American Library.

Duplessis, R. S. (1997). *Transitions to Capitalism in Early Modern Europe*. Cambridge: Cambridge University Press.

Florence, P. S. (1961). *The Logic of British and American Industry* (rev. edn). London: Routledge & Kegan Paul.

Hannah, L. (1976). *Management Strategy and Business Development: An Historical and Comparative Study*. London: Macmillan Press.

Henderson, W. O. (1961). *The Industrial Revolution on the Continent*. London: Frank Cass & Co.

Horwitz, M. J. (1992). *The Transformation of American Law, 1780–1860*. New York: Oxford University Press.

Israel, J. (1995). *The Dutch Republic: Its Rise, Greatness, and Fall 1477–1806*. Oxford: Oxford University Press.

Katz, M. B., Doucet, M. J., and Stern, M. J. (1982). *The Social Organization of Early Industrial Capitalism*. Cambridge, MA: Harvard University Press.

Lachmann, L. M. (1994). *Expectations and the Meanings of Institutions*. London: Routledge.

Landes, D. S., Mokyr, J., and Baumol, W. J. (eds) (2010). *The Invention of Enterprise: Entrepreneurship from Ancient Mesopotamia to Modern Times*. Princeton: Princeton University Press.

Lewis, D. L. (2008). *God's Crucible: Islam and the Making of Europe, 570–1215*. New York: W. W. Norton.

Kennedy, H. (2007). *The Great Arab Conquests: How the Spread of Islam Changed the World We Live In*. Philadelphia: Da Capo Press.

MacMillan, M. (2009). *Dangerous Games: The Uses and Abuses of History*. New York: Modern Library.

McCloskey, D. N. (2006). *The Bourgeois Virtues: Ethics for an Age of Commerce*. Chicago: University of Chicago Press.

McCloskey, D. N. (2010). *Bourgeois Dignity: Why Economics Can't Explain the Modern World* (vol. ii of *The Bourgeois Era*). Chicago: University of Chicago Press.

McCraw, T. K. (2007). *Prophet of Innovation: Joseph Schumpeter and Creative Destruction*. Cambridge, MA: Belknap Press.

Mokyr, J. (2002). *The Gifts of Athena: Historical Origins of the Knowledge Economy*. Princeton: Princeton University Press.

O'Driscoll, G. P., and Rizzo, M. J. (1996). *The Economics of Time and Ignorance* (New Introduction edn). London: Routledge.

Pollard, S. (1968). *The Genesis of Modern Management*. Harmondsworth: Penguin Books.

Saliba, G. (2007). *Islamic Science and the Making of the European Renaissance*. Cambridge, MA: MIT Press.

Schumpeter, J. A. (1975). *Capitalism, Socialism and Democracy* (3rd edn). New York: Harper & Row.

Shackle, G. L. S. (1979). *Imagination and the Nature of Choice*. Edinburgh: Edinburgh University Press.

Spulber, D. F. (2009). *The Theory of the Firm: Microeconomics with Endogenous Entrepreneurs, Firms, Markets, and Organizations*. Cambridge: Cambridge University Press.

Steinfeld, R. J. (1991). *The Invention of Free Labor: The Employment Relations in English and American Law and Culture, 1350–1870*. Chapel Hill, NC: University of North Carolina Press.

Sumida, J. T. (2008). *Decoding Clausewitz: A New Approach to 'On War'*. Lawrence, KS: University Press of Kansas.

Swedberg, R. (ed.) (1991). *Joseph A. Schumpeter: The Economics and Sociology of Capitalism*. Princeton: Princeton University Press.

Swedberg, R. (ed.) (2000). *Entrepreneurship: The Social Science View*. Oxford: Oxford University Press.

Vaughn, K. I. (1994). *Austrian Economics in America: The Migration of a Tradition*. Cambridge: Cambridge University Press.

von Clausewitz, C. (1962). *War, Politics and Power: Selections from 'On War' and 'I Believe and Profess'*, tr. E. M. Collins. Chicago: Henry Regnery and Co.

Williamson, O. E., and Winter, S. G. (eds) (1991). *The Nature of the Firm: Origins, Evolution, and Development*. New York: Oxford University Press.

## D.3 Recent Management Thought

Alvesson, M., and Willmott, H. (2012). *Making Sense of Management: A Critical Introduction* (2nd edn). London: Sage.

Augier, M., and March, J. G. (2011). *The Roots, Rituals, and Rhetorics of Change*. Stanford, CA: Stanford University Press.

Burns, T., and Stalker, G. M. (1961). *The Management of Innovation*. London: Tavistock Publications.

Clements, J. D. (2012). *Corporations are Not People: Why They Have More Rights than You Do and What You Can Do about it*. San Francisco: Brett-Koehler Publishers.

Drucker, P. F. (1955). *The Practice of Management*. London: Heinemann.

Hartmann, T. (2010). *Unequal Protection: How Corporations Became 'People'—and How You can Fight Back* (2nd edn). San Francisco: Berrett-Koehler.

Heald, M. (1988). *The Social Responsibilities of Business: Company and Community, 1900–1960*. New Brunswick, NJ: Transaction Books.

Heracleous, L. (2003). *Strategy and Organization: Realizing Strategic Management*. Cambridge: Cambridge University Press.

Khurana, R. (2007). *From Higher Aims to Hired Hands: The Social Transformation of American Business Schools and the Unfulfilled Promise of Management as a Profession*. Princeton: Princeton University Press.

Losurdo, D. (2011). *Liberalism: A Counter-History*, tr. G. Elliott. London: Verso.

MacIntyre, A. (2007). *After Virtue: A Study in Moral Theory* (3rd edn). Notre Dame, IN: University of Notre Dame Press.

Middleton, J. (2003). *The Ultimate Strategy Library: The Fifty Most Influential Strategic Ideas of All Time*. Chichester: Capstone Publishing.

Mintzberg, H. (1973). *The Nature of Managerial Work*. New York: Harper & Row.

Mintzberg, H. (2004). *Managers Not MBAs: A Hard Look at the Soft Practice of Managing and Management Development*. San Francisco: Berrett-Koehler Publishers.

Morgan, G. (1997). *Images of Organization* (new edn). Thousand Oaks, CA: Sage.

Mowles, C. (2011). *Rethinking Management: Radical Insights from Complexity Sciences*. London: Gower.

Normann, R. (1977). *Management for Growth*. New York: John Wiley & Sons.

O'Connor, E. S. (2011). *Creating New Knowledge in Management: Appropriating the Field's Lost Foundations*. Stanford, CA: Stanford Business Books.

Pettigrew, A. M. (1985). *The Awakening Giant: Continuity and Change in Imperial Chemical Industries*. Oxford: Basil Blackwell.

Porter, T. M. (1986). *The Rise of Statistical Thinking 1820–1900*. Princeton: Princeton University Press.

Porter, T. M. (1995). *Trust in Numbers: The Pursuit of Objectivity in Science and Public Life*. Princeton: Princeton University Press.

Standing, G. (2011). *The Precariat: The New Dangerous Class*. London: Bloomsbury.

Witzel, M. (2011). *A History of Management Thought*. Abingdon: Routledge.

Witzel, M., and Warner, M. (eds.) (2013). *The Oxford Handbook of Management Theorists*. Oxford: Oxford University Press.

## D.4 Rhetoric

Conley, T. M. (1990). *Rhetoric in the European Tradition*. Chicago: University of Chicago Press.

Fairhurst, G. T. (2011). *The Power of Framing: Creating the Language of Leadership*. San Francisco: Jossey-Bass.

Giglioni, P. P. (1972). *Language and Social Context: Selected Readings*. Harmondsworth: Penguin Books.

Grant, D., Hardy, C., Oswick, C., and Putnam, L. L. (eds) (2004). *The Sage Handbook of Organizational Discourse*. London: Sage.

Heracleous, L., and Jacobs, C. D. (2012). *Crafting Strategy: Embodied Metaphors in Practice*. Cambridge: Cambridge University Press.

Leith, S. (2012). *Words Like Loaded Pistols: Rhetoric from Aristotle to Obama*. New York: Basic Books.

Lucaites, J. L., Condit, C. M., and Caudill, S. (eds) (1999). *Contemporary Rhetorical Theory: A Reader*. New York: Guilford Press.

McCloskey, D. N. (1998). *The Rhetoric of Economics* (2nd edn). Madison, WI: University of Wisconsin Press.

Putnam, L. L., and Nicotera, A. M. (eds) (2009). *Building Theories of Organization: The Constitutive Role of Communication*. New York: Routledge.

Taylor, J. R., and Van Every, E. J. (2000). *The Emergent Organization: Communication as its Site and Surface*. Mahwah, NJ: Lawrence Erlbaum Associates.

Toulmin, S. E. (2003). *The Uses of Argument* (updated edn). Cambridge: Cambridge University Press.

van Eemeren, F. H., and Houtlosser, P. (eds) (2002). *Dialectic and Rhetoric: The Warp and Woof of Argumentation Analysis*. Dordrecht: Kluwer.

Weigand, E. (ed.) (2008). *Dialogue and Rhetoric*. Philadelphia: John Benjamins.

Zappavigna, M. (2013). *Tacit Knowledge and Spoken Discourse*. London: Bloomsbury.

# Index